RETHINKING CORRECTIONS

To my sons, Jonathan and Eithan: May you have the insight to be tolerant and understanding of others' needs.

—L. Gideon

To my parents and my wife for their never-ending support.

—H.-E. Sung

RETHINKING CORRECTIONS

Rehabilitation,

Reentry, and

Reintegration

LIOR GIDEON
John Jay College of Criminal Justice

HUNG-EN SUNG
John Jay College of Criminal Justice

Los Angeles | London | New Delhi
Singapore | Washington DC

1/11/12
Lan
$52-

Copyright © 2011 by SAGE Publications, Inc.

For information:

SAGE Publications, Inc.
2455 Teller Road
Thousand Oaks,
   California 91320
E-mail: order@sagepub.com

SAGE Publications Ltd.
1 Oliver's Yard
55 City Road
London EC1Y 1SP
United Kingdom

SAGE Publications India Pvt. Ltd.
B 1/I 1 Mohan Cooperative
   Industrial Area
Mathura Road, New Delhi 110 044
India

SAGE Publications Asia-Pacific Pte. Ltd.
33 Pekin Street #02-01
Far East Square
Singapore 048763

Printed in the United States of America.

Library of Congress Cataloging-in-Publication Data

Rethinking corrections : rehabilitation, reentry, and reintegration / editors, Lior Gideon, Hung-En Sung.
     p. cm.
Includes bibliographical references and index.
ISBN 978-1-4129-7018-1 (cloth)
ISBN 978-1-4129-7019-8 (pbk.)
   1. Criminals–Rehabilitation. 2. Corrections. 3. Ex-convicts.
4. Community-based corrections. I. Gideon, Lior. II. Sung, Hung-En, 1968-
HV9275.R48 2011
365'.7—dc22   2009043897

This book is printed on acid-free paper.

10   11   12   13   14   10   9   8   7   6   5   4   3   2   1

Acquisitions Editor:	Jerry Westby
Editorial Assistant:	Eve Oettinger
Production Editor:	Karen Wiley
Copy Editor:	Carol Anne Peschke
Typesetter:	C&M Digitals (P) Ltd.
Proofreader:	Andrea Martin
Indexer:	Diggs Publication Services
Cover Designer:	Arup Giri
Marketing Manager:	Carmel Withers

Brief Contents

Detailed Contents

Preface

Although the topic of rehabilitation, reentry, and reintegration is not a new one, it has become a more pressing issue worldwide. In American society alone, the number of offenders returning to the community after serving a term of prison incarceration has risen to around 700,000 annually, resulting in nearly 7 million formerly incarcerated people who are estimated to be released back to their home communities in the next decade. Fortunately, continuous experimentation in new rehabilitation approaches and the evaluation of these treatment and service innovations in the past two decades have yielded a very rich, albeit poorly integrated, body of research literature on successful policies, effective models, and best practices in corrections. This book fills a void in the literature for training future correctional professionals by providing an accessible collection of state-of-the-art empirical studies and theoretical discussions. It is hoped that readers of this book will be exposed to findings from the most recent and rigorous research and learn to develop critical thinking in the complex issues of rehabilitation, reentry, and reintegration, with help from some of the most prominent experts in the field.

Acknowledging the complexity of the rehabilitation and reintegration process, this book seeks to present a more complete spectrum of these processes, beginning with the assessment stage, followed by specific intervention modalities, through a discussion of a theoretical model that defines and incorporates the three common concepts of rehabilitation, reentry, and reintegration. Specifically, this book explores the challenges experienced by convicted offenders during rehabilitation and reintegration and suggests relevant policy implications. The book uses a unique approach that examines what the public think our policy should be in regard to convicted offenders. At the same time, it presents an examination of convicted offenders from the beginning stages of incarceration—intake and risk and need assessment—through their release to the community, including the barriers they experience in the community, such as postrelease supervision and the need to obtain legitimate employment and adequate health care, negotiate their social surroundings, and rebuild family life. In the concluding chapter, a theoretical discussion is presented in an effort to clarify what rehabilitation, reentry, and reintegration are and how they are related to one another.

The book has 16 chapters, including an introduction and conclusion to fit a semester-based course and thus to be used as a primary textbook. Each chapter focuses on a specific stage or aspect of the rehabilitation and reintegration process using original evidence-based conceptual material not published elsewhere. Each chapter is followed by discussion questions and supplementary readings that will promote critical thinking and class discussion. However, the astute reader will find each chapter in this book is also linked to the others. Consequently, the chapters of the book can be divided into six different sections:

- General discussion on offenders (chapter 1)
- Theoretical framework (mainly chapters 2–4)
- Diversion and suspension of sentencing (chapters 5 and 6)
- Prison-based and community interventions (chapters 7–10)
- Postrelease practices and barriers faced by released offenders (chapters 11–14)
- Theory and curricula (chapters 15 and 16)

A key feature of the book is an integrative summary with conclusions regarding the main findings and concepts across all the chapters. In this summary chapter we suggest a theory that will clear the mist of confusion about what the different stages of the reentry process are.

We wish you an invigorating experience that will reinforce your understanding of the topics discussed in this book, and if you are a first-time student of corrections, we hope this book will change how you think about corrections and offenders.

Lior Gideon

Hung-En Sung

Acknowledgments

The idea for this book came from another comparative corrections text that the first editor was working on. That text was not published but gave life to a new idea. The process was invigorating, and we had the opportunity to work with ambitious people; some were practitioners, some scholars, and some both. Their names appear on the chapters they contributed. Each one of them inspired us and taught us a great deal, from a different approach and perspective. However, we all share a common understanding that something must be done to address the current crisis in our correctional system and in the way we deal with criminals.

Equally important to this project are the people who made it possible. We would like to thank Jerry Westby, Sage's executive editor, and his assistant, Eve Oettinger, as well as the editorial team for their impeccable work, including production editor Karen Wiley and copy editor Carol Anne Peschke. Jerry and Eve were our lighthouse in the stormy and fickle sea of scholarship. In particular, Jerry gave us a guiding hand in arranging contributions to the text, and he provided good advice and reassurance whenever the need arose. Jerry believed in our work and in this project, and this is all we could ask for. Eve was always available to us and was very quick to find solutions and answers to all our queries. With her very studious and insightful comments Carol provided us with invaluable support. Her masterful editing helped bridge the different voices of contributors, thus improving the chapters dramatically, and for that we are thankful. We also want to thank Marlene Lipson, our personal editor, for her preliminary work on some of the chapters. We were truly blessed by our team of editors!

One of our many concerns was the review stage. This was not an easy task because each contributor has a different writing style, and sometimes these styles pulled in different directions. By now it is obvious that we succeeded in drawing them together. However, this would not have been possible without the input of our colleagues, who shared their ideas and criticism with one aim in mind: to improve this project. Their input was insightful and helped us and our contributors to revise their work while aligning the chapters to convey the idea of this book in a coherent fashion. In no particular order, we would like to express our gratitude to Karin Dudash, Cameron University; Kent Kerley, University of Alabama; Jessie Krienert, Illinois State University; Jodi Lane, University of Florida; Natasha Frost, Northeastern University; Deborah Baskin, California State University at Los Angeles; Jeb Booth, Salem State College; Terry Campbell, Kaplan University School of Criminal Justice; Sharon Green, Louisiana State University at Shreveport; Patricia Joffer, South Dakota University; Eric Metchik, Salem State College; Tom Rutherford, West Virginia University at Parkersburg; Gaylene Armstrong, Sam Houston State University; Shannon M. Barton, Indiana State University; Susan F. Brinkley, University of Tampa; and Peggy Maynes, Kaplan University and Iowa Department of Corrections. This book is the result of a truly peer-reviewed effort, and for this we are grateful.

Special thanks to Lior Gideon's son, Jonathan Gideon, who searched the Web to find the photo that is now the cover of this book. Jonathan, you are amazing!

CHAPTER 1

Corrections in an Era of Reentry

Lior Gideon

Recent data published by the Bureau of Justice Statistics (2009) indicate that on June 30, 2008, more than 2.3 million people were incarcerated in federal or state prisons or held in local jails. Consequently, the number of inmates released from prisons and returned to their home communities was calculated at around 700,000. Krisberg and Marchionna (2006) also presented this number in an early work. Consequently, the number of prison inmates expected to be released and returned to their local communities will reach an astonishing 7 million people in the next decade (This calculation is also presented in Wilkinson & Rhine, 2005.) Travis (2005) calculated that 1,700 inmates are released every day. This number increases to 1,918 inmates released every day when more recent data from the Bureau of Justice Statistics are used. Petersilia (2003) reviewed earlier Bureau of Justice Statistics data from 2000 and determined that 93% of all inmates will eventually return home. A recent examination of Bureau of Justice Statistics data reveals a slightly higher estimate, stating, "At least 95% of all State prisoners will be released from prison at some point; nearly 80% will be released to parole supervision" (Bureau of Justice Statistics, 2009). Correspondingly, the Bureau of Justice Statistics (2009) observed an increase in the number of people released to parole supervision, documenting 824,365 people on parole as of December 31, 2007.

Petersilia's (2005) interpretation of parole data indicates that the number of incarcerated people who will be released back to the community is expected to grow in future years. This increase will result from two causes: The total number of incarcerated people is increasing, and more inmates will "max out" from long prison terms (Petersilia, 2005). In fact, recent data published by the Bureau of Justice Statistics (2009) on incarceration numbers from the last two decades reveal a dismal reality in which more Americans are being sentenced to prison terms than ever before, with a corresponding increase in people being released on parole supervision, as can be seen in Figure 1.1.

Interestingly, a large portion of the incarceration surge took place during a time in American history when crime dropped the most: 1992–2006. Most prisons in the country are now occupied beyond capacity, and this situation will worsen in the face of a significant growth in crime, as may be expected in

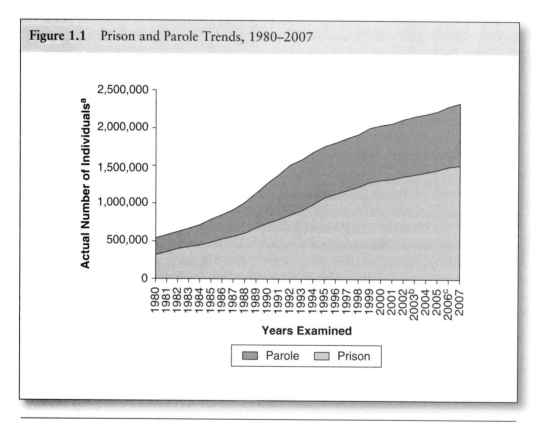

Figure 1.1 Prison and Parole Trends, 1980–2007

Source: Bureau of Justice Statistics (2009). *Key facts at a glance: Correctional populations.* Retrieved September 2, 2009, from http://www.ojp.usdoj.gov/bjs/glance/tables/corr2tab.htm

[a]Because some offenders may have multiple statuses (i.e., held in a prison or jail but remain under the jurisdiction of a probation or parole authority) totals in 2000–2004 exclude probationers held in jail or prison; totals in 2005–2006 exclude probationers and parolees held in jail or prison; and the total in 2007 excludes probationers and parolees held in jail or prison, probationers who were also under parole supervision, and parolees who were also under probation supervision. For these reasons, details do not sum to total.

[b]The 2003 probation and parole counts were estimated and may differ from previously published numbers.

[c]Oklahoma did not provide community supervision data for 2007; therefore, all data for Oklahoma were estimated. Maine and Nevada did not provide prison data for 2007; therefore, all prison data for Maine and Nevada were estimated.

the near future as the economy worsens. Unless we change our sentencing practices, our prison system is doomed to collapse.

Additionally, data on recidivism show that most offenders leaving prison are likely to be rearrested within 3 years of release; nearly 80% of prisoners are likely to be rearrested within a decade of release (Freeman, 2003). Studies conducted around the world suggest that rearrest may occur within the first year after release if no support is available to the released offender (Hassin, 1989).

With such a staggering number of people being incarcerated and eventually released back to the community—and the high risk of rearrest and reincarceration—rehabilitation, reentry, and reintegration have become a newfound concern for policymakers, criminologists, and those involved in corrections. According to Austin (2001), prisoner reentry has become "the 'new buzzword' in correctional reform" (p. 314). It is in this context that this book aims to present a renewed discourse on the subject. A thoughtful synthesis of current data and past studies supports an argument that rehabilitation and reintegration efforts should begin early, perhaps as early as the trial stage and during preparation of the presentence report. This chapter briefly introduces some of the main themes covered by this book, allowing the reader to understand the scope of work covered and how this understanding may translate into correctional practice.

OFFENDER CHARACTERISTICS AND NEEDS

Nationally, it is estimated that 31% of offenders were unemployed before arrest, 40% are functionally illiterate, 19% are illiterate, and 13% have some type of mental health problem (Petersilia, 2003, p. 35). In chapter 13, Tarlow cites related data on employment barriers. Similarly, studies demonstrate that most inmates are poorly educated, lack vocational skills, struggle with drug and alcohol abuse, and often suffer from some form of mental illness (Petersilia, 2003; Travis, 2005). Additionally, the incidence of serious mental illnesses, such as schizophrenia, major depression, bipolar disorder, and post-traumatic stress disorder, is believed to be two to four times higher among prisoners than in the general population (Golembeski & Fullilove, 2005; Petersilia, 2003; St. Gerard, 2002). Furthermore, Wynn (2001) argues that more than 265,000 mentally ill Americans are in prison. She argues that "the correctional system has become the biggest psychiatric hospital in the world" (Wynn, 2001, p. 100). Offenders are still being returned to society and are expected to succeed despite limited assistance (sometimes no assistance at all) in dealing with these problems, including factors that are often associated with future criminality. In addition, offenders are often expected to make many arrangements on their own, sometimes while they are still incarcerated. Most of the main issues, such as finding housing and employment, are left solely up to them, and for many offenders this is beyond their comprehension (Taxman, Douglas, & Bryne, 2000). This is why a statement made by Martin Horn, the former commissioner of corrections for the City of New York, calling for a shift in accountability from the facility to the inmates, sounds self-defeating. Specifically, Horn (in Wynn, 2001) argues that the correctional system should reduce its expectations and responsibilities for correcting inmates; the inmate, not corrections, should be held responsible for his or her own postrelease behavior.

THE PARADOX OF PRISON AS AN AGENT OF REHABILITATION AND REINTEGRATION

In its current state, prison is not an appropriate place for rehabilitation. The current model of prison operations is based solely on incapacitation and not on inmate rehabilitation or preparation for a successful release (Seiter, 2004). Relying on previous studies and her own professional experience, Wynn (2001) argues that what prison has always done is to give those who already have problems many more. However, scholars argue that even with rehabilitation goals in mind, prisons still do not deter repeat offenders. In fact, the corrections system creates a revolving door of justice (Freeman, 2003; Petersilia, 2003; Travis, 2005). Similarly, as prisons become overcrowded, many correctional officials are forced to release offenders early, causing a backfire effect (Walker, 2006). Moreover, the practice in the United States of spending billions of dollars to lock up offenders for increasingly longer periods of time has proven ineffective; therefore, it has been suggested that these funds be spent on programs that improve the success rate of prisoners' reentry to society. Furthermore, the high recidivism rates suggest that the existing model of "corrections" is not solving the crime problem; if anything, it is only perpetuating it. This paradox is discussed in multiple contexts throughout this chapter. Additionally, chapter 6 by Porter discusses diversion programs, with an emphasis on programs in practice—treatment courts (e.g., drug, mental health, and domestic violence courts), Treatment Alternatives for Street Crime (TASC), and shock incarceration or boot camps—as ways to reduce the growing incarceration rates and the lessons learned from such alternatives as they have been implemented.

PAROLE DISCOURSE EFFECT ON REENTRY

Before the 1970s, the American corrections system focused on parole and indeterminate sentencing for the purpose of rehabilitating the offender. However, parole and indeterminate sentencing came under attack by a group of crime control advocates in conjunction with several scholars who initiated change in the American criminal justice system. For example, James Q. Wilson (in Walker, 2006) argued for a revival of interest in deterrence and incapacitation. He wanted to abandon rehabilitation as the purpose of corrections: "Wicked people exist. Nothing avails except to set them apart from innocent people" (Walker, 2006, p. 22). Wilson and others had a major influence on how America felt about parole and rehabilitation programs; by 1995, only 26% of the American population surveyed thought that the primary purpose of prison should be rehabilitation (Petersilia, 2003, p. 65).

Kadela and Seiter (2003) maintain that the current model of prison and prisoner reentry focuses on punishment, deterrence, and incapacitation in order to prevent future crimes; rehabilitation and preparation for a successful release are not recognized. Many states have opted to abolish parole. The federal government and 15 states have decided to deny parole boards the authority to make release decisions, thus eliminating the major function of parole boards. Parole boards ensure supervision of parolees and their attendance in treatment programs that benefit the offenders. Many states still have a form of mandatory supervision under determinate sentencing; nevertheless, it is less individualized and is based on risk rather than the needs of the offenders, setting supervision levels based primarily on offenders' history of criminal behavior (Kadela & Seiter, 2003; Petersilia, 2003; Travis, 2005).

As a result, discretionary parole is no longer the mechanism used to determine whether offenders will be released. Petersilia (2003) states that most inmates are being released automatically on a mandatory basis without ever appearing before a parole board, whereas previously parole release was considered an incentive for many inmates to participate in rehabilitative programs. This provides a better understanding of why some prisoners decide not to participate in programs offered at their institutions. Preparing inmates for release has rarely been an organizational concern for prison administrators at many institutions; the primary goal of such prisons is to maintain order using the allocated funds provided by the legislature (Austin, 2001). Moreover, an increase in prison populations caused by changes in sentencing guidelines has resulted in a more punitive approach to crime reduction. As a result, local and state governments are reallocating funds previously designated for public health, employment, and education programs to construction and management of new jails and prisons (Austin, 2001). Consider this: In the 1990s federal spending on employment and training programs was cut nearly in half while spending on correctional facilities increased by 521% (Golembeski & Fullilove, 2005, p. 1702), resulting in more prisoners being released without individualized help in finding employment or housing (Petersilia, 2003).

Kadela and Seiter (2003) argue that longer prison terms do not produce a safer or healthier community and usually hinder a successful reintegration into society. For example, Newman (2002) found that length of incarceration does not have a positive effect on recidivism.

Prisons do not have the necessary funding or staff to facilitate rehabilitation programs for offenders. In addition, lack of adequate program space results in classes and counseling sessions being held in open dorms or recreation spaces that are not equipped for such purposes (Austin, 2001). For these reasons, many facilities are ill prepared to offer adequate treatment and rehabilitation programs, which may also account for the inmates' lack of motivation to fully participate in such programs and services. In addition, with parole not being used as often as it once was, many offenders are being released without supervision requirements. Most inmates are released directly from the facility with no regard for their rehabilitation or concern for the reentry process (Austin, 2001; Travis, 2005).

To further illustrate this concept, consider how Washington, D.C., and Nevada deal with offender reentry. Washington, D.C., has been identified as providing the most comprehensive prerelease planning effort in the country. As of July 1, 2000, the Offender Accountability Act required all inmates released from their prison system to be assessed for risks and needs. Washington, D.C., is among the most active in terms of requiring offenders at release time to spend time at prerelease centers, with at least 30% of offenders adhering to this requirement (Austin, 2001, p. 326). However, Nevada has no formal prerelease program. The parole agency operated a small program until it was canceled because of budget cuts. Inmates are given only $25 and transportation to the city in which they intend to reside. They are further stigmatized by requirements to report to their local law enforcement agency and to carry a card that identifies them as ex-convicts (Austin, 2001). According to Taxman et al. (2000), the traditional process for releasing offenders in Nevada has not changed in the last 20 years.

This comparison illustrates how different jurisdictions deal with released offenders. Often offenders are expected to make as many arrangements as they can before they leave prison. Critical tasks such as finding a home and employment are left solely up to them, and for many offenders these tasks are beyond their abilities (Taxman et al., 2000). Similarly, studies have demonstrated that most inmates are poorly educated, lack vocational skills, struggle with drug and alcohol abuse, and often suffer from some type of mental illness, so programs to address these problems are crucial (Petersilia, 2003; Travis, 2005). The incidence of serious mental illnesses, such as schizophrenia, major depression, bipolar disorder, and posttraumatic stress disorder, is two to four times higher among prisoners than in the general population (Golembeski & Fullilove, 2005; Petersilia, 2003; St. Gerard, 2002). Despite these problems, offenders are still released back into society, left to struggle to succeed, and expected not to revert to criminality.

As mentioned previously, in its current state prison is not an appropriate place for rehabilitation. Moreover, scholars argue that, even with rehabilitation goals in mind, prisons still do not deter offenders; in fact, the corrections system creates a revolving door of justice (Freeman, 2003; Petersilia, 2003; Travis, 2005). Moreover, as prisons become overcrowded, many untreated offenders are being released before the end of their sentence. This practice perpetuates the notion of a punitive society that is guided by "getting tough on crime," with public safety policies that end up backfiring (Walker, 2006). Furthermore, recidivism data show that most incarcerated people are not rehabilitated, and consequently a majority of released prisoners are likely to be rearrested within 3 years after their release. Specifically, about 75–80% of released prisoners are likely to be rearrested within a decade of release (Freeman, 2003). Additionally, Petersilia (2003) indicates that nearly one quarter of inmates released from prisons in 1994 returned to prison for a new crime within 3 years of their release. According to Hassin (1989) and Petersilia (2003), risk of recidivism is highest in the first year after release. These recidivism rates suggest that our current model for corrections is not solving the crime problem and may be perpetuating it. Moreover, the practice of spending billions of dollars on incarcerating offenders for longer and longer periods of time has been ineffective. A new approach should be considered wherein such expenditures are used for programs that improve the success rate of prisoner reentry. "It must be considered whether such decisions are creating a revolving door of offenders who will be committed to prison time and again, as they continuously fail in the community" (Seiter, 2004, p. 87). The American corrections system is not aiding offenders in rehabilitation, reentry, or reintegration efforts. There are many different approaches to rehabilitation and reentry advancement that may help offenders reintegrate while minimizing the revolving door phenomenon. In chapter 12, Taxman discusses the historical development of parole and the different parole practices currently in use and their effectiveness in reintegration.

OFFENDER NEEDS AND DIFFERENT APPROACHES TO REHABILITATION

As discussed in more detail in the chapters that follow, released offenders encounter many impediments to success in reintegration and often experience increasing difficulties upon return to the community (for further discussion about the barriers to reintegration, see chapter 14). For example, many states deny convicted felons the right to vote, and others limit their employment options by banning them from certain professions (Petersilia, 2003; Taxman et al., 2000; Travis, 2005). Moreover, ex-offenders are denied access to student loans, drivers' licenses, and benefits such as welfare, food stamps, and public housing (Travis, 2005). Kadela and Seiter (2003) further affirm this claim by stating that "the world to which they return is drastically different from the one they left regarding availability of jobs, family support, community resources, and willingness to assist ex-offenders" (p. 361). Released prisoners often return to the communities from which they came, many of which are characterized by poverty, social decay, and scarce employment opportunities. Some face multifaceted challenges such as finding housing, employment, and funding to attend school. One might well ask how offenders can be expected to return to society and make a successful life for themselves without being rehabilitated or appropriately prepared for reentry. These problems are magnified when society continues to belittle ex-offenders, denying them the benefits of the social safety net and forms of assistance that could facilitate their recovery and reentry into a law-abiding society (Lowenkamp & Latessa, 2005; Petersilia, 2001, 2003, 2005; Travis, 2005).

Educational and Vocational Training Programs

To demonstrate the need for educational and vocational programs, Wilson, Gallagher, Coggeshall, and MacKenzie (1999) completed a meta-analysis comparing nonparticipants with program participants. They found strong support for offenders who participated in educational and vocational programs. The study concluded that those who participated in correction-based education, vocation, and work programs recidivated at a lower rate than nonparticipants. Tischler (1999) describes one correction-based program at the Bath Institution in Ontario, Canada, where the assistant warden was known for introducing the concept of offender rehabilitation at a time when the focus of incarceration was simply to lock people up. The program focuses on academic skills, teamwork, employment skills, and personal management skills. "Bath Institution places a serious emphasis on being a place for change and not just a warehouse for stagnant offenders" (Tischler, 1999, p. 74). In another example, the state of Texas created a separate school district to offer education services to the prison population (a full description of this program appears in chapter 8). Even with most offenders having low levels of education and many being functionally illiterate, it was reported in 2000 that nearly 5,000 Texas prisoners took the

General Educational Development (GED) test; 67% passed, and most were enrolled in basic literacy courses (Austin, 2001). Education programs open new doors for many offenders who want to rehabilitate themselves and continue on a successful path in life (Davis, 2000).

Prison-Based Drug Treatment Programs

Drug treatment programs are also in demand in many facilities. For instance, almost 68% of jail inmates are dependent on drugs or alcohol. Unfortunately, only 15–18% of substance-abusing inmates receive treatment or participate in other substance abuse programs after entering jail (La Vigne, Solomon, Beckman, & Dedel, 2006; see chapter 7). Recent research studies suggest that prisoners are more likely to reoffend if they are unemployed, use drugs or abuse alcohol, and have extensive criminal histories (La Vigne et al., 2006; Petersilia, 2001, 2003; Travis, 2005). Similarly, Prendergast and Wexler (2004) assert that about 70% of people in state prisons need substance abuse treatment, but 45% of them are not being offered any kind of treatment; the lack of adequate substance abuse treatment in many facilities may contribute to high rates of recidivism. In a study completed by the National Center on Addiction and Substance Abuse at Columbia University in 1996, it was found that 70–85% of state prison inmates needed some level of substance abuse treatment, but only 13% actually received any treatment. (See chapter 7 for further discussion of this report and other substance abuse treatment modalities.)

The close tie between substance abuse and crime has led many scholars and policymakers to turn to treatment as a way to reduce the adverse public health and safety consequences of drugs (Inciardi, Martin, & Butzin, 2004; Inciardi, Martin, Butzin, Hooper, & Harrison, 1997; Prendergast & Wexler, 2004). In the light of the "nothing works" doctrine adopted by many legislators and corrections officials in the late 1960s and early 1970s, the work of Martinson suggested that, with few exceptions, there is little evidence to show that correctional treatment works. "The idea that nothing works entered professional and popular thinking, engendering deep pessimism about society's ability to rehabilitate offenders" (Prendergast & Wexler, 2004, p. 4). Despite the Martinson report, several studies suggest that some treatment programs do work, and two types of substance abuse treatment programs have developed in prison settings: therapeutic community (TC) programs and cognitive-behavioral programs (see chapters 4 and 7 for further discussion of these modalities). In the 1990s, the TC model was adapted to correctional environments, where it became the primary approach for treating substance abuse problems among inmates (see chapter 7).

Therapeutic Communities

TCs are especially effective in a correctional institution because they are structured as total treatment environments isolated from the rest of the prison population. The reason they are so effective is because they segregate prisoners from the drugs, violence, and other aspects of prison life commonly associated with ineffective rehabilitation efforts (see Gideon, Shoham, & Weisburd, in press; Shoham, Gideon, Weisburd, & Vilner, 2006). The TC has been the modality most often implemented in prison settings because of previous successes, and it has been the focus of several large-scale studies in the past decade (Prendergast & Wexler, 2004). For example, Wexler, De Leon, Thomas, Kressel, and Peters (1999) indicate that TCs that provide aftercare produce large positive outcomes, whereas TCs alone only show small and mostly nonsignificant effects (also see Shoham et al., 2006). Similarly, Inciardi et al. (1997) studied prison TC evaluations to assess the effects of prison TC substance abuse treatment followed by either work release or aftercare treatment. Their findings suggest that treatment programs with some type of postrelease aftercare decrease recidivism, as measured by arrests and lower levels of drug use (Inciardi et al., 1997). Similarly, Wexler et al. (1999) indicate that inmates who were randomly assigned to treatment as a condition of parole had significantly lower recidivism rates than the nontreatment control group. Other studies examining TCs also support the notion that TCs are most effective for those who remain in treatment the longest (Simpson, Savage, & Lloyd, 1979). A study by Inciardi et al. (2004) indicates that long-term treatment in correctional settings can have a major impact on the potential for relapse and recidivism among drug-involved offenders. This outcome could be surprising because these programs target the most difficult of all substance abusers: "They are the most drug involved, the most criminally involved, and the most socially dysfunctional. As such, positive changes typically occur in small increments" (Inciardi et al., 2004, p. 15). Similar findings were also found in a study of prison-based TCs in Israel (Shoham et al., 2006).

TC treatment programs are not the only approach to reducing substance abuse in offenders. Cognitive–behavioral programs offer advantages over TC programs in that they are less expensive and easier to implement. Prendergast and Wexler (2004) indicate that "this approach to treating offenders begins with the premise that criminals commit crimes because they think differently than non-criminals, because they lack appropriate social skills, or because they operate from a lower level of moral development" (p. 8). The main goal of cognitive–behavioral programs is to change the thought process and behavioral patterns that may encourage criminal activities. Cognitive–behavioral pro-grams focus on problem solving and negotiations, skill training, rational–emotive therapy, and so forth (see chapter 4). Studies also suggest positive results in reducing reoffending. For instance, Pearson, Lipton, Cleland, and Yee (2002) conducted a meta-analysis of 69 studies that examined the effectiveness of behavioral and cognitive treatment in reducing recidivism for offenders. The study indicated a 12% difference in recidivism between offenders in cognitive–behavioral treatments and those in the comparison group. Similar results were found by Allen, MacKenzie, and Hickman (2001), with reductions in recidi-vism associated with a cognitive–behavioral treatment. Allen and colleagues' research signaled to policymakers that the "nothing works" idea is no longer valid. In order for substance abusers to be fully rehabilitated, it is necessary for them to be enrolled in effective programs. Instead of incarcerating substance-abusing people and releasing them untreated—and often in worse condition than when they entered prison—we need to provide funding for these types of institutional programs.

Faith-Based Programs

Another approach to rehabilitating offenders is faith-based prison programs (see chapter 11). These are inexpensive approaches to correctional treatment and have been receiving increased attention. In recent years, faith-based pro-grams have become more interesting to corrections officials, although research on these types of prison-based programs is just beginning to develop. However, studies suggest that religion is one of the coping methods inmates may find use-ful in a harsh prison environment (Clear et al., 1992; Clear & Sumter, 2002; Kerley, Matthews, & Schulz, 2005; O'Connor & Perreyclear, 2002). Having a better understanding of the value of religious programs can help a correctional administrator make more informed decisions in difficult financial times. Religious programs have also served as a way of dealing with the psychologi-cal and physical deficiencies that are often effects of imprisonment (Dammer, 2002). Kerley and colleagues (2005) conducted a study on faith-based prison programs at one of the nation's largest state prisons, in Mississippi. Their study found that inmates who participated in the program were somewhat less likely to experience negative emotions and were less likely to engage in fights with fellow inmates and staff. Furthermore, they found a decrease in feelings of anger, bitterness, and coldness, similar to the findings of Clear et al. (1992), who administered a self-report questionnaire to a nonrandom sample of 769 inmates in 20 prisons from 12 states. Clear and his colleagues were trying to determine whether an inmate's religiousness was related to prison adjustment and the number of disciplinary infractions for which they were cited. Kerley and colleagues' (2005) results showed positive effects on offenders' behavior. Likewise, an earlier study by Clear and Sumter (2002) found a significant relationship between inmate religiousness and various measures of inmate adjustment to the prison environment. The study also found that higher levels of inmate religiousness are associated with fewer self-reported disciplinary confinements. Additional findings suggest that correctional theory and practice ought to include active religious participation to reduce factors associated with prison infractions (O'Connor & Perreyclear, 2002).

Clearly these programs are much needed to aid in prisoners' rehabilitation and reintegration initiatives. However, budget cuts and an overall lack of designated funds have prevented many correctional institutions from establishing such programs. This is practically inconceivable, but sadly true, even when $50 billion is spent on corrections each year (Petersilia, 2003; Seiter, 2004). Petersilia (2005) indicates that funding is spent on hiring more prison staff, constructing new prisons, and meeting the rising costs of health care, leaving very little funding for treatment and work programs. As a result, not enough money is left to fund these supportive programs. Despite the knowledge that these programs can be effective, legislators continue to withdraw funding for reentry initiatives, leaving prisoners to be released into a situation that is many times worse than what they experienced before they entered prison. These cutbacks are legislative decisions that are supported by false perceptions (chapter 2). Legislators sometimes wrongly assume that the public will have more of a conservative outlook regarding how to handle criminals (Petersilia, 2003; Travis, 2005). "On the whole, we are people who do not really expect deviants to change very much as they are processed through the control agencies we provide for them, and we are often reluctant to devote much of the community's resources to the job of rehabilitation" (Adler & Adler, 2003, p. 17). Furthermore, it is believed that the shortage of rehabilitative programs is largely the result of public dislike for these programs, the belief these programs will not work, and the overall popularity of punitive measures that are commonly associated with the public's fear of crime (Golembeski & Fullilove, 2005; Zimring, Hawkins, & Kamin, 2001). "Ultimately, public opinion on crime and punishment is a complex mix of perception, reason, emotion, and social ideals of justice, one that cannot be readily reduced to political slogans or newspaper headlines" (Warr, 1995, p. 302).

However, emerging evidence shows that public opinion has calmed in its clamor for more punitive policies. Petersilia (2003) cites several public opinion polls that suggest this promising conversion. For instance, a Hart poll conducted in 2002 found that nearly two thirds of all Americans agree that the best way to reduce crime is to rehabilitate offenders through job training and educational programs while they are still in prison. Likewise, Petersilia (2003) reveals findings by the Public Agenda Foundation, which conducted several series of focus groups on prisoner reentry in 2002. They discovered that Americans are frustrated with our prison system and believe that many inmates are released with only minimal survival skills (Petersilia, 2003, p. 233). Other research indicates that the public may be more liberal in its attitudes toward offenders, a surprising change from the conservative ideologies of the past. The research further implies that a majority of Americans, 85%, believe that it is important to rehabilitate offenders, and 90% still believe it is important for offenders to serve time (Sims & Johnston, 2004).

A study by the National Council of Crime and Delinquency (Krisberg & Marchionna, 2006) examined a sample of 1,039 voters regarding public attitudes toward prisoner rehabilitation and reentry. It found that the overwhelming majority supported rehabilitation as a major goal of incarceration. Additionally, participants appeared to understand that current correctional practices are not working, that prisoners are facing enormous barriers to successful reintegration, and that rehabilitative services should be provided as means of reducing crime. For instance, most thought that job training, drug treatment, mental health services, family support, mentoring, and housing assistance were all very important services for rehabilitating offenders. Also, participants thought that a lack of life skills, the experience of being in prison, and obstacles to reentry are precursors to a return to criminality. Moreover, the study found that 78% either "strongly support" or "support" the implementation of the Second Chance Act (Krisberg & Marchionna, 2006). Similar results were found in a recent study that used a nonrandom public opinion survey conducted by Gideon and Loveland that examined level of punitiveness and support for rehabilitative endeavors among New Yorkers and residents of the tri-state area (see chapter 2).

Likewise, recent polls suggest that Americans are becoming more aware of the hardships prisoners face during and after incarceration. In addition, they realize that incarceration should be coupled with rehabilitation and reentry efforts to promote successful reintegration into society. Unfortunately, budget constraints have kept several prisons from fully implementing such programs. At the same time, "get tough" policies are continuously marketed to support more punitive strategies to solve the crime problem, counteracting efforts to revise penological ideologies that have governed correctional practice for more than three decades.

POLICY IMPLICATIONS

"We must accept the reality that to confine offenders behind walls without trying to change them is an expensive folly with short-term benefits—winning the battles while losing the war. It is wrong. It is expensive. It is stupid" (former U.S. Supreme Court chief justice Warren Burger, in Petersilia, 2003, p. 93). This quote says it all. Society has begun to realize that locking away its offenders is a partial solution at best. Prison is not an appropriate place to rehabilitate offenders. According to Ortmann (2000), the prisonization process experienced by inmates during their incarceration prevents them from being rehabilitated while incarcerated. In fact, Elliot Currie (2002) argues that the tendency for incarceration to make some criminals worse is one of the best established findings in criminology. Currie maintains that prisons are schools for crime, so very little or no rehabilitation can be found in these institutions. Conversely, numerous studies support the idea of prison-based treatment and rehabilitation (Andrews, 1990; Cullen, 1985; Gendreau & Ross, 1987; Greenwood & Zimring, 1985; Hamm & Schrink, 1989; Inciardi et al., 1997; Lipton, Franklin, & Wexler, 1992). Additionally, studies cited in this chapter support the notion that there are treatment programs and interventions that do promote rehabilitation. In the following chapters such evidence will be described in detail. Each chapter shows how programs such as prison-based substance abuse treatment, prison-based TCs, educational and vocational training, cognitive–behavioral treatment, faith-based programs, diversion programs, and adequate medical and psychiatric attention all show promising results in terms of their effect on rehabilitation, reentry, and successful reintegration.

Policymakers should embrace the results of these studies and the changes in public opinion that support rehabilitation for convicted offenders. Policymakers should advocate for a larger investment in treating and rehabilitating offenders while they are incarcerated because such practices will ease the transition from jail or prison back into the community and will provide released offenders with a true opportunity to reintegrate as productive members of the normative, noncriminal community.

To that end, the chapters of this book discuss rehabilitation and reintegration initiatives in different stages of the criminal justice system, from the beginning of the intake process, where offenders are assessed for their risks and needs; through diversion programs, as appropriate; through the prison-based treatment experiences available to offenders; and concluding with the community supervision strategies offered upon release and the impediments these offenders experience after release. Each chapter concludes with a policy implication section that summarizes the potential benefits of the practice discussed in the chapter and describes how such practice can affect policy, with the hope that such knowledge will find its way into future policies as they are being developed for public safety.

DISCUSSION QUESTIONS

1. Discuss the various impediments released offenders face in their effort to reintegrate into society.

2. Discuss why some scholars argue that prison is not an appropriate place for rehabilitation.

3. Discuss the different approaches to prison-based treatment in this chapter. Can you relate your discussion to any specific type of offenders? How?

4. Discuss how policymakers can use public opinion polls to change existing penological policies.

5. Discuss Warren Burger's statement, "We must accept the reality that to confine offenders behind walls without trying to change them is an expensive folly with short-term benefits—winning the battles while losing the war. It is wrong. It is expensive. It is stupid." Do you agree with this statement? Why or why not?

REFERENCES

Adler, A. P., & Adler, P. (2003). *Constructions of deviance: Social power, context and interaction.* Belmont: Thompson and Wadsworth.

Allen, L. C., MacKenzie, D. L., & Hickman, L. (2001). The effectiveness of cognitive behavioral treatment for adult offenders: A methodological, quality-based review. *International Journal of Offender Therapy and Comparative Criminology, 45*(4), 498–514.

Andrews, D. A. (1990). Does correctional treatment work? A clinically relevant and psychologically informed meta-analysis. *Criminology, 28*(3), 369–404.

Austin, J. (2001). Prisoner reentry: Current trends, practices, and issues. *Crime & Delinquency, 47*(3), 314–334.

Bureau of Justice Statistics. (2009). *Reentry trends in the United States.* Retrieved September 2, 2009, from http://www.ojp.usdoj.gov/bjs/reentry/reentry.htm

Clear, T. R., Stout, B. D., Dammer, H. R., Kelly, L., Hardyman, P. L., & Shapiro, C. (1992). *Does involvement in religion help prisoners adjust to prison?* National Council on Crime and Delinquency Focus report no. NCJ 151513, pp. 1–7.

Clear, T. R., & Sumter, M. T. (2002). Prisoners, prison, and religion: Religion and adjustment to prison. *Journal of Offender Rehabilitation, 35,* 127–159.

Cullen, F. T. (1985). Attribution, salience, and attitudes toward criminal sanctioning. *Criminal Justice and Behavior, 12*(3), 305–331.

Currie, E. (2002). Rehabilitation can work. In T. Gray (Ed.), *Exploring corrections: A book of readings*. Boston: Allyn & Bacon.

Dammer, H. R. (2002). The reasons for religious involvement in the correctional environment. *Journal of Offender Rehabilitation, 35,* 35–58.

Davis, C. (2000, December). Education: A beacon of hope for the incarcerated. *Correction Today, 62*(7), 14.

Freeman, R. (2003, May). *Can we close the revolving door? Recidivism vs. employment of ex-offenders in the U.S.* Urban Institute Reentry Roundtable, Washington, DC.

Gendreau, P., & Ross, B. (1987). Revivification of rehabilitation: Evidence from the 80's. *Justice Quarterly, 4*(3), 349–408.

Gideon, L., Shoham, E., & Weisburd, D. L. (in press). Changing prison to therapeutic milieu: Evidence from the Sharon prison. *The Prison Journal.*

Golembeski, C., & Fullilove, R. (2005). Criminal justice in the city and its associated health consequences. *American Journal of Public Health, 95*(10), 1701–1706.

Greenwood, P. W., & Zimring, F. E. (1985). *One more chance: The pursuit of promising intervention strategies for chronic juvenile offenders.* Santa Monica, CA: A report prepared for the U.S. Office of Juvenile Justice and Delinquency Prevention.

Hamm, M. S., & Schrink, J. L. (1989). The conditions of effective implementation: A guide to accomplishing rehabilitative objectives in corrections. *Criminal Justice and Behavior, 16*(2), 166–182.

Hassin, Y. (1989). Notes on rehabilitation of released offenders in the community. *Studies in Criminology, 17*(1), 43–49.

Inciardi, J., Martin, S., & Butzin, C. (2004). Five-year outcomes of therapeutic community treatment of drug-involved offenders after release from prison. *Crime & Delinquency, 50*(1), 88–107.

Inciardi, J. A., Martin, S. S., Butzin, C. A., Hooper, R. M., & Harrison, L. D. (1997). An effective model of prison-based treatment for drug-involved offenders. *Journal of Drug Issues, 27,* 261–278.

Kadela, R. K., & Seiter, P. R. (2003). Prisoner reentry: What works, what does not, and what is promising. *Crime & Delinquency, 49*(3), 360–388.

Kerley, K., Matthews, T., & Schulz, J. (2005). Participation in Operation Starting Line, experience of negative emotions, and incidence of negative behavior. *International Journal of Offender Therapy and Comparative Criminology, 49*(4), 410–426.

Krisberg, B., & Marchionna, S. (2006). *Attitudes of US voters toward prisoner rehabilitation and reentry policies.* Retrieved May 9, 2007, from http://www.nccd-crc.org/nccd/pubs/2006april_focus_zogby.pdf

La Vigne, N., Solomon, A. L., Beckman, K. A., & Dedel, K. (2006). *Prisoner reentry and community policing: Strategies for enhancing public safety.* U.S. Department of Justice Office of Community Oriented Policing Services. Retrieved April 29, 2009, from http://www.urban.org/UploadedPDF/411061_COPS_reentry_monograph.pdf

Lipton, D. S., Franklin, G. P., & Wexler, H. K. (1992). Correctional drug abuse treatment in the United States: An overview. In F. M. Tims & C. Leukefeld (Eds.), *Drug abuse treatment in prison and jails* (pp. 8–29). Rockville, MD: National Institute on Drug Abuse.

Lowenkamp, C. T., & Latessa, E. (2005). Confronting recidivism: Inmate reentry and the Second Chance Act. In *Reentry today: Programs, problems, & solutions, 2006* (pp. 99–112). Alexandria, VA: American Correctional Association.

Newman, D. J. (2002). Prisons don't work. In T. Gray (Ed.), *Exploring corrections: A book of readings* (pp. 243–249). Boston: Allyn & Bacon.

O'Connor, T. P., & Perreyclear, M. (2002). Prison religion in action and its influence on offender rehabilitation. *Journal of Offender Rehabilitation, 35,* 11–33.

Ortmann, R. (2000). The effectiveness of social therapy in prison: A randomized experiment. *Crime and Delinquency, 23,* 591–601.

Pearson, F. S., Lipton, D. S., Cleland, C. M., & Yee, D. S. (2002). The effects of behavioral/cognitive–behavioral programs on recidivism. *Crime & Delinquency, 48*(3), 476–496.

Petersilia, J. (2001). Prisoner reentry: Public safety and reintegration challenges. *The Prison Journal, 81*(3), 360–375.

Petersilia, J. (2003). *When prisoners come home: Parole and prisoner reentry.* New York: Oxford University Press.

Petersilia, J. (2005). Confronting recidivism: Inmate reentry and the Second Chance Act. In *Reentry today: Programs, problems, & solutions, 2006* (pp. 25–34). Alexandria, VA: American Correctional Association.

Prendergast, M. L., & Wexler, H. K. (2004). Correctional substance abuse treatment programs in California: A historical perspective. *The Prison Journal, 84*(1), 8–35.

Seiter, R. (2004). Inmates reentry: What works and what to do about it. In *Reentry today: Programs, problems, & solutions, 2006* (pp. 77–90). Alexandria, VA: American Correctional Association.

Shoham, E., Gideon, L., Weisburd, L. D., & Vilner, Y. (2006). When "more" of a program is not necessarily better: Drug prevention in the Sharon prison. *Israel Law Review, 39*(1), 105–126.

Simpson, D. D., Savage, J., & Lloyd, M. R. (1979). Follow-up evaluation of treatment of drug abuse during 1969 to 1972. *Archives of General Psychiatry, 36,* 772–780.

Sims, B., & Johnston, E. (2004). Examining public opinion about crime and justice: A statewide study. *Criminal Justice Policy Review, 15*(3), 270–293.

St. Gerard, V. (2002, October). New effort to reintegrate offenders. *Corrections Today, 64*(6), 29.

Taxman, F. S., Douglas, Y., & Bryne, J. M. (2000). *Offender's views of reentry: Implications for processes, program, and services.* New Orleans, LA: Bureau of Governmental Research.

Tischler, E. (1999). Making a place of change. *Corrections Today, 61*(4), 74.

Travis, J. (2005). *But they all come back: Facing the challenges of prisoner reentry.* Washington, DC: The Urban Institute Press.

Walker, S. (2006). *Sense and non-sense about crime and drugs: A policy guide.* Belmont, CA: Thomson Wadsworth.

Warr, M. (1995, Summer). Poll trends: Public opinion on crime and punishment. *The Public Opinion Quarterly, 59*(2), 296–310.

Wexler, H. K., De Leon, G., Thomas, G., Kressel, D., & Peters, J. (1999). The Amity prison TC evaluation. *Criminal Justice & Behavior, 26*(2), 147–167.

Wilkinson, R. A., & Rhine, E. (2005). Confronting recidivism: Inmate reentry and the Second Chance Act. In *Reentry today: Programs, problems, & solutions, 2006* (pp. 17–22). Alexandria, VA: American Correctional Association.

Wilson, B. D., Gallagher, A. C., Coggeshall, B. M., & MacKenzie, L. D. (1999). Corrections-based education, vocation, and work programs. *Corrections Management Quarterly, 3*(4), 8–18.

Wynn, J. (2001). *Inside Rikers: Stories from the world's largest colony.* New York: St. Martin's Griffin.

Zimring, F. E., Hawkins, G., & Kamin, S. (2001). *Three strikes and you're out in California: Punishment and democracy.* Oxford: Oxford University Press.

CHAPTER 2

Public Attitudes Toward Rehabilitation and Reintegration

How Supportive Are People of Getting-Tough-on-Crime Policies and the Second Chance Act?

Lior Gideon and Natalie Loveland

The people we love to hate are those we know very little about. Most of us admit that we know very little about offenders but simultaneously argue that they should be locked behind bars. Very few laypersons are familiar with current policies or the difficulties released offenders often encounter upon their release. This chapter examines public attitudes toward offenders' rehabilitation and reintegration while examining punitiveness and support of the Second Chance Act—an act that was signed by President George W. Bush in April 9, 2008—in regard to public knowledge and familiarity with offender-related policies.

It is estimated that about 700,000 people in the United States will be leaving prison and returning to their communities this year (Krisberg & Marchionna, 2006). However, the Bureau of Justice Statistics continues to present data suggesting that incarceration rates are increasing, and so is the number of people being released back to their communities. Figure 2.1 shows the increase in the number of people being admitted to correctional facilities between 1980 and June 30, 2007 (the last date for which data were available from the Bureau of Justice Statistics). As mentioned in chapter 1, such incarceration rates also affect the number of people being released on parole supervision.

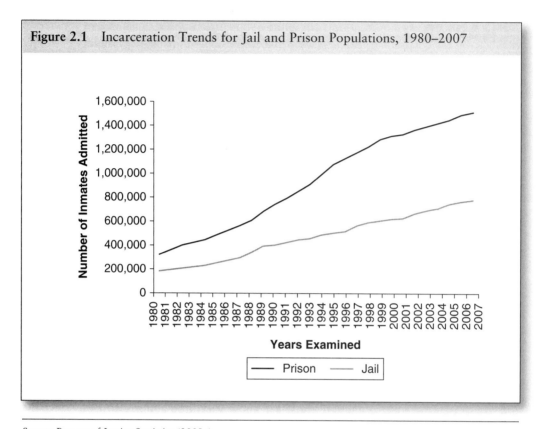

Figure 2.1   Incarceration Trends for Jail and Prison Populations, 1980–2007

Source: Bureau of Justice Statistics (2008a).

Petersilia (2005) states that the number of incarcerated people who will be released back to their home communities is expected to grow in future years.

According to both Petersilia (2005) and Travis (2005), and according to the Bureau of Justice Statistics, "at least 95% of all State prisoners will be released from prison at some point" (Bureau of Justice Statistics, 2008b). However, as mentioned by Travis (2005), reintegration and reentry have risen to public awareness only recently, with punitive approaches to crime control dominating public attitudes and, as a result, public policy. Policies such as the "war on crime" and "war on drugs" have resulted in tough-on-crime policies, which in turn resulted in an imprisonment binge in the 1980s and 1990s, as can be seen in Figure 2.1. Such incarceration binges led to the steep increase in the number of people being incarcerated and therefore those who are exiting the prison system today (Irwin & Austin, 2006). In fact, De Parle (2007, p. 33) refers to this incarceration binge as "the American prison nightmare," with daily counts reaching more than 2.3 million people behind bars (Harrison & Beck, 2006; Sabol, Couture, & Harrison, 2007). Consequently, most communities are ill prepared to accommodate those released from jails and prisons, and they do not have the knowledge or support to do so (see Clear, 2007, for a discussion on community consequences of mass incarceration).

Similarly, policymakers' perceptions of the public's fear and distrust in the ability of the government to protect them from criminal threats produced "the perfect storm of punitive expansion" (Zimring & Johnson, 2006, p. 265). Such perceptions may very well be accounted for by a lack of understanding of the public's true fear of crime and criminals and its attitudes toward prisoner rehabilitation, reentry, and reintegration practices. Zimring, Hawkins, and Kamin (2001) argue that "in punishment of street criminals, *vox populi* is rarely accused of undue leniency" (p. 188). Furthermore, they argue, "the essential element of the way in which the public opinion applies to questions of penal policy is that citizens tend to express . . . [an] attitude toward criminals, a non-proportional hostility" (Zimring et al., 2001, p. 201). Such a gap between the public's true concerns and the way in which those concerns are interpreted by policymakers leads toward much harsher policies that in turn create more impediments for successful reintegration and rehabilitation. In fact, Tonry (2006) argues that "politicians typically led public opinion about crime rather than followed it, in effect raising public fears and anxieties and then proposing harsh, simplistic solutions to ameliorate them" (p. 4). Such practice can also be attributed to the unstoppable "get tough" movement that dominated academic scholarship, according to which incarceration is the ideal method of punishment (Listwan-Johanson, Lero-Jonson, Cullen, & Latessa, 2008). A different perspective, focusing on community consequences of incarceration, started appearing in the mid-1980s and early 1990s and called for reevaluation of the consequences of mass incarceration. Up to that time, scholars were trained to show what didn't work as opposed to what worked in correctional practice. In fact, Cullen and Gendreau (2001) argue that such ideology has affected the creation of knowledge that "reveals the foolishness of numerous correctional interventions" (p. 314). This, they argue, "has been dysfunctional to the extent that it has inhibited academic criminology's ability to create an evidence-based agenda for how best to correct offenders" (Cullen & Gendreau, 2001, p. 314). As a result, the years after the Martinson (1974) report were characterized by an increase in the number of offenders being incarcerated and by an increase in the length of sentences (Austin, 2001).

However, previous studies have shown that such a punitive approach does not reflect what the public actually thinks (Applegate, Cullen, & Fisher, 1997,

2002; Brown, 1999; Cohn, Barkan, & Halteman, 1991; Cullen, Clark, Cullen, & Mathers, 1985; Dowler, 2003; Lambert, 2005; Levenson, Brannon, Fortney, & Baker, 2007; Listwan-Johanson et al., 2008; McIntyre, 1967; Wanner & Caputo, 1987; Warr, 1995). Therefore, knowledge of public attitudes toward prisoners' rehabilitation and reintegration in general and the degree to which they support rehabilitation, reintegration, and reentry programs can help policymakers approach the problem effectively.

CORRECTIONAL STAFF ATTITUDES TOWARD INMATES

Offenders' reintegration and reentry has become a popular topic in recent years. However, many may view it as a renewed discussion of treatment and rehabilitation practices of the 1960s and 1970s. As Johnson (1960, p. 356) noted, "the rehabilitation bureaucracy hopes to return its 'clients' to the outside world prepared to play socially-approved roles." Such discussion was violently put down by the Martinson report of the early 1970s, and the work since then has attempted to examine what works and what is promising in criminal justice practice.

One major advance that has been made in regard to rehabilitation and reintegration of offenders is the Second Chance Act, signed by President George W. Bush in April 2008. "The Second Chance Act expands federal support for adult and juvenile offender reentry demonstration projects and supports post-release drug treatment" (Anonymous, 2006a, p. 4). This bill and similar legislation will improve prisoner reentry.

Rehabilitation's effectiveness in improving offender behavior has been questioned—from Martinson's (1974) "Nothing Works" article to the shift to truth-in-sentencing. Corrections staff, the general public, and offenders must all be motivated for a rehabilitation program to succeed. Specifically, replacing the traditional custodial role with a new "humane enthusiast" role can improve success rates for offenders (Johnson, 1960). This is contrary to most correctional practice; increasingly, there has been a focus on "risk management" and the "new penology," in which offenders are addressed as a group, shifting away from their individual identities and needs (Rhine, 1997). It appears that this approach has deep roots in the past. For example, Hazelrigg (1967) compared self-report surveys from inmates with surveys of staff perceptions and found that staff perceptions of incarcerated offenders are governed largely by unfavorable, stereotypical images of the inmates. It is possible that common stereotypes of the inmate population result from the conflicting nature of the corrections job, as suggested by O'Leary and Duffee (1971), who developed a typology of management control, including reform, restraint, rehabilitation, and reintegration measures. Furthermore, they found that rehabilitation and reintegration programs will be viewed by correctional staff as a necessary deceitful practice to maintain institutional order while they prepare inmates for reintegration (O'Leary & Duffee, 1971). This is especially true when it is time for prisoners to be released and reintegrated back into society. A study of parole officers identified job training or vocational rehabilitation, substance abuse treatment, and residential facilities and halfway houses as essential ingredients of successful reintegration (Seiter, 2004). However, Seiter (2004) also found that correctional staff see improving parolees' chances of success as an aspect of their job as important as monitoring, supervising, or controlling.

However, a later study that used surveys administered to prison staff shows that most prison staff do not identify preparation for reentry and reintegration as part of their job responsibilities. Consequently, many inmates who return to the community after incarceration are ill prepared for the transition.

The American Correctional Association fully supports evidence-based practices for reentry of ex-offenders. "Reentry programs enhance public safety, help prepare offenders for transition to responsible citizenship, can help reduce future criminal behavior, remove barriers that make it difficult for offenders to reenter their communities, and develop necessary support for the community" (Anonymous, 2006b, p. 88). The association encourages agencies at the federal, state, and local levels to implement certain policies to aid offenders' reentry. Some of these policy suggestions include advocating for the review and revision of existing laws that inhibit successful reentry, initiating individualized transitional planning during intake to the facility, and helping offenders access appropriate housing upon release (see Anonymous, 2006b).

THE SECOND CHANCE ACT

In his 2004 State of the Union address, President George W. Bush said, "America is the land of the second chance, and when the gates of the prison open, the path ahead should lead to a better life." This statement paved the way for a renewed discussion of prisoners' rehabilitation and reintegration. For the first time in decades, Congress was poised to pass a bill that aims to make current offenders' and ex-offenders' lives easier by allocating federal funds to rehabilitation and reentry programs. "Invisible punishments" (Travis, 2005) have been imposed on offenders who are reintegrating back into their communities, putting a wall between the ex-offender and society. For instance, ex-offenders are denied benefits such as student loans, drivers' licenses, welfare, food stamps, and public housing eligibility (Travis, 2005). Additionally, a lack of funds prevented the implementation of previously proposed rehabilitation programs by correctional agencies, which could have provided services to offenders with mental illness or substance abuse problems (Austin, 2001; Petersilia, 2003).

Furthermore, 31% of offenders were unemployed before arrest, 40% are functionally illiterate, 19% are illiterate, and 13% have some type of mental health problem (Petersilia, 2003, p. 35). If these problems are ignored during incarceration, these offenders are more likely to be reincarcerated. Specifically, with an estimated 700,000 inmates being released from prisons back to their communities each year, employment issues must be addressed before release (for an in-depth discussion of employment barriers for released offenders, see chapter 13). Furthermore, soaring recidivism rates result from the fact that most inmates being released do not receive rehabilitation services and therefore are likely to be rearrested within 3 years of release (Freeman, 2003).

Chronology of the Second Chance Act

In light of these alarming data, both Democrats and Republicans decided to sponsor the Second Chance Act of 2007, a unique proposal to expand reentry services for people leaving prison and returning to society. (The bill was first introduced in 2005 but was returned to the House of Representatives for amendments before its final approval by the president on April 9, 2008.) The Second Chance Act has been deemed the first comprehensive legislation attempting to address the multifaceted problems offenders face during and after incarceration. Additionally, it is striking that members of the Republican Party are showing strong support for the implementation of the act despite their more punitive approach to prison reform in the past. Senator Arlen Specter (R-PA), chairman of the Senate Judiciary Committee, and Senator Joe Biden (D-DE), were the lead sponsors of the bill. The bill was introduced to the House (H.R. 1704) in April and the Senate (S. 1934) in October 2005. The Second Chance Act has been supported by more than 200 organizations and has broad bipartisan support, with 113 co-sponsors in the House and 34 in the Senate (Re-Entry Policy Council, 2007).

Despite every effort to move the Second Chance Act through the 109th congressional session, the legislation stalled in the Senate. The act faced opposition from Oklahoma senator Tom Coburn (R). Senator Coburn objected to the bill on the grounds that there is no federal role in prisoner reentry. Furthermore, he argued that individual states have the resources to reduce recidivism and improve reentry on their own. Because of these objections, he placed a hold on the bill to prevent it from reaching the floor for further consideration. The 109th congressional session adjourned leaving the act undecided. In January 2007, the 110th congressional session convened, and the Second Chance Act was reintroduced to the U.S. House of Representatives on March 20, 2007. The House bill (H.R. 1593) was passed by the full Judiciary Committee only a month after being reintroduced.

Nevertheless, the Second Chance Act was postponed by the Democratic leadership and placed on the suspension calendar in order to ensure enough Republican votes for swift passage of the bill. Additionally, members of the Senate Judiciary Committee completed a markup of S. 1060, the Second Chance Act of 2007. The committee reviewed several different amendments to the act and accepted the amendment introduced by Senator Jon Kyl (R-AZ). The amendment excludes sex offenders from the early release program for elderly prisoners. A resolution was made in December 2007 to address the Senate's concerns. The resolution included new language to change the match for state and local government reentry grants and clarified the eligibility requirements for elderly release programs. Despite these minor technical changes, after months of delay the Second Chance Act was finally passed by the U.S. House of Representatives on November 13, 2007, with a 347–62 vote.

The Second Chance Act of 2007 was finally passed by the U.S. Senate on March 11, 2008. President Bush signed the Second Chance Act of 2007 on April 9, 2008. Assemblyman Jeffrion Aubry, Justice Center board member and chair of the New York State Assembly Correction Committee, made a noteworthy statement at the signing of the Second Chance Act: "The signing of the Second Chance Act is a celebrated moment for policymakers who know that, if properly funded, this legislation will increase public safety, improve lives, and make more effective use of taxpayers' dollars" (Re-Entry Policy Council, 2008).

Essence of the Second Chance Act

The Second Chance Act will provide $191 million for prisoner rehabilitation, reentry, and reintegration programs, including $65 million in grants to state and local governments for reentry initiatives, $15 million to nonprofit organizations to provide mentoring and other transitional services, $1 million for state research grants, $10 million for reentry task forces and several drug treatment provisions, $5 million for career training, $20 million for education at prisons and jails, and $20 million for prison-based and family treatment programs (Re-Entry Policy Council, 2008). Additionally, the Second Chance Act could eventually save American taxpayers millions of dollars by reducing recidivism rates and consequently lowering arrest and incarceration rates. Currently, the annual cost of incarcerating a prisoner exceeds $20,000, a number that increased sixfold between 1982 and 2002. Former senator and current vice president Joe Biden, co-sponsor of the act, stated that it is "a relatively modest investment in offender reentry efforts [that] compares very well with the alternative—building more prisons for these ex-offenders to return to if they are unable to successfully reenter their communities. An ounce of prevention, as they say, is worth a pound of cure" (Press release, 2007).

Furthermore, the Second Chance Act encourages collaboration of the criminal justice, public health, and social service systems to allow access to resources and opportunities to promote successful reentry. The partnership of these systems will continue to reduce recidivism by providing tools to address multifaceted issues, such as drug abuse and mental health issues. Additionally, the act calls for services such as public assistance, public housing, health and mental services, education, and job training; which are all associated with preventing further recidivism and allowing for a smoother transition back into society (Pogorzelski, Blitz, Pan, & Wolff, 2005; Wilkinson & Rhine, 2005).

Additionally, O'Hear (2007) points out that grant recipients are required to "develop a reentry strategic plan not only containing measurable performance outcomes, but must have a 50 percent reduction in recidivism rates over five years" (p. 76). Similarly, performance levels are measurable through increased employment, education, and housing opportunities to offenders who are released back into the community. "In short, the Second Chance Act repudiates the notion that recidivism reduction is best achieved through deterrent threats alone and calls for the delivery of services to former prisoners, not in a minimal or grudging way but in a systematic, proactive fashion" (O'Hear, 2007, p. 76). The Second Chance Act is a reentry movement that could be classified as having a "harm-reductionist flavor e.g., therapeutic jurisprudence, restorative justice, and, to some extent, victim's rights" (O'Hear, 2007, p. 77). In other words, O'Hear suggests that the Second Chance Act could weaken legalism's hold on penal law and policy. He states that such legalism has consisted of astonishing harshness in sentencing and a tendency to view offenders as "undifferentiated, willful lawbreakers" and not as "individual human beings with unique needs and limitations" (O'Hear, 2007, p. 77).

These problems do not disappear while offenders are in prison. The Second Chance Act provides for programs and services that will aid in rehabilitation efforts and encourage positive participation in society upon release. In addition, the act eliminates what Travis (2005) calls "invisible punishments" that continue to alienate the prisoner from his or her community by excluding access to public benefits such as temporary assistance for needy families, general assistance, food stamps, and public housing. These types of assistance are needed by many in society who are in transition, not just ex-offenders. It is reasonable to assume that ex-offenders need to rely more on public assistance than the average person, but they are the ones constantly denied access. The act will counter the effects of three decades of get-tough-on-crime policies, which have made it extremely difficult for ex-offenders to reenter the normative, noncriminal community and could explain why so many recidivate (Pogorzelski et al., 2005). Farabee (2007) believes that the funding the Second Chance Act provides to state and local correctional agencies could reduce recidivism. Furthermore, Farabee states that "by requiring that these efforts be independently evaluated using intent-to-treat, randomized designs, this legislation could make history by putting us on the slow but solid path of real progress" (p. 137).

The Second Chance Act also aims at minimizing the undesirable effects of institutionalization. Most offenders have a hard time coping in the real world; many may come to believe they are doomed to a life of crime and punishment (Maruna, 2001). Often it is very difficult for offenders to adjust after spending time on the inside. According to Goffman (1957), a "stripping process" occurs among inmates. During this process, the penal system tries to remove all personal identity, including any possessions with which the inmate may have identified himself. Furthermore, all other ties, such as family, occupational, and educational attachments, are severed.

The Second Chance Act will provide jobs, education, drug treatment, and other types of aid in hopes that offenders can help themselves, support their families, and improve society overall. In many ways this act is an implementation of Braithwaite's (1989) reintegrative shaming theory.

PUBLIC SUPPORT FOR THE SECOND CHANCE ACT AND REHABILITATION INITIATIVES

In a public opinion study that examined public attitudes toward rehabilitation, punitiveness, and support of the Second Chance Act, a sample of 879 respondents from various sectors in New York and the Tri-State Region (including parts of New York, New Jersey, and Connecticut) was examined. The sample was drawn between September 2007 and February 2008 from residents of these areas, resulting in a sample that does not differ significantly from the actual population of New York and the Tri-State Region. Self-administered questionnaires included five domains: knowledge, feeling, hypothetical action, attitude, and legal compliance. The first four domains were necessary to examine the dependent variable: attitudes toward rehabilitation, punitiveness, and support of the Second Chance Act. The survey had 99 items and took about half an hour to complete on average.

The sample included slightly more females (about 54%), with about 61% of the sample being single, divorced, or separated and 61% being Christians. In terms of race, about half of the participants were White (50.8%), 15.2% were Black, and 11.7% were Hispanic. The majority of those who responded were employed full time or part time during the survey (67.3%) and had a high level of education— 15.4 years—on average. A plurality of the participants in the sample identified themselves as Democrats (49.9%), with 17.5% Republicans and 23.2% Independent. Although this sample is not representative of the entire U.S. population, it provides a substantial review of public attitudes on rehabilitation, punitiveness, and support of the Second Chance Act; this study may provide a good indicator of what the public thinks about how released offenders should be treated.

The startling fact that nearly 700,000 inmates will be released from prison to their home communities may explain why the public fears for its safety. Such concern may be attributed to the fact that the public knows that recidivism rates are high and that most offenders are not being treated while incarcerated. As can be seen in Figure 2.2, about 85% of respondents reported being concerned about the fact that about 700,000 inmates will be released from prison to their home communities. Such concern may also be explained by the fact that most communities are ill prepared to accommodate those released from jails and prisons, and they do not have the knowledge or support to do so (Clear, 2007). In other words, Figure 2.2 illustrates that the public understands the difficulties faced by inmates and the receiving community. In fact, 68% of the inmates surveyed by Braucht and Bailey-Smith (2006) reported being worried about their reentry needs as their release date approached. Strangely enough, only 24% asked for help, including assistance with finding housing.

The New York City and Tri-State Region survey found that about 83% of the public is supportive of the Second Chance Act of 2007 (Figure 2.3) and thus support offenders' rehabilitation and reintegration. Such support indicates a weakening of the "penal harm" movement that governed criminal justice policy over the past three decades (Listwan-Johanson et al., 2008). "The persistence of rehabilitative attitudes among the public, burgeoning doubts about harsh justice. . . . They make a formidable case for guarded optimism that mass imprisonment is running out of steam both ideologically and intellectually" (Downes, 2008, p. 420). Indeed, such a conclusion is indicated by the fact that 93% of representatives from New York supported the act. The act symbolizes a new era in how our society deals with criminals. As previously mentioned, the act allocates funds to examine reintegration practices and thereby allows for hope that the penal harm movement and its get-tough policies will be reevaluated and, within time, will change to address the needs of offenders while maintaining public safety.

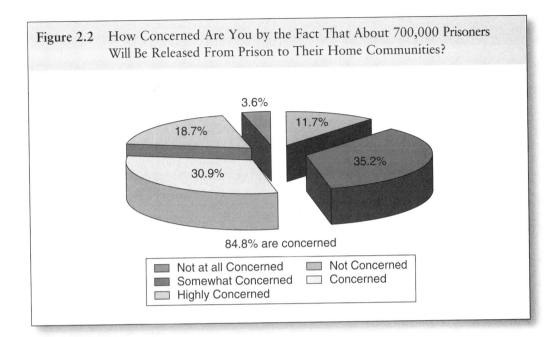

Figure 2.2   How Concerned Are You by the Fact That About 700,000 Prisoners Will Be Released From Prison to Their Home Communities?

84.8% are concerned

- Not at all Concerned
- Somewhat Concerned
- Highly Concerned
- Not Concerned
- Concerned

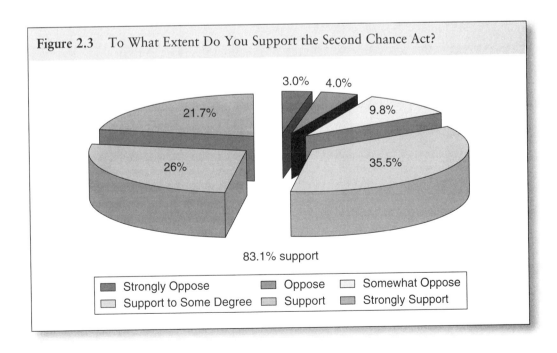

Figure 2.3   To What Extent Do You Support the Second Chance Act?

83.1% support

- Strongly Oppose
- Support to Some Degree
- Oppose
- Support
- Somewhat Oppose
- Strongly Support

Despite the public support for the Second Chance Act, lower levels of support were observed for sexual offenders. When asked whether they support the Second Chance Act for sex offenders, a majority of the respondents said they either "strongly disagree" or "disagree" with the Second Chance Act. As can be seen in Figure 2.4, the public tend to be more supportive of reintegration of non–sex offenders. When it comes to sex offenders the public is reluctant to support such policies as the Second Chance Act. In that regard, it is important to note that sex offenders are characterized by extremely low recidivism rates, as mentioned by Palermo (2009). In fact, Palermo (2009, p. 3) argues that high recidivism rates—of more than two thirds of released inmates—were observed for non–sex offenders, whereas only 5.3% of sex offenders were rearrested for another sex offense in the 3-year period that followed their release.

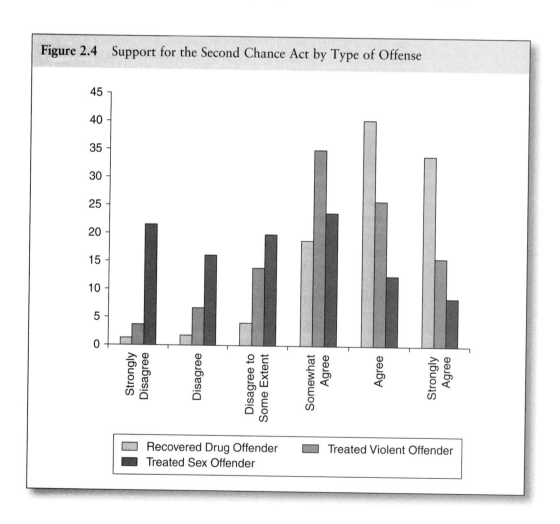

Figure 2.4   Support for the Second Chance Act by Type of Offense

Such results suggest that the public and policymakers should be educated more about the risk posed by convicted and treated sexual offenders. Chapters 3 and 9 deal with the risk and need assessments of such offenders. Findings of previous studies show that knowledge and familiarity with offenders are statistically significant predictors of punitiveness and support for rehabilitation: The more knowledge a person has, the less punitive and more supportive of rehabilitation he or she will be. Stereotypical attitudes toward offenders were found to have the opposite effect, which suggests that stigma may result in less support for rehabilitation and more punitiveness. It was also found, as in other studies (Brown, 1999; Cullen et al., 1985; Dowler, 2003; Lambert, 2005; Sundt, Cullen, Applegate, & Turner, 1998), that level of education was significantly associated with support for rehabilitation (and thus for the Second Chance Act). Consequently, one can argue that higher levels of education will reduce stigma, which may increase support for rehabilitation and reintegration.

GENDER, RACE, AND POLITICAL AFFILIATION

When gender and race were examined, results from the New York and Tri-State Region did not find gender to have a significant effect on level of punitiveness and support for rehabilitation (also an indicator of support for the Second Chance Act) (Table 2.1). However, as in previous studies, women tended to be less punitive and more supportive of rehabilitation than men. This is similar to Applegate et al.'s (1997) findings.

Table 2.1	Differences in Level of Punitiveness and Support for Rehabilitation by Gender, Race, and Political Affiliation	
	Punitiveness	**Rehabilitation**
Gender	Not significant $T = -1.406$	Not significant $T = .688$
Race	H > W > AA $F = 2.32^*$	AA > H > W $F = 6.113^{**}$
Political affiliation	R > Independent > D $F = 12.5^{**}$	D > Independent > R $F = 11.75^{**}$
$^*p < .05.$	$^{**}p < .01.$	

Notes: H = Hispanic; W = White; AA = African American; R = Republican; D = Democrat; Independent = not affiliated with any party.

Findings from the New York and Tri-State Region suggest that race does have a significant effect on attitudes toward rehabilitation and punitiveness. Specifically, African Americans are more supportive of rehabilitation than Hispanics and Whites (see Table 2.1). Whites had a strong positive effect when examined in regard to punitiveness and a strong negative effect when examined in regard to rehabilitation. However, when race was examined along with education it was found that education had a reverse effect on level of punitiveness and support for rehabilitation. Specifically, White educated respondents are less punitive than any of the other ethnic categories. This interaction was found to be significant only for punitiveness.

Finally, political affiliation was found to have a significant effect (see Table 2.1). Republicans are tougher on crime and thus tend to be more punitive and less supportive of rehabilitation. Although not significant, Democrats exhibit the opposite tendency. In fact, of those who voted for the Second Chance Act, 62.8% were Democrats and only 37.1% were Republicans.

Public attitudes are often cited as major obstacles to the implementation of policies (Skovron, Scott, & Cullen, 1989). Therefore, public opinion surveys play an important role in decisions about correctional practices, and the Second Chance Act is no exception. Examination of New Yorkers' and Tri-State Region residents' attitudes revealed that the public is concerned about crime but is also supportive of rehabilitation initiatives. In addition, results from the New York and Tri-State Region are consistent with findings by other scholars, who found that the public supports rehabilitation of offenders (Cullen, Skovron, Scott, & Burton, 1990; Krisberg & Marchionna, 2006; McCorkle, 1993; Skovron et al., 1989; Sundt et al., 1998).

POLICY IMPLICATIONS

Measurements of public opinions and attitudes must include a thorough measure of knowledge, feeling, and potential action in order to reliably assess such issues as punitiveness and support for rehabilitation and reintegration policies and legislation. As the study presented in this chapter found, the more knowledge people have of inmate-related topics, the less punitive they are. Consequently, the public should be provided with more accurate information about correctional practices, inmates, and the actual recidivism rates of different offender categories. Additionally, the public should be educated about the rehabilitation and reintegration barriers faced by released offenders and how such impediments may backfire, causing more harm to public safety than good. As mentioned by Clear (2007), this harm affects primarily the communities to which the offenders return. Addressing concerns about the large numbers of inmates who will be released back to their communities may result in less punitiveness and more support for reintegration. This support may lead to what Braithwaite (1989) calls reintegrative shaming, through which people have the opportunity to redeem themselves.

DISCUSSION QUESTIONS

1. Discuss the effect of the last decade's incarceration binge on the Second Chance Act of 2005.

2. How can policymakers benefit from measuring public attitudes when considering new legislation? Specifically, why should politicians and policymakers consider public opinions, and, if so, how should they interpret their results?

3. Discuss some of the barriers to successful reintegration that the Second Chance Act targets.

4. Discuss the effect of public opinion polls on both policies and public perceptions. According to Zimring, Hawkins, and Kamin (2001) and Tonry (2006), what shapes the public's perceptions, and how are such perceptions being abused by politicians and policymakers?

SUGGESTED WEB SITES

Reentry Policy Council:
http://reentrypolicy.org/search?states=NY&keyword=Jeffrion+Aubry

Second Chance Act of 2007 (H.R. 1593):
http://www.govtrack.us/congress/bill.xpd?bill=h110-1593

Suellentrop, C. (2006). *The Second Chance Act: The right has a jailhouse conversion.* http://realcostofprisons.org/blog/archives/2006/12/the_second_chan_1.html

SUGGESTED READINGS

Erikson, S. R. (1976). The relationship between public opinion and state policy: A new look at some forgotten data. *American Journal of Political Science, 20,* 25–36.

Haghighi, B., & Lopez, A. (1998). Gender and perception of prisons and prisoners. *Journal of Criminal Justice, 26*(6), 453–464.

Johnston, E., & Sims, B. (2004, September). Examining public opinion about crime and justice: A statewide study. *Criminal Justice Policy Review, 15*(3), 270–293.

Kadela, R. K., & Seiter, P. R. (2003, July). Prisoner reentry: What works, what does not, and what is promising. *Crime & Delinquency, 49*(3), 360–388.

Lowenkamp, C. T., & Latessa, E. (2005). Confronting recidivism: Inmate reentry and the Second Chance Act. In *Reentry today: Programs, problems, & solutions, 2006* (pp. 99–112). Alexandria, VA: American Correctional Association.

Page, I. B., & Shapiro, Y. R. (1983). Effects of public opinion on policy. *The American Political Science Review, 77*(1), 175–190.

Page, I. B., Shapiro, Y. R., & Dempsey, R. G. (1987). What moves public opinion? *The American Political Science Review, 81*(1), 23–44.

Petersilia, J. (2001). Prisoner reentry: Public safety and reintegration challenges. *The Prison Journal, 81*(3), 360–375.

Sims, B., & Johnston, E. (2004). Examining public opinion about crime and justice: A statewide study. *Criminal Justice Policy Review, 15*(3), 270–293.

REFERENCES

Anonymous. (2006a, March 24). Panel approves funds for reentry programs. *Corrections Digest, 37*(11), 4.

Anonymous. (2006b, October). Policies and resolutions. *Corrections Today, 68*(6), 87–89.

Applegate, B. K., Cullen, F. T., & Fisher, B. S. (1997). Public support for correctional treatment: The continuing appeal of the rehabilitative ideal. *The Prison Journal, 77*(3), 237–258.

Applegate, B. K., Cullen, F. T., & Fisher, B. S. (2002). Public views toward crime and correctional policies: Is there a gender gap? *Journal of Criminal Justice, 30*(2), 89–100.

Austin, J. (2001). Prisoner reentry: Current trends, practices, and issues. *Crime & Delinquency, 47*(3), 314–334.

Braithwaite, J. (1989). *Crime, shame, and reintegration.* Cambridge: Cambridge University Press.

Braucht, G. S., & Bailey-Smith, K. (2006, June). Reentry surveys: A reality check. *Corrections Today, 68*(3), 88–89.

Brown, S. (1999). Public attitudes toward the treatment of sex offenders. *Legal and Criminological Psychology, 4*(2), 232–252.

Bureau of Justice Statistics. (2008a). *Key facts at a glance: Correctional populations.* Retrieved January 26, 2009, from http://www.ojp.usdoj.gov/bjs/glance/tables/corr2tab.htm

Bureau of Justice Statistics. (2008b). *Reentry trends in the United States.* Retrieved February 3, 2009, from http://www.ojp.usdoj.gov/bjs/reentry/reentry.htm

Clear, T. R. (2007). *Imprisoning communities: How mass incarceration makes disadvantaged neighborhoods worse.* Oxford: Oxford University Press.

Cohn, S. F., Barkan, S. E., & Halteman, W. A. (1991). Punitive attitudes toward criminals: Racial consensus or racial conflict? *Society for the Study of Social Problems, 38*(2), 287–296.

Cullen, F. T., Clark, G., Cullen, J., & Mathers, R. (1985). Attributes, salience, and attitudes toward criminal sanctioning. *Criminal Justice and Behavior, 12*(3), 305–331.

Cullen, F. T., & Gendreau, P. (2001). From nothing works to what works: Changing professional ideology in the 21st century. *The Prison Journal, 81*(3), 313–338.

Cullen, F. T., Skovron, S. E., Scott, J. E., & Burton, V. S. Jr. (1990). Public support for correctional treatment: The tenacity of rehabilitation ideology. *Criminal Justice and Behavior, 17*(1), 6–18.

De Parle, J. (2007, April 12). The American prison nightmare. *New York Review of Books, 54,* 33–36.

Dowler, K. (2003). Media consumption and public attitudes toward crime and justice: The relationship between fear of crime, punitive attitudes, and perceived police effectiveness. *Journal of Criminal Justice and Popular Culture, 10*(2), 109–126.

Downes, D. (2008). Editor's introduction to "Cracks in the penal harm movement." *Criminology and Public Policy, 7*(3), 419–422.

Farabee, D. (2007). For the Second Chance Act, great strides will come in small steps. *Federal Sentencing Reporter, 20*(2), 136–137.

Freeman, R. (2003, May). *Can we close the revolving door?: Recidivism vs. employment of ex-offenders in the U.S.* Urban Institute Reentry Roundtable. Washington, DC: Urban Institute.

Goffman, E. (1957). Characteristics of total institutions. *Symposium on Preventive and Social Psychiatry, 84,* 43–64.

Harrison, P., & Beck, A. J. (2006). *Prison and jail inmate at midyear 2005.* Washington, DC: Bureau of Justice Statistics.

Hazelrigg, L. E. (1967). An examination of the accuracy and relevance of staff perceptions of the inmate in the correctional institution. *Journal of Criminal Law, Criminology, and Police Science, 58*(2), 204–210.

Irwin, J., & Austin, J. (2006). It's about time: America's imprisonment binge. In E. J. Latessa & A. M. Holsinger (Eds.), *Correctional contexts: Contemporary and classical readings* (pp. 901–905). Los Angeles, CA: Roxbury.

Johnson, E. H. (1960). Bureaucracy in the rehabilitation institution: Lower level staff as a treatment resource. *Social Forces, 38*(4), 355–359.

Krisberg, B., & Marchionna, S. (2006). *Attitudes of US voters toward prisoner rehabilitation and reentry policies.* Retrieved December 30, 2008, from http://www.nccd-crc.org/nccd/pubs/2006 april_focus_zogby.pdf

Lambert, E. (2005). Worlds apart: The views on crime and punishment among white and minority college students. *Criminal Justice Studies, 18*(1), 99–121.

Levenson, J., Brannon, Y., Fortney, T., & Baker, J. (2007). Public perceptions about sex offenders and community protection policies. *Analyses of Social Issues and Public Policy, 7*(1), 137–161.

Listwan-Johanson, S., Lero-Jonson, C., Cullen, F. T., & Latessa, E. J. (2008). Cracks in the penal harm movement: Evidence from the field. *Criminology and Public Policy, 7*(3), 423–465.

Martinson, R. (1974, Spring). What works? Questions and answers about prison reform. *Public Interest,* pp. 22–54.

Maruna, S. (2001). *Making good: How ex-convicts reform and rebuild their lives.* Washington, DC: American Psychological Association.

McCorkle, R. (1993). Research note: Punish and rehabilitate? Public attitudes toward six common crimes. *Crime and Delinquency, 39*(2), 240–252.

McIntyre, J. (1967). Public attitudes toward crime and law enforcement. *Annals of the American Academy of Political and Social Science, 374*(1), 34–46.

O'Hear, M. M. (2007). The Second Chance Act and the future of reentry reform. *Federal Sentencing Reporter, 20*(2), 75–83.

O'Leary, V., & Duffee, D. (1971). Correctional policy: A classification of goals designed for change. *Crime & Delinquency, 17*(4), 373–386.

Palermo, G. B. (2009). Reintegration and recidivism. *International Journal of Offender Therapy and Comparative Criminology, 53*(1), 3–4.

Petersilia, J. (2003). *When prisoners come home: Parole and prisoner reentry.* New York: Oxford University Press.

Petersilia, J. (2005). Confronting recidivism: Inmate reentry and the Second Chance Act. In *Reentry today: Programs, problems, & solutions, 2006* (pp. 25–34). Alexandria, VA: American Correctional Association.

Pogorzelski, W., Blitz, C., Pan, K., & Wolff, N. (2005, October). Behavioral health problems, ex-offender reentry polices, and the "Second Chance Act." *American Journal of Public Health, 95*(10), 1718–1724.

Press release. (2007, March). *Second Chance Act would prevent ex-cons from becoming repeat offenders.* Retrieved April 25, 2007, from http://biden.senate.gov

Re-Entry Policy Council. (2007). *Re-entry legislation Second Chance Act of 2005.* Retrieved April 25, 2007, from http://www.reentrypolicy.org/reentry/Second_Chance_Act_of_2005.aspx

Re-Entry Policy Council. (2008). *Re-entry legislation informational resources on the Second Chance Act of 2007.* Retrieved February 5, 2009, from http://www.reentrypolicy.org/government_affairs/second_chance_act

Rhine, E. E. (1997). Why "what works" matters under the "broken windows" model of supervision. *Federal Probation, 66*(2), 38–42.

Sabol, W. J., Couture, H., & Harrison, P. M. (2007). *Prisoners in 2006.* Washington, DC: Bureau of Justice Statistics.

Seiter, R. (2004). Inmate reentry: What works and what to do about it. In *Reentry today: Programs, problems, & solutions, 2006* (pp. 77–90). Alexandria, VA: American Correctional Association.

Skovron, S. E., Scott, J. E., & Cullen, F. T. (1989). The death penalty for juveniles: An assessment of public support. *Crime and Delinquency, 35*(4), 546–561.

Sundt, J. L., Cullen, F. T., Applegate, B. K., & Turner, M. G. (1998). The tenacity of the rehabilitation ideal revisited: Have attitudes toward offenders treatment changed? *Criminal Justice and Behavior, 25*(4), 426–442.

Tonry, M. (2006). *Thinking about crime: Sense and sensibility in American penal culture.* Oxford: Oxford University Press.

Travis, J. (2005). *But they all come back: Facing the challenges of prisoner reentry.* Washington, DC: The Urban Institute Press.

Wanner, R. A., & Caputo, T. C. (1987). Punitiveness, fear of crime, and perceptions of violence. *Canadian Journal of Sociology, 12*(4), 331–344.

Warr, M. (1995, Summer). Poll trends: Public opinion on crime and punishment. *The Public Opinion Quarterly, 59*(2), 296–310.

Wilkinson, R. A., & Rhine, E. (2005). Confronting recidivism: Inmate reentry and the Second Chance Act. In *Reentry today: Programs, problems, & solutions, 2006* (pp. 17–22). Alexandria, VA: American Correctional Association.

Zimring, F. E., Hawkins, G., & Kamin, S. (2001). *Punishment and democracy: Three strikes and you're out in California.* Oxford: Oxford University Press.

Zimring, F. E., & Johnson, D. T. (2006). Public opinion and the governance of punishment in democratic political systems. *The Annals of the American Academy of Political and Social Science, 605*(1), 265–280.

CHAPTER 3

Treatment of Offender Populations

Implications for Risk Management and Community Reintegration

Elizabeth L. Jeglic, Christian Maile, and
Cynthia Calkins-Mercado

Traditionally, one of the goals of incarceration has been rehabilitation. However, there has been a great debate in the literature about the efficacy of different treatment interventions for offenders and the ability of these treatments to decrease recidivism rates. In the 1950s and 1960s there was some evidence that treating offenders worked (Bailey, 1966; Logan, 1972). However in 1974, Martinson conducted a review of 230 treatment studies and concluded that nothing works in the treatment of offenders (Martinson, 1974). These findings supported the growing movement in the criminal justice system from a rehabilitative approach to a punitive one.

While the field moved away from rehabilitation, criminal justice researchers became interested in developing a theory to explain why some treatments worked and others did not (Andrews et al., 1990). This resulted in the development of the risk–need–responsivity (RNR) model for evaluating program effectiveness (Andrews, Bonta, & Hoge, 1990). The RNR model has been empirically supported as a means of effectively evaluating offender treatment programs (Andrews & Bonta, 1998). The basic principles of RNR are that correctional interventions must be structured on three core rehabilitation principles: risk, need, and responsivity. The risk principle addresses the fact that offender treatments must change according to the offender's risk to the community. In other words, offenders who are identified as being at high risk to reoffend should receive the most intensive treatment available, whereas offenders identified as low risk should receive less intensive treatment. According to the need principle, effective offender therapies must primarily address the offender's criminogenic needs and attempt to modify his or her dynamic risk factors (risk factors that are amenable to change). Lastly, the responsivity principle addresses the need for offender treatment therapies to match an offender's learning style, motivation level, and cultural background (Andrews & Bonta, 1998; Ward, Vess, & Collie, 2006). Programs that adhered to all three principles of the RNR model saw 17% and 35% decreases in recidivism for residential and community programs, respectively (Andrews & Bonta, 2006).

In order to adequately address these three principles for the purposes of treatment, researchers needed assessment instruments. These assessment instruments targeted the domains of offender risk level, dynamic criminogenic factors such as prosocial beliefs and cognitive distortions, and individual factors that could influence treatment outcome (Andrews & Bonta, 2006).

Finally, after the assessment and treatment of an offender, the final phase of rehabilitation is reintegration back into the community and risk management. Traditionally risk management has assumed a one-size-fits-all model. However, with the success of the RNR model of treatment, alternatives to risk management that adhere to this model and thus continue to target the RNR principles upon release are also being developed (Conroy, 2006).

Although the overarching goal of well-designed and well-executed rehabilitation programs is to use research to inform practice, that is not always the case in the criminal justice system. This chapter reviews the current state of assessment and treatment of violent offenders, sex offenders, perpetrators of intimate partner violence, juvenile offenders, female offenders, and offenders with serious mental illness and addresses how these affect risk management and community integration.

VIOLENT OFFENDERS

Violent offenders are among the most dangerous offenders in the criminal justice system, having been arrested, convicted, and imprisoned for felony crimes such as robbery, assault, rape, and homicide. Violent offenders are also among the most common type of offenders in the national prison system and constitute 49% of the state prison population. In addition, violent offenders accounted for approximately 53% of the growth of the state prison population for the 10-year period of 1990–2000. Moreover, the majority of violent offenders (70%) have a prior arrest record, and more than half (56%) have been arrested for a previous violent felony. It is clear that successful treatment and rehabilitation of such a prolific and persistent group of offenders are of great value to society.

Assessment for Treatment

The development and implementation of any treatment program for offenders start with a thorough assessment of the individual offender. Because treatment success in forensic settings is most often measured by subsequent reductions in offender recidivism rates, the measurement of an offender's risk of recidivism is an integral part of the development of any treatment plan. A number of such instruments have been developed over the last decade and generally fall into two categories: risk assessment instruments that measure static (i.e., historical or invariant) variables, such as the Violence Risk Appraisal Guide (Quinsey, Harris, Rice, & Cormier, 1998), and risk assessment instruments that incorporate both static and dynamic variables (variables related to reoffending that change over time, such as pro-criminal attitudes), such as the History, Clinical, Risk 20 (Webster, Douglas, Eaves, & Hart, 1997), the Violence Risk Scale (Wong & Gordon, 2006), and the Level of Service Inventory (Andrews & Bonta, 1995). Dynamic risk assessment instruments are favored in the development of treatment plans because they allow for the targeting of specific variables that are theoretically amenable to change. Although the Hare Psychopathy Checklist–Revised (Hare, 1991) and its screening version, the Psychopathy Checklist: Screening Version, are often used in risk assessment procedures, the presence of psychopathy is often considered only one significantly predictive clinical variable, albeit a powerful one, among a panoply of variables related to recidivism risk and therefore is not considered to be a standalone risk assessment instrument.

Treatment Techniques

Over the last 20 years or so, research on the development, implementation, and evaluation of treatment program effectiveness for violent offenders has proliferated (Polaschek & Dixon, 2001). With regard to the specific structure of treatment for violent offenders, research has demonstrated support for cognitive–behavioral and social learning theory–based intervention programs (Cullen & Gendreau, 1989; Quinsey, Harris, Rice, & Cormier, 2006). Although they contain many of the same elements as nonviolent offender treatment models, violent offender treatment programs typically encourage the development of offenders' insight into the functional role of their violent behavior and attempt to teach offenders alternative behavioral strategies that will allow them to navigate conflict more effectively. An example of such a program was designed and implemented by Polaschek and Dixon (2001) with a New Zealand sample of violent offenders. It consisted of several components consistent with these theoretical approaches targeting anger management, communication skill training, and the acquisition of parenting, interpersonal, social problem solving, and general life skills. In addition, substance abuse and health education were incorporated into the program, concurrent with individual therapy sessions. Although this particular program consisted of up to four 90-minute sessions per day, 5 days per week for 3 months, recommendations for treatment duration vary. Gendreau and Goggin (1997) recommend that intense treatment should last for at least 4 months, with a minimum of 100 contact hours, whereas others argue that in order for a significant reduction in recidivism to be demonstrated, treatment should last at least 6 months (Bush, 1995).

In addition, researchers caution that special consideration must be exercised when treatment programs for psychopathic violent offenders are developed (Hare, 1999). Hare suggests that when dealing with psychopathic offenders, cognitive–behavioral treatment should deemphasize empathy development in favor of targeting the development of appropriate attributional styles (i.e., teaching offenders to accept sole responsibility for their actions rather than blaming victims). Additionally, psychopathic offenders' repertoires of behavioral responses should be expanded, enabling them to fulfill their needs using more prosocial methods.

Treatment Effectiveness

Surprisingly little research has investigated the effectiveness of treatment and rehabilitation programs designed to reduce recidivism in violent offenders (Polaschek & Dixon, 2001). Historically, what little research has been done regarding the effectiveness of offender rehabilitation and treatment has been less than optimistic (Andrews et al., 1990; Serin & Brown, 1996, 1997). However, reexamination of prior research (Andrews et al., 1990) and current research using more sophisticated methods, with greater scientific rigor, have provided much more promising results.

Some of the first violent offender treatment effectiveness data emerged from two studies conducted at the Vermont Department of Corrections cognitive-based treatment program, initiated in 1988. Both studies indicated that this treatment program significantly decreased rates of parole violation and rearrest in a group of violent offenders (Bush, 1995; Henning & Frueh, 1996). Similarly, preliminary results from the New Zealand treatment program mentioned earlier demonstrated positive treatment effects, resulting in a significant reduction in the frequency and severity of reoffense in offenders released to the community (lower risk) and a significant reduction in the severity of reoffense in the parole sample (higher risk) (Polaschek & Dixon, 2001).

However, the most current results come from several studies published in England and Canada. These studies found that intervention programs based on the RNR treatment philosophy, incorporating cognitive–behavioral and social learning theory–based techniques embedded in a relapse prevention framework were effective in reducing rates of high-risk offender recidivism 2 years after release (Di Placido, Simon, Witte, Gu, & Wong, 2006; Fylan & Clarke, 2006; Wong, Gordon, & Gu, 2007; Wong et al., 2005). More specifically, treated offenders demonstrated a significant reduction in serious institutional infractions and a decrease in commission of serious violent offenses after release. Interestingly, these same studies demonstrated modest positive treatment effects, in terms of harm reduction, for offenders with elevated levels of psychopathy. Although treatment did not significantly reduce overall rates of recidivism or the frequency of reoffense in high-psychopathy offenders, it did result in a decrease in severity of reoffenses. Such findings may be welcome news in a field that is largely doubtful of its ability to induce therapeutic change in a subset of notoriously treatment-resistant offenders (Hare, 1998; Losel, 1998; Rice, Harris, & Cormier, 1992).

Risk Management

Despite the promising results of these most recent studies, there is a general consensus in the clinical and research communities that in order for any therapeutic gains to be maintained, treatment must not end upon an offender's release (Marshall, Eccles, & Barbaree, 1993; Tate, Reppucci, & Mulvey, 1995). Effective treatment modalities must be implemented as comprehensive, ongoing treatment programs that continue after release, often necessitating the involvement of a therapeutic community environment and careful monitoring by parole or probation offices.

SEXUAL OFFENDERS

Although sexual offenders are often treated as a monolithic group, they are quite heterogeneous with regard to offense patterns, characteristics, and risk for future offending. Therefore, most typological distinctions make reference to age of victim (adult vs. child), gender of victim, nature of offense (e.g., contact vs. noncontact offense), or level of fixation (i.e., how intense and exclusive is the interest in deviant sexual behavior). Assessment strategies and treatment interventions may thus necessitate different techniques, and risk management strategies must take into account variation in motivations and patterns, because these factors can be important in estimating the risk of recidivism.

Assessment for Treatment

An offender's risk level is an important consideration before treatment services are provided. The RNR model posits that offenders who pose the highest risk of reoffense should receive the most intensive treatment services (Andrews & Bonta, 1998). A number of risk assessment tools have been developed to specifically assess risk for recidivism among sex offenders. Although these tools are critical in assessing an offender's risk for reoffending before release or other change in custodial status, such risk-related information is also an important consideration for pretreatment planning, insofar as these tools are used to determine which sex offenders need the most intensive treatment services.

Although general measures of cognitive ability (e.g., the Wechsler Adult Intelligence Scale [Wechsler, 1997]) or personality style (e.g., the Minnesota Multiphasic Personality Inventory [Butcher, Dahlstrom, Graham, Tellegen, & Kaemmer, 1989]) are often used before treatment to enhance understanding of offender motivational or personality structure or to match learning or interpersonal style to treatment groups or program offerings, a number of specialized assessment instruments have also been developed for use with this population. The Multiphasic Sex Inventory–II (Nichols & Molinder, 1984) is a self-report inventory that includes an assessment of deviant sexual history and interests and an examination of thought patterns and other behavioral and emotional characteristics related to deviant sexual interest. The Abel Assessment for Sexual Interest (Abel, Huffman, Warberg, & Holland, 1998), a computer-based screening measure, was designed to identify the presence of deviant sexual interest in children. Involving a series of images of children, adolescents, and adults of varying age ranges, this screening tool includes a measure of visual reaction time to images of these various sexual interest subgroups, allowing evaluators to compare viewing time with established norms. Given that evaluees are not aware that the viewing time is being measured, the Abel measure may be of particular utility in assessing deviant sexual interest where honest disclosure may be an issue.

The penile plethysmograph (PPG), which includes a measure of blood flow to the penis and other measures of physiological arousal, is perhaps the most direct measure of sexual response and interest. Through presentation of video or audio stimuli involving suggestive sexual content, the PPG allows the identification of those who have a physiological response to inappropriate or deviant sexual stimuli. Although its use in legal settings may be problematic (Barker & Howell, 1992), the PPG can provide an important measure of pre-treatment and post-treatment response and, like the Abel measure, may be particularly useful where disclosure is of concern.

Treatment Techniques

The relapse prevention model, adopted from the substance abuse literature, aims to help sex offenders recognize their offense patterns, toward the goal of identifying cognitive, emotional, and situational factors that lead to offending. The aim of this model is to allow offenders to proactively intervene in their offense cycle so as to prevent reoffense. Cognitive–behavioral therapy (CBT), a short-term and typically time-limited set of techniques, involves strategies to modify both behavioral habits and cognitive assumptions that may be linked to some form of, in this case, sexual deviance. CBT techniques, which are often used in relapse prevention models, focus on identifying and modifying thoughts, behaviors, or feelings that have some link to sexually deviant behavior. Because CBT has received a great deal of empirical support, it is generally considered to be an efficacious form of therapy with this population. The central tenet of the good lives model approach to the treatment of sex offenders is enhancement of human well-being. By focusing on the development of prosocial behaviors and the acquisition of human goods (e.g., intimacy, safety, creativity, or education), the treatment reduces motivation to reoffend.

Treatment Efficacy

Doubt remains as to the effectiveness of sex offender treatment. Although the field has evolved greatly over the past couple of decades (Ward, Mann, & Gannon, 2007) and evidence suggests that newer treatment models are more effective than older forms of therapy (Hanson et al., 2002), the question as to whether sex offender treatment works continues to arouse debate. However, researchers have generally found that sex offender treatment can reduce both sexual and general recidivism (Hall, 1995; Hanson et al., 2002; Looman, Dickie, & Abracen, 2005).

Hanson et al. (2002), who conducted a meta-analysis of 43 sexual offender treatment outcome studies, found that 12.3% of sex offenders who completed treatment sexually recidivated (i.e., committed a new sexual offense, typically defined in these studies as rearrest or reconviction), whereas 16.8% of those who did not complete treatment sexually recidivated over the follow-up period (average 46 months). Moreover, Hanson et al. reported recidivism rates of 9.9% for offenders who completed more modern forms of treatment (e.g., CBT) and 17.4% for offenders who did not receive these newer forms of treatment. Similar sexual and nonsexual recidivism reduction rates based on CBT interventions have also been identified by other researchers (e.g., Barbaree & Seto, 1997; Gallagher, Wilson, Hirschfield, Coggeshall, & MacKenzie, 1999; Hanson, 2000; Looman, Abracen, & Nicholaichuk, 2000; Marshall, Barbaree, & Eccles, 1991; McGrath, Cumming, Livingston, & Hoke, 2003; McGrath, Hoke, & Vojtisek, 1998; Nicholaichuk, Gordon, Deqiang, & Wong, 2000; Scalora & Garbin, 2003). A more recent meta-analysis showed that sexual offender treatment programs that adhered to RNR principles showed the largest reduction in both sexual and nonsexual recidivism (Hanson, Bourgon, Helmus, & Hodgson, 2009).

This finding supports Andrews and Bonta's (1998) contention under the RNR model that effective treatment programs should target offenders who are deemed to be at highest risk to recidivate, focus on treating criminogenic needs, and be responsive to unique offender learning styles. Given evidence of lower rates of recidivism associated with more modern treatment models, CBT techniques and the RNR framework are among the most promising models of treatment with this population.

Risk Management

Given heightened concern about reoffense with this population, evaluation of sex offenders typically involves an evaluation of recidivism risk. Because clinical judgment (or a more subjective, impressionistic approach) has been shown to be inferior to actuarial decision making (or a more statistically based, formal approach) to risk assessment (Grove et al., 2000; Hanson & Morton-Bourgon, 2004), adherence to best practices implies the use of empirically validated risk tools. The development of these tools has relied on the work of Hanson and Bussiere (1998), Hanson and Morton-Bourgon (2004), Hanson et al. (2002), and others in identifying individual factors (e.g., age) or offense characteristics (e.g., gender of victim, use of violence) that most strongly correlate with recidivism. Whereas some risk assessment instruments provide overall risk scores based on the combined weightings of a set number of risk factors, such as the Sex Offender Risk Appraisal Guide (Quinsey et al., 1998), Rapid Risk Assessment for Sex Offence Recidivism (Hanson, 1997), Minnesota Sex Offender Screening Tool–Revised (Epperson et al., 1999), and Static-99 (Hanson & Thornton, 2000), others, such as the Sexual Violence Risk–20 (Boer, Hart, Kropp, & Webster, 1997) and the Risk for Sexual Violence Protocol (Hart et al., 2003), use a structured professional judgment approach that provides decision makers with structured guidelines for considering a list of empirically validated factors but does not provide probabilistic estimates of risk based on the combination of such factors.

Comparative analyses of the utility of specific risk instruments have been undertaken elsewhere (see Barbaree, Seto, Langton, & Peacock, 2001; Harris et al., 2003), and although each instrument seems to have its particular strengths, as yet there appears to be no single instrument with a well-accepted superior predictive capability, although each has a demonstrated reliability and predictive validity that exceeds that of clinical judgment. Continued refinement of these instruments should enhance our predictive capabilities in the realm of recidivistic sexual violence, but at present such instruments seem to provide decision makers with the best available evidence regarding likelihood of recidivism. Indeed, Janus and Prentky (2003) highlight the transparency, accountability, and consistency that actuarial tools bring to the risk-finding process and suggest that actuarial risk assessment provides the most accurate indication of long-term reoffense risk.

INTIMATE VIOLENCE OFFENDERS

Intimate partner violence is an all too common social phenomenon, with a yearly average of approximately 511,000 women and 105,000 men reporting having experienced violence at the hands of an intimate between 2001 and 2005 (Catalano, 2007). Furthermore, 22% of women report experiencing intimate partner violence at some point in their lives (Tjaden & Thoennes, 1998). Intimate partner violence has serious psychological and physical sequelae for victims and has been estimated to cost the U.S. government approximately $5.8 billion annually in direct (e.g., health care) and indirect (e.g., lowered productivity) costs (National Center for Injury Prevention and Control, 2003). It is clear that treatment and prevention programs targeting intimate violence are vital.

Assessment for Treatment

Research into the assessment of intimate violence offenders has not enjoyed the same allocation of resources often devoted to the study of other offender populations (Geffner & Rosenbaum, 2001), such as sex or violent offenders. However, the limited body of literature examining this issue suggests that the risk factors for intimate violence recidivism may be similar to those for peer violence, such as exposure to family and community violence, attachment difficulties, and child abuse (Moffitt, Krueger, Caspi, & Fagan, 2000; Wolfe & Feiring, 2000). A handful of risk assessment instruments have been specifically designed for use with intimate violence offenders. The three most widely used are the Spousal Assault Risk Assessment Guide (Kropp, Hart, Webster, & Eaves, 1999), a 20-item checklist of clinical variables comprising five broad risk domains (intimate violence history, criminal history, psychosocial adjustment, characteristics of index offense, and other); the Revised Conflict Tactics Scale (Straus, Hamby, Boney-McCoy, & Sugarman, 1996), a 36-item self-report measure that assesses the degree to which intimate partners attack each other, physically and psychologically, and their use of more adaptive methods of conflict resolution (e.g., reasoning and negotiation); and the Danger Assessment Scale (Campbell, 1986), a 14-item dichotomous yes/no scale assessing the presence of factors found to be empirically associated with battery-related homicide.

However, researchers have noted that risk assessment of intimate violence is an understudied area, and current instruments have questionable predictive validity and should serve only as adjuncts to a comprehensive clinical assessment (Geffner & Rosenbaum, 2001).

Treatment Techniques

The first intervention program for intimate violence offenders began in the mid-1970s, with the number of such programs proliferating in subsequent decades because of the growing awareness in the legal community of the need for such treatment programs (Geffner & Rosenbaum, 2001; Scott, 2004). However, despite such growth the scientific community did not become involved in the development, implementation, and evaluation of such programs until well into the 1980s (Babcock, Green, & Robie, 2004). Although there has been growing demand and interest in intimate violence offender interventions, many of the programs currently offered lack standardization and, unfortunately, lack sufficient empirical support to warrant their continued use

(Babcock et al., 2004). Among the most common intimate violence offender programs are those founded in feminist-based psychoeducation and cognitive–behavioral principles.

The bulk of programs offered as intimate violence prevention programs can be roughly categorized as following the feminist psychoeducational model, often referred to as the Duluth model after its originator, the Duluth Domestic Abuse Intervention Program in Minnesota (Babcock et al., 2004; Pence & Paymar, 1993). This paradigm, founded in social work theory, is often viewed as an educational rather than a true therapeutic approach (such as the cognitive–behavioral approaches) because of its avoidance of diagnostic labels and other psychological constructs. This model posits that intimate partner violence stems from an offender's patriarchal views coupled with the differential power dynamic between men and women (Dobash & Dobash, 1977; Pence & Paymar, 1993). The goal of this psychoeducational model, conducted almost exclusively in a group format, is to challenge the offender's existing views and replace them with more egalitarian beliefs, thereby effecting a reduction in intimate violent behavior (Babcock et al., 2004).

Less prevalent than the feminist psychoeducational intervention model are programs derived largely from cognitive–behavioral psychological theory. Like the Duluth model, cognitive–behavioral interventions are conducted almost exclusively in a group format and target the development of offenders' insight into the functional role that intimate partner violence plays in their lives (Babcock et al., 2004). Techniques that are commonly used in cognitive–behavioral interventions include skill training aimed at enhancing assertiveness, communication, social skills, and anger management strategies. However, critics point out that many intimate violence offender programs labeled as CBT use a range of techniques that would not be used in true cognitive–behavioral therapies and more closely resemble psychoeducational models, such as the Duluth model, rather than traditional CBT (Dunford, 2000). Indeed, many researchers argue that most programs offered to intimate violence offenders are paradigmatic hybrids, blending elements of feminist psychoeducational models and cognitive–behavioral approaches (Gregory & Erez, 2002; Whitaker et al., 2006).

Treatment Effectiveness

Historically, research regarding the effectiveness of intimate violence offender treatment programs has been hampered by several factors. First, before individual states mandated treatment for all intimate violence offenders, engagement in voluntary treatment programs was abysmally low (Geffner &

Rosenbaum, 2001). Furthermore, more recent research suggests that the intimate violence offender population is much more heterogeneous than previously believed. An identified subset of these offenders are viewed as highly treatment resistant because of their reluctance to initially engage in treatment and to remain in treatment once engaged, with some estimates suggesting that 50–75% of these offenders drop out early in treatment (Daly & Pelowski, 2000; Geffner & Rosenbaum, 2001). Only with the advent of mandatory treatment has enrollment in intimate violence offender treatment programs reached a level conducive to empirical scrutiny.

Second, early research on treatment effectiveness with intimate violence offenders has been plagued by methodological flaws including poor operationalization of outcome variables (Whitaker et al., 2006). In other words, measurement of treatment success has varied widely, precluding comparisons across studies. Typically, treatment effectiveness has been measured by a reduction in a partner's use of physical violence, through self- or partner report, criminal complaints, or offender rearrest (Gregory & Erez, 2002; Scott, 2004).

Despite these challenges, recent research has emerged elucidating intimate violence offender treatment program effectiveness, although the results have been less than optimistic. For instance, recent meta-analyses and other outcome studies have consistently found small effect sizes for such programs (Davis & Taylor, 1999; Dunford, 2000; Green & Babcock, 2001; Levesque & Gelles, 1998), regardless of the treatment modality, with average effect sizes of approximately 5% reductions in rates of recidivism (Babcock et al., 2004). Proponents of intimate violence offender treatment argue that although such a modest reduction in reoffense rates may seem inconsequential, a reduction of even 5% would equate to approximately 44,000 fewer women being physically abused each year. However, critics point out that even these modest treatment gains apply only to recidivism in terms of physical abuse, with other studies demonstrating that treatment is even less effective in reducing other forms of intimate partner violence such as psychological or verbal abuse (Gondolf, 2002). Taylor, Davis, and Maxwell (2001) provide more optimistic findings, concluding that when offenders are categorized and excluded from analysis based on low treatment motivation, a significant effect for treatment on reoffense rates does emerge. That is, for offenders who express interest in and actively engage in the treatment process, significant therapeutic gains can be made.

Risk Management

Currently, treatment programs for intimate violence offenders are designed to be universally applicable. With the surge of interest and research in the development, implementation, and evaluation of such programs, there has been a move to assess and refer individual offenders to programs specifically designed to suit their individual capacities and criminogenic needs (Holtzworth-Munroe, 2001). It is believed that such a paradigmatic shift, consistent with the RNR model, would lead to better risk management services for intimate violence offenders.

JUVENILE OFFENDERS

With more than 2.2 million juvenile arrests in 2006, juvenile offenders are responsible for a significant proportion of criminal offenses, accounting for 17% of all violent offenses and 26% of all property crimes in the United States (Snyder, 2008). In the last 20 years, the rate of juvenile violent offenses, including homicide, has increased dramatically. Moreover, because of the current age distribution of the general population, it has been estimated that the juvenile arrest rate will have doubled in the 15-year period of 1996 to 2010 (Office of Juvenile Justice and Delinquency Prevention, 1996; Sickmund, Snyder, & Poe-Yamagata, 1997).

Assessment for Treatment

The assessment of juvenile offenders for risk of recidivism and treatment planning has been hampered by a disproportionate allocation of resources to the study of adult offender populations. Although the risk assessment of adult offenders has generally shifted from reliance on subjective clinical judgment to more objective actuarial methods, the risk assessment of juvenile offenders has been slow to follow suit (Hoge, 2002). Only recently has research into the development and validation of juvenile assessment instruments accelerated. In the last decade, numerous structured instruments specifically designed for use with juvenile offenders have been developed.

Among the more commonly used risk assessment instruments are the Youth Level of Service/Case Management Inventory (Hoge & Andrews, 2001), a structured clinical inventory consisting of 42 items and 8 subscales that can be administered with minimal training; the Child and Adolescent Functional Assessment Scale (Hodges, 1994, 1999), a structured instrument designed to ascertain impairments in emotional and behavioral functioning associated with recidivism; the Structured Assessment of Violence Risk in Youth (Borum, Bartel, & Forth, 2003), a 30-item structured instrument designed to assess four major domains (historical, social/contextual, and individual risk factors and protective factors); and the Hare Psychopathy Checklist–Youth Version (Hare, Forth, & Kosson, 1994), a 20-item adaptation of the adult version designed to measure the presence of psychopathic traits in juveniles, particularly older juveniles. It should be noted that the use of this instrument with juveniles remains controversial because of concerns about the construct validity of juvenile psychopathy (Hoge, 2002).

Treatment Techniques

Numerous treatment modalities have been developed and implemented with juvenile offenders, but the bulk of empirical data appears to favor two approaches: treatments based in cognitive–behavioral and social learning theory and family system therapy.

Intervention programs grounded in cognitive–behavioral and social learning principles target maladaptive thought processes and impairments in social problem-solving skills found to be linked with the onset and maintenance of antisocial behavior (Tarolla, Wagner, Rabinowitz, & Tubman, 2002). Although the specific techniques used in any given cognitive–behavioral treatment program can vary somewhat, many programs use a number of the following techniques in a group therapy format: cognitive skill training, cognitive restructuring, interpersonal problem solving, social skill training, anger management, moral reasoning, victim impact, substance abuse counseling, behavior modification, and relapse prevention (Landenberger & Lipsey, 2005). Supplemental individual therapy is often offered to maintain active therapeutic engagement and to reduce attrition. Some researchers and clinicians have criticized the use of CBT-based approaches as too narrow in their focus, arguing that such treatment modalities ignore the role of dysfunctional family relationships, deviant peer groups, and negative school and neighborhood environments in the etiology and maintenance of juvenile antisocial behavior (Borduin et al., 1995).

These critics argue that for juvenile offender treatment to be effective, treatment must be customized to fit the needs and capabilities of the individual offender, his family, and his environment (e.g., school, neighborhood); take a holistic approach, allowing the multiple determinants of juvenile antisocial behavior to be targeted for intervention concurrently; and be provided in a number of settings (e.g., home and community) to ensure optimal generalization of newly acquired skills and produce more stable therapeutic change (Tarolla et al., 2002; Tate et al., 1995). Treatment programs based in family system theory were developed to provide such a comprehensive approach to juvenile offender treatment. Although a variety of treatments fall under the broad umbrella of family system therapy, all such treatment programs attempt to enhance family communication styles and use techniques such as behavioral contracting, rule clarification, and positive reinforcement to achieve desired behavioral outcomes.

Among the most successful family system treatment approaches is multisystemic therapy (MST), developed in the 1980s by Henggeler et al. (1986). This treatment seeks to keep the family intact while addressing a number of issues believed to be related to the juvenile offense cycle, such as maladaptive cognitive styles and attitudes, social and relational difficulties (at both the immediate micro and larger macro levels), and symptoms of mental illness (e.g., depression), if relevant. MST uses numerous empirically supported treatment approaches including techniques based in cognitive–behavior therapy, social learning, strategic and structural family therapy, and behavioral training for the juvenile's parents or primary caregivers.

Treatment Effectiveness

Research suggests that without treatment, 60–96% of juvenile offenders will reoffend within approximately 1 year of arrest (Jenson & Howard, 1998; Lattimore, Visher, & Linster, 1995; Lewis, Yeager, Lovely, Stein, & Cobham-Portorreal, 1994). Despite skepticism about the effectiveness of treatment with juvenile offenders, recent advances in intervention development and implementation have provided promising results for both cognitive–behavioral, social learning–based, and family system therapy.

Mounting literature supports the effectiveness of cognitive–behavioral approaches in enhancing social problem-solving skills and regulating impulsive behavior, reducing rates of reoffense among juvenile offenders (Andrews et al., 1990; Dowden & Andrews, 2003; Gendreau & Ross, 1979; Larson, 1990; Lipsey & Wilson, 1998; Redondo, Sanchez-Meca, & Garrido, 1999). Redondo and colleagues found that CBT programs, in general, produced a mean reduction in recidivism rates among treated juvenile offenders of 25%. Moreover, this effect resulted in a 50% reduction for treated offenders who received programs optimally configured to include the most effective components (i.e., those that included anger management and interpersonal effectiveness as targets). Interestingly, treatment programs that included victim impact and behavior modification components were found to be less effective. Furthermore, CBT-based approaches appeared to be most effective with higher-risk juvenile offenders, directly contradicting clinical lore suggesting that high-risk offenders are untreatable (Landenberger & Lipsey, 2005).

Similarly, a significant body of literature supports the use of more holistic family system approaches (Kazdin, 1987; Shadish et al., 1993), particularly MST (Borduin, 1999; Henggeler, 1996; Schoenwald, Ward, Henggeler, Pickrel, & Patel, 1996). MST has been demonstrated to produce both short-term and long-term reductions in recidivism among juvenile offenders, including persistent and seriously violent ones (Borduin et al., 1995). More specifically, it was found that 14 months after referral for MST services, juvenile offenders had been rearrested 50% fewer times than their treatment-as-usual counterparts (Henggeler, Melton, & Smith, 1992). Furthermore, MST-treated juvenile offenders had an overall reincarceration rate of 20%, compared with 68% for their treatment-as-usual counterparts. Finally, treatment effectiveness has been maintained for follow-up periods of up to 4 years, with MST-treated juvenile offenders being arrested at much lower rates than the offenders who received treatment as usual; when rearrest did occur, the MST-treated offenders committed significantly less serious crimes (Borduin et al., 1995).

Risk Management

As with treatment of all offenders, treatment of juvenile offenders should be viewed as an ongoing, dynamic process following the RNR paradigm. That is, intensity of treatment should be matched to the perceived risk of the juvenile offender, and criminogenic factors should be targeted for treatment, with the assumption that they may change as the juvenile develops (Borum & Verhaagen, 2006). Furthermore, only empirically supported treatments should be implemented, treatment should be customized to suit the unique capabilities and characteristics of the individual juvenile offender and his or her environment, and both treatment providers and community supervision agents should continually monitor, reassess, and modify intervention programs to ensure that treatment gains are maintained.

FEMALE OFFENDERS

Little research has focused on the treatment of female offenders, which may stem from the fact that females offend at much lower rates than do males, making up 8–18% of the total population of offenders (Bonta, Pang, & Wallace-Capretta, 1995). Given their lower rates of offending, research has either neglected female offender populations or treated them similarly to male offender populations, with little attention paid to whether motivations for offending or crime patterns and recidivism are distinct for female offenders. Therefore, it is not known whether the needs and patterns of female offenders are unique.

Assessment for Treatment

Given that female offenders may have unique life experiences and responsibilities (e.g., pregnancy, childcare) (Koons, Burrow, Morash, & Bynum, 1997) and may be affected more frequently by certain life events (e.g., child sexual abuse, domestic violence, adult sexual assault) and clinical syndromes (e.g., depression or posttraumatic stress disorder) (Poels, 2007), it stands to reason that gender-specific issues warrant attention in a clinical evaluation. Indeed, although measures of personality, cognitive functioning, substance abuse history, or mood dysfunction are likely to be the same as those used with male offenders, a full and comprehensive evaluation should consider the unique needs and obstacles that female offenders may face both in accessing treatment and in benefiting from services offered. Although gender-specific measures are seldom used, at least some evidence suggests that economic disadvantage and social relationships may have differential impact on risk for offending among men and women (Heilbrun et al., 2008).

Treatment Techniques

Given the aforementioned unique needs of female offenders, some suggest that more gender-responsive treatment services be offered (Koons et al., 1997; Morash, Bynum, & Koons, 1998). For example, like their male counterparts, female inmates may be cut off from family and supportive networks. However, this separation could be particularly difficult for mothers with young children, and maintaining family contacts and connections may be an especially important treatment target for females (Monster & Micucci, 2005). However, some evidence suggests that specific programming for causes of female criminality may not be offered in correctional settings (Monster & Micucci, 2005), although there is a shift toward offering more gender-specific programming (Heilbrun et al., 2008). Moreover, evidence suggests that most treatment programming may be based on patterns of male offending (Monster & Micucci, 2005). However, little is known about whether the existing treatment literature or existing treatment programs can be simply extended to female offenders or whether different models of treatment should be used with this population.

Treatment Efficacy

Little research has specifically examined the effectiveness of treatment for female offenders. Using meta-analytic techniques, Dowden and Andrews (1999) examined 26 studies that investigated the effectiveness of corrections-based treatment for female offenders, finding support for the RNR model of treatment. Indeed, Dowden and Andrews found larger treatment effects for programs that directed more treatment services to higher-risk (rather than lower-risk) female offenders and larger treatment effects in programs that focused on criminogenic (vs. noncriminogenic) needs. Specifically, focus on interpersonal criminogenic needs (family process or antisocial associate variables) was most strongly associated with reduced reoffending. Program focus on antisocial cognition and self-control deficits also had a significant association with reduced reoffending (Dowden & Andrews, 1999). Notably, although substance abuse and basic education may intuitively appear to be important treatment targets, Dowden and Andrews did not find these variables to be associated with treatment outcomes in female offenders. Importantly, no research has looked specifically at treatment responsivity in female offenders, specifically whether women may have particular learning or interpersonal styles that affect recidivism rates (Dowden & Andrews, 1999). Although what works with female offenders may in many ways be an extension of what works with male offenders, more research attention, particularly with regard to issues of treatment responsivity, is needed in this area.

Risk Management

Because their pathway to crime may be different, it stands to reason that risk assessment should also consider unique risk factors predictive of future offending among women who commit crime. Unfortunately, given a dearth of research identifying risk correlates for female offenders, little is known about whether there are specific and unique risk factors for this population. Therefore, risk assessment tools may lack predictive utility if applied to female offenders. Although identified factors that predict future offending for male offenders may be similar to those that predict future offending for female offenders, this is not necessarily the case. Moreover, even if the factors are similar, their levels of association with future offending and combinations may be quite different. Although at least some evidence suggests that risk factors may be generally similar for male and female offenders (Heilbrun et al., 2008; Loucks & Zamble, 2000), there do appear to be at least some distinctions in pathways to and maintenance of offending (Heilbrun et al., 2008). As with any population or subgroup not well represented in the developmental samples on which risk assessment tools are based, it may be premature to extend risk estimates to female offenders without a more established normative comparison group (Poels, 2007). Clearly, more research is needed that establishes how males and females differ, and this research can be used to extend or develop genderspecific assessment tools and develop or enhance more gender-responsive programming.

OFFENDERS WITH SERIOUS MENTAL DISORDERS

Mental illness is prevalent among forensic populations. Since the deinstitution-alization movement of the latter half of the 20th century, a significant increase in the number of people with severe and persistent mental illness in the prison system has been observed (Lamb & Weinberger, 2008). These mental illnesses include bipolar disorder, major depression, and psychotic disorders such as schizophrenia (American Psychiatric Association, 2004). In the United States, the numbers of people with mental illness in prisons vary according to the method used to assess prevalence. For instance, the Bureau of Justice Statistics (2006) reported that approximately 55% of male offenders and 73% of female offenders in state prison had a diagnosable mental illness based on self-report, and others have estimated the prevalence of mental illness among prison inmates to be approximately 16% based on mental health service records (Ditton, 1999). However, it is believed that only about one third of offenders with mental illness receive any treatment for their mental illness while they are incarcerated (Bureau of Justice Statistics, 2006).

Assessment for Treatment

Inmates are generally screened for mental illness at intake (Beck & Maruschak, 2001). Currently there appears to be no standard approach for assessing mental illness among offenders. Practices include clinical interviews and assessments and actuarial approaches (Adams & Ferrandino, 2008). The overarching goal of these assessments is to identify offenders who need mental health treatment and to assess their needs and security level.

Several measures have been used to assess need based on the RNR model. One such measure is the Level of Service Inventory–Revised (Andrews & Bonta, 1995), a rating scale designed to assess the risk for general recidivism. However, this instrument was designed for use with the general prison population and not specifically for mentally ill offenders (Long, Webster, Waine, Motala, & Hollin, 2008). More recently, scales specifically designed to assess treatment needs (Camberwell Assessment of Need; Thomas et al., 2003) and security needs (Operationalized Risk Factors; Brown & Lloyd, 2008) among mentally disordered offenders have been developed. Both scales have been found to be useful and improve mentally ill offenders' access to care (Brown & Lloyd, 2008; Long et al., 2008).

Treatment Techniques

The primary line of treatment for mentally ill offenders is psychotropic medication. It is estimated that 73% of state prisons distribute medications to offenders in their facilities, resulting in 114,400 inmates receiving psychotropic drugs during their incarcerations (Beck & Maruschak, 2001).

Recently more focus has been placed on psychological interventions for mentally ill offenders with the passage of the Mentally Ill Offender Treatment and Crime Reduction Act of 2004 in the United States. This act provides funding to train correctional and mental health staff to treat mentally ill offenders and provides mentally ill offenders with greater access to mental health treatment both while incarcerated and when released into the community (American Psychological Association, 2004). Such interventions include in vivo training of goal-directed actions for offenders with treatment-resistant schizophrenia (Hodel & West, 2003), CBT for long-term inpatients with psychotic disorders and forensic histories (Garrett & Lerman, 2007), dialectical behavior therapy for offenders with borderline personality disorder characteristics (Linehan, 1993), and the Dangerous and Severe Personality Disorder Programme (Mullen, 2007).

Some prisons have developed therapeutic communities (TCs). Generally TCs in prisons are usually separate from the general population and are considered therapeutic milieus. In this environment offenders develop prosocial skills that can be used to transition back into the community (Adams & Ferrandino, 2008). Although TCs traditionally have been used to treat offenders with substance use disorders (see Linhorst, Knight, Johnston, & Trickey, 2001), these programs also have been modified to treat other types of offenders, including those with mental illness (Saum et al., 2007). Staff in the TC environment receive specialized training on how to deal with mentally ill people, and many TC programs have elements of aftercare to help offenders with mental illness in the community (Wormith et al., 2007).

Another form of treatment for people with mental illness is the mental health court. These courts were established in an effort to divert people with serious mental illness from prisons and jails (Slate & Johnson, 2008). The goal of these programs is to provide these people with the treatment and services they need in an effort to prevent recidivism (Lamb & Weinberger, 2008). Traditionally, mental health courts heard cases of mentally ill people who were accused of misdemeanor crimes, but some courts are also hearing cases of mentally ill people who have been charged with violent felonies (Fisler, 2005). Mental health courts differ from traditional courtrooms in that all those involved (such as the judge, prosecutors, and defense counsel) have had training and experience in working with people with mental illness. Furthermore, they are familiar with community mental health resources, and they make every attempt to provide mental health treatment and support to offenders once they are released from jail and reenter the community (Lamb & Weinberger, 2008).

Treatment Efficacy

Evidence suggests that people with severe mental illness benefit from treatment, which lowers their recidivism rate (Swanson et al., 2006). However, a substantial proportion of people with mental illness who commit crimes are resistant to psychiatric treatment (Draine, Solomon, & Meyerson, 1994; Laberge & Morin, 1995). For example, they may refuse referrals, miss appointments, refuse to take medication, and abuse substances. The failure to participate or adhere to treatment can substantially interfere with treatment success (Lamb & Weinberger, 1998). Therefore, programs that meet the specific needs of those with mental illness are likely to have the greatest success. For example, Griffith, Hiller, Knight, and Simpson (1999) found that TCs were the most cost effective for those at highest risk for recidivism, such as those with mental illness. Furthermore, Lees, Manning, and Rawlings (1999) found that TCs significantly decreased recidivism rates for offenders with borderline personality disorder and other mental disorders. The outcome research on mental health courts is still in its infancy, but preliminary studies have found that mentally ill offenders who successfully completed mental health court programs were less likely to recidivate and engage in future acts of violence than those who did not participate in mental health court programs (McNeil & Binder, 2007).

Risk Management

A recent development in risk management for offenders with mental illness is the emergence of assertive community treatment for forensic populations

(FACT). FACT is based on assertive community treatment (ACT), with the primary goal of preventing reincarceration. ACT is designed to prevent repeat hospitalizations for mental illness by providing a clinical team to help these people in the community around the clock (Morrissey, Meyer, & Cuddeback, 2007). Whereas ACT programs target clients of local hospitals and mental health agencies, FACT teams target county jails. The effectiveness of ACT has been well established (see Bond, Drake, Mueser, & Latimer, 2001). In theory FACT should operate on the same premises as ACT but with mentally ill forensic outpatients; however, in practice, resources are not available for FACT programs to adhere to ACT guidelines. Preliminary uncontrolled findings suggest that FACT programs decrease arrests and hospitalization and reduce yearly service costs (see Morrissey et al., 2007, for review).

COMMUNITY REINTEGRATION AND RISK MANAGEMENT

Each year, more than half a million offenders are released back into the community (Office of Justice Programs, 2004); however, many of these offenders eventually relapse and return to prison (Langan & Levin, 2002). A question that is frequently asked of researchers and policymakers is, "How can we stop this revolving door?" Although there are no easy answers to this question, one solution appears to lie in the RNR model. Offender treatment based on the principles of the RNR model has been found to reduce recidivism. Not only can these principles be used in prison-based programs, they can also be applied to relapse prevention and community reentry programs. For example, information garnered from intake screenings such as offender risk level, mental health status, and level of need can inform discharge planning and ensure that appropriate resources are available to the offender upon release (Hammett, Roberts, & Kennedy, 2001). This information can then be used to tailor reentry programs to coincide with offenders' periods of increased risk (Motiuk & Serin, 1998). Agencies should work together with the criminal justice system to more seamlessly provide services to meet the needs of released offenders (Wormith et al., 2007).

In addition to assessment, correctional treatment must be connected to reintegration efforts so that skills that are learned in prison can be practiced and reinforced in the community. Furthermore, changes that may occur within correctional treatment should be assessed and incorporated into the release plan (Serin & Kennedy, 1997).

Taxman, Young, and Byrne (2004) developed a list of six principles for successful reentry based on the most current research literature on the RNR model:

- Emphasizing informal social control such that family, friends, and community members are enlisted to prevent the offender from reoffending
- Ensuring sufficient duration of the intervention, because behavior change takes a long time, and continuing prison-based initiatives in the community can give offenders the 12–24 months they need to learn new skills and behaviors
- Providing sufficient dosage of the intervention so that the intensity and frequency of the programming meet the offender's risk level and needs
- Providing comprehensive, integrated, and flexible services designed to address the psychosocial needs of the offender
- Ensuring continuity in behavior change interventions such that interventions that are started in prison are continued into the community with aftercare programming
- Providing clear communication of offender responsibility and expectations so that the offender is involved with the development of rules and sanctions, thus ensuring more accountability

Offenders should be active participants in the development of the treatment and reintegration plan, and adherence to these principles decreases the risk of recidivism (Taxman, 2004).

Although most current reintegration programming is based on the RNR model, several reentry programs based in the restorative justice movement have gained prominence recently. One example is the Options to Parole Suspension project in Canada, whose goal is to prevent offenders released on parole from returning to prison. This program enlists professionally supported volunteers in the community to work with high-risk sex offenders. The goal of these types of reintegration programs is to empower stakeholders (Wilson, Huculak, & McWhinnie, 2002; also see chapter 9, this book).

POLICY IMPLICATIONS

At present, a large portion of the burden of preventing recidivism falls on the criminal justice system through the use of sanctions and monitoring. However, treatment removes some of this burden because unlike all other methods of containing offenders, treatment prevents recidivism by making the offenders responsible for their own actions, providing them the tools to restrain themselves from committing further crimes (Beck & Klein-Saffran, 1990; Levenson, 2003). This benefits offenders as they learn new skills and become more self-sufficient, and it also alleviates some of the financial, physical, and psychological burdens caused by repeat offenders. Many researchers advocate active participation by offenders in their rehabilitation and reintegration plans (Taxman, 2004). It is assumed that if offenders are stakeholders in their treatment, they will assume a greater level of accountability.

Currently, treatment for many offenders is not a mandated component of incarceration. Consequently, offenders may complete their sentences without addressing any of their criminogenic needs. Additionally, for many offenders treatment is not designed to adhere to the principles of the RNR model. Numerous studies have demonstrated that treatment based on the RNR model can decrease recidivism (see Andrews et al., 1990, for review), and therefore it is unclear why some offenders are not participating in treatment at all or are participating in treatment programs that have no empirical support.

Many of the laws pertaining to offenders that have been enacted in recent years were developed in response to public pressure and outcry (Petrunik, 2002). Most of these laws are designed to contain and monitor offenders, not to provide treatment. However, several studies have found that the public is supportive of rehabilitation efforts (Brown, 1999; McCorkle, 1993; Valliant, Furac, & Antonowicz, 1994). For example, Gideon and Loveland (chapter 2) found in a public opinion survey of residents in New York and the Tri-State Region that about 80% of respondents supported the Second Chance Act and thus are supportive of rehabilitation initiatives. Although the public and policymakers may support treatment in theory, very few people are vocal advocates for it. Therefore, researchers must educate stakeholders about the importance of empirically supported treatment methods in the reduction of recidivism so that these types of rehabilitation and reintegration programs are provided to all offenders.

DISCUSSION QUESTIONS

1. Why do you think that not all rehabilitation programs adhere to the RNR model?

2. What would be the advantages and disadvantages of a generic rehabilitation program that could be adapted to meet the needs of various offender populations?

3. How can the transition from prison to the community be made in such a way as to minimize the risk of recidivism?

4. What facets of treatment are most important for risk management?

5. How can we use assessment to facilitate offender reentry?

SUGGESTED READINGS

Andrews, D., Zinger, I., Hoge, R., Bonta, J., Gendreau, P., & Cullen, F. (1990). Does correctional treatment work? A clinically relevant and psychologically informed meta-analysis. *Criminology, 28,* 369–404.

Cullen, F. T., & Gendreau, P. (1989). The effectiveness of correctional rehabilitation: Reconsidering the "nothing works" debate. In L. Goldstein & D. L. McKenzie (Eds.), *The American prison: Issues in research policy* (pp. 23–44). New York: Plenum.

Gendreau, P., & Goggin, C. (1997). Correctional treatment: Accomplishments and realities. In P. Van Voorhis, M. Braswell, & D. Lester (Eds.), *Correctional counseling and rehabilitation* (3rd ed., pp. 271–279). Cincinnati, OH: Anderson.

Gendreau, P., & Ross, R. R. (1979). Effective correctional treatment: Bibliotherapy for cynics. *Crime and Delinquency, 25,* 463–489.

Henning, K., & Frueh, B. C. (1996). Cognitive behavioral treatment of incarcerated offenders: An evaluation of the Vermont Department of Correction's cognitive self-change program. *Criminal Justice and Behavior, 23,* 523–541.

Martinson, R. (1974). What works? Questions and answers about prison reform. *The Public Interest, 35,* 22–54.

Motiuk, L. L., & Serin, R. (1998). Situating risk assessment in the reintegration potential framework. *Forum on Corrections Research, 10*(1), 19–22.

Wormith, J., Althouse, R., Simpson, M., Reitzel, L., Fagan, T., & Morgan, R. (2007). The rehabilitation and integration of offenders: The current landscape and some future directions for correctional psychology. *Criminal Justice and Behavior, 34,* 879–892.

REFERENCES

Abel, G. G., Huffman, J., Warberg, B., & Holland, C. L. (1998). Visual reaction time and plethysmography as measures of sexual interest in child molesters. *Sexual Abuse: A Journal of Research and Treatment, 10,* 81–95.

Adams, K., & Ferrandino, J. (2008). Managing mentally ill inmates in prisons. *Criminal Justice and Behavior, 35*(8), 913–927.

American Psychiatric Association. (2004). *Mental illness and the criminal justice system: Redirecting resources toward treatment, not containment.* Arlington, VA: Author.

American Psychological Association. (2004). *The American Psychological Association applauds passage of the Mentally Ill Offender Treatment and Crime Reduction Act of 2004.* Washington, DC: Author.

Andrews, D. A., & Bonta, J. (1995). *The LSI-R: The Level of Service Inventory–Revised.* Toronto: Multi-Health Systems.

Andrews, D. A., & Bonta, J. (1998). *The psychology of criminal conduct* (2nd ed.). Cincinnati, OH: Anderson.

Andrews, D. A., & Bonta, J. (2006). *The psychology of criminal conduct* (4th ed.). Newark, NJ: LexisNexis.

Andrews, D., Bonta, J., & Hoge, R. (1990). Classification for effective rehabilitation: Rediscovering psychology. *Criminal Justice and Behavior, 17*(1), 19–52.

Andrews, D., Zinger, I., Hoge, R., Bonta, J., Gendreau, P., & Cullen, F. (1990). Does correctional treatment work? A clinically relevant and psychologically informed meta-analysis. *Criminology, 28,* 369–404.

Babcock, J. C., Green, C. E., & Robie, C. (2004). Does batterers' treatment work? A meta-analytic review of domestic violence treatment. *Clinical Psychology Review, 23,* 1023–1053.

Bailey, W. C. (1966). Correctional outcome: An evaluation of 100 reports. *Journal of Criminal Law, Criminology and Police Science, 57,* 153–160.

Barbaree, H. E., & Seto, M. C. (1997). Pedophilia: Assessment and treatment. In D. R. Laws & W. T. O'Donoghue (Eds.), *Sexual deviance: Theory, assessment, and treatment* (pp. 175–193). New York: Guilford.

Barbaree, H. E., Seto, M. C., Langton, C. M., & Peacock, E. J. (2001). Evaluating the predictive accuracy of six risk assessment instruments for adult sex offenders. *Criminal Justice and Behavior, 28,* 490–521.

Barker, J. G., & Howell, R. J. (1992). The plethysmograph: A review of recent literature. *Bulletin of the American Academy of Psychiatry and Law, 20,* 13–25.

Beck, A. J., & Maruschak, L. M. (2001). *Mental health treatment in state prisons, 2000.* Bureau of Justice Statistics special report. Washington, DC: Government Printing Office.

Beck, J. L., & Klein-Saffran, J. (1990). Home confinement and the use of electronic monitoring with federal parolees. *Federal Probation, 54,* 23–24.

Boer, D. P., Hart, S. D., Kropp, P. R., & Webster, C. D. (1997). *Manual for the Sexual Violence Risk–20.* Vancouver: The British Columbia Institute Against Family Violence.

Bond, G. R., Drake, R. E., Mueser, K. T., & Latimer, E. (2001). Assertive community treatment: Critical ingredients and impact on patients. *Disease Management and Health Outcomes, 9*(3), 141–159.

Bonta, J., Pang, B., & Wallace-Capretta, S. (1995). Predictors of recidivism among incarcerated female offenders. *The Prison Journal, 73,* 277–294.

Borduin, C. M. (1999). Multisystemic treatment of criminality and violence in adolescents. *Journal of American Academy of Child and Adolescent Psychiatry, 38,* 242–249.

Borduin, C. M., Mann, B. J., Cone, L. T., Henggeler, S. W., Fucci, B. R., Blaske, D. M., et al. (1995). Multisystemic treatment of serious juvenile offenders: Long-term prevention of criminality and violence. *Journal of Consulting and Clinical Psychology, 63*(4), 569–578.

Borum, R., Bartel, P., & Forth, A. (2003). *Manual for the Structured Assessment for Violence Risk in Youth (SAVRY) version 1.1.* Tampa: Florida Mental Health Institute, University of South Florida.

Borum, R., & Verhaagen, D. (2006). *Assessing and managing violence risk in juveniles.* New York: Guilford.

Brown, C. S. H., & Lloyd, K. (2008). OPRISK: A structured checklist assessing security needs for mentally disordered offenders referred to high security psychiatric hospitals. *Criminal Behaviour and Mental Health, 18,* 190–202.

Brown, S. (1999). Public attitudes toward the treatment of sex offenders. *Legal and Criminological Psychology, 4,* 239–252.

Bureau of Justice Statistics. (2000). *Intimate partner violence.* Washington, DC: U.S. Department of Justice, NCJ-178247.

Bureau of Justice Statistics. (2006). *Prison and jail inmates at midyear 2005.* Washington, DC: U.S. Department of Justice, NCJ-213133.

Bush, J. (1995). Teaching self-risk management to violent offenders. In J. McGuire (Ed.), *What works: Reducing reoffending—Guidelines from research and practice* (pp. 139–154). Chichester: Wiley.

Butcher, J. N., Dahlstrom, W. G., Graham, J. R., Tellegen, A., & Kaemmer, B. (1989). *The Minnesota Multiphasic Personality Inventory-2 (MMPI-2): Manual for administration and scoring.* Minneapolis: University of Minnesota Press.

Campbell, J. (1986). Nursing assessment for risk of homicide with battered women. *Advances in Nursing Science, 8,* 36–51.

Catalano, S. (2007). *Intimate partner violence in the United States.* Bureau of Justice Statistics. Retrieved April 27, 2009, from http://www.ojp.usdoj.gov/bjs/pub/pdf/ipvus.pdf

Conroy, M. A. (2006). Risk management of sex offenders: A model for community intervention. *Journal of Psychiatry & Law, 34,* 5–24.

Cullen, F. T., & Gendreau, P. (1989). The effectiveness of correctional rehabilitation: Reconsidering the "nothing works" debate. In L. Goldstein & D. L. McKenzie (Eds.), *The American prison: Issues in research policy* (pp. 23–44). New York: Plenum.

Daly, J. E., & Pelowski, S. (2000). Predictors of dropout among men who batter: A review of studies with implication for research and practice. *Violence and Victims, 15,* 137–160.

Davis, R. C., & Taylor, B. G. (1999). Does batterer treatment reduce violence? A synthesis of the literature. *Women and Criminal Justice, 10*(2), 69–93.

Di Placido, C., Simon, T., Witte, T., Gu, D., & Wong, S. C. P. (2006). Treatment of gang members can reduce recidivism and institutional misconduct. *Law and Human Behavior, 30*(1), 93–114.

Ditton, P. M. (1999). *Special report: Mental health and treatment of inmates and probationers.* Washington, DC: U.S. Department of Justice, Bureau of Justice Statistics.

Dobash, R. E., & Dobash, R. P. (1977). Wives: The appropriate victims of marital violence. *Victimology, 2,* 426–442.

Dowden, C., & Andrews, D. A. (1999). What works for female offenders: A meta-analytic review. *Crime & Delinquency, 45,* 438–452.

Dowden, C., & Andrews, D. A. (2003). Does family intervention work for delinquents? Results of a meta-analysis. *Canadian Journal of Criminology and Criminal Justice, 45*(3), 327–342.

Draine, J., Solomon, P., & Meyerson, A. T. (1994). Predictors of reincarceration among patients who received psychiatric services in jail. *Hospital and Community Psychiatry, 45,* 163–167.

Dunford, F. W. (2000). The San Diego Navy experiment: An assessment of interventions for men who assault their wives. *Journal of Consulting and Clinical Psychology, 68,* 468–476.

Epperson, D. L., Kaul, J. D., Huot, S. J., Hesselton, D., Alexander, W., & Goldman, R. (1999). *Minnesota Sex Offender Screening Tool–Revised (MnSOST-R) technical paper: Development, validation, and recommended risk level cut scores.* Retrieved September 1, 2009, from http://www.psychology.iastate.edu/faculty/epperson/TechUpdatePaper12-03.pdf

Fisler, C. (2005). Building trust and managing risk: A look at a felony mental health court. *Psychology, Public Policy and the Law, 11*(4), 587–604.

Fylan, F., & Clarke, J. (2006). *Violence reduction strategy.* York: Her Majesty's Prison Full Sutton.

Gallagher, C. A., Wilson, D. B., Hirschfield, P., Coggeshall, M. B., & MacKenzie, D. L. (1999). A quantitative review of the effects of sex offender treatment on sexual reoffending. *Corrections Management Quarterly, 3,* 19–29.

Garrett, M., & Lerman, M. (2007). CBT for psychosis for long-term inpatients with a forensic history. *Psychiatric Services, 58*(5), 712–713.

Geffner, R. A., & Rosenbaum, A. (2001). Domestic violence offenders: Treatment and intervention standards. *Journal of Aggression, Maltreatment, and Trauma, 5*(2), 1–9.

Gendreau, P., & Goggin, C. (1997). Correctional treatment: Accomplishments and realities. In P. Van Voorhis, M. Braswell, & D. Lester (Eds.), *Correctional counseling and rehabilitation* (3rd ed., pp. 271–279). Cincinnati, OH: Anderson.

Gendreau, P., & Ross, R. R. (1979). Effective correctional treatment: Bibliotherapy for cynics. *Crime and Delinquency, 25,* 463–489.

Gondolf, E. W. (2002). *Batterer treatment systems: Issues, outcomes, and recommendations.* Thousand Oaks, CA: Sage.

Green, C., & Babcock, J. (2001, July). *Does batterers' treatment work? A meta-analytic review of domestic violence treatment.* Paper presented at the 7th International Family Violence Research Conference, University of New Hampshire, Portsmouth.

Gregory, C., & Erez, E. (2002). The effects of batterer intervention programs: The battered women's perspective. *Violence Against Women, 8*(2), 206–232.

Griffith, J. D., Hiller, M. L., Knight, K., & Simpson, D. D. (1999). A cost-effectiveness analysis of in-prison therapeutic community treatment and risk classification. *The Prison Journal, 79*(3), 352–368.

Grove, W. M., Zald, D. H., Hallberg, A. M., Lebow, B., Snitz, E., & Nelson, C. (2000). Clinical versus mechanical prediction: A meta-analysis. *Psychological Assessment, 12,* 19–30.

Hall, G. C. N. (1995). Sexual offender recidivism revisited: A meta-analysis of recent treatment studies. *Journal of Consulting and Clinical Psychology, 63*(5), 802–809.

Hammett, T. M., Roberts, C., & Kennedy, S. (2001). Health-related issues in prisoner reentry. *Crime & Delinquency, 47,* 390–410.

Hanson, R. K. (1997). *The development of a brief actuarial risk scale for sexual offense recidivism.* User report 97-04. Ottawa: Department of the Solicitor General of Canada.

Hanson, R. K. (2000). What is so special about relapse prevention? In D. R. Laws, S. M. Hudson, & T. Ward (Eds.), *Remaking relapse prevention with sex offenders* (pp. 27–38). Thousand Oaks, CA: Sage.

Hanson, R. K., Bourgon, G., Helmus, L., & Hodgson, S. (2009). *A meta-analysis of the effectiveness of treatment for sexual offenders: Risk, need, and responsivity.* Corrections research user report no. 2009-01. Ottawa: Public Safety Canada.

Hanson, R. K., & Bussiere, M. T. (1998). Predicting relapse: A meta-analysis of sexual offender recidivism studies. *Journal of Consulting and Clinical Psychology, 66,* 348–362.

Hanson, R. K., Gordon, A., Harris, A. J. R., Marques, J. K., Murphy, W., Quinsey, V. L., et al. (2002). First report of the Collaborative Outcome Project on the effectiveness of psychological treatment for sex offenders. *Sexual Abuse: A Journal of Research and Treatment, 14,* 159–194.

Hanson, R. K., & Morton-Bourgon, K. (2004). *Predictors of sexual recidivism: An updated meta-analysis.* User report 2004-02. Ottawa: Public Safety and Emergency Preparedness Canada.

Hanson, R. K., & Thornton, D. (2000). Improving risk assessment for sex offenders: A comparison of three actuarial scales. *Law and Human Behavior, 24,* 119–136.

Hare, R. D. (1991). *The Hare Psychopathy Checklist–revised.* Toronto: Multi-Health Systems.

Hare, R. D. (1998). *Without conscience: The disturbing world of the psychopaths among us.* New York: Guilford.

Hare, R. D. (1999). Psychopathy as a risk factor for violence. *Psychiatric Quarterly, 70*(3), 181–197.

Hare, R. D., Forth, A., & Kosson, D. S. (1994). *The Psychopathy Checklist: Youth version.* Vancouver: University of British Columbia, Department of Psychology.

Harris, G. T., Rice, M. E., Quinsey, V. L., Lalumiere, M. L., Boer, D., & Lang, C. (2003). A multisite comparison of actuarial risk instruments for sex offenders. *Psychological Assessment, 15,* 413–425.

Hart, S. D., Kropp, P. R., Laws, D. R., Klaver, J., Logan, C., & Watt, K. A. (2003). *The Risk for Sexual Violence Protocol (RSVP): Structured professional guidelines for assessing risk of sexual violence.* Vancouver: The British Columbia Institute Against Family Violence.

Heilbrun, K., DeMatteo, D., Fretz, R., Erickson, J., Yasuhara, K., & Anumba, N. (2008). How "specific" are gender-specific rehabilitation needs? An empirical analysis. *Criminal Justice and Behavior, 35,* 1382–1397.

Henggeler, S. W. (1996). Treatment of juvenile offenders: We have the knowledge. *Journal of Family Psychology, 10,* 137–141.

Henggeler, S. W., Melton, G. B., & Smith, L. A. (1992). Family preservation using multisystemic therapy: An effective alternative to incarcerating serious juvenile offenders. *Journal of Consulting and Clinical Psychology, 60,* 953–961.

Henggeler, S. W., Rodick, J. D., Borduin, C. M., Hanson, C. L., Watson, S. M., & Urey, J. R. (1986). Multi-systemic treatment of juvenile offenders: Effects on adolescent behavior and family interaction. *Developmental Psychology, 22,* 132–141.

Henning, K., & Frueh, B. C. (1996). Cognitive behavioral treatment of incarcerated offenders: An evaluation of the Vermont Department of Corrections cognitive self-change program. *Criminal Justice and Behavior, 23,* 523–541.

Hodel, B., & West, A. (2003). A cognitive training for mentally ill offenders with treatment-resistant schizophrenia. *The Journal of Forensic Psychiatry & Psychology, 14*(3), 554–568.

Hodges, K. (1994). *Manual for the Child and Adolescent Functional Assessment Scale.* Ypsilanti: Eastern Michigan University, Department of Psychology.

Hodges, K. (1999). Child and Adolescent Functional Assessment Scale (CAFAS). In M. F. Maruish (Ed.), *The use of psychological testing for treatment planning and outcome assessment* (2nd ed., pp. 631–660). Mahwah, NJ: Erlbaum.

Hoge, R. D. (2002). Standardized instruments for assessing risk and need in youthful offenders. *Criminal Justice and Behavior, 29*(4), 380–396.

Hoge, R. D., & Andrews, D. A. (2001). *The Youth Level of Service/Case Management Inventory (YLS/CMI): Intake manual and item scoring key.* Ottawa: Carleton University.

Holtzworth-Munroe, A. (2001). Standards for batterer treatment programs: How can research inform our decisions? *Journal of Aggression, Maltreatment, & Trauma, 5*(2), 165–180.

Janus, E. S., & Prentky, R. A. (2003). The forensic use of actuarial risk assessment with sex offenders: Accuracy, admissibility and accountability. *American Criminal Law Review, 40,* 1443–1449.

Jenson, J. M., & Howard, M. O. (1998). Youth crime, public policy, and practice in the juvenile justice system: Recent trends and needed reforms. *Social Work, 43,* 324–334.

Kazdin, A. E. (1987). Treatment of antisocial behavior in children: Current status and future directions. *Psychological Bulletin, 102,* 187–203.

Koons, B. A., Burrow, J. D., Morash, M., & Bynum, T. (1997). Expert and offender perceptions of program elements linked to successful outcomes for incarcerated women. *Crime & Delinquency, 43,* 512–532.

Kropp, P. R., Hart, S. D., Webster, C., & Eaves, D. (1999). *Spousal Assault Risk Assessment Guide: User's manual.* Vancouver: Multi-Health Systems.

Laberge, D., & Morin, D. (1995). The overuse of criminal justice dispositions: Failures of diversionary policies in the management of mental health problems. *International Journal of Law and Psychiatry, 18,* 389–414.

Lamb, H. R., & Weinberger, L. E. (1998). Persons with severe mental illness in jails and prisons: A review. *Psychiatric Services, 49,* 483–492.

Lamb, H. R., & Weinberger, L. E. (2008). Mental health courts as a way to provide treatment to violent persons with severe mental illness. *Journal of the American Medical Association, 300*(6), 722–724.

Landenberger, N. A., & Lipsey, M. W. (2005). The positive effects of cognitive–behavioral programs for offenders: A meta-analysis of factors associated with effective treatment. *Journal of Experimental Criminology, 1,* 451–476.

Langan, P. A., & Levin, D. J. (2002). *Recidivism of prisoners released in 1994.* Washington, DC: Bureau of Justice Statistics, U.S. Department of Justice.

Larson, J. D. (1990). Cognitive–behavioral therapy with delinquent adolescents: A cooperative approach with the juvenile court. *Journal of Offender Counseling, Services and Rehabilitation, 16,* 47–64.

Lattimore, P. K., Visher, C. A., & Linster, R. L. (1995). Predicting rearrest for violence among serious youthful offenders. *Journal of Research in Crime and Delinquency, 32,* 54–83.

Lees, J., Manning, N., & Rawlings, B. (1999). *Therapeutic community effectiveness. A systemic international review of therapeutic community treatment for people with personality disorders and mentally disordered offenders.* CRD report 17. York: NHS Centre for Reviews and Dissemination, University of York.

Levenson, J. S. (2003). Policy interventions designed to combat sexual violence: Community notification and civil commitment. *Journal of Child Sexual Abuse, 12,* 17–52.

Levesque, D. A., & Gelles, R. J. (1998, July). *Does treatment reduce recidivism in men who batter? A meta-analytic evaluation of treatment outcome.* Paper presented at Program Evaluation and Family Violence Research: An International Conference, Durham, NH.

Lewis, D. O., Yeager, C. A., Lovely, R., Stein, A., & Cobham-Portorreal, C. S. (1994). A clinical follow-up of delinquent males: Ignored variables, unmet needs, and the perpetuation of violence. *Journal of the American Academy of Child and Adolescent Psychiatry, 33,* 518–528.

Linehan, M. M. (1993). *Cognitive behavioral treatment of borderline personality disorder.* New York: Guilford.

Linhorst, D. M., Knight, K., Johnston, J. S., & Trickey, M. (2001). Situational influences on the implementation of a prison-based therapeutic community. *The Prison Journal, 81,* 436–453.

Lipsey, M. W., & Wilson, D. B. (1998). Effective intervention for serious juvenile offenders: A synthesis of research. In R. Loeber & D. P. Farrington (Eds.), *Serious and violent juvenile offenders: Risk factors and successful interventions* (pp. 313–345). Thousand Oaks, CA: Sage.

Logan, C. H. (1972). Evaluation research in crime and delinquency: A reappraisal. *Journal of Criminal Law, Criminology and Police Science, 63*, 378–387.

Long, C. G., Webster, P., Waine, J., Motala, J., & Hollin, C. (2008). Usefulness of the CANFOR-S for measuring needs among mentally disordered offenders resident in medium or low secure hospital service in the UK: A pilot evaluation. *Criminal Behavior and Mental Health, 18*, 39–48.

Looman, J., Abracen, J., & Nicholaichuk, T. P. (2000). Recidivism among treated sexual offenders and matched controls: Data from the Regional Treatment Centre (Ontario). *Journal of Interpersonal Violence, 15*, 279–290.

Looman, J., Dickie, I., & Abracen, J. (2005). Responsivity issues in the treatment of sexual offenders. *Trauma, Violence, & Abuse, 6*(4), 330–353.

Losel, F. (1998). Treatment and management of psychopaths. In D. J. Cooke, A. E. Forth, & R. D. Hare (Eds.), *Psychopathy: Theory, research, and implications for society* (pp. 303–354). Dordrecht, the Netherlands: Kluwer.

Loucks, A., & Zamble, E. (2000). Predictors of criminal behavior and prison misconduct in serious female offenders. *Empirical and Applied Criminal Justice Review, 1*, 1–47.

Marshall, W. L., Barbaree, H. E., & Eccles, A. (1991). Early onset and deviant sexuality in child molesters. *Journal of Interpersonal Violence, 6*, 323–336.

Marshall, W. L., Eccles, A., & Barbaree, H. E. (1993). A three-tiered approach to the rehabilitation of incarcerated sex offenders. *Behavioral Sciences and the Law, 11*, 441–455.

Martinson, R. (1974). What works? Questions and answers about prison reform. *The Public Interest, 35*, 22–54.

McCorkle, R. C. (1993). Research note: Punish and rehabilitate? Public attitudes toward six common crimes. *Crime & Delinquency, 39*(2), 240–252.

McGrath, R. J., Cumming, G., Livingston, J. A., & Hoke, S. E. (2003). Outcome of a treatment program for adult sex offenders: From prison to community. *Journal of Interpersonal Violence, 18*(1), 3–17.

McGrath, R. J., Hoke, S. E., & Vojtisek, J. E. (1998). Cognitive–behavioral treatment of sex offenders: A treatment comparison and long-term follow-up study. *Criminal Justice and Behavior, 25*, 203–225.

McNeil, D. E., & Binder, R. L. (2007). Effectiveness of a mental health court in reducing criminal recidivism and violence. *American Journal of Psychiatry, 164*, 1395–1403.

Moffitt, T. E., Krueger, R. F., Caspi, A., & Fagan, J. (2000). Partner abuse and general crime: How are they the same? How are they different? *Criminology, 38*, 199–232.

Monster, M., & Micucci, A. (2005). Meeting rehabilitative needs at a Canadian women's correctional centre. *The Prison Journal, 85*(2), 168–185.

Morash, M., Bynum, T. S., & Koons, B. A. (1998). *Women offenders: Programming, needs and promising approaches.* Washington, DC: National Institute of Justice, Research in Brief.

Morrissey, J., Meyer, P., & Cuddeback, G. (2007). Extending assertive community treatment to criminal justice settings: Origins, current evidence, and future directions. *Community Mental Health Journal, 43*(5), 527–544.

Motiuk, L. L., & Serin, R. (1998). Situating risk assessment in the reintegration potential frame-work. *Forum on Corrections Research, 10*(1), 19–22.

Mullen, P. E. (2007). Dangerous and severe personality disorder and in need of treatment. *The British Journal of Psychiatry, 192,* s3–s7.

National Center for Injury Prevention and Control. (2003). *Cost of intimate partner violence against women in the United States.* Atlanta: Centers for Disease Control and Prevention.

Nicholaichuk, T., Gordon, A., Deqiang, G., & Wong, S. (2000). Outcome of an institutional sexual offender treatment program: A comparison between treated and matched untreated offenders. *Sexual Abuse: A Journal of Research and Treatment, 12,* 139–154.

Nichols, H. R., & Molinder, I. (1984). *The Multiphasic Sex Inventory manual.* Fircrest, WA: Nichols & Molinder.

Office of Justice Programs. (2004). *Reentry.* Washington, DC: Author.

Office of Juvenile Justice and Delinquency Prevention. (1996). *Combating violence and delinquency: The National Juvenile Justice Action Plan.* Washington, DC: Author.

Pence, E., & Paymar, M. (1993). *Education groups for men who batter: The Duluth model.* New York: Springer-Verlag.

Petrunik, M. G. (2002). Managing unacceptable risk: Sex offenders, community response, and social policy in the United States and Canada. *International Journal of Offender Therapy & Comparative Criminology, 46,* 483–511.

Poels, V. (2007). Risk assessment of recidivism of violent and sexual female offenders. *Psychology, Psychiatry, & Law, 14,* 227–250.

Polaschek, D. L. L., & Dixon, B. G. (2001). The Violence Prevention Project: The development and evaluation of a treatment programme for violent offenders. *Psychology, Crime, & Law, 7,* 1–27.

Quinsey, V. L., Harris, G. T., Rice, M. E., & Cormier, C. A. (1998). *Violent offenders: Appraising and managing risk.* Washington, DC: American Psychological Association.

Quinsey, V. L., Harris, G. T., Rice, M. E., & Cormier, C. A. (2006). *Violent offenders: Appraising and managing risk* (2nd ed.). Washington, DC: American Psychological Association.

Redondo, S., Sanchez-Meca, J., & Garrido, V. (1999). The influence of treatment programmes on the recidivism of juvenile and adult offenders: A European meta-analytic review. *Psychology, Crime, & Law, 5,* 251–278.

Rice, M. E., Harris, G. T., & Cormier, C. A. (1992). An evaluation of a maximum security thera-peutic community for psychopaths and other mentally disordered offenders. *Law and Human Behavior, 16,* 399–412.

Saum, C. A., O'Connell, D. J., Martin, S. S., Hiller, M. L., Bacon, G. A., & Simpson, D. D. (2007). Tempest in a TC: Changing treatment providers for in-prison therapeutic communities. *Criminal Justice and Behavior, 34,* 1216–1234.

Scalora, M. J., & Garbin, C. (2003). A multivariate analysis of sex offender recidivism. *International Journal of Offender Therapy and Comparative Criminology, 47*(3), 309–323.

Schoenwald, S. K., Ward, D. M., Henggeler, S. W., Pickrel, S. G., & Patel, H. (1996). Multisystemic therapy treatment of substance abusing or dependent adolescent offenders: Costs of reducing incarceration, inpatient, and residential treatment. *Journal of Child and Family Studies, 5,* 431–444.

Scott, K. L. (2004). Predictors of change among male batterers: Application of theories and review of empirical findings. *Trauma, Violence, & Abuse, 5*(3), 260–284.

Serin, R. C., & Brown, S. (1996). Strategies for enhancing the treatment of violent offenders. *Forum of Corrections Research, 8,* 45–48.

Serin, R. C., & Brown, S. (1997). Treatment programs for offenders with violent histories: A national survey. *Forum of Corrections Research, 9,* 35–38.

Serin, R. C., & Kennedy, S. (1997). *Treatment readiness and responsivity: Contributing to effective correctional programming.* Ottawa: Correctional Services of Canada.

Shadish, W. R., Montgomery, L. M., Wilson, P., Wilson, M. R., Bright, I., & Okwumabua, T. (1993). Effects of family and marital psychotherapies: A meta-analysis. *Journal of Consulting and Clinical Psychology, 61,* 991–1002.

Sickmund, M., Snyder, H. N., & Poe-Yamagata, E. (1997). *Juvenile offenders and victims: 1997 update on violence.* Washington, DC: Office of Juvenile Justice and Delinquency Prevention.

Slate, R. N., & Johnson, W. W. (2008). *Criminalization of mental illness.* Durham, NC: Carolina Academic Press.

Snyder, H. (2008). *Juvenile arrests 2006.* Office of Juvenile Justice and Delinquency Prevention. Retrieved April 27, 2009, from http://www.ncjrs.gov/pdffiles1/ojjdp/221338.pdf

Straus, M. A., Hamby, S. L., Boney-McCoy, S., & Sugarman, D. B. (1996). The Revised Conflict Tactics Scales (CTS2): Development and preliminary psychometric data. *Journal of Family Issues, 17*(3), 283–316.

Swanson, J., Swartz, M., van Dorn, R., Elbogen, E., Wagner, R., Rosenheck, R., et al. (2006). A national study of violent behavior in persons with schizophrenia. *Archives of General Psychiatry, 63,* 490–499.

Tarolla, S. M., Wagner, E. F., Rabinowitz, J., & Tubman, J. G. (2002). Understanding and treating juvenile offenders: A review of current knowledge and future directions. *Aggression and Violent Behavior, 7,* 125–143.

Tate, D. C., Reppucci, N. D., & Mulvey, E. P. (1995). Violent juvenile delinquents: Treatment effectiveness and implications for future action. *American Psychologist, 50*(9), 777–781.

Taxman, F. S. (2004). The offender and reentry: Supporting active participation in reintegration. *Federal Probation, 68*(2), 31–35.

Taxman, F. S., Young, D., & Byrne, J. (2004). Transforming offender reentry into public safety: Lessons from OJP's Reentry Partnership Initiative. *Justice Policy and Research, 5*(2), 101–128.

Taylor, B. G., Davis, R. C., & Maxwell, C. D. (2001). The effects of a group batterer treatment program in Brooklyn. *Justice Quarterly, 18,* 170–201.

Thomas, S. D. M., Harty, M. A., Parrott, J., McCrone, P., Slade, M., & Thornicroft, G. (2003). *CANFOR: Camberwell Assessment of Need—Forensic version.* London: Gaskell.

Tjaden, P., & Thoennes, N. (1998). *Prevalence, incidence, and consequences of violence against women: Findings from the National Violence Against Women Survey.* Washington, DC: U.S. Department of Justice.

Valliant, P. M., Furac, C. J., & Antonowicz, D. H. (1994). Attitudes toward sex offenders by female undergraduate university students enrolled in a psychology program. *Social Behavior and Personality, 22*(2), 105–110.

Ward, T., Mann, R. E., & Gannon, T. A. (2007). The good lives model of offender rehabilitation: Clinical implications. *Aggression and Violent Behavior, 12,* 87–107.

Ward, T., Vess, J., & Collie, R. M. (2006). Risk management or goods promotion: The relationship between approach and avoidance goals in treatment of sex offenders. *Aggression and Violent Behavior, 11*(4), 378–393.

Webster, C., Douglas, D., Eaves, D., & Hart, S. (1997). *HCR-20. Assessing risk for violence* (Version 2). Vancouver: Simon Fraser University and Forensic Psychiatric Services Commission of British Columbia.

Wechsler, D. (1997). *Wechsler Adult Intelligence Scale* (3rd ed.). San Antonio, TX: The Psychological Corporation and Harcourt Brace.

Whitaker, D. J., Morrison, S., Lindquist, C., Hawkins, S. R., O'Neil, J. A., Nesius, A. M., et al. (2006). A critical review of interventions for the primary prevention of perpetration of partner violence. *Aggression and Violent Behavior, 11,* 151–166.

Wilson, R. J., Huculak, B., & McWhinnie, A. (2002). Restorative justice innovations in Canada. *Behavioral Sciences & the Law, 20*(4), 363–380.

Wolfe, D. A., & Feiring, C. (2000). Dating violence through the lens of adolescent romantic relationships. *Child Maltreatment, 5,* 360–363.

Wong, S. C. P., & Gordon, A. (2006). The validity and reliability of the Violence Risk Scale: A treatment friendly violence risk assessment tool. *Psychology, Public Policy, and Law, 12,* 279–309.

Wong, S. C. P., Gordon, A., & Gu, D. (2007). Assessment and treatment of violence-prone forensic clients: An integrated approach. *British Journal of Psychiatry, 190*(49), s66–74.

Wong, S. C. P., Van der Veen, S., Leis, T., Parrish, H., Gu, D., Usher Liber, E., et al. (2005). Reintegrating seriously violent and personality disordered offenders from a super-maximum security institution into the general offender population. *International Journal of Offender Therapy and Comparative Criminology, 49*(4), 362–375.

Wormith, J., Althouse, R., Simpson, M., Reitzel, L., Fagan, T., & Morgan, R. (2007). The rehabilitation and integration of offenders: The current landscape and some future directions for correctional psychology. *Criminal Justice and Behavior, 34,* 879–892.

CHAPTER 4

Major Rehabilitative Approaches

Hung-En Sung and Lior Gideon

THEORETICAL MODELS OF REHABILITATION

Successful correctional interventions are clinically effective, politically relevant, and theoretically meaningful. The idea of theoretical models is most often discussed in the context of scientific methods (see Jupp, 1989). Because evidence-based correctional models usually are programs or practices that are based on a distinct conceptual framework, have been tested by independent and rigorous evaluation research, and have produced consistent patterns of positive results, the identification of a theoretical model constitutes the first step in the development of evidence-based correctional practices.

This chapter introduces major rehabilitative approaches that provide the dominant paradigms and frameworks of current correctional practices that support the intervention modalities presented in the chapters that follow. Our discussion begins with a description of the basic elements of a theoretical model of rehabilitation.

Elements of a Theoretical Model of Rehabilitation

A theory of rehabilitation is a set of coherent hypotheses proposed to solve the problem of criminal recidivism and related adverse consequences. It usually contains an explicit theory of causation for criminal recidivism and an implicit theory of treatment that is logically derived from the former. The basic function of a theory of rehabilitation is to impose order and predictability on our discrete observations of criminal careers and to guide public policymaking with reasoned and tested arguments.

Some might object to the use of theoretical models on the grounds that formal propositions involve such drastic simplifications of the complexity of rebuilding a law-abiding and productive citizen that they cannot possibly deepen our understanding in this regard. We offer three counterarguments to such objections.

First, the fact that models are simplifications of complexity is not a shortcoming but a virtue. This is precisely what a good theory of rehabilitation should accomplish: to get to the heart of the intrigue, problems of recidivism and desistance, by identifying the key causal linkages.

Second, the essential action of theoretical models of rehabilitative change is to create a thought experiment on lifestyle transformation. That is, the model fulfills a need to specify the underlying assumptions about why some offenders recidivate whereas others desist from crime, the conditions that should be treated as parameters, and the ways in which rehabilitative interventions would work. Furthermore, it is essential to understand that the success of a theory of rehabilitation is not a matter of rigid truth but is determined when it is useful in increasing our ability to explain recidivism reduction while expanding our therapeutic options.

Finally, lurking behind every rehabilitative intervention or correctional program is a tacit formal theory. All explanatory arguments about patterns of recidivism contain assumptions about human nature, beliefs about determinants of human behavior, and expectations about how the most promising interventions fit together. Ignoring implicit assumptions is surely more dangerous than formal modeling, which not only enhances the depth of our knowledge of the abstract propositions but also makes it much easier to pinpoint their weaknesses and reconstruct them in light of empirical feedback.

Empirical and Clinical Importance of Theoretical Models

Rehabilitative interventions and correctional programs that produce the best results among supervised criminal offenders are characterized by high program integrity (Colorado Division of Criminal Justice, 2007). By *program integrity* we mean the degree to which a program is implemented in practice, as intended by its underlying theory and original design; it is different from *program effectiveness,* which is the extent to which the stated goals are achieved. The first indicator of program integrity in correctional practices is whether or not the program adopts a specific theoretical model of criminal behavior in the design of the intervention, and the second indicator is the fidelity of program implementation in practice as intended in theory and design, as judged by the extent to which a particular program is conducted. Next, we will present the main conceptual approaches adopted in correctional settings.

COGNITIVE–BEHAVIORAL APPROACHES

Cognitive–behavioral therapy (CBT) is a diverse family of treatment interventions, which are rooted in the merging of behavioral modification, cognitive therapy, and social learning theory. Behaviorism proposes that human behavior is either induced by sensorial cues or determined by its consequences. Just as behavioral patterns are conditioned by rewards or punishments in previous experiences, they are also susceptible to planned change through careful administration of rewards and punishments. Alternatively, cognitive therapists assert that maladaptive behavior has been shaped by experience, but they assert that self-defeating behaviors are the result of unproductive thought patterns relating to these past experiences. Social learning theorists believe that behavior is learned and can be unlearned not only through conditioning but also through modeling and imitation. The amalgamation of these theories renders a particular understanding that sees cognition (e.g., beliefs, expectations, ideas, and attitudes) modeled in social situations during one's upbringing as influential antecedents and powerful consequences of human behaviors.

Learning of Criminal Thinking and Behaviors

Despite their many differences, different types of CBT share some fundamental commonalities. To begin, it is assumed that human emotions and behaviors are determined and shaped by cognitive habits such as beliefs and thoughts (Lipsey, Landenberger, & Wilson, 2007; Milkman & Wanberg, 2007). Factors outside the mind of the individual, such as family events, situational contingencies, and other people, are believed to be less influential on the person's feelings and acts than established patterns of perceptions and thinking. This assumption shifts the emphasis of treatment away from changing social relations or external circumstances to changing the way people think and feel about things, values, others, and themselves.

Gresham Sykes and David Matza (1957) first proposed that delinquents develop a special collection of rationalizations for their antisocial behavior to silence the voice of their conscience. Such rationalizations permit juveniles to temporarily neutralize their commitment to social norms, freeing them to commit delinquent acts. Five basic techniques of neutralization are identified: denial of responsibility, denial of injury, denial of the victim, condemnation of the condemners, and appeal to higher loyalties.

Samuel Yochelson and Stanton Samenow (1976, 1977) formalized an etiological theory of criminal thinking with practical clinical implications. They developed a system of 52 thinking errors that underlie the criminal behaviors of most offenders. Several prominent elements of the criminal thinking are a schema of entitlement, fascination with power and control, sentimentality, overoptimism, cognitive indolence, and overvaluation of the present. Other notable thinking errors include self-justificatory thinking, misapprehension of situational cues, dislodgment of responsibility, and immature ethical reasoning. People with such cognitive distortions may misperceive neutral situations as threats, interpret benign remarks as disrespectful or hostile, thirst for immediate gratification, and confuse wants with needs. These patterns of perception and reasoning often become consolidated by offenders' involvement in a criminal subculture.

This thread of inquiry highlights the importance of thought, choice, and personal responsibility, which have been largely overlooked by mainstream criminological research. Criminal thinking has been scientifically validated as a distinguishable and useful empirical construct that is highly correlated with past maladaptive behaviors and criminal activities as well as statistically significantly predictive of future deviance, including criminal recidivism. Instruments such as the Psychological Inventory of Criminal Thinking Styles, an 80-item self-administered questionnaire designed to assess deviant cognitive patterns, have been developed and tested for research and clinical use (Walters, 2002).

Modeling and Reinforcement of Prosocial Behaviors

Lasting transformation in the offender requires a focus on thinking and not on behavior. Reckless offenders may clean up certain areas of their lives, but unless there is a change in their cognitive habits, there will be no change across the many aspects of their relationships and social functions (Lipsey et al., 2007; Milkman & Wanberg, 2007). Readiness to be held accountable signals the first commitment to change.

Criminal justice–based CBT programs focus on personal responsibility and seek to help offenders to visualize the thinking processes and choices that immediately preceded their antisocial activities. Change begins when offenders learn to self-monitor thinking and to single out and modify problem cognitive habits. All CBT interventions deploy structured techniques for fostering prosocial cognitive skills and reorganizing cognition in areas where offenders' thinking is distorted.

In general, CBT programs seek to achieve cognitive modification within a short period of time. On average, a treatment regimen of no more than 20 sessions is prescribed to criminal offenders. Therapists have a focused agenda for each session, and special techniques and concepts are applied during treatment. The goal of therapy is to suppress maladaptive behaviors through unlearning of undesired cognition and to model prosocial behaviors through the learning of positive attitudes and healthy reasoning skills. The premise of the CBT interventions is that when offenders understand how and why they are doing well, they acquire the skills to maintain their confirmative and normative behavior and thus continue to do well.

Offenders in treatment are encouraged to closely examine their thoughts and to directly confront their own beliefs. The therapist is to provide new information that directly challenges the accuracy and legitimacy of clients' old cognitive habits and to guide them to change their thinking to be in line with the reality of the situation. Role play and practice in real situations are the most widely used tools to practice and consolidate prosocial behaviors supported by cognitive habits newly learned in group discussions, multimedia sessions, and reading assignments.

Implementation and Evaluation of Cognitive–Behavioral Interventions (CBT)

CBT programs have been extensively experimented with and evaluated among juvenile offenders, substance-abusing offenders, violent offenders, sex offenders (as explained in chapter 3), and violent and sexual offenders (see chapter 9). In contrast to traditional CBT interventions that are somewhat egocentric, correction-based CBT interventions are essentially sociocentric. Rather than asking clients to identify their own problems and helping them to fulfill their inner goals and expectations, therapists and educators direct offenders' attention to self-control and responsibility toward others and the community. A recent review by the National Institute of Corrections concludes that six CBT programs are most commonly used in correctional settings (Milkman & Wanberg, 2007):

Aggression Replacement Training (ART). This program is intended to control hostility and aggression among juvenile delinquents. In recent times, the strategy has been replicated among adult offenders. ART provides offenders with prosocial tools to use in stressful situations and skills to manage hostile urges conducive to aggressive behaviors. It consists of three training stages, each targeting the behavioral, affective, and cognitive factors, respectively:

Social skill training teaches interpersonal techniques to handle anger-provoking situations, anger control training models effective habits to reduce hostile feelings and anger by enhancing self-control competencies, and moral reasoning training consists of a set of procedures intended to increase the offender's ability to value fairness and justice and to empathize with the pain and needs of others.

Criminal Conduct and Substance Abuse Treatment: Strategies for Self-Improvement and Change (SSC). SSC provides a standardized and structured approach to the rehabilitation of adult substance-abusing offenders. When compared with other CBT strategies, SSC intervention is unusually long and requires 9 to 12 months of rigorous programming. The SSC curriculum comprises 12 treatment modules organized around three phases of recovery. These phases are Challenge to Change, in which the offender engages in a reflective–contemplative process aimed at the development of motivation to change and positive therapeutic alliance; Commitment to Change, in which the offender is shown new cognitive and behavioral patterns and asked to practice these skills to foster a law-abiding and drug-free lifestyle; and Ownership of Change, in which the offender actively consolidates both the internalization of prosocial thinking and the stabilization of new behaviors in different settings and social situations.

Moral Reconation Therapy (MRT). Originally developed for substance-abusing offenders, MRT has since been applied to drunk drivers and offenders who commit violence against women. Moral reconation is the continuous evaluation and adjustment of decisions about behaviors based on socially accepted values. MRT seeks to address the fundamental obstacle in the rehabilitation of offenders: their failure to replicate new attitudinal and conduct patterns learned in therapeutic settings in noncontrol environments. This failure to implement prosocial thinking and behaviors in high-risk situations causes recidivism and is caused by deficient personality traits in treated offenders.

Reasoning and Rehabilitation (R&R). R&R is a CBT strategy derived from the idea that cognitive deficits in the offender have an important social dimension and that important people in the offender's life must be involved in the process of skill acquisition. Offenders are taught specific reasoning skills such as thinking before acting, anticipating consequences of actions, and considering alternative behaviors. The combination of these cognitive habits is expected to enhance self-control, conflict solving, social perspectives, and communitarian attitudes. Typical R&R therapy operates in groups of six to eight and takes 8 to 12 weeks.

Relapse Prevention Therapy (RPT). RPT was initially designed to prevent and manage substance use relapse after addiction therapy. This program teaches offenders to anticipate and cope with relapse and to see their substance abuse as what they *do* rather than who they *are*. RPT teaches clients monitoring and management of their own thoughts and behaviors. Relapse is less likely when a person is alert to meaningful cues, avoids high-risk situations, and controls internal cravings. Successful experiences enhance the sense of self-efficacy and increase abstinence from problem behaviors. Even when relapse occurs, the person is trained to immediately apply damage control procedures to minimize adverse consequences and to remain engaged in the therapeutic process.

Thinking for a Change (T4C). Rather than targeting specific types of offenders, T4C is designed for the general offender population. It combines cognitive reorganization, interpersonal skills, and conflict resolution to enhance awareness of self and others. The strategy begins with an introspective examination of one's patterns of thinking and feelings, perceptions, and orientations. This reflective process is constantly reinforced and constitutes the backbone of the intervention. Different social and problem-solving skills are offered and practiced as effective alternatives to antisocial behaviors. The program starts with a 15-minute induction session to remind the offender of his or her obligation to stay committed to the change process. The T4C curriculum contains 22 lessons of 1 to 2 hours each, designed for groups of 8 to 12 participants. Lessons are sequential, highly interactive, and offered twice a week.

A growing body of research shows that CBT approaches with offenders reduce recidivism (Box 4.1). A meta-analysis of 69 evaluations of traditional behavioral programs and CBT interventions found that the CBT programs were more successful in reducing reoffending than the behavioral interventions. The average decrease in reoffending hovered around 30% for participants of CBT programs (Pearson, Lipton, Cleland, & Yee, 2002). CBT programs that kept participants for a longer period of time, employed better-trained staff, targeted high-risk offenders, and emphasized quality control such as the enforcement of attendance and compliance rules were found to yield better results. Small pilot CBT programs for demonstration purposes tend to produce more positive outcomes than established programs, suggesting that the maintenance of the integrity of CBT principles in large correctional settings remains a daunting challenge (Milkman & Wanberg, 2007).

Box 4.1	**Cognitive–Behavioral Therapy and Community Supervision for Juvenile Sex Offenders**

The Juvenile Rehabilitation Administration (JRA) of the Washington State Department of Human and Social Services uses a combination of CBT and community supervision to promote rehabilitation of juvenile sex offenders and to prevent new harms to the community by treated offenders.

JRA offers a residential care program for juvenile sex offenders based on CBT principles. A continuum of treatment and intervention provides services from adjudication to discharge in four specialized institutions. Assessment, treatment, and transitional services are delivered under the CBT Integrated Treatment Model, which targets the following core areas of intervention: defining and taking responsibility, victim empathy, family support and education, social skills, sex education, anger and aggression management, arousal reconditioning, overcoming past trauma, and relapse prevention.

In order to achieve improvements in these core areas of intervention, JRA managers use a collection of therapeutic tools to weaken antisocial attitudes and behaviors and to foster new prosocial patterns of thinking and conduct among youths under treatment. These therapeutic tools include Washington State Sex Offender Risk Level Classification, multimodal CBT interventions through individual and group sessions, and CBT curricula such as *Pathways and Roadmaps* by Tim Kahn and *Relapse Prevention Workbook for Youth in Treatment* by Charlene Steen. Treated juvenile offenders routinely receive 24 to 36 months of parole supervision, which includes electronic monitoring, continued treatment by community-based therapists, and random polygraph tests.

Whereas research-informed CBT services are made available to rehabilitate offenders, strict measures have also been adopted to protect public safety. Washington State sex offender laws require that juvenile sex offenders be subject to civil commitment if judged to be sexually violent predators and that they register with law enforcement when released to the community. Offenders under posttreatment community supervision are assigned a risk level classification for purposes of community notification by law enforcement. Risk Level I offenders pose the lowest risk for reoffense, and upon request law enforcement may disclose information to victims or community members who live near the offender's residence. Risk Level II offenders are of moderate risk for reoffense. In these cases, law enforcement may disclose information to schools; daycare centers; businesses serving primarily children, women, and vulnerable adults; and neighbors and community groups near the offender's residence. Lastly, Risk Level III offenders are considered of highest risk for reoffense, and law enforcement may disclose information to the public at large. This may include Web site posts, newspaper articles, and community notification flyers where the offender resides.

In 2007, approximately 142 juvenile sex offenders were in JRA residential care on any given day, and 291 were under parole supervision. Sex offenders represented 17.2% of the juvenile residential population and 38.8% of the juvenile parole population.

Source: Compiled from online materials published by the Washington State Department of Human and Social Services at http://www.dshs.wa.gov.

MULTISYSTEMIC APPROACH

Multisystemic Therapy (MST) was conceived as a rehabilitative intervention for juvenile offenders by Scott W. Henggeler (1989). MST was conceived as a reaction to the theoretical vacuum and empirical blindness that affected the fields of family therapy and family-based services for adolescent offenders at that time. Although focused on the family, programs available to supervised juveniles rarely addressed the known causes of youthful deviant behaviors, and the programs were inaccessible for the youths most in need.

The MST model is based on Urie Bronfenbrenner's (1979) theory of human ecology and pragmatic family systems. MST mobilizes family therapy, individual counseling for a particularly troubled child of a family, and other community services, such as childcare and academic support. This approach emphasizes flexibility and recognizes that each family system is distinct and responds to a unique set of challenges. Most importantly, it is developed to directly attack the etiological determinants of juvenile delinquency reported in criminological literature.

Dysfunctional Systems as Criminogenic Factors

The basic tenet of MST is that human behavior is determined by multiple interactions between the child and his or her social environment, composed of family, peers, school, neighborhood, and other community settings. Because of shared causal pathways, different forms of antisocial behaviors such as substance abuse, delinquency, and sexual promiscuity tend to develop within overlapping and dysfunctional social systems. Five interdependent systems are identified: individual, family, peer, school, and community (Henggeler, 2002). Different correlates of deviant behaviors are found in each of these systems. Problem behavior is a function of deficit in any of the pertinent systems and deficits or conflicts that characterize the interfaces between systems (e.g., family–school relations, family–neighborhood relations).

At the individual level, low verbal skills, acceptance of deviant values, psychiatric symptoms, and tendency to attribute hostile intentions to others increase the risk of deviance. Determinants at the family level include lack of monitoring, ineffective discipline, low warmth, high conflict, and parental deviance such as substance abuse and criminality. Association with deviant peers, alienation from prosocial peers, and poor social skills are also precursors of antisocial behaviors. Academic failure, dropout, low commitment to education, and poor school environment (e.g., low morale and inadequate management) pose unique hazards. Finally, at the neighborhood level, high residential mobility, low community cohesion, and presence of criminal subcultures can exacerbate disadvantages in other social systems and encourage deviance. The primary purpose of MST is to reduce problem and antisocial behaviors among adolescents by decreasing weaknesses and enhancing strengths in the multiple social systems in which a young life develops.

Rebuilding Social Systems for Change

MST services are usually delivered by teams of three master's-level clinicians who are supervised by a doctoral-level mental health professional. Although MST programs target individual, family, peer, school, and community variables simultaneously, the family of the troubled youth is most often considered as the unit of intervention. In this family preservation model, services are delivered to the family, with targeted activities undertaken with or on behalf of individual members of the family. A typical intervention lasts up to 5 months. Meetings are flexibly scheduled to meet the family's needs, and services are tailored for each family member and delivered in the home.

MST teams routinely contemplate a set of different interventions such as cognitive–behavioral strategies directed at individual beliefs and attitudes, various family therapies, and parenting training. These therapeutic components disrupt dysfunctional patterns of communication and relationships within the family and cause them to settle back into a healthier and more adaptive direction. A frequent purpose is to improve parents' capacity to oversee the activities and whereabouts of their teenage children and to reinforce their responsible behaviors. At the peer level, the adolescent is trained to avoid delinquent and substance-using peers and to associate with positive friends and find satisfaction in these friendships. Parents are taught to maintain a fluid communication with schoolteachers and staff to promote better monitoring of and assistance in their children's academic performance.

Quality assurance mechanisms are routinely imposed to maximize program fidelity and effectiveness. Common mechanisms include a 5-day orientation for administrators and clinicians, weekly onsite supervision by a senior professional, quarterly booster training, weekly consultation with MST experts, and ongoing centralized review of caregiver reports.

Implementation and Evaluation

Swenson, Henggeler, and Schoenwald (2000) review eight evaluations that examined MST for serious juvenile offenders using randomized control and comparison groups. Summarizing 10 years of research, they conclude that rigorous studies of youths with severe antisocial behavior unambiguously show the short-term impact of MST to improve family relations and the long-term ability of MST to reduce rearrest, nondelinquent problem behaviors, and violent acts.

Because of better results than those yielded by traditional interventions, MST has been identified as a cost-saving intervention model for juvenile offenders (Aos, Phipps, Barnoski, & Lieb, 1999). In a comparative study, MST produced an average net gain of $61,068 per treated youth, as compared to the net loss of $7,511 reported for juvenile boot camp (Henggeler, 2002). These findings have boosted MST as one of the best rehabilitation models for juvenile offenders and may also have far-reaching implications for reentry and reintegration programs for released adult inmates.

THERAPEUTIC COMMUNITY

The modern therapeutic community (TC) is a new application of an ancient concept. The communal practices of an ascetic religious lifestyle were designed and implemented to combat human weaknesses of greed, cruelty, lust, selfishness, and laziness by the Jewish Qumran community and a number of Christian monastic groups. Change of lifestyle and the maintenance of a transformed lifestyle were thought to require strict adherence to the rules and teaching of the community. Reacting to the perceived failure of mainstream psychiatric institutions in the wake of World War II, structured communal living with a participative and group-based approach was introduced to treat chronic mental illnesses, personality disorders, and substance addiction.

In 1969 the first TC established in a prison was created at Marion Federal Penitentiary. Known as the Aesklepieion program, this prison-based TC was designed for serious felons transferred from a maximum security facility, Alcatraz (Wexler & Love, 1994). Other federal prisons followed suit and created TC units on their premises. But this movement in federal prisons ended within a decade as a result of a general loss of confidence in rehabilitation triggered by the Martinson report (1974). Connecticut and Virginia state prisons were the first state facilities to adopt TC programs. Although plagued by suspicion from the correctional establishment and public mistrust, some of these state programs, such as the Stay'n Out program in New York, survived the backlash against rehabilitative interventions through the 1980s. The model was revived as a promising strategy to combat the crowding of prisons by drug-abusing offenders in the 1990s. It remains popular among correctional administrators today. Unlike TC programs in non–criminal justice settings that emphasize permissiveness, communality, and democratic participation, criminal justice–based TCs tend to be much more hierarchical, more authoritarian, and confrontational. Prison-based TCs and other substance abuse programs are discussed at length in chapter 7.

Deviant Behaviors Versus Deviant People

TC philosophy sees criminal behavior or problem conduct such as drug abuse or sexual deviance as a symptom of a complex malady of the whole person, not the essence of the disorder, and therefore treats it with a holistic approach (De Leon, 2000). Self-destructive behavior, self-defeating thinking, and negative emotions disrupt the lifestyle of the offender. Lifestyle is defined as the multifaceted expression of the psychosocial being of the offender, including the ways he or she behaves, thinks, manages feelings, interacts with others, and perceives himself or herself and the world. A lifestyle malfunctions when a negative identity is developed and deviant coping skills such as lying and manipulation are deployed with lasting psychological, social, legal, and economic harms to the person.

This disordered lifestyle is defined by the failure of the person to assume responsibility for his or her actions and decisions. The very act of seeking or agreeing to participate in treatment is interpreted as a call for help that interrupts the person's troubled way of living. Taking responsibility implies that the offender makes a voluntary decision to cease criminal acts as a prerequisite for transformation. How and when a person arrives at this decision varies enormously. Some offenders make that conscious determination only when health, legal, and family pressures have reached a crisis. For others, the decision evolves gradually in a process of awakening, without external coercion.

The TC environment is available to help the offender at every step of the awakening and transformation process. The goals are to create changes in both lifestyle and personal identity.

Communal Living as Therapy

Communal living is both the context and the tool in the therapeutic process. Both staff and residents are seen as agents of change. The transformation unfolds as a developmental process of multidimensional learning in the intimate climate of group affiliation and loyalty. According to De Leon (2000), "The community teachings, which are collectively termed right living, consist of moral injunctions, values, beliefs, and recovery prescriptions" (p. 84). Learning the right way of living entails practice in a real community, and TC provides an around-the-clock setting in which residents can be monitored in all their routines: how they work, relate to peers and counselors, maintain personal hygiene, and participate in group and community meetings. Helping residents become invested in a peer self-help community is a fundamental step in preparing them to engage in the world outside.

TCs are residential centers that adopt a hierarchical organization with progress phases that represent growing levels of responsibility and privilege. Peer influence, calibrated through a number of group activities, is used to help residents internalize social norms and externalize healthier social skills. Besides the role of the group as a primary catalyst of transformation, another basic TC ingredient is self-help. *Self-help* means that offenders in rehabilitation contribute to their own transformation. *Mutual self-help* implies that offenders also take partial responsibility for the change of other residents by mentoring and sponsoring peers, who in turn could reinforce an offender's own rehabilitation (see Gideon, in press).

TC treatment typically comprises three major phases. Phase 1, known as induction and early treatment, usually encompasses the first month of treatment and introduces the resident to the subculture of the treatment setting. The new resident learns the rules, nurtures trust with counselors and peers, begins an evaluation of needs, starts to appreciate the nature of problem behaviors, and works on readiness for change. Phase 2 is the main treatment stage and models prosocial attitudes and behaviors through a progression of increasing levels of achievement, responsibility, and privilege. Although ancillary services meeting legal, vocational, and psychosocial needs are routinely made available to residents, mutual self-help remains the backbone of TC intervention. The last stage, Phase 3, is the phase of reentry, which is designed to aid the resident's departure from the TC and return to the community. Post-residential aftercare services such as self-help groups, family counseling, and vocational guidance are often made available to TC graduates.

Implementation and Evaluation

The TC model has shown a surprising versatility in serving criminal populations with special needs (De Leon, 1997). It has been modified to provide childcare services for mothers, developmental guidance for teenagers, psychiatric services for offenders with co-occurring disorders, and connections to medical care for offenders with HIV and AIDS. Clinical practices and management style often are customized in terms of disciplinary measures, group dynamics, and level of confrontation.

The most widely examined TC programs are those intended for substance-abusing offenders. For more than three decades, the National Institute on Drug Abuse (2006) has funded and conducted several national studies of drug abuse treatment, and the National Institute of Justice (Stohr et al., 2003) has funded evaluations of individual TC interventions for criminal offenders. These studies, large and small, agree that graduation from a TC is associated with lower levels of criminal recidivism, substance use relapse, and unemployment (see studies on the following prison-based TCs: Stay'n Out in New York, Forever Free in California, KEY/CREST in Delaware, Amity in California, New Vision in Texas, and the Sharon TC in Israel [Box 4.2]). The major threat to the cost-effectiveness of TC intervention is the high dropout rate among participants. Many TC participants do not stay in treatment long enough to benefit from the therapy, which wastes taxpayers' money and lessens the visible impact on crime rates.

Box 4.2	**The Sharon Therapeutic Community: Prison-Based TC in Israel**

In response to the increase in the number of substance-abusing offenders returning to prison after release, the Israeli Prison System developed the first prison-based TC in late 1993. The first stage was done informally by segregating cell blocks for prisoners who expressed their desire to free themselves of drug abuse. One cell at a time, in each cell block, was converted to a drug-free barracks where inmates were segregated from the rest of the prison population. Inmates in the segregated drug-free cell blocks had a different prison routine—inmates were assigned to different jobs and programs—resulting in no contact with the rest of the prison population. In the next stage, a detoxification unit was built to accommodate the increasing number of substance-abusing inmates who wanted to join the program. Thus, the therapeutic model came to life. About a year later the entire prison population was changed from general population inmates to substance-abusing inmates who expressed a desire to recover from drug addiction. The Sharon Prison has become the only TC in Israel for the treatment and rehabilitation of substance-abusing inmates. The program draws from innovative programs in the United States, such as the KEY/CREST, Amity, New Vision, Stay'n Out, and Forever Free. Specifically, the Sharon program adopted the model of a TC that combines residence and incarceration with an around-the-clock, intensive educational experience, with a clear separation between the treatment staff and the inmates and with the aim of changing an inmate's lifestyle, identity, behavioral patterns, and self-confidence and improving his ability to solve problems. In that regard the Sharon TC program aims to desocialize and resocialize participants in order to better their lives. In an outcome evaluation study published by Shoham, Gideon, Weisburd, and Vilner (2006), it was found that the program reduced recidivism rates (according to official police data) and substance abuse (according to self-reported accounts).

Source: For full details about the Sharon program and its outcome evaluation, see Shoham, Gideon, Weisburd, and Vilner (2006).

INTENSIVE COMMUNITY SUPERVISION

Intensive Community Supervision (ICS) is a development of traditional community corrections (i.e., probation and parole) that first emerged in the late 1970s, when prison overcrowding and fiscal crises across jurisdictions demanded a cost-effective solution.[1]

ICS refers to probation and parole programs that build on a foundation of rigorous monitoring (see chapters 5 and 12). These community-based sanctions are variously labeled as intensive monitoring, alternative penalties, intermediate sanctions, and intermediate punishments. There are ICS interventions that take the form of diversion programs designed to reroute prison-bound offenders to the community, as an alternative or an adjunct to prison sentences. Others are enhancement programs—such as graduated sanctioning and electronic monitoring—developed to make regular probation or parole programs more coercive and incapacitating. Intensive supervision is indicated for offenders who are too dangerous to be put on regular probation or parole but not so dangerous that they could not be handled in the community under a surveillance regimen more stringent than that found in regular community supervision.

ICS proponents find in this particular mode of punishment an intermediate penal option between the humane but ineffective sanction of probation and the harsh and expensive (and inconsistently effective) choice of incarceration. Others see it as a useful and just method to relieve the pressure from an overcrowded prison system and overextended government budgets. Most ICS programs entail some combination of weekly contacts with a supervising officer, curfew, random drug tests, electronic monitoring, home confinement, and a very strict enforcement of release conditions (e.g., treatment participation, maintenance of a job, community service). Although therapeutic and human services are often routine components of ICS programs, they never constitute the defining core of this correctional strategy. These features are expected to catalyze the right dosage of punitiveness and control to prevent recidivism among supervised offenders.

Rational Choice, Deterrence, and Incapacitation

The idea that regular probation and parole practices should be made much more punitive and intrusive shares some assumptions with the classic school of penology represented by Cesare Beccaria and Jeremy Bentham. The tenets of *classical theory* include the belief that a human being is a rational agent, capable of instrumental calculation, and the view that a person freely chooses all his or her behavior. With all other circumstances held equal, a person's choice will be directed toward the optimization of personal satisfaction and the minimization of pain. Individual decision making can be manipulated through the perception and understanding of the potential consequences that follow a behavior.

From this perspective, criminal behavior should be seen as a result of an offender's decision to risk severe punishment after taking into account his or her own desire for pleasure and the chance of being caught in the criminal act. Therefore, the imposition of coercive sanctions on an offender can in theory deter future criminal behaviors. Moreover, if the criminal justice sanction is intrusive enough, it can significantly neutralize the capacities for criminal offending among at-risk people and thus decrease the chance of recidivism. Whereas other theories highlight the importance of nurturing self-control through effective parenting and high-quality schooling in crime prevention, the rational choice theory emphasizes the promise of formal controls imposed by state agencies in extinguishing antisocial behaviors among supervised offenders.

Surveillance and Control as Therapy

Enhanced supervision is said to prevent crime through close scrutiny, thereby reducing the need for future imprisonment. Monitoring and contacts are provided as therapeutic controls or constraints of deviant behaviors with lasting effects. Frequent meetings between the offender and the monitoring officer can be seen as brief interventions that manipulate negative reinforcements and expectations affecting offender behavior (Taxman, 2002). In fact, in his study of released participants of a prison-based TC, Gideon (2009) found that the majority of respondents were in favor of supervision after release, and they identified supervision with support and guidance as an essential condition for their successful reintegration. Supervised offenders are deterred from committing new offenses because surveillance increases the chance of getting caught and being sent to prison. They are constrained from committing crimes during their sentences because the supervision conditions limit their opportunities.

An implicit extension of this argument assumes that the suppression of criminality would continue beyond the expiration of the community sanction because the maturation process has had a chance to set in. Having been exposed to the consequences of both an unrestrained criminal lifestyle and an artificially induced law-abiding lifestyle, the formerly supervised offender would be able to rationally assess the positive and negative consequences of his or her future actions and then behave in his or her own self-interest (MacKenzie, 2006). The transformative process, which begins with the offender's compliance with the release conditions and supervision rules, is reinforced by the rapport between the offender and the supervision officer and can develop into respect for social codes of civility and legal norms after sentence completion (Taxman, 2002).

Implementation and Evaluation

Although the earliest evaluations of intensive community supervision programs completed in the early 1980s reported recidivism reductions and cost savings in some jurisdictions, the methodological design of these studies was seriously weakened by the lack of matched controls (General Accounting Office, 1990). The first large-scale experimental evaluation of ICS programs was conducted by RAND researchers between 1986 and 1991 (Petersilia & Turner, 1993). This federally funded project involved 14 sites in nine states and randomly assigned eligible adult offenders to either traditional processing or ICS programs. Results show that ICS programs were too small to reduce prison overcrowding because ICS programs admit hundreds of offenders, whereas prison populations ran into tens of thousands. As a matter of fact, the closer surveillance required by the ICS model, which was able to more quickly detect technical violations of release conditions, increased the number of prison inmates in a few states. This unintended consequence also led to higher costs of program maintenance: ICS programs were not less expensive than incarceration.

Investigators hypothesized that the effectiveness of ICS in reducing recidivism hinges on small caseloads and frequent contacts. Having supervision officers manage smaller caseloads would allow frequent meetings, closer scrutiny, and more positive rapport to develop, which in turn could produce better outcomes. Evaluation results were quite disappointing. Smaller caseloads did not result in lower recidivism rates than regular caseloads (Petersilia & Turner, 1993; Taxman, 2002). Furthermore, when ICS participants were compared with offenders supervised under regular probation and parole regimens, increased contacts did not cause a steeper decline in criminality as measured by arrests for new offenses and technical violations (MacKenzie, 2006). However, one clear benefit of ICS programs was improved public safety: The intense monitoring prompted early detection and arrest of ICS recidivists, which could be interpreted as an increase in accountability. However, the fundamental lesson learned from ICS remains this: Surveillance and control by themselves contribute very little to recidivism reduction if they do not incorporate therapeutic and service components (Taxman, 2002). Consequently, Taxman developed the seamless system of supervision in collaboration with the Maryland Department of Corrections. This model corresponded with the need to incorporate treatment with ICS (see chapter 12).

CASE MANAGEMENT

Case management is an experimental approach of service delivery developed by nurses and social workers in the late 1960s and early 1970s (Prins, 1999). It is a participatory process of diagnosis, scheduling, advocacy, and services that promote healthy and productive lifestyles among people with multiple problems. As the use of community corrections in lieu of incarceration became more widespread and the number of released inmates returning to their communities increased, correctional agencies began to incorporate case management techniques to serve these populations. Criminal justice agencies across the country have adopted a variety of case management techniques with the ultimate goal of reducing recidivism; they include measures to address psychiatric needs, physical and mental disabilities, homelessness, unemployment, HIV and AIDS, and other severe health problems among supervised offenders. Today's correctional professionals who provide pretrial monitoring, rehabilitative programming, reentry support, and community supervision for released inmates must be proficient in case management.

Risk Factors and Protective Factors

Case management adopts an actuarial approach to recidivism and views it as a result of cumulated risks. Risks are factors statistically associated with a greater likelihood of committing new criminal offenses detected in past criminological research. Unaddressed criminogenic factors such as substance abuse, unemployment, lack of self-control, certain mental illnesses and personality disorders, deficient life skills, and deviant peers or lack of prosocial support are seen as major recidivism risks.

Equally important to the concept of risk factors is that of protective factors. Protective factors can be either satisfactorily met criminogenic factors or the resilience of an offender against future recidivism. *Resilience* is understood as a dynamic process in which offenders mobilize available resources to exhibit positive behavioral adaptation when they encounter significant recidivism risks. Resilience is a two-way construct related to the exposure of recidivism risks and the positive behavioral responses to those risks. Positive responses include social competence or success at coping with stress and adversity and at experiencing excitement and satisfaction in life without engaging in criminal activities.

Efforts at reducing recidivism through risk assessment–based and risk control–oriented case management are most often offered to substance-abusing offenders, mentally ill or disabled offenders, and inmates in need of transitional care (Healey, 1999). Case management services are believed to be best suited to these criminal justice populations.

Coordination and Delivery of Multiple Services

Corrections from this perspective involve *rehabilitation:* the use of externally available services to relearn social functioning, basic life skills, and conventional norms and to regain equilibrium and well-being. Some sentenced offenders have never acquired functional lifestyles. For these people, case management is usually their first exposure to adequate resources for orderly living.

Change involves *habilitation:* developing for the first time the human and social capital for a productive life.

An ideal administration of case management consists of seven interconnected stages: intake, assessment, classification, referral, intervention, evaluation, and advocacy (Enos & Southern, 1996). Intake initiates the case management process by establishing a rapport with the offender, providing orientation, and offering a discussion about penalties for noncompliance. It can be performed through face-to-face interviews, printed brochures, or a videotaped presentation. Assessment normally involves face-to-face meetings and history taking and may include drug use assessment or psychiatric screening, home visits, and interview of key informants such as family members and employers (for the importance of intake and risk assessment, see chapter 3). Overall, violent offenders, particularly sex offenders and domestic batterers, demand more detailed scrutiny than public order or property offenders. Classification, on the other hand, includes both risk assessment and service matching. An offender's suitability for treatment is determined and ranked; those diagnosed to be unsuitable for treatment could be institutionalized or receive no services.[2] Classifications center on risk assessments based on the person's mental health and criminal histories and his or her community ties.

Referral is usually conducted in collaboration with contracted external service providers. Parolees may be referred to halfway houses that stabilize community ties and offer substance abuse programs, behavior counseling, psychiatric care, and vocational training and job development assistance. Inmates due for release may be referred to community-based services to ensure continuity of services. Other areas of service include medical care, housing, welfare assistance, and HIV and AIDS support. The case manager matches intervention opportunities to the offender's diagnosed needs. The offender is expected to show his or her commitment by complying with service requirements and engaging in the transformative process.

Close monitoring of and effective graduated sanctions for offenders who fail to comply with service requirements are key components of successful case management. Examples of graduated sanctions include intensified court appearances, use of electronic monitoring devices, or brief incarcerations to coerce the acceptance of program objectives. Close surveillance may include frequent drug tests, regular phone contacts or personal meetings between the case manager and the offender, and close tracking of the offender's progress and compliance with previously agreed conditions. The intensity of surveillance usually decreases over time.

Evaluation seeks to determine whether the goal of recidivism reduction has been achieved. Other indicators of behavioral improvement such as substance use abstinence and stable employment may also be adopted to assess response to the intervention. A few types of advocacy on behalf of the offender are often required of case managers, who may have to make recommendations to the judge, negotiate accessible services, seek priority placements at programs with waiting lists, and arrange visitation with children no longer in the offender's custody.

Implementation and Evaluation

No systematic examination of case management evaluations has ever been published, the popularity of the intervention notwithstanding. However, evidence from specific programs suggests that although the case management model has promise, its impact can easily be canceled out by faulty implementation and inadequate dosage. It also appears that case management programs specifically designed for offenders with targeted special needs produce much better outcomes than generic programs serving a wide variety of offenders. As Sutherland (1939) observed regarding effective delivery of correctional intervention, the key to success is individualization.

The Bay Area Services Network (BASN) offers case management, drug use counseling, and referrals to other human services for addicted parolees in San Francisco. Using a quasi-experimental design, researchers detected no difference between BASN participants and control parolees in program length, use of social and health resources, frequency of drug use, or rearrests. Nevertheless, number of meetings with a case manager and program length were low among BASN participants overall. In analyses focusing on BASN participants, researchers reported that participants with a stronger case management dosage had lower drug use and involvement in property crime (Longshore, Turner, & Fain, 2005). Effects of strong dosage persisted even when motivation was held constant. In other words, case management may have exercised favorable effects on recidivism and drug use when delivered in a sufficient dosage.

A recent review of 27 evaluations of intensive case management (ICM) programs for mentally ill offenders indicated that case management could reduce recidivism under the right conditions, but the causal dynamics are rather complex (Loveland & Boyle, 2007). The review focused on two groups of programs: general ICM programs for mentally ill offenders and ICM programs specifically developed as a component of a jail diversion intervention for mentally ill offenders. Evaluators reported that general ICM programs rarely led to reductions in recidivism over time. General ICM programs that included an integrated addiction treatment component had mixed results but a trend toward reductions in rearrests and reincarceration over time for offenders with co-occurring mental illness and substance use disorders. Mixed results were reported for jail diversion interventions with an ICM program, with some yielding significant reductions in recidivism.

POLICY IMPLICATIONS

The major appeal of evidence-based programs is their promise of effectiveness. Despite enormous attention placed on the question of what works in correctional practices, issues surrounding theoretical grounding and program integrity are critical but rarely discussed. In the short run, federal, state, and local governments should require all correctional demonstration programs funded with special grants to identify and adhere to a tested theoretical model or a group of mutually coherent models in the conceptualization, design, implementation, and evaluation of these innovations. Staying true to the guiding theoretical model and the theoretically driven design increases implementation fidelity, without which the promised outcomes are hard to realize. In the long run, all correctional programs supported by regular budget lines should meet a requirement of theoretical grounding to help ensure the achievement of satisfactory integrity and expected impact.

In order to maintain the integrity of a theoretically grounded design, the following steps should be taken. First, at the program planning stage, the basic conceptual underpinnings of the program (including causal explanations of and therapeutic changes expected in criminal recidivism and criminogenic recurrence of substance abuse, mental illness, or unemployment) must be explicitly stated in published materials. Program staff should discuss the theoretical assumptions and theoretically inspired program protocols in depth so that each member of the team understands the intervention and what makes it effective. If adaptation from the original model is needed, conceptual justifications should be developed for these modifications.

Second, at the implementation stage, administrative and clinical staff should be thoroughly trained to understand the protocols and program curriculum built on the original theoretical model. Job descriptions should include a short statement explaining how each specific position relates to the larger enterprise of promoting changes in the offender population. When revisions are made to the program during its regular operation, detailed manuals documenting necessary adaptations and their justificatory rationale should be prepared and disseminated among the staff. Rigid fidelity leads to interventions that are irrelevant or even inappropriate for meeting community needs, but program modifications without clear etiological and therapeutic justifications are simply blind and cannot be measured or duplicated.

Third, evaluation research should focus on the measurement of empirical indicators that are directly derived from the conceptual model and that validate key outcomes of the program. When properly done, both the underlying theory and the implemented intervention can be assessed at the same time.

DISCUSSION QUESTIONS

1. As a rule, serious criminal offenders tend to be less responsive to interventions, but once engaged in the change process, they produce the largest reductions in recidivism. In contrast, nonserious offenders are more susceptible to planned change but tend to yield minor reductions in criminal involvement. Which group of offenders should receive most rehabilitative resources and services? Why?

2. Which rehabilitative approaches could be more promising in changing chronic, hard-core criminals and which rehabilitative approaches may be more suitable for occasional offenders? Why?

3. Please explain which set of causal assumptions about criminal behaviors you like the most. Do you equally enthusiastically accept the rehabilitative practices derived from it?

4. Why is it important to base a correctional program on an explicit rehabilitative model?

5. None of the discussed approaches explicitly engages the issue of treatment settings. What could be the advantages and disadvantages associated with offering programs in prisons as opposed to the community, and vice versa?

NOTES

1. Probation is a court-sanctioned nonincarcerative disposition through which an adjudicated offender is placed under the supervision, monitoring, and care of a supervision officer in lieu of imprisonment, as long as the probationer meets certain standards of conduct. Parole, instead, deals with adult prisoners conditionally released to community monitoring, whether by parole board decision or by mandatory conditional release after serving a prison term. They are subject to being returned to prison for rule violations or other offenses.

2. In more and more jurisdictions, the "suitability for treatment" test has been replaced with the assumption that all offenders benefit from services, even those predicted to be at highest risk for recidivism and those who are incarcerated for a long period of time (Prins, 1999).

SUGGESTED READINGS

Andrews, D. A., & Dowden, C. (2005). Managing correctional treatment for reduced recidivism: A meta-analytic review of programme integrity. *Legal and Criminological Psychology, 10,* 173–187.

Cunningham, P. B. (2002). Brief overview of multisystemic therapy in treating serious and chronic delinquents. *Juvenile Correctional Mental Health Report, 2,* 33–46.

De Leon, G. (2000). *The therapeutic community: Theory, model, and method.* New York: Springer.

Gondolf, E. W. (2008). Implementation of case management for batterer program participants. *Violence Against Women, 14,* 208–225.

Hansen, C. (2008). Cognitive–behavioral interventions: Where they come from and what they do. *Federal Probation, 72,* 43–49.

Paparozzi, M. A., & Gendreau, P. (2005). Intensive supervision program that worked: Service delivery, professional orientation, and organizational supportiveness. *The Prison Journal, 85,* 445–466.

Pearson, F. S., Lipton, D. S., Cleland, C. M., & Yee, D. S. (2002). The effects of behavioral/cognitive–behavioral programs on recidivism. *Crime and Delinquency, 48,* 476–496.

Swenson, C. C., Henggeler, S. W., Taylor, I. S., & Addison, O. W. (2009). *Multisystemic therapy and neighborhood partnerships: Reducing adolescent violence and substance abuse.* New York: Guilford.

Zhang, S. X., Roberts, R. E. L., & McCollister, K. E. (2009). Therapeutic community in a California prison: Treatment outcomes after 5 years. *Crime and Delinquency,* 0011128708327035v1.

REFERENCES

Aos, S., Phipps, P., Barnoski, R., & Lieb, R. (1999). *The comparative costs and benefits of programs to reduce crime: A review of national research findings with implications for Washington State.* Olympia: Washington State Institute for Public Policy.

Bronfenbrenner, U. (1979). *The ecology of human development: Experiments by design and nature.* Cambridge, MA: Harvard University Press.

Colorado Division of Criminal Justice. (2007, August). *Evidence based correctional practices.* Washington, DC: National Institute of Corrections.

De Leon, G. (1997). *Community as method: Therapeutic communities for special populations and special settings.* Westport, CT: Praeger.

De Leon, G. (2000). *The therapeutic community: Theory, model, and method.* New York: Springer.

Enos, R., & Southern, S. (1996). *Correctional case management.* Cincinnati, OH: Andersen.

General Accounting Office. (1990). *Intermediate sanctions: Their impacts on prison crowding, costs, and recidivism are still unclear.* Washington, DC: Author.

Gideon, L. (2009). What shall I do now? Released offenders' expectations for supervision upon release. *International Journal of Offender Therapy and Comparative Criminology, 53*(1), 43–56.

Gideon, L. (in press). Drug offenders' perceptions of motivation: The role of motivation in rehabilitation and reintegration. *International Journal of Offender Therapy and Comparative Criminology.*

Healey, K. M. (1999). *Case management in the criminal justice system.* Washington, DC: National Institute of Justice.

Henggeler, S. W. (1989). *Delinquency in adolescence.* Thousand Oaks, CA: Sage.

Henggeler, S. W. (2002). Effective family-based treatment for juvenile offenders: Multisystemic therapy and functional family therapy. In H. E. Allen (Ed.), *Risk reduction: Interventions for special needs offenders* (pp. 223–244). Lanham, MD: American Correctional Association.

Jupp, V. (1989). *Methods of criminological research*. London: Routledge.

Lipsey, M. W., Landenberger, N. A., & Wilson, S. J. (2007, August). *Effects of cognitive–behavioral programs for criminal offenders*. Nashville, TN: Vanderbilt Institute for Public Policy Studies.

Longshore, D., Turner, S., & Fain, T. (2005). Effects of case management on parolee misconduct: The Bay Area Services Network. *Criminal Justice and Behavior, 32,* 205–222.

Loveland, D., & Boyle, M. (2007). Intensive case management as a jail diversion program for people with a serious mental illness: A review of the literature. *International Journal of Offender Therapy and Comparative Criminology, 51,* 130–150.

MacKenzie, D. L. (2006). *What works in corrections: Reducing the criminal activities of offenders and delinquents*. New York: Cambridge University Press.

Martinson, R. (1974, Spring). What works? Questions and answers about prison reform. *The Public Interest,* pp. 22–54.

Milkman, H., & Wanberg, K. (2007, May). *Cognitive–behavioral treatment: A review and discussion for corrections professionals* (NIC 021657). Washington, DC: National Institute of Corrections.

National Institute on Drug Abuse. (2006). *Principles of drug abuse treatment for criminal populations: A research-based guide*. Rockville, MD: Author.

Pearson, F. S., Lipton, D. S., Cleland, C. M., & Yee, D. S. (2002). The effects of behavioral/cognitive-behavioral programs on recidivism. *Crime and Delinquency, 48,* 476–496.

Petersilia, J., & Turner, S. (1993). Intensive probation and parole. In M. Tonry (Ed.), *Crime and justice: Reviews of research* (pp. 281–336). Chicago: The University of Chicago Press.

Prins, H. (1999). *Will they do it again? Risk assessment and management in criminal justice and psychiatry*. New York: Routledge.

Shoham, E., Gideon, L., Weisburd, D. L., & Vilner, Y. (2006). When "more" of a program is not necessarily better: Drug prevention in the Sharon Prison. *Israeli Law Review, 39*(1), 105–126.

Stohr, M. K., Hemmens, C., Baune, D., Dayley, J., Gornik, M., Kjaer, K., et al. (2003). *Residential substance abuse treatment for state prisoners* (NCJ 199948). Washington, DC: National Institute of Justice.

Sutherland, E. H. (1939). *Principles of criminology* (3rd ed.). Chicago: J. B. Lippincott.

Swenson, C. C., Henggeler, S. W., & Schoenwald, S. K. (2000). Family-based treatments. In C. Hollin (Ed.), *Handbook of offender assessment and treatment* (pp. 205–220). New York: Wiley.

Sykes, G. M., & Matza, D. (1957). Techniques of neutralizations: A theory of delinquency. *American Sociological Review, 22,* 664–670.

Taxman, F. S. (2002). Supervision: Exploring the dimensions of effectiveness. *Federal Probation, 66,* 14–26.

Walters, G. D. (2002). The Psychological Inventory of Criminal Thinking Styles (PICTS): A review and meta-analysis. *Assessment, 9,* 278–291.

Wexler, H. K., & Love, C. T. (1994). Therapeutic communities in prison. In F. M. Tims, G. De Leon, & N. Jainchill (Eds.), *Therapeutic community: Advances in research and application* (pp. 181–208). Rockville, MD: National Institute on Drug Abuse.

Yochelson, S., & Samenow, S. (1976). *The criminal personality*. Vol. I: *A profile for change*. Lanham, MD: Jason Aronson.

Yochelson, S., & Samenow, S. (1977). *The criminal personality*. Vol. II: *The change process*. Lanham, MD: Jason Aronson.

CHAPTER 5

Probation

An Untapped Resource in U.S. Corrections

Doris Layton MacKenzie

Probation has been an integral part of corrections since its inception more than 100 years ago. It is the most common form of criminal sentencing in the United States. In 2006, more than 7.2 million adults, or 3.2% of the adult population, was incarcerated in prisons or jails or serving time in the community on probation or parole (Glaze & Bonczar, 2007). The majority of these were serving sentences of probation. As shown in Figure 5.1, 58% of the correctional population, or more than 4.2 million adults, were on probation in 2006.

Probation is a sentence requiring offenders to serve a period of correctional supervision in the community, generally in lieu of incarceration. The judge often sentences a defendant to prison or jail and then suspends the sentence in favor of probation. In such cases, prison or jail has been legally imposed but is held in abeyance; it can be reinstated if the probationer fails to abide by the requirements of supervision. Some courts combine probation with a sentence of incarceration into a split sentence. Seventy percent of those who entered probation supervision in 2006 were sentenced to probation without a term of incarceration (Glaze & Bonczar, 2007). Nearly a quarter were sentenced to a combination of probation and incarceration.

When on probation the offender must comply with an extensive list of probation conditions as specified by the court. The sentencing judge is responsible for enumerating the conditions required of the probationer. Some judges also authorize probation officers to set other conditions as deemed proper. If the probationer violates the conditions of probation, the judge may decide to

Figure 5.1 U.S. Correctional Population, 2006

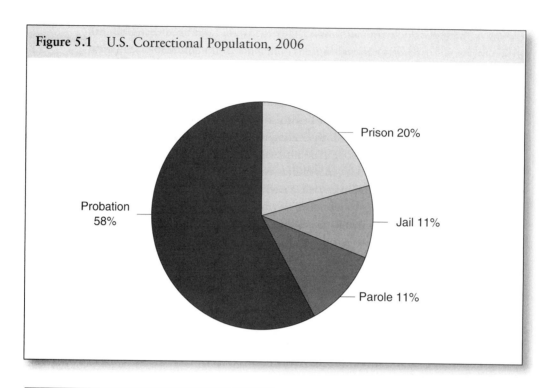

Prison 20%

Jail 11%

Parole 11%

Probation 58%

Source: Bureau of Justice Statistics (2008).

revoke or terminate the probation. The court retains authority to supervise the offender, modify conditions, and resentence if the probationer violates the terms of probation.

The advantages of probation from the perspective of the offender are the ability to remain in the community and protection from the negative impacts that could come with incarceration. From the system point of view, probation is an alternative that is substantially cheaper than prison.

Yet probation faces several challenges. Since the start probation has been viewed as being soft on crime. This was a strong disadvantage during the punitive, tough-on-crime atmosphere of the 1980s and 1990s. In response, probation agencies developed intermediate sanctions designed to appropriately punish and control their charges. However, these sanctions were disappointingly ineffective in reducing recidivism. The criminal justice system's focus on control and punishment also led to dramatic increases in the number of probationers without a corresponding increase in funding. Caseloads grew, and many probationers were revoked and sent to prison, increasing the problem of prison crowding. Little money was available for treatment and services. During this time probation agencies focused on managing aggregates of individuals for risk instead of providing individualized treatment plans (Feeley & Simon, 1992).

There are some hopeful signs for the future of probation. New initiatives such as specialized courts have been developed to address the identified needs of specific types of offenders. To the degree finances permit, evidence-based treatment programs are being used to address the needs or deficits of offenders. Carefully planned reporting systems help to manage caseloads so the offenders most at risk receive the most attention. Information management systems are being developed to improve the use of data in problem solving. This chapter begins with an overview of probation agencies' work and responsibilities.

RESPONSIBILITIES OF PROBATION AGENCIES

Probation agencies have two major responsibilities: investigation and supervision. Investigation involves obtaining information about the defendant and preparing a presentence investigation report (PSI). In comparison, supervision involves oversight of probationers while they are on community supervision.

Investigation

During criminal justice processing, beginning when the offender first interacts with the police, the probation agent collects information needed by decision makers. The agent investigates to determine whether the defendant can be released on his or her own recognizance or bail. If the case goes to court, between the time of conviction and sentencing the agent must prepare a PSI documenting the offender's past criminal history and characteristics of the current crime.

Typically, the PSI includes information on the seriousness of the crime, the defendant's risk, the defendant's personal circumstances (e.g., employment, family, housing), a summary of the legally permissible sentencing options, and a sentencing recommendation. If a prison sentence is recommended, the PSI includes information on the recommended sentence length. In the case of a recommendation for probation the PSI includes recommendations on both sentence length and conditions of probation.

The PSI becomes very important in sentencing decisions because this is the information the judge receives about offenders and their crimes. Research demonstrates that the information the judge has about the defendant is usually limited to the information contained in the PSI, and there is a high correlation between the probation officer's recommendations in the PSI and the judge's sentencing decision (Petersilia, 1997).

Decision makers throughout the criminal justice system use the information provided in the PSI. Probation officers, responsible for supervision, use it for initial classifications of risk and needs, which determine the supervision intensity and treatment plan. If offenders are sentenced to jail or prison, the PSI follows them and is used for security and custody classification in prisons and eventually for release decisions.

Supervision

The second major task of the probation agent is to supervise offenders once they are sentenced to probation. Depending on the supervision requirements, the agent meets with the probationer, checks on the probationer's employment, makes collateral contacts (e.g., family, treatment providers), and conducts drug tests. The agent may also assist the probationer in finding housing, employment, or needed social services. The agent is responsible for completing risk and need classification instruments to determine what supervision level is appropriate for each probationer and what treatment services would be most appropriate.

THE ORGANIZATION OF PROBATION

Probation is administered by more than 2,000 separate agencies (Abadinsky, 2008). These agencies differ by whether services are delivered by the executive or the judicial branch of government, how they are funded, and whether they are primarily a federal, state, or local function. Most states combine probation and parole into one statewide agency, but others have separate probation agencies. In other jurisdictions, the responsibility for probation rests with a local agency administered by the court or a county executive branch.

Debates continue about whether probation should be administered by the judicial or executive branch of government and whether it should be the responsibility of municipal, county, or state jurisdictions (Petersilia, 1997). Some argue in favor of local administration by the courts because this allows greater diversity. A local court will be able to implement more innovative programming and will be less restricted by state bureaucratic control. On the other hand, statewide probation is more closely coordinated with other components of the corrections system, which helps with funding and decision making because other correction functions are under the control of the executive branch of the state.

THE AMERICAN PROBATION AND PAROLE ASSOCIATION

The American Probation and Parole Association (APPA) is an international association of members who are actively involved with probation, parole, and community-based corrections for both adults and juveniles. Association members come from all levels of government including local, state or provincial, legislative, executive, judicial, and federal agencies as well as educators, volunteers, and concerned citizens with an interest in criminal and juvenile justice. It has grown to become a voice for thousands of practitioners including line staff, supervisors, and administrators.

APPA was first discussed in 1974, when probation practitioners expressed frustration over the lack of national representation for their field. The Probation Committee of the American Correctional Association recommended that probation start a national-level association. However, almost immediately the organizers realized parole was a "twin" of probation and should be included in the same organization. The new organization, named the American Probation and Parole Association, began in Louisville, Kentucky, in 1975, with more than 3,000 individual members in 1999. Since its inception, APPA has been an active organization holding annual meetings and training institutes and publishing a journal, *Perspectives*.

CHARACTERISTICS OF PROBATIONERS

Most probationers are convicted of nonviolent offenses; about half are sentenced to probation for felonies and about half for misdemeanors. According to a recent survey by the Bureau of Justice Statistics, a large percentage of probationers are serving time on probation for substance-related violations (Glaze & Bonczar, 2007). More than a quarter (27%) were convicted of a drug law violation, and 16% were convicted of driving while intoxicated. Most probationers (73%) were serving time for nonviolent offenses (including substance-related violations). Property offenses (larceny and theft 13%, burglary 5%, and motor vehicle theft 1%) accounted for a large proportion of the probationers. Sixteen percent of the probationers were convicted of assaults, including sexual assaults (2%), domestic violence (5%), and other assaults (9%).

In 2006, 24% of probationers were female, a much larger percentage of females than in any other correctional sanction. The majority of probationers were White (55%) and male (76%). In 2006, 29% were Black, and 13% were Hispanic or Latino (of either race).

Box 5.1   Sentencing in Finland

In 1950 Finland was a poor war-ridden agricultural country. The country was struggling to get out from under the impact of 25 years of war (Lappi-Seppala, 2007). The incarceration rate of approximately 200 per 100,000 inhabitants was four times higher than that of the other Nordic countries. The Finns made a concentrated effort to change this situation and over the next 25 years were successful in reducing the incarceration rate to about 60 prisoners per 100,000 people, approximately the same as in the other Nordic countries. This change in penal severity cannot be explained by differences in crime rates. Lappi-Seppala attributes the change to public sentiments, welfare provisions, income equality, political influences, and legal expectations.

Lowering the incarceration rate meant that a higher proportion of sentenced offenders had to receive community alternatives. They decided to use imprisonment for only the most serious crimes. Today, the majority of penalties are less severe alternatives in the community. Probation agents are responsible for enforcing these sanctions. Community sanctions include supervision of conditionally sentenced offenders, juvenile punishment, community service, and supervision of parolees. Prison sentences of up to 2 years may be imposed conditionally (suspended sentence). Two alternative sanctions frequently used in Finland are day fines and community service.

Fines have become one of the principal alternative punishments. These are imposed as day fines. This system, first adopted by Finland in 1921, aims to ensure equity for offenders of different levels of income and wealth. The number of day fine points is determined on the basis of the seriousness of the offense committed; the amount of the fine is based on the financial situation of the offender. So similar offenses committed by offenders with different income levels will result in similar overall severity considering the income differences.

Community service is another frequently used alternative. It has had a strong impact on the number of prison sentences. Community service is used as an independent sanction. In order to ensure that community service did not have a net-widening effect on the system, a two-step procedure was initiated. First the court has to make a sentencing decision without considering community service as an option. Under specific conditions prescribed by law, if the sentence is unconditional imprisonment not exceeding 8 months, then the court can commute the sentence to community service. The probation agent prepares a suitability assessment on the capability of the accused to complete the service. The length of service varies from 20 to 200 hours depending on the length of the prison term. Offenders sentenced to community service perform unpaid work for public good in a job approved by the probation service. They may continue to live at home and work or attend school. Their community service is completed during their leisure time.

CONDITIONS OF PROBATION

Probation is a period of conditional release to the community. In return for their freedom, probationers agree to abide by standard release conditions and any special release conditions that have been imposed. Standard release conditions tend to be very similar across jurisdictions, requiring probationers to report to the probation officers at specific times, to work or go to school, to support dependents, to refrain from moving without permission, to permit residential or workplace visits by probation officers, and so forth. Special conditions of probation are tailored to meet the needs or life circumstances of individual probationers. Such conditions include drug testing, substance abuse treatment, mental health counseling, or community service. Financial conditions such as court costs, supervision fees, or restitution are also commonly imposed.

Conditions of probation generally fall into one of three categories: treatment oriented, control oriented, and punishment oriented (MacKenzie & Souryal, 1997). Additionally some restorative justice principles have been brought into the practice of probation through the use of community service and restitution. The following sections discuss these different types of conditions of probation.

Treatment-Oriented Conditions

Consistent with the rehabilitation model of probation, treatment-oriented conditions are intended to facilitate long-term behavioral change. Through the presentence investigation and classification systems, the presumed needs of offenders are identified. A treatment plan is then developed and special conditions are used to address the identified needs. For example, offenders believed to have problems with drugs or alcohol are required to attend substance abuse treatment as a condition of probation. Assuming that drug use is related to criminal behavior and that the substance abuse treatment program can effectively curb drug use, the likelihood of further criminal behavior should be substantially reduced as drug use declines. Hence, treatment-oriented conditions are utilitarian in nature, promising to reduce future criminal activity.

Control-Oriented Conditions

As the name suggests, control-oriented conditions are intended to control or restrain the behavior of probationers in the community. There are several types of control-oriented conditions. One type limits the opportunity of probationers to commit further crime. Such conditions include curfews and prohibitions against associating with certain people or frequenting certain areas or establishments. Another type of control-oriented condition limits a probationer's privacy, thereby increasing the risk of detection. Examples of this type of condition might include submitting to searches or permitting visits to the home or workplace. A third type of control-oriented condition that tends to overlap with treatment-oriented conditions entails mandatory employment or education. Such conditions can be considered control oriented simply in that employment and education typically provide supervision and take up a great deal of a probationer's time. In short, control-oriented conditions are those that seek to regulate probationer behavior in the community in an attempt to prevent crime during the period of supervision.

Punishment-Oriented Conditions

Punishment-oriented conditions that do not fall into the treatment- or control-oriented category are commonly imposed. They typically involve physical or economic sanctions such as community service, restitution, court costs, and supervision fees. Imposed as punishment, they are intended to reflect the seriousness of the crime.

Restorative Conditions

Restorative justice is a philosophy of jurisprudence that attempts to restore victims, offenders, and communities to their situation before the crime (Braithwaite, 1998). Although there have been few programs directly using restorative programs for adult probationers, some believe that community service and restitution are representative of restorative justice principles. Both of these are common conditions of probation.

PROBATION REVOCATION

Probation status can be revoked for either a new crime or a technical violation of the conditions of probation. Conditions of probation are essentially a list of things required of the probationer. This is part of the contract with the court. The court agrees to permit offenders to serve sentences in the community if they abide by the required conditions. When probationers do not comply with the conditions of their probation they are considered to have violated the contract, and they can be punished. Technical conditions are requirements that would not be criminal offenses if the person were not on probation.

A substantial number of probationers fail to comply with release conditions and are consequently arrested and disciplined. Many of those who begin probation do not successfully complete their sentence. For example, in 2006, only 57% of the probationers who left probation exited successfully (Glaze & Bonczar, 2007). Eighteen percent were incarcerated: 4% for a new crime, 9% for probation violations, and 5% for other reasons. Four percent absconded, and another 12% were considered to have ended their probation unsatisfactorily (another 8% left for other reasons, including death, but were not considered to have successfully completed supervision).

In seeking to control the behavior of probationers and to ensure that they comply with the technical conditions of probation, probation officers possess a wide range of sanctions. Sanctions range in severity from warnings to placement in a residential center to revocation. Revocation is the most serious sanction available to probation agencies. The threat of revocation and presumably incarceration is intended to serve as a deterrent. Specifically, it is hypothesized that the threat of revocation will deter probationers from violating the conditions of supervision. Secondarily, the threat of revocation is often used as a means of coercing treatment. In other words, absent the threat of revocation, probationers may be less likely to attend counseling or treatment.

OFFICER DISCRETION

Probation officers have traditionally exercised a great deal of discretion in choosing between the various sanctions available to them. Clear, Harris, and Baird (1992) reviewed prior research and concluded that the magnitude of officer discretion is considerable. In summarizing the scant research literature on probation officer responses, they found that officers had a great deal of discretion, and even within the same office responses to similar situations varied widely; officers tailored their decisions to gain the approval of immediate supervisors; and officers became more punitive in their attitudes in the late 1970s and 1980s (Harris, Clear, & Baird, 1989).

Clear et al.'s (1992) evaluation of six probation agencies supported the conclusions of earlier research. They, too, found that officers possess a great deal of discretion, resulting in wide variation in officer responses to similar offenses. Variation in probation officer responses may result from factors such as an officer's attitude toward rehabilitation. For example, officers who support rehabilitation may be willing to overlook minor violations in order to establish an effective supervision relationship (Clear et al., 1992).

However, it should be noted that although probation officers have a great deal of discretion in sanctioning probationers, their role in the revocation process may be more limited. Clear et al. (1992) discovered, contrary to popular belief, that individual agents may have little control over the decision to revoke or over the consequences of the revocation order. Higher administrators in the probation department, department policies, and court officials have the final decision-making authority.

Not only is there a great deal of variation *within* probation departments in responding to technical violations, but there appears to be a great deal of variation *between* probation departments as well. For example, Clear et al.'s (1992) evaluation of six probation agencies revealed that the conditions necessary for revocation varied widely between jurisdictions. Probation officer responses within an agency appear to be shaped by organizational policy and tradition.

Organizational policy refers to the formal sanction policies. Differences in organizational policy between jurisdictions include the availability of alternatives to revocation, the type of supervisory review of case records and officer decisions, and the requirements for initiation of the revocation process (Clear et al., 1992). Organizational policy obviously can have a major impact on individual probation officer responses. For example, in jurisdictions where there is a great deal of supervisory review, probation officers exercise less discretion, and patterns of responses to violations are more likely to be shaped by the supervising officer.

Equally important as organizational policy in shaping probation officer responses is organizational tradition. According to Clear et al. (1992), sanctioning policy reflects the "workability" of formal policy, the availability of resources, and the relationship between the probation agency and the judicial branch of government. For example, probation officers report that they sometimes fail to strictly adhere to formal policy, such as the reporting of all violations, if they believe that it is in the best interests of the probationer not to do so. In sum, Clear et al. (1992) conclude that decisions about sanctions and revocations are best understood in the context of the local legal culture, a finding comparable to those for police and court decision making.

HISTORY OF PROBATION

Probation is usually considered to have begun in the United States in 1841, when John Augustus, an owner of a Boston boot-making company, asked the Boston Police Court whether he could post bail for a man charged with being a common drunk. Augustus asked the judge to defer sentencing for 3 weeks. Augustus promised to take responsibility for the man during this time. He took the man into his home, found him a job, and made him sign a pledge that he would stop drinking. At the end of this short period, the man appeared before the court and was given a nominal fine. Augustus continued to provide such voluntary assistance to men, women, and children for the next 15 years, until his death in 1859. By the time he died in 1859, he had helped nearly 2,000 prisoners. He used his own money for bail or received financial aid from other residents of Boston who believed in his cause; several of these followers continued the program after his death. Most of Augustus's charges were accused or convicted of violating Boston's vice or temperance laws.

Augustus's work became a model for modern probation. He reported a careful procedure for selecting his candidates, limiting assistance to first-time offenders who had demonstrated remorse and willingness to change (Augustus, 1972). Thus, he introduced the concepts of risk assessment and classification. He believed offenders could be rehabilitated while on probation, and this would be better than letting them spend time in prison or jail.

Based on the work of Augustus, in 1878 Massachusetts authorized the mayor of Boston to hire a probation officer. Two years later, every city in Massachusetts was using a probation officer, and by 1890 every court in the state had one. Probation gradually spread to other jurisdictions. By 1922, 22 states had probation in their systems, and by 1957 all states had statutes authorizing the use of probation for adults.

FROM SOCIAL SERVICE TO LAW ENFORCEMENT AND BACK

Since the inception of probation, there has been a debate about the appropriate model of probation (Abadinsky, 2008; O'Leary, 1987). For example, jurisdictions and individual agents vary in whether they focus on rehabilitation or incapacitation and control in their management policies and interactions with inmates.

John Augustus's original probationary work was voluntary and focused on the need for rehabilitation for "common criminals," most of whom were accused of violating Boston's vice or temperance laws. Other volunteer officers were drawn from church groups. When governments took over the responsibility for probation, they often hired people with law enforcement backgrounds to serve as probation officers. These officers had a very different perspective about their work and their role as probation officers. Thus, individual agents differed in perspectives, and depending on the correctional philosophy of the time, there have been changes in perspective across time.

The law enforcement perspective stresses the legal authority and enforcement aspects of their roles. Agents working under this model are apt to emphasize their authority and firmness, rule abidance, and enforcement of conditions and rules. Agents with a more therapeutic perspective emphasize their role in helping the probationer make changes toward a more law-abiding life. Agents view themselves as case workers who are responsible for counseling probationers, helping them connect with community services, and identifying appropriate community treatment programs.

CHANGES IN CORRECTIONAL PHILOSOPHY

Probation was originally conceived in humanitarian terms, as a second chance or an opportunity for reform. Not surprisingly, the enactment of many probation statutes coincided with the Progressive Era (1900–1920) in correctional history. Progressive reformers dismissed penal policies of the previous century as prohibitively rigid and advocated the adoption of the medical model in conjunction with indeterminate sentencing. During this period probation officers assumed responsibility for changing offenders. Attention focused on the offender, not the offense, in an attempt to prevent future crimes. Probation officers possessed discretion and the power to use coercive means if deemed necessary to further the process of rehabilitation (O'Leary, 1987). The philosophy of the Progressive movement remained largely unchallenged until the early 1970s, at which time it became the target of fierce attack (Cullen & Gendreau, 2000; MacKenzie, 2006).

Time of Optimism

The 1960s began with great optimism about the promises of a new frontier. There was a belief that we could solve the problems of the world. We could walk on the moon. We could create a more equitable order. And we could solve the crime problem. By the end of the decade the belief in this "great society" gave way to a despairing distrust of the state.

In the 1950s and 1960s, corrections in the United States focused on rehabilitating offenders. An indeterminate system of sentencing permitted judges wide leeway in deciding the type and length of sentence. Probation agents prepared the presentence report with recommendations for the appropriate sentence. Parole boards had wide discretion about when offenders would be released, based on when the board thought they had been rehabilitated and were at low risk for committing additional crimes. Offenders were often required to show evidence that they had participated in rehabilitation programs.

The system was responsible for changing lawbreakers into law abiders. The expectation was that offenders would be treated during their time under correctional supervision. Through this treatment they would be rehabilitated, and as a result they would not continue in their criminal activities in the future.

President Johnson's Blue Ribbon Panel

The strong emphasis on rehabilitation is demonstrated by the recommendations made by a panel of experts formed in response to President Lyndon Johnson's 1965 address to the U.S. Congress. He called for the establishment of a blue ribbon panel to examine the problems of crime in our nation (President's Commission on Law Enforcement and Administration of Justice, 1967). A short list of some of the recommendations made by the Commission in regard to probation demonstrates the strong emphasis on rehabilitation:

- Probation services should be available for felons and for adult misdemeanants who need or can profit from community treatment.
- All jurisdictions should aim for an average ratio of 35 offenders per probation officer.
- Probation officers should actively intervene on behalf of offenders to connect them with community institutions.
- The officer must be a link between the offender and the community, a mediator when there is trouble, and an advocate in regard to bureaucratic policies that screen offenders out.
- Correctional authorities should develop more community programs to provide special, intensive treatment as an alternative to institutionalization.
- Classification of offenders should be used to determine their needs and problems so appropriate treatment plans can be designed.

Obviously, the panel believed in the need for and value of treatment and was advocating an increase in the use of such programs for offenders.

Times Are Ripe for Change

The philosophy of corrections changed radically in the 1970s. This change is often attributed to an article, "What Works? Questions and Answers About Prison Reform," prepared by Robert Martinson (1974). This article, summarizing the work of Martinson and his colleagues (Lipton, Martinson, & Wilks, 1975), provided an extremely pessimistic assessment of the existing rehabilitation programs. His words, "With few and isolated exceptions, the rehabilitative efforts that have been reported so far have had no appreciable effect on recidivism" (Martinson, 1974, p. 25), were subsequently reduced to the core idea that "nothing works" in correctional rehabilitation.

A rigorous debate ensued about the correctness of Martinson's conclusion (Cullen & Gendreau, 2000; Palmer, 1975, 1992). Many said these results did not mean that rehabilitation programs could never work to change offenders. Instead, the findings demonstrated that the programs were so poorly implemented and studies were so inadequately designed that it was impossible to tell what worked. Well-designed programs studied with adequate research designs might be able to demonstrate how to rehabilitate offenders. Others argued many of the programs studied did reduce recidivism, and in his conclusion Martinson failed to take fair consideration of these programs. Despite the debate about the relevance of the conclusions, the "nothing works" philosophy had a major impact on corrections.

Although Martinson's work may be the most visible impetus for change, other factors were probably equally influential (Cullen & Gendreau, 2000; Cullen & Gilbert, 1982; MacKenzie, 2006). Cataclysmic changes occurred in the larger society from the mid-1960s until the mid-1970s. Civil rights, women's rights, questions about the war in Vietnam, urban riots, Watergate, and prison riots led many to question whether social institutions could be trusted. The times were ripe for change, and this had a direct effect on correctional philosophy, which, in turn, had an enormous influence on the practice of probation (Cullen & Gilbert, 1982).

The Justice Model: Let the Punishment Fit the Crime

If social institutions couldn't be trusted to treat people fairly, then the extreme power given to the courts and corrections, which was inherent in the indeterminate model of sentencing, was not justified. Furthermore, if rehabilitation programs were not effective, then it was unfair to force offenders into treatment. The justice model of corrections was the proposed solution to the problems of sentencing and corrections. From this perspective, sentences should be decided on the basis of fair and just sentencing policies based on a retributive notion of punishment. The power of the courts and correctional officials would be limited. From this perspective, a criminal should receive a deserved punishment for a crime; the sentence should fit the crime. Interest focused on justice, ensuring the legal rights of offenders and protection of inmates from coerced rehabilitation programs (Cullen & Gendreau, 2000; MacKenzie, 2006).

Perhaps the largest policy change was the move from an indeterminate sentencing model to determinate sentencing. Under this model, sentencing for a crime would carry a clearly identified sentence length, not a broad minimum and maximum; parole release would be eliminated; and sentence lengths would be determined by guidelines considering only the past history of criminal activity and the current crime of conviction.

Individualized decisions were discouraged, thus eliminating discretion and the resulting disparity. One argument for eliminating judicial discretion was that judges didn't always make their own decisions about sentencing because they based their decisions on recommendations made by probation agents as part of the PSI.

Guidelines were designed as a grid, with past criminal history and severity of current crimes marking the rows and columns. Judges were expected to find the appropriate cell and give the sentence listed. At first the guidelines applied only to sentences of incarceration, but later states included probation and intermediate sentencing options in the grid.

Crime Control: Incapacitation and Deterrence

By the 1980s, fueled in part by the crime increase in the late 1970s, the focus changed from the justice model to crime control through incapacitation and deterrence. No longer was the focus on a just and fair sentence for the crime committed, without consideration of other factors. Now the focus was on how to keep offenders from continuing to commit crimes, either by controlling them or by making the punishment so onerous that the criminals themselves (specific deterrence) or others in the general population (general deterrence) would be deterred from committing crimes.

The "war on drugs" expanded criminal sanctions for drug crimes. Legislatures passed mandatory sentencing laws increasing the length of sentences for certain crimes. "Three strikes," or life incarceration for someone convicted of three felonies, was advocated as a way to incapacitate habitual criminals for life. There was an emphasis on getting tough on crime.

IMPACT OF PHILOSOPHICAL CHANGES ON PROBATION

The philosophical changes had a major impact on probation agencies. Although many people worried about the rising incarceration rates and the enormous costs associated with this rise, they failed to notice that probation was also growing without a corresponding increase in budget to accommodate this large increase in probationers. As shown in Figure 5.2, probation increased dramatically during this time. From 1980 to 2005 the number of people under probation supervision increased from 1.1 million to 4.2 million. This dramatic increase and the change in philosophy had a direct impact on the availability of treatment and individualized programs.

Probation moved away from the emphasis on rehabilitation and services, as proposed by the President's Crime Commission, to a focus on control of offenders. Instead of giving officers time for counseling and providing services, smaller

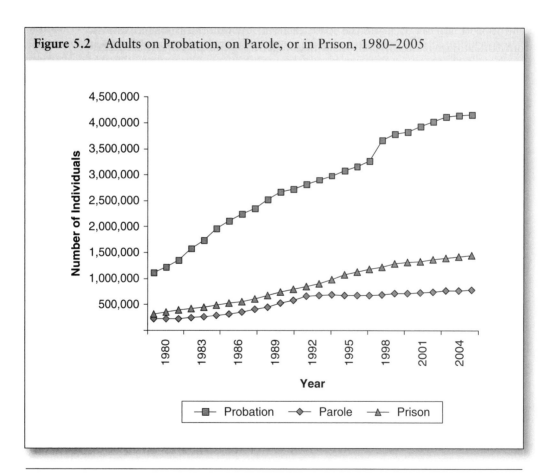

Figure 5.2   Adults on Probation, on Parole, or in Prison, 1980–2005

Source: Bureau of Justice Statistics. Retrieved on Sep. 25, 2009 from http://www.ojp.usdoj.gov/bjs/glance/tables/corr2tab.htm

caseloads were designed to control offenders so they would be caught and punished for criminal activity. Intermediate punishments became popular. These punishments, variously called intermediate sanctions, community corrections, correctional options, or alternative punishments, were designed to be more serious than traditional probation but less serious than prison (Byrne, Lurigio, & Petersilia, 1992; Morris & Tonry, 1990). Rather than being limited to a choice of either prison or ordinary probation, offenders could be given one of a variety of sanctions that ranged between prison and ordinary probation in severity. Intensive supervised probation (ISP), correctional boot camps, electronic monitoring (EM), house arrest, drug testing, and day reporting were some of the more popular sanctions used to increase control over probationers. Most of these came under the administrative authority of probation departments.

The shift in the philosophy and practice of probation came at a time when the institution of probation was demoralized (Tonry, 1990). Not only was probation publicly perceived as merely a slap on the wrist (as it has been by some since the days of John Augustus), but faith in its ability to rehabilitate had slowly eroded. The reemergence of intermediate punishments and the control philosophy in general therefore seemed to have given probation managers an opportunity to restore probation's credibility, impact, and material resources (Tonry, 1990). Most of the sanctions emphasized the punishment, incapacitation, or deterrence aspect of the sanction and not increased treatment or services.

Intensive Supervised Probation

One obvious byproduct of the new sentencing philosophy was the reemergence of ISP. First implemented in the 1960s, the early ISPs were attempts at discovering the caseload size that would maximize the intensity of supervision (Clear & Hardyman, 1990). Intensity was assumed to be related to successful outcome. The second wave of ISPs surfaced in the mid-1980s despite the unenthusiastic findings of the earlier movement. The number of programs grew dramatically, and by 1990 almost every state in the nation had developed some type of ISP program.

ISP increased the conditions of probation by requiring more meetings with supervising agents, more collateral contacts with employers or family, and more frequent drug and alcohol tests. The emphasis was on control of the offender, with rapid responses to misbehavior or violations of probation. Risk assessment became important as a tool to decide which offenders were most at risk for recidivating so that workloads could be adjusted to more intensively supervise these offenders.

The growth in the number of ISP programs was in part a result of early research suggesting that ISP led to a significant decrease in reincarcerations and rearrests (MacKenzie, 2006). However, these initial results were not supported by later, more rigorous studies of intensive supervision programs (Latessa, Travis, Fulton, & Stichman, 1998; Petersilia & Turner, 1993). A recent meta-analysis of studies of probation and parole programs by MacKenzie found the programs were not effective in reducing recidivism. In fact, in their study, Petersilia and Turner found that offenders on ISP may be revoked more often for technical violations.

Electronic Monitoring (EM)

With advances in technology came the ability to electronically monitor offenders while they were in the community on probation. Today, most offenders on EM are on what may be described as curfew checking systems, equipment that establishes whether an offender is at a fixed place at a specific time. The remaining offenders are on Global Positioning System tracking that can report offender locations to an agency as frequently as every minute (Renzema, 2003). Often EM is combined with house arrest or the requirement that the offender remain at home unless given permission to leave to work, visit doctors, or attend other agent-sanctioned activities. The monitoring gives the agent knowledge about whether the offender leaves the house during periods when this is not permitted. As was found with the ISP programs, EM was not effective in reducing later criminal activities of probationers (MacKenzie, 2006).

Impact of Intermediate Sanctions on Recidivism

Intermediate sanctions were designed to be cost-effective alternatives to incarceration and to increase the control and punitiveness of community sanctions (Clear & Braga, 1995; Petersilia, 1998; Tonry & Lynch, 1996). Research has demonstrated that they do indeed increase the requirements of supervision. However, to successfully reduce costs they need to divert offenders from prison to community alternatives or substantially reduce recidivism. This has not occurred. Many programs have widened the net to increase penalties and requirements for offenders who would otherwise have been on standard probation.

Most intermediate sanctions have focused on increasing control, not on increased therapeutic programming, with the result that they have not reduced recidivism. Using systematic reviews and meta-analysis, MacKenzie (2006) examined the effectiveness of correctional programs and management strategies on recidivism. Research evidence demonstrated that programs such as cognitive skills, drug treatment, education, and sex offender treatment that included human service components were effective in reducing recidivism. In contrast, no programs or interventions focusing on punishment, deterrence, or control were found to reduce recidivism. Intermediate sanctions such as boot camps, ISP, and EM, which were popular during the period when corrections focused on incapacitation and deterrence, were not effective in reducing recidivism.

Box 5.2   Community Corrections in China

In China, prisons are the punishment of choice. A strong punishment ideology combined with a social control philosophy has resulted in incarceration for the majority of sentenced offenders. Many people who might receive probation in the United States are sent to prison or to labor camps. Until recently, community corrections was seldom used as a sanction in China.

A significant number of offenders who would be criminal cases in the United States bypass the Chinese criminal justice system when they are sent to the labor camps. Labor camps are an option police have for sending minor offenders to a secure facility for "reeducation through labor." Under Chinese law, the police have the discretion to decide, without judicial proceedings, to send a person to the labor camps, where they can be kept for up to 3 years. People sent to the labor camps might be punished for minor offenses such as petty theft, fighting, shoplifting, vandalism, or drug involvement. In the United States these offenders might be sentenced to probation.

The currently operating community corrections programs in China began in 2003 when the Supreme People's Procuratorate, Ministry of Public Security, and Ministry of Justice promoted the development of experimental projects in community corrections. The pilot programs were first developed in Beijing, Shanghai, Tianjin, Shejiang, Jiangsu, and Shandon. By 2007, at least 18 pilot programs had been started.

Before the initiation of these pilot programs, probation and parole were seldom used in many jurisdictions. Earlier community correction programs were operating at the time of the revolution in 1949 and legally established in 1979. However, during this time few people were placed on community corrections. Most offenders who were on community corrections had served a lengthy period of time in prison and then were released to the community. Public security or the police were responsible for these offenders, but there was little supervision after the offender registered with the police. At this time the Ministry of Justice and the Ministry of Public Security were in charge of the program.

(Continued)

(Continued)

The new community corrections programs are the responsibility of the Ministry of Justice, the Ministry of Public Security, and the districts (counties). The district is expected to provide supervision and assistance to the offenders while they are in the community. The assistance is expected to be based on a social worker model in which the supervising agent is responsible for assisting offenders in their adjustment to the community. Similar to community corrections in the United States, China's community corrections agents assess the offender's risk level and plan treatment and surveillance accordingly.

PROBATION AND CRIMINAL ACTIVITY

Since the beginning of probation, one of the arguments in favor of keeping people in the community was to protect them from being negatively influenced by prison and prisoners. Prison removes people from the community, often destroying ties with significant others and disrupting employment. In prison, offenders associate with other prisoners who may be more hardened criminals. Upon release, they must reintegrate into the community; reestablishing contacts with family and friends and finding employment and housing are just some of the challenges they face (for a summary of the barriers of reintegration, see chapter 14). Thus, one reason for using probation as a sanction is that prison may be more criminogenic, leading to increased criminal activities after sanctioning. Another argument in favor of probation is that such supervision and suspended sentences are expected to have a positive impact on offenders so they will not continue to commit crimes. Several studies have examined these issues.

Prison Versus Probation: Impact on Recidivism

In a Campbell Collaboration systematic review, Killias (2006) assessed the relative effects of custodial sanctions (imprisonment) and noncustodial (alternative or community sanctions, most often probation). The question was whether custodial and noncustodial sanctions have different effects on the rates of reoffending. After an intensive search of the research literature, he found 27 comparisons of noncustodial and custodial sanctions. The reoffending rates after a noncustodial sentence were significantly lower than after a custodial sentence for 11 comparisons, the reverse was true for 2 studies, and for 14 comparisons there was no significant difference. These results suggest that non-custodial sentences were less criminogenic.

However, many of the studies examined by Killias (2006) were quasi-experimental designs and many of the noncustodial offenders probably were at lower risk for recidivism, a possible reason for the significant differences. Taking this into consideration, Killias conducted a meta-analysis including only the five strongest research designs. He found no differences between sanctions. Thus, there is little evidence that probation keeps people from being negatively or positively influenced by prison.

The Impact of Probation on Criminal Activity

Although probation may be no more or less effective than prison, it may have an impact on criminal activities. According to MacKenzie and her colleagues, arrest and a sentence of probation may significantly reduce the criminal activities of offenders (MacKenzie, Browning, Priu, Skroban, & Smith, 1998; MacKenzie, Browning, Skroban, & Smith, 1999). In a self-report study of criminal activities of probationers, they found offenders' criminal activities were dramatically reduced when their activities in the year before arrest were compared with their activities after arrest and probation. In comparison to the year before arrest, there were fewer offenders who committed crimes during probation, and both the annualized rate of criminal activity for these offenders and the proportion of months when offenders committed crimes declined. For example, 18.7% of the offenders admitted to stealing (thefts) in the year before arrest, but only 1.9% continued to steal after they were on probation, and the number of thefts declined from 43 per year to 10.5 per year. Similarly, 28% of the offenders admitted assaulting someone before their arrests, but only 14% assaulted in the year after arrest. These declines occurred for all the self-reported crimes examined (burglary, theft, forgery, robbery, assault, drug dealing), but they were greatest for property offenses and drug dealing. Forgery was not significantly associated with a decline in offending. However, the research could not distinguish whether the decline in criminal activity began at arrest before sentencing or whether it was due to the sentence itself. What is clear is that the criminal activities of these offenders dramatically declined when they were arrested and placed on probation.

Three basic types of conditions of probation were set for the probationers in the study by MacKenzie et al. (1999): financial and community service conditions that were set by the sentencing court, special conditions regarding treatment and drug screening that may be set by the courts or probation department, and standard conditions such as travel and gun possession restrictions that apply to all probationers. Most of the probationers, 96%, had at least one type of financial obligation to the court. Ninety-two percent of the probationers were required to pay court costs.

One reason for setting control-oriented conditions of probation is to reduce the criminal activities of offenders while they are being supervised. MacKenzie and colleagues found that self-reported violations of probation were associated with criminal activity. Criminal activity was greater during periods when the offenders were violating their conditions of probation. However, increases in the intrusiveness of conditions, in the agent's knowledge of misbehavior, or in how the agent responded to misbehavior were not associated with either criminal activity or violations of conditions. So although violations were associated with criminal activity, whether the agent knew about the violations or sanctioned the offender did not reduce criminal activity or limit violations.

This study is important for probation because it suggests that arrest and probation do reduce criminal activity, so it may not be necessary for U.S. jurisdictions to incarcerate so many offenders. In addition, violations of conditions of probation (e.g., drug use, heavy drinking, travel outside area, breaking curfew) are associated with criminal activity. The problem is that agent knowledge of and response to these violations did not change the behavior. It may be that the agents need more options for responding to misbehavior or that the responses need to address the therapeutic needs of the probationers and not just punish them.

NEW DEVELOPMENTS IN PROBATION AND COMMUNITY CORRECTIONS

Exciting new developments in probation bring promise for the future success of community corrections programs. What stands out in these new developments is the recognition of the need to focus on evidence. The exact form of this evidence differs, but the underlying theme is that information can be used to determine the most effective way to treat and manage offenders. Increasingly, probation departments are recognizing the importance of using evidence to support their management decisions. Evidence-based corrections is a philosophy arguing in favor of using research evidence to guide policy decisions. Research clearly indicates that therapy and treatment from a human service perspective are more effective in changing offenders than are the recent deterrence and punishment interventions. Specialized courts are a good example of how probation departments have increased the focus on treatment.

Specialized Courts

Probation agencies have become important members of the teams for the new specialized or problem-solving courts. These courts focus on the issues relevant to particular types of offenders. Currently, there are courts for drug-involved offenders, domestic batterers, offenders with mental health problems, and family issues. In general these courts begin with a careful classification assessment to identify offenders who are appropriate for the court program. The earliest specialized courts, the treatment drug courts, which began in 1989 in Dade County, Florida, are the models for most other courts.

Treatment drug courts are specialized courts that focus on drug-involved offenders who are assessed to be in need of treatment (National Association of Drug Court Professionals, 2009). Some argue that drug courts are one of the major justice reforms of the 20th century in the United States (Goldkamp, White, & Robinson, 2000). They represent a paradigm shift away from the punitive orientation toward drug-related crime that had been so prominent in the 1980s, as exemplified by the "war on drugs." From the perspective of the crime control strategy, arrests and punishments for drug offenses were expected to be effective in reducing illegal drug use and sales. The problem was that many of those arrested were users and addicts. The strategy did not include any treatment for the offenders, who became enmeshed in the net of control, and many of them served sentences without receiving treatment for their problems.

Drug courts were introduced in order to address these problems. The courts are a management strategy designed to use the authority of the courts to reduce crime by changing defendants' drug-using behaviors. The goal is to reduce drug use and criminal activity. These goals are accomplished by engaging and retaining drug-involved offenders in supervision and treatment programs. Probation agents are responsible for identifying appropriate offenders for the drug courts. These defendants are diverted to drug courts in exchange for the possibility of dismissed charges or reduced sentences. Judges preside over drug court proceedings and monitor the progress of the defendants; they arrange sanctions for noncompliance with program requirements and rewards for compliance.

Prosecutors, defense attorneys, treatment providers, probation agents, and others work in collaboration instead of in the more usual court adversarial roles. In comparison to other traditional courtrooms, the drug court model is less punitive and more healing and restorative. The focus is not on the disposition of the case but on rehabilitating drug-involved defendants. Sanctions for continued drug use often involve more intensive treatment rather than time in jail. Probation agents are responsible for supervising drug court participants and reporting their behavior to the court during the regularly scheduled status hearings, where the judge monitors the behavior of the defendants.

Meta-analyses examining the effectiveness of drug courts have demonstrated that the courts reduce recidivism. Almost all of the 26 studies examined by MacKenzie (2006) found drug court participants had lower recidivism than the comparison groups. The research could not distinguish which particular aspects of the courts led to the positive outcomes. More research is needed to identify whether treatment exposure, sanctions, appearance before the judge, or some combination of these is the important drug court component that reduced recidivism (Belenko, 1998). Diversion programs and specialized courts are discussed in length in chapter 6.

Box 5.3   Allegheny County Mental Health Court, Pennsylvania

Mental health courts are based on the more familiar drug court model. Both offer offenders with a behavioral health diagnosis a special criminal court that diverts them to treatment rather than incarceration. The goals of the Allegheny County Mental Health Court are to maintain effective communication between behavioral health and criminal justice systems, reduce the revolving door of recidivism for this population, and help the offenders obtain treatment, housing, and community support services.

The mental health court relies on participation of the Allegheny County Department of Human Services, the Office of Behavioral Health, the Allegheny County Court of Common Pleas, the Office of the Public Defender, the Office of the District Attorney, and the Office of Probation and Parole. After spending decades watching people with serious mental health problems enter and reenter the criminal justice system with little hope of eventual community reintegration, personnel from the Department of Human Services, the court, and the Office of Probation and Parole agreed to support the mental health court.

According to Allegheny County Jail, in 2001 the jail was the third largest mental health facility in southwestern Pennsylvania; inmates with mental illness accounted for 20–25% of the jail population. Several issues led the county to experiment with a special Mental Health Court (MHC) to deal with offenders with mental illness. First, offenders with mental health problems typically were kept in jail longer than other offenders before their trial because of high bail bonds, limited resources, and society's general fear of people with mental illness. Second, once in jail, they were at risk of losing their medical assistance, Social Security Income benefits, case management services, and other critical benefits. Third, many were at risk for losing their housing, a basic necessity that is often in short supply for those with mental illness.

MHC was designed as a specialty court with its own judge, assistant district attorney, public defender, court monitor, forensic support specialist, and probation liaison so the court could more carefully monitor the progress of offenders and develop expertise related to mental illness and treatment. MHC intervention is essentially probation with close supervision and mandatory treatment. Offenders must agree to participate in outpatient treatment. A mandatory element of the offender's probation is a court-approved service plan intended to promote recovery and guide treatment. Most service plans stipulate where offenders live, and they must take their medications as prescribed, must refrain from using drugs and alcohol, and have periodic meetings with case managers, probation officers, doctors, and forensic specialists.

MHC participants do not receive any priority for access to behavioral health services in the community; however, they do get extra support and supervision from the MHC program. Once they are released to serve their probation, MHC participants are supervised by a Special Service Unit probation officer and the MHC probation liaison. At least every 3 months, participants are required to attend periodic reinforcement hearings before an MHC judge, where the liaison updates the court on how the MHC participants are progressing. If offenders have complied with the requirements, they may be rewarded with gift cards or a reduction in the term of probation. When offenders have not complied with stipulations, team members determine how best to assist them in meeting their goals.

Evidence-Based Corrections

Correctional systems have begun to turn more of their attention to research. Evidence-based corrections is a philosophy emphasizing the importance of developing programs that have been demonstrated to be effective through rigorous scientific research (MacKenzie, 2000, 2001). There is now a body of research literature showing the ineffectiveness of correctional programs that only increase control and punishment. Effective programs have human service components that provide treatment (MacKenzie, 2006). Important in evidence-based corrections is the quality and quantity of information available.

Compstat for Community Corrections

Compstat is a procedure for increasing the use of objective data to focus on desired outcomes. Probation agencies do a poor job of measuring and managing information about their performance (Pew Foundation, 2007). Compstat (short for *compare statistics*) is a comprehensive model used for measuring and managing police operations in New York City. It is based on the following principles: Gather accurate and timely information, deploy resources rapidly, use effective tactics, and conduct follow-up and assessment monitoring. Perhaps as important as the principles are the key dynamics created at the frequent Compstat meetings: peer pressure; real-time, objective data; focus on outcomes; responsibility and authority; rewards and reprimands; and normative consequences. Some people credit Compstat with significantly reducing crime in New York City, although others debate whether Compstat can be credited with this.

The New York City Department of Probation developed a version of Compstat, called Statistical Tracking, Analysis and Reporting System (STARS) using the principles as a model for community corrections. The probation department tracks the commission of crimes by people on probation and has monthly face-to-face meetings where top managers' efforts are reviewed. Community corrections is interested primarily in reducing the numbers and types of new crimes committed by offenders under supervision. However, equally important are strategies and activities that help reduce offenders' risk factors and thereby reduce their likelihood of reoffending. For example, getting addicted offenders to attend and complete substance abuse treatment and getting unemployed offenders jobs are important in turning them away from criminal activity.

From the perspective of community corrections, STARS consists of gathering information about offenders. Agencies need to know the risk levels of offenders and their individual deficits or needs. Once agents know who is most likely to reoffend and what factors contribute to reoffending, resources can be deployed to those who pose a high risk; low-risk cases can receive less attention and resources. Caseloads for the most risky offenders can be kept low so these offenders can be monitored more closely. Resources can be focused on high-risk offenders at the times when they are most at risk (e.g., soon after sentencing for probationers). This system relies on clear, up-to-date information about the individual probationers. This information is presented at the meetings, so there is a clear indication of the success or failure of the district in reducing criminal activity and improving life conditions for probationers.

No evaluation of STARS has been completed, but preliminary findings about the arrests of probationers are promising. Community supervision agencies in Georgia, Maryland, and the District of Columbia have also instituted Compstat-like information management systems.

New York's Automated Kiosk Reporting System

Many low-risk offenders receive little supervision during their time on probation. In order to reduce the costs of supervision and more appropriately allocate resources, several jurisdictions have developed automated reporting or kiosk systems for use in supervising low-risk offenders (Wilson, Naro, & Austin, 2007). Kiosks are similar in appearance to bank automated teller machines. The system uses a personal computer with a touch-screen system, a biometric hand scanner, and a small printer to generate a receipt.

In an effort to deal with the problem of serious budget cuts and large caseloads, in the mid-1990s the New York City Department of Probation developed and tested an automated reporting system for low-risk offenders. In response to its initial success, the department expanded the use of the kiosk reporting system, and by 2003 all probationers who had been assessed as low risk for recidivism were assigned to report to kiosks.

The probationer must report to the probation office to attend an initial orientation session. During the orientation probationers are required to register with the system, told their responsibilities on probation, and shown a videotape demonstrating how to use the kiosk system. Subsequently, probationers are required to visit the office kiosk each month and answer a short list of questions. If new issues come up (such as an arrest) or the probationer is randomly selected for drug testing, the probationer is required to stay for a meeting or drug test. Kiosk attendants ensure that the probationer stays to report to an officer if required.

Kiosks are expected to allow probation departments to redistribute limited resources, to be a critical element in a comprehensive data management strategy, and lead to better or equal outcomes than reporting directly to a probation officer. Wilson et al. (2007) examined the effectiveness of the New York kiosk system. They found that the system increased reporting and decreased caseloads for high-risk offenders. By assigning low-risk cases to kiosk reporting, the department was able to devote more attention to high-risk offenders. Arrest rates for both high-risk and low-risk probationers declined slightly.

The preliminary research suggests that the kiosk system may be a viable method for managing probation populations. Of course, any agency planning to use this system must have a valid and reliable risk assessment instrument (Wilson et al., 2007). Equally important is a strong protocol for assigning probationers to high- and low-risk categories for supervision.

SUMMARY AND POLICY IMPLICATIONS

In some ways probation might be thought of as the neglected stepchild of corrections. Given the enormous costs of prison and politicians' fear of being accused of being soft on crime, probation has not received a great deal of support. For a short time there was hope that intermediate sanctions might be successful in reducing crime, but this did not prove to be the case. Yet probation is a critically important part of the U.S. correctional system—an untapped resource. It is often offenders' first sentence for a crime. A majority of those sentenced to the U.S. correctional system serve their time on probation. Research suggests that probation can and does reduce future criminal activity.

Other developed countries use community options for offenders instead of relying so heavily on incarceration. There is every reason to believe that the United States could reduce the prison population without a corresponding increase in crime. Certainly some of the following would be important in increasing the effectiveness of probation:

- Increased use of information to make decisions, providing direct, clear, and timely feedback with the goal of improving methods for implementing programs, strategies, and interventions
- Careful classification and risk assessment using valid and reliable instruments to ensure that probationers at different risk levels receive the appropriate interventions and programs
- The increased use of evidence-based corrections so programs with demonstrated effectiveness are provided, particularly programs with therapeutic programming and human service components
- A move away from a focus on control and punishments, as was popular during the "get-tough" period of the past
- New and innovative programs such as specialized courts, day fines, and community service focusing on the needs of particular types of offenders

Jurisdictions have begun to rethink probation. Many in the United States have argued that we do not need to incarcerate such a large percentage of our population. There are alternatives, and other developed countries have successfully used them instead of incarcerating such large proportions of the population. People continue to worry about what our high incarceration rates have done to our inner-city communities and minority populations (Clear, 2007). Offenders released from prison face enormous problems during reentry. Probation eliminates some of these problems. If we spent more on treatment options or the type of programs with demonstrated effectiveness, we would reduce the problems of reentry (MacKenzie, 2006). This chapter discussed some of the things that might be done to rethink probation. Perhaps the most important is to provide the necessary funding so intensive programming is available for those on probation. Instead of worrying about offenders when they are released from prison, we should send fewer to prison.

DISCUSSION QUESTIONS

1. Do you believe that probation is in a better position than traditional incarceration to achieve the seemingly conflicting goals of control, punishment, and treatment? Why or why not?

2. According to the Bureau of Justice Statistics, about half of those sentenced to probation were convicted of felonies and nearly 27% of all probationers were convicted of violent offenses. Which factors should determine whether an offender should be sentenced to probation: severity of crime, threat to public safety, motivation and readiness for change, or community ties? Please justify your answer.

3. There has been an uneasy struggle between the trend to model probation as a law enforcement function and the push to conceptualize probation from a social service approach. What kind of academic training and professional skills would help probation officers succeed in their duties? How should their job performance be evaluated? By the number of technical violations detected, the number of new offenses avoided, the level of satisfaction of the probationers, or the approval of the community? Why?

4. What are the advantages or disadvantages of using technological innovations such as electronic monitoring and kiosk reporting systems? What role do they play in the monitoring and rehabilitation of supervised probationers?

REFERENCES

Abadinsky, H. (2008). *Probation and parole: Theory and practice.* Upper Saddle River, NJ: Pearson.

Augustus, J. (1972). *John Augustus' original report of his labors: 1852.* Montclair, NJ: Patterson Smith.

Belenko, S. R. (1998). Research on drug courts: A critical review. *National Drug Court Institute Review, 1,* 1–42.

Braithwaite, J. (1998). Restorative justice. In M. Tonry (Ed.), *The handbook of crime & punishment.* Oxford: Oxford University Press.

Bureau of Justice Statistics. (2008). *Sourcebook of criminal justice statistics.* Washington, DC: Author.

Byrne, J. M., Lurigio, A. J., & Petersilia, J. (Eds.). (1992). *Smart sentencing: The emergence of intermediate sanctions.* Newbury Park, CA: Sage.

Clear, T. R. (2007). *Imprisoning communities: How mass incarceration makes disadvantaged neighborhoods worse.* Oxford: Oxford University Press.

Clear, T. R., & Braga, T. A. (1995). Community corrections. In J. Q. Wilson & J. Petersilia (Eds.), *Crime.* San Francisco: Institute for Contemporary Studies.

Clear, T. R., & Hardyman, P. M. (1990). The new intensive supervision movement. *Crime and Delinquency, 36,* 42–60.

Clear, T. R., Harris, P. M., & Baird, S. C. (1992). Probationer violations and officer response. *Journal of Criminal Justice, 20,* 1–12.

Cullen, F. T., & Gendreau, P. (2000). Assessing correctional rehabilitation: Policy, practice, and prospects. In J. Horney (Ed.), *Criminal justice 2000: Volume 3. Policies, processes, and decisions of the criminal justice system.* Washington, DC: U.S. Department of Justice, National Institute of Justice.

Cullen, F. T., & Gilbert, K. E. (1982). *Reaffirming rehabilitation.* Cincinnati: Anderson.

Feeley, M. M., & Simon, J. (1992). The new penology: Notes on the emerging strategy of corrections and its implications. *Criminology, 30*(4), 449–470.

Glaze, L. E., & Bonczar, T. P. (2007). *Probation and parole in the United States, 2006.* Washington, DC: Bureau of Justice Statistics Bulletin, U.S. Department of Justice.

Goldkamp, J., White, M., & Robinson, J. (2000). *Retrospective evaluation of two pioneering drug courts: Phase I findings from Clark County, Nevada, and Multnomah County, Oregon.* Philadelphia: Crime and Justice Research Institute.

Harris, P. M., Clear, T. R., & Baird, S. C. (1989). Have community supervision officers changed their attitudes toward their work? *Justice Quarterly, 6*(2), 233–246.

Killias, M. (2006). Improving impact evaluations through randomised experiments: The challenge of the NRC Report for European Criminology. *Journal of Experimental Criminology, 2/3,* 375–391.

Lappi-Seppala, T. (2007). Penal policy in Scandinavia. In M. Tonry (Ed.), *Crime, punishment, and politics in comparative perspective.* Chicago: University of Chicago Press.

Latessa, E., Travis, L., Fulton, B., & Stichman, A. (1998). *Evaluating the prototypical ISP: Final report.* Cincinnati, OH: University of Cincinnati, Division of Criminal Justice.

Lipton, D., Martinson, R., & Wilks, J. (1975). *The effectiveness of correctional treatment: A survey of treatment evaluation studies.* New York: Praeger.

MacKenzie, D. L. (2000). Evidence-based corrections: Identifying what works. *Crime and Delinquency, 46*(4), 457–471.

MacKenzie, D. L. (2001). Corrections and sentencing in the 21st century: Evidence-based corrections and sentencing. *The Prison Journal, 81*(3), 299–312.

MacKenzie, D. L. (2006). *What works in corrections: Reducing the criminal activities of offenders and delinquents.* Cambridge: Cambridge University Press.

MacKenzie, D. L., Browning, K., Priu, H., Skroban, S. B., & Smith, D. A. (1998). *Probationer compliance with conditions of supervision.* Final report. Washington, DC: National Institute of Justice, U.S. Department of Justice.

MacKenzie, D. L., Browning, K., Skroban, S., & Smith, D. (1999). The impact of probation on the criminal activities of offenders. *Journal of Research in Crime and Delinquency, 36,* 423–453.

MacKenzie, D. L., & Souryal, C. (1997). Probationer compliance with conditions of supervision. In J. W. Marquart & J. Sorensen (Eds.), *Correctional contexts: Contemporary and classical readings*. Los Angeles: Roxbury.

Martinson, R. (1974). What works? Questions and answers about prison reform. *Public Interest, 35*, 22–54.

Morris, N., & Tonry, M. (1990). *Between prison and probation: Intermediate punishments in a rational sentencing system*. New York: Oxford University Press.

National Association of Drug Court Professionals. (2009). *What are drug courts?* Retrieved January 4, 2009, from http://www.nadcp.org/learn/what-are-drug-courts

O'Leary, V. (1987). Probation: A system in change. *Federal Probation, 51*(4), 8–11.

Palmer, T. (1975). Martinson revisited. *Journal of Research in Crime and Delinquency, 12*, 133–152.

Palmer, T. (1992). *The re-emergence of correctional intervention*. Newbury Park, CA: Sage.

Petersilia, J. (1997). Probation in the United States. In M. Tonry (Ed.), *Crime and justice: A review of the research* (Vol. 22, pp. 149–200). Chicago: University of Chicago Press.

Petersilia, J. (1998). Probation and parole. In M. Tonry (Ed.), *The handbook of crime and punishment*. New York: Oxford University Press.

Petersilia, J., & Turner, S. (1993). Intensive probation and parole. In M. Tonry & N. Morris (Eds.), *Crime and justice: A review of research* (Vol. 17, pp. 281–335). Chicago: University of Chicago Press.

Pew Foundation. (2007). *You get what you measure: Compstat for community corrections*. Public safety policy brief. Retrieved January 4, 2009, from http://www.pewcenteronthestates.org/uploadedfiles/You%20Get%20What%20You%20Measure.pdf

President's Commission on Law Enforcement and Administration of Justice. (1967). *Task force report: Corrections*. Washington, DC: U.S. Government Printing Office.

Renzema, M. (2003). *Electronic monitoring's impact on reoffending*. Retrieved August 20, 2004, from http://www.campbellcollaboration.org/doc-pdf/elecmon.pdf

Tonry, M. (1990). State and latent functions of ISP. *Crime and Delinquency, 36*(1), 174–191.

Tonry, M., & Lynch, M. (1996). Intermediate sanctions. In M. Tonry (Ed.), *Crime and justice: A review of research* (Vol. 20). Chicago: University of Chicago Press.

Wilson, J. A., Naro, W., & Austin, J. F. (2007). *Innovations in probation: Assessing New York City's automated reporting system*. Washington, DC: The JFA Institute. Retrieved December 12, 2008, from http://www.nyc.gov/html/prob/downloads/pdf/kiosk_report_2007.pdf

CHAPTER 6

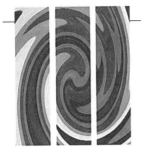

Diversion Programs

Rachel Porter

Diversion programs are used to divert people accused or convicted of crimes away from incarceration and into alternative punishments. These programs provide sentencing options for prosecutors and judges and a mechanism for reducing jail and prison populations for corrections officials. For the most part current diversion programs have a rehabilitative focus, targeting problems that may underlie crime, such as drug addiction, unemployment, and mental illness. These programs seek to keep people out of jail and prison. They are based on the belief that incarceration alone is likely to increase the chance of reoffending and other dysfunction—the same assumption that motivates many reentry programs. Long before reformers focused on the community impact of prisoner reentry, diversion programs were engaged with rehabilitating offenders in their community instead of removing them through incarceration.

True diversion programs serve as an alternative to incarceration. By reducing reliance on incarceration, diversion programs also aim to reduce criminal justice system costs (incarceration costs more than diversion programs on a per capita and annual basis) and may reduce reoffending. The goals of diversion include reducing costs, reducing prison overcrowding, rehabilitating offenders, maintaining public safety, decreasing recidivism, and reducing reliance on incarceration as a punishment. These goals may complement or compete with each other; many are very difficult to achieve once the theory of diversion meets the realities of implementing diversion programs.

Diversion programs respond to competing demands in the policy arena that reflect the local political and cultural climates. In most cases, diversion programs are designed to address concerns that crime rates are too high, that criminals must be held accountable, and that the public safety must be protected—the tough-on-crime position. At the same time, administrators and policymakers implementing diversion programs try to respond to the apparent failure of incarceration to reduce reoffending. To reduce recidivism, diversion programs often address the underlying health, social, and economic problems that research has shown to be criminogenic—problems that may contribute to individual decisions to commit crimes.

The first section of this chapter will discuss the goals and rationale of diversion programs, including differences between jail and prison diversion and between programs designed to divert offenders from incarceration at sentencing (front-end programs) and programs designed to divert people from prolonged jail or prison stays after they have been incarcerated (back-end programs). The next section will describe some of the most commonly implemented front-end diversion programs: alternative-to-incarceration programs, problem-solving courts, and boot camps. The final section will summarize the policy issues associated with diversionary programs.

THE CONTEXT AND GOALS OF DIVERSION: PUNITIVE ALTERNATIVES TO IMPRISONMENT

The question of how best to respond to violations of the law has occupied societies for centuries. The challenge is to satisfy the desire for retribution while avoiding the excesses of revenge and to increase social order, preferably by convincing people not to commit future crimes (deterrence). Banishment, corporal punishment, fines, imprisonment, and rehabilitation have all been used and debated, and in the United States and elsewhere all these methods remain in use, although we commonly avoid discussion of the first two (Garland, 1990; Harris, 1985; Ignatieff, 1981).

Diversion first developed in the late 19th century in response to concerns that incarceration was inappropriate and counterproductive for youth who were being arrested, prosecuted, and punished without recognition of their special status as children. As "child saving," diversion programs provided alternatives to "Jim Crow juvenile justice" that nonetheless provided social control, often targeting black youth in particular (Ward, 2009). Alternative punishments emerged as a means of sanctioning children who committed crimes while avoiding the damaging effects of being incarcerated with adults and in the same way as adults (Feld, 1998; Zimmering, 1998). Diversion was intended to "do good by doing less harm," avoiding the corrupting impact of incarceration on youth sanctioned for committing a crime or, later, for status offenses, the noncriminal acts such as truancy that could land juveniles in custody. This goal of reducing harm has sometimes been coupled with the interventionist goal of rehabilitation, but the two are distinct and possibly in opposition (Zimmering, 2000).[1]

Diversion programs may have different goals and different government stakeholders who are interested in them. Correspondingly, these programs vary with regard to when they are used (at what point in criminal case processing) and who is eligible to enter them. The stage of case processing and eligibility criteria complement the goals of the specific program and reflect the concerns of the local or state government that provides financial and structural support. Three significant issues for diversion programs are considered in this section: the stage of case processing at which the program operates, diversion program goals, and diversion program impacts on public safety. At the end of the chapter these issues are revisited in light of their policy implications.

The Stages of Case Processing

Once a person is arrested, there are multiple points at which he or she may be offered a diversion program. The broadest distinction is whether the diversion is offered before trial as an alternative sentence or offered after a sentence has been imposed and partially served. Much of this volume is devoted to the latter variation, sometimes called back-end programs, which divert incarcerated offenders from a portion of their sentence. This chapter focuses on front-end programs that typically require defendants to plead guilty to a criminal charge and agree to complete a program in lieu of incarceration.

Participation in front-end diversion programs is most often negotiated as a condition of a deferred sentence, with the understanding that the guilty plea will be voided and the charges will be dropped (or in some cases lessened to a lower charge) upon successful program completion. As part of the pretrial agreement, the defendant admits guilt for a specific charge that carries a stated term of incarceration. However, the judge holds the custodial sentence in abeyance, permitting the offender to attend the diversion program. The defendant agrees that if he or she fails to complete the program, he or she will be punished by having to serve the stated term of incarceration. In negotiating such plea agreements, some prosecutors and judges insist that defendants plead guilty to charges that carry lengthier sentences than the charges they would offer absent the diversion alternative. They believe the harsher sentence motivates defendants to remain law-abiding while attending the program. If the offender completes the program successfully, the court may void the original guilty plea. At that point, the judge will either dismiss the case or permit the offender to plead guilty to a lesser offense with a sentence of time served or probation.

In addition to the deferred sentence, judges typically have two less common mechanisms for placing offenders in programs. First, a judge may order placement as part of a sentence. This might be common practice if not for the fact that many felony charges carry mandatory prison sentences; state legislatures have made laws restricting judicial discretion. Even in states that do not mandate incarceration for certain types of offenses, sentencing guidelines may put political pressure on judges to adhere to recommended jail and prison specifications. To sentence a defendant to a diversion program directly, when the defendant is charged with a crime that typically carries a jail or prison term, the judge would need the prosecutor to reduce the charge or otherwise permit a noncustodial sentence. Second, a judge may order a defendant into a diversion program as a condition of release from detention even before the defendant has entered a plea. This might occur if the prosecutor is insisting on a plea to high-level felony. The judge could release the defendant, mandate program attendance, and adjourn the case for several months. In this way, the judge would hope to show the prosecutor that the defendant is suitable for program placement instead of incarceration and convince the prosecutor to accept a plea to a lesser charge.

Diversion Program Goals

The two aims of diversion are to divert offenders from the harms of incarceration and toward rehabilitative interventions designed to change the behavior (and often the character) of the offender. Community-based interventions promise to produce better outcomes than traditional incarceration because they prevent the prison culture from derailing the rehabilitation process (Natarajan & Falkin, 1997). To varying degrees, incarcerated offenders become socialized to the inmate subculture that values solidarity among fellow inmates and resists official correctional goals (Sykes & Messinger, 1960). The threat of peer violence and the deprivation of basic needs also force many inmates to seek protection and privileges through gang affiliation. This climate is not conducive to effective rehabilitative treatment. More recent scholarship reveals that the removal of able bodies from disadvantaged neighborhoods further exacerbates familial stresses, destroys social ties, and deteriorates the socioeconomic fabric of the community (Clear, 2007; Pager, 2007). The continued reliance on mass incarceration will further reduce the ability of inner cities to support the reentry of returning ex-offenders unless an effort to expand the use of alternatives to incarceration is sustained.

Although the goals of diversion from incarceration and treatment in the community are similarly cast as alternatives to simple (i.e., nontherapeutic) incarceration, they differ from each other in important ways, including their measures of success. Straight diversion programs, such as those that seek to reduce prison overcrowding or those that seek to spare youth from the damaging experiences of the adult criminal justice system, have a corresponding goal: to reduce the use of incarceration. That goal can be measured in terms of sentencing patterns for various offenses (Belenko, Schiff, Phillips, & Winterfield, 1994). However, diversion programs that also seek to change offender behavior, called interventionist programs, have additional goals beyond the negative impacts of incarceration and reductions in system costs. Specifically, interventionist program goals include reducing problematic behavior such as drug use, out-of-marriage pregnancy, and vagrancy and reducing illegal activity or recidivism (Mears, Winterfield, Hunsake, Moore, & White, 2003). To measure the impact of these interventionist efforts, researchers must track and monitor offenders over time to assess whether they use drugs or gain and keep jobs, for example, and whether they are arrested for new crimes. Most current programs that are labeled as diversion programs are interventionist in their orientation. This reflects both program administrators' interest in rehabilitation and policymakers' interest in maintaining public safety while avoiding the perception that they are soft on crime (Porter, 2002; Tonry, 1996).

Because of the overwhelming interventionist trend, diversion programs that target jail-bound defendants overwhelmingly seek to rehabilitate them. Diversion programs can be divided by severity of the offense and of the likely punishment. Less severe crimes, especially misdemeanors, are more likely to meet eligibility criteria for straight diversion programs, that is, those with little or no focus on rehabilitation or reducing recidivism. This is because judges and prosecutors are more likely to release an offender perceived as posing a low risk to communities than to release an offender with a dangerous record into a diversion program without assurances that the program will change behavior and reduce the risk of reoffending. For example, if a judge uses community service instead of simple time served (in a jail or other detention facility before arraignment) to punish a person accused of shoplifting lipstick, the person has no greater chance to reoffend, so the judge is taking little risk because the person would probably be sentenced to no additional jail time (incapacitation) absent the community service. Unfortunately, this type of diversion is used for offenses that are not likely to lead to jail sentences because they are so minor, so there is no diversion in the true sense of the term. Under the guise of diversion, many alternative sentences do not divert offenders from incarceration; they are simply alternative punishments that seek therapeutic or restorative results as well as retribution. This phenomenon, sometimes called net widen-ing, has been both criticized as unnecessarily increasing the reach of the crimi-nal justice system and lauded as effectively addressing minor offending without increasing costs (Belenko et al., 1994; Fagan & Malkin, 2003; Macallair & Roche, 2001; Svirdoff, Rottman, Weidner, & Curtis, 2000; Thompson, 2002).

More severe crimes, including more serious misdemeanors and some felony offenses, meet the eligibility criteria for most interventionist diversion pro-grams, and it is these programs that may truly divert offenders from jail, and sometimes from prison.[2] In the United States very serious offenses, such as vio-lent crimes, are almost never eligible for diversion programs. Other societies have used diversion for violent crimes and indeed for the most serious crimes, such as the Truth and Reconciliation Commission that addressed the mass atrocities committed under the racist apartheid regime in South Africa (Gibson, 2006; Skelton, 2002). Because of the concern that offenders placed in diversion programs could commit serious new offenses while in those programs, prose-cutors, judges, and policymakers are anxious to establish that programs pro-viding therapeutic mandates also monitor their participants and report back to the sentencing judge about individual compliance and progress. All the pro-grams discussed in the next section fit this interventionist model, which seeks rehabilitation while incorporating a strong monitoring component.

The interventionist model of diversion programs was the perfect setup for the "what works?" and "nothing works" literature of the end of the 20th century (Andrews et al., 1990; Austin & Irwin, 1993; Martinson, 1974; Petersilia, 1999; Sherman et al., 1998; Taxman, 1999; and, more recently, MacKenzie, 2006). Those who evaluate these programs look for the same signs of effect: Does behavior change for the better? Do program participants stop using drugs, stay married, pay child support, keep a job, and stop committing crime? Treatment used in diversion programs may last for months or years, but these interven-tionist programs are all used in the hope that they will decrease recidivism.

Does this make sense? As discussed in detail in other chapters, offenders typically have a range of problems in addition to their apparent willingness to break the law. Typically they have less education, fewer job skills, fewer social and economic resources, poorer physical and mental health, and weaker fam-ily ties than people who do not break the law. Once they complete their sen-tence they probably have one more disadvantage: a criminal record. It is a tall order indeed to expect that people who enter or even complete a diversion program will translate that achievement into lifetime change. And yet that is what happens for some program participants: generally between 20% and 70% of people who complete these programs (this figure varies depending on program length, content, eligibility, implementation, and individual characteristics such as readiness for treatment and perceived legal pressure) (Ward, Day, Howells, & Birgden, 2004; Young, 2002). The percentage of program participants who remain arrest-free after program completion is smaller, but here there has been some success (Belenko, Foltz, Lang, & Sung, 2004; Government Accountability Office [GAO], 2005). The GAO analyzed 23 evaluations of adult drug court programs and found that across studies, the recidivism rates among drug court program participants were generally between 10 and 30 percentage points lower than those of the comparison groups. The GAO also reported that recidivism reductions occurred for drug court participants who had committed different types of offenses. However, when multiple needs are present, even diversion programs may fall short of delivering significant and lasting gains. A recent review of 27 intensive case management–based jail diversion programs for serious mentally ill offenders concluded that although community-based intensive case management seems to offer a greater chance of reducing rearrests and reincarcerations, diversion per se is probably not enough to keep many of these people off their criminal paths (Loveland & Boyle, 2007).

A key problem is that some participants of diversion programs—indeed most—probably do not reduce their criminal activity after community-based intervention. The interventionist model looks for a linear relationship between therapeutic intervention and behavior change. Because behavior (such as crime) depends on many factors, holding interventionist programs accountable for participants' behavior during the period of attendance—to say nothing of the post-program period—is as much wishful thinking as it is evidence-based science.

Diversion Program Impacts on Public Safety

A central concern of any diversion program is ensuring participant eligibility and screening out people who present an unacceptable risk of reoffending. No judge, prosecutor, or policymaker wants to be the one who lets a convicted offender out of jail if that offender goes on to commit a high-profile crime. In truth this almost never happens, but the possibility that a participant in a diversion program could commit a horrible crime such as murder carries great power in judicial policymaking. Public safety is a hypothetical concern in many respects, but it is one that dominates decisions about diversion sentences.

Judges are often on their own in determining when to use diversion programs. Few refer to any particular policy that guides deterrence decision making or report any significant discussion among peers about the process of assessing risk to public safety or a defendant's potential success in treatment. Few judges and almost no prosecutors interviewed in a 4-year study of alternatives to incarceration in New York expressed strong views about the effectiveness of specific programs in reaching and rehabilitating offenders. Preferences, if they exist for judges and prosecutors, typically reflect personal familiarity with the representatives of those programs (Porter, 2002).

Nevertheless, judges and prosecutors often use common language to describe defendants whom they are not likely to place in a diversion program. Because their primary concern is that offenders placed in diversion might threaten public safety (or under the glare of media attention could be perceived as a threat to public safety), they are likely to exclude defendants whose charges include violence or the use of weapons. They are much less likely to offer program placement to repeat felony offenders or to those with violent histories. Some prosecutors and judges report that they are less likely to offer placement to those with histories of absconding or violating probation or parole. Prosecutors in particular are less likely to agree to a diversion program for an offense they believe has great public visibility, such as a drug crime near a school, drug dealing in a grocery, or any offense in a community that has been complaining about similar offenses. Yet research suggests that public safety and criminal history are not always aligned. In an analysis of a ground-breaking drug treatment program for serious felony offenders initiated by the district attorney in Brooklyn, New York, researchers found that recidivism could be controlled even when these offenders were placed in community-based treatment programs (Dynia & Sung, 2000; Young, Fluellen, & Belenko, 2004). Some prosecutors and many judges are more willing to use diversions when the defendant appears to have committed the offense under the influence of illegal substances or to support an addiction. Prosecutors might consent to a charge reduction in order to avoid going to trial, especially when they want to protect a witness or when the evidence against the defendant is weak (Tonry & Lynch, 1996).

Generally, policymakers see nonresidential diversion programs as less secure and posing greater risks to public safety. Offenders in these programs are likely to reside in the same communities where they have obtained drugs and committed crimes in the past. Residential program settings are also often preferred because they are perceived as more punitive. Terms such as *difficult, rigorous,* and *intensive* are used to describe the regimen of residential therapeutic communities; these programs usually require participant stays of a year or more, which some liken to a jail sentence. Some research has found that judges and prosecutors with extended exposure to outpatient treatment, such as those who work in drug courts, are more willing to endorse nonresidential programs (National Institute of Justice, 2006). The intertwined roles of treatment and supervision continue to influence the structure and use of diversion programs, requiring compromise and leaps of faith from policymakers, court actors, and service providers alike.

DIVERSION PROGRAM DESCRIPTIONS

This section describes three of the most common forms of diversion programs. The first is independent alternatives to incarceration (ATIs), including such national programs as Treatment Alternatives to Street Crime (TASC) and Drug Treatment Alternative to Prison (DTAP). Then it describes drug courts, the effort at systemic change in case processing that started about 20 years ago in Miami and has become a national effort. Finally we describe boot camps, the demanding semi-prisons designed to provide a quick and unforgiving combination of punishment and therapy.

Alternatives to Incarceration

ATI programs provide therapeutic or other constructive programming (e.g., job training) and supervision for offenders who are placed in the ATI by a judge. They may be residential or day programs and may require full-time or part-time activities. They typically have both clinical and nonclinical staff and work to address participants' needs, as determined in extensive assessments conducted shortly after program entry. Unlike some other intermediate sanctions, ATIs try to admit only defendants who would otherwise be incarcerated. ATIs can be individual programs working with their own representatives in the courts individually or in coordinated alliances of programs. Or they can be coordinated by agencies such as TASC that act as liaisons or brokers between an array of treatment providers and the court, which works best when the courts can maintain significant legal jeopardy (i.e., for people convicted of serious offenses facing incarceration sentences) (Anglin et al., 1996). ATIs can also be operated by prosecutors, who often have the greatest control over eligibility because sentencing mandates and plea negotiations are determined largely by prosecutorial decisions. In both cases the treatment providers or the treatment liaisons must rely on word of mouth among defense attorneys and sympathetic judges to get cases. Judges rarely systemically seek out these diversion programs, and their use is never systematic across judges. ATIs are never a local policy that can be relied on for all cases of a specified eligibility.

Some have promoted ATIs as less expensive than jail but still punitive, depriving offenders of their freedom at least during program hours. Others have emphasized the value of the services ATIs provide to a needy population that would otherwise repeat a cycle of crime and incarceration. By offering drug treatment, literacy classes, family counseling, and employment training, ATI programs might change the circumstances and improve the skills of participants and in so doing may reduce the likelihood that they will commit crimes again. Still others more modestly assert that by dealing with offenders out of jail, the ATIs can at least avoid disrupting the positive roles participants play in their families and communities, roles such as parenting or supporting others through legitimate employment. Several of these uses of ATIs are similar to the goals of other intermediate sanctions, such as drug courts and probation alternatives.

In design, ATI programs fulfill all these purposes. They maintain their punitive elements by holding participants accountable for absences and misconduct. They monitor costs to keep ATIs less expensive than incarceration—not as easy as it seems if a 12-month treatment program replaces a 2- or 3-month jail sentence and if those who fail midcourse are returned to jail for longer than the jail sentence they would have received otherwise. They deliver treatment and social services to address the wide range of problems that may contribute to future offending while preserving the positive roles of their participants in families and communities. In practice, however, these purposes sometimes conflict, and program operators must balance punishment and treatment while staying within their budgets and meeting their contractual targets for enrollments and successful completions. Moreover, the program operators strike this balance differently over time, as one purpose or another becomes more important to the system as a whole.

Judges in most states are not required by legislation or sentencing guidelines, nor are they encouraged, to send offenders to ATI programs. In the absence of such formal encouragement, budget and justice officials have few mechanisms to shift large numbers of offenders away from jail sentences, even if the alternative sentences save money and reduce crime. These officials may try to promote alternative sentences publicly and privately, but the use of alternative programs is left to the initiative of individual judges, prosecutors, or defense lawyers. In this regard ATIs are dramatically different from the drug courts discussed next, and because of the difference, ATIs process many fewer cases.

Box 6.1   Diversion Programs in New York

Between 1967, when the first diversion program in New York opened, and the early 1980s New York was dotted with small programs offering judges a treatment option instead of incarceration. These programs were independent and not coordinated, and the city had no real system of alternatives to incarceration (ATC). New York State's Alternatives to Incarceration Act of 1984 brought increased funding and government management to this array of experiments. The act provided funds for programs that diverted convicted offenders from jail terms of at least 180 days. While experimentation continued with other private and public funds, the 1984 act created a dedicated funding stream that continues to support New York City's ATI system to this day. The act came in the middle of the largest expansion of jail and prison capacity in New York State history. The rhetoric of rehabilitation had been largely abandoned, leaving punishment for crime as an end in itself and rapidly growing in popularity. Between 1980 and 1990, for example, the New York City Department of Correction increased its spending on the city's jails by more than 450% (Porter, Lee, & Lutz, 2002). In this context, ATI program operators emphasized their role in diverting offenders who would otherwise go to jail or prison. At the same time, the ATIs responded to some judges' and prosecutors' frustration with their limited sentencing options.

By the time New York City's ATI system was restructured in 1997 to divert offenders from jails and prisons more effectively, the pressure to do so was waning. The population in New York City's jails had declined, and corrections officials found themselves more focused on long-term population maintenance than on rapid construction. At the same time, interest in treatment to reduce future offending was revived because information about the effectiveness of drug treatment and the growth of problem-solving courts focused policymakers on such options as anger management, batterer treatment, and cognitive–behavioral therapies for various antisocial behaviors—although not all these treatments were demonstrated to work. Additionally, the much-lauded Drug Treament Alternative to Prison program, which successfully (Belenko et al., 2004; Dynia & Sung, 2000) diverted second-time felony offenders to lengthy residential drug treatment instead of certain prison terms, has spurred interest in a wide range of treatment regimens to match the therapeutic needs and the criminal profile (essentially the current crime coupled with criminal history) of offenders entering the criminal justice system.

(Continued)

(Continued)

The diversion system in New York City differs from that of other localities nationwide in at least three ways. First, its programs are more carefully targeted than most alternative sentences in the United States, typically screening offenders to maximize the chance that the programs admit only those genuinely bound for jail or prison. Defendants whose charges carry potential jail time but who are likely to receive only probation are screened out. Second, diversion in New York emphasizes treatment and on-site supervision as opposed to around-the-clock surveillance, avoiding such devices as electronic bracelets. Programs typically target specific populations, such as substance abusers, women, or youth. Third, the city does not rely on the government's probation or corrections department but has a wide array of nonprofit organizations that are fluent in the dual responsibilities of treatment and supervision.

Drug Courts and Other Problem-Solving Models

In 1989 the first drug court opened in Miami. It was designed to institutionalize and standardize the potentially coercive element of the criminal court to encourage defendants to enter drug treatment. The court model reflected the consternation among some court actors that a revolving door of drug use, arrest, sentencing, and release did little to reduce drug use or the crime associated with drug use. The drug court model was to place offenders in treatment in exchange for a lesser or no conviction and monitor their compliance through regular communication between therapeutic (drug treatment) staff and the judge and between the judge and the offender (Casey & Rottman, 2000; Drug Courts Program Office, 1997).

More than any other alternative sanction, the drug court model has been absorbed into mainstream sentencing across the United States: Today there are more than 2,100 drug courts. The drug court model has been used to develop courts addressing other problems seen as underlying criminal offending, such as mental health courts, domestic violence courts, and prison reentry courts. Where alternatives to incarceration rely on individual program recognition by individual judges, the problem-solving model includes an extensive planning phase that results in specific eligibility, plea mechanism, and legal jeopardy criteria before the court begins hearing cases. Once a jurisdiction opens a drug court, all eligible cases should go through that court and should be assigned therapeutic alternatives instead of jail or prison.

Drug courts use the coercive power of the judge and of a jail sentence in the event of failure to complete the program to place defendants in drug treatment and monitor them until they complete treatment. In this regard they are very much like the ATIs, TASC, and DTAP programs discussed earlier. Also like these programs, drug courts try to address the broader needs of defendants and try to place them in treatment that works for them. To maintain this kind of flexibility, drug courts have successfully institutionalized four components: a court coordinator, a network of treatment providers, graduated sanctions (and rewards), and a data system to track participant behavior.

The court coordinator is the resource to the judge in a drug court who makes sure that each participant is assessed, placed in appropriate treatment, and tracked weekly (or more often) for treatment attendance and behavior compliance including drug testing. The coordinator ensures that the reports about the participant are delivered regularly to the judge and that those reports are reliable. It would be difficult or impossible for a judge to manage a case-load of any significance without a coordinator, so this person plays a key role in maintaining a drug court, but it is a full-time job. Drug treatment (as discussed in chapter 7) can be delivered through various models ranging from 12-step programs that are entirely volunteer run (e.g., Alcoholics Anonymous) to 2-year residential treatment programs. Ideally drug courts have multiple treatment options from which to choose in order to retain a participant whose addiction is too great for a low-intensity treatment model, for example, or a participant who is too independent and high functioning to do well in a residential program with many restrictions. However, developing a network of programs can be challenging. Not all communities have a range of treatment programs; not all treatment programs have been tested or evaluated, and their models may be ineffective; and not all treatment programs are as devoted to public health and public safety as they are to making money (in this case through government contracts). For these reasons, the court coordinator should regularly monitor and meet with treatment providers to assess their commitment, capacity, and efficacy.

Drug courts emphasize the accountability of participants (Longshore et al., 2001; Porter, in press; Rossman, Zweig, & Roman, 2008), and to do so they promise an elaborate system of mandates, sanctions, and rewards. Participants report back to the judge weekly, and the judge confronts those who skip a therapy session, drug testing, or other mandate. Unless the participant can provide a compelling (to the judge) reason for the poor attendance, she or he is sanctioned, perhaps by having to write an essay, perhaps spending the day in court observing proceedings, or perhaps, for more serious or repeated failures to comply, a short jail stay. These sanctions are complemented by rewards that are typically less tangible—applause or congratulations from the judge, for example—but are similarly intended to sustain compliance. Indeed, many evaluations of drug courts include descriptions of participants who have never had positive interactions with authority before being spoken with and congratulated by a drug court judge, and this type of positive interaction may be one of the most striking and innovative elements of drug courts, although it is unrelated to the concept of diversion.

Finally, drug courts maintain data systems that allow them to track participants quickly and easily. Data are a critical element of any program that claims an interventionist or diversionary purpose. This is because only by tracking participant activities, mandates, and sanctions over time can a court claim to understand any impact it has on participant outcomes such as drug use and recidivism and on court and jail expenditures. Without an electronic monitoring system these outcomes would have to be tallied individually, and no court has the money, time, or staff to do that kind of detailed data collection (Rempel, 2005; SEARCH, 2003).

More than any other diversion effort, drug courts are focused on system change, and the planning for these courts ideally involves all court stakeholders (i.e., judges, prosecutors, defense attorneys, and service providers or community representatives) so that their design includes systemic impact, not just impact on individual cases. At the same time, in order to achieve comprehensive eligibility, drug courts require collaboration between prosecutors and the judiciary, a partnership that is uncommon in criminal case processing. Because the prosecutor's office agrees to eligibility criteria before the drug court hears cases, there is a strong pull away from more serious cases such as crimes classified as violent (which may or may not involve actual violence) and other crimes that the prosecutor refuses to include, such as crimes that take place near a school. Consequently, although drug courts have shown terrific success in developing a model that affects more cases than TASC or other ATIs (Huddleston, Freeman-Wilson, Marlowe, & Roussell, 2005), it is likely that the minority of these cases would be destined for jail or prison sentences absent the drug court. In other words, drug courts' dominance has buried the issue of net widening and significantly complicated the question of diversion. As interventions, the research literature suggests that drug courts have been effective in reducing recidivism (GAO, 2005), but researchers have yet to examine the extent to which these courts truly divert offenders from any incarceration, much less from state prison (Porter, 2001).

Box 6.2	**Gender Disparities?**

Increases in the numbers of girls and women entering the criminal justice system are a cause for concern. Indeed, the rate of growth for female arrestees is significantly higher than for males. It is important to note that the actual numbers of girls and women in the criminal justice system are much smaller than the numbers of boys and men, which is why small numeric increases can yield very large percentage increases. That said, the criminal justice system was designed largely for male defendants, and diversions are similarly focused on boys and men. A study by the American Bar Association and the National Bar Association (2001) found that girls were more often ineligible for alternative sentencing programs and that those programs were designed for boys and did not adequately address girls' needs. Social assumptions about women and girls may affect how they are treated by police, judges, prosecutors, and corrections officials (Chesney-Lind & Sheldon, 1998).

At the same time, there is evidence that women and girls receive greater leniency throughout the criminal justice process, from arrest through sentencing (Farrell, 2001), with some research suggesting that the disparity may be attributable largely to women with dependent children (Koons-Witt, 2002). Although much research is still needed to examine the nuances of gender and criminal case processing, and existing research suggests that findings vary with race, the literature suggests that breaking out defendants by gender may privilege a small minority of offenders (i.e., girls and women) and wrongly—if unintentionally—focus attention away from concerns about lifestyle and family that affect boys and men.

Boot Camps

Boot camps are militaristic short-term incapacitation programs that originated in 1983 in Georgia and Oklahoma. They became increasingly popular throughout the 1980s and 1990s and operate now for both juveniles and adults and in federal, state, and local jurisdictions (MacKenzie, 2006).

In general, they feature a rigid daily routine emphasizing physical activity. However, there is variation between the programs in regard to their emphasis on rehabilitation and aftercare. There are three generations of boot camps, the earliest of which (e.g., "Scared Straight" or shock incarceration programs) followed a military model of early rising, a long day of activity, strict restrictions, physical activity as punishment, and a graduation ceremony upon completion of the program (Parent, 2003). The goal of these programs is learned strict social control to decrease recidivism. The second generation maintains the rigid structure but incorporates rehabilitation into daily program content through programs such as drug treatment and educational services. This style of boot camp also uses intensive supervision, largely as a response to concerns about public safety. The third generation sought to further advance the public safety and rehabilitation components by including an aftercare component that mandated therapeutic contact with the offender after release.

Because of the differences in implementation between boot camps and methodological issues, evaluating their overall impact on recidivism has been difficult. Wilson, MacKenzie, and Mitchell (2005) conducted a meta-analysis of boot camps. Of the 43 studies reviewed, most were plagued with methodological flaws and did not reveal any significant difference, and those that were significant did not yield consistent results or indicate that boot camps affected recidivism.

The lack of methodological rigor and inconclusive results were echoed in another study by MacKenzie (2006) that reviewed 14 studies of boot camps for adults and 17 studies of boot camps for youth. She found no conclusive evidence that boot camps have a significant impact on recidivism. However, MacKenzie suggests that adult aftercare may be a promising program component that warrants further investigation.

More recent studies, such as Wells, Minor, Angel, and Stearman (2006) and Kurlycheck and Kempinen (2006), using quasi-experimental methods, have found a reduction in recidivism associated with boot camp programs with an aftercare component. MacKenzie, Bierie, and Mitchell (2007) conducted an experiment with random assignment on a therapeutic boot camp in Maryland and found that boot camp graduates were significantly less likely to reoffend. However, other recent research has not yielded such positive findings. Duwe and Kerschner (2008) found that Minnesota's Challenge Incarceration Program (which includes aftercare) did not affect recidivism rates, although it did affect time to reoffending.

The popularity of boot camps has declined because of the disappointing findings about their effectiveness, movement away from their original ideological focus on discipline and punishment, and concern that they recklessly endanger the well-being of participants (Cullen, 2005; MacKenzie & Armstrong, 2004; Simon, 1995). Although they arose to fulfill the desire to be tough on crime and reduce prison overcrowding, there is little evidence that boot camps are effective at reducing recidivism (Cullen, 2005; Duwe & Kerschner, 2008).

Program Impact

Do these diversion programs work? They can be evaluated in at least three distinct categories (which can also be used in combination): diversions intended to keep people out of jail or prison because of the harms and costs associated with the latter, diversions intended to respond to the underlying causes of criminal offending through therapeutic and behavioral interventions, and diversions intended to demonstrate public accountability for huge court caseloads and swelling prison and jail populations. ATIs, drug courts, and boot camps each satisfy some of the standards suggested in these models and fail to satisfy others. If a diversion engages in net widening, then it fails the first set of goals. If a diversion addresses and engages with participant problems, it may succeed in the second. If a diversion program maintains low recidivism rates—even if it engages in net widening—it may succeed in the third, which is also the most common measure of success for these programs.

Table 6.1 provides a sample of findings from studies looking at various diversion programs. All these studies use recidivism as a principal measure for two reasons. First, court stakeholders and policymakers are eager to demonstrate accountability of programs that release convicted offenders. Second, recidivism, especially when measured by conviction data, is by far the easiest indicator of success or failure for researchers to capture, given the challenges of tracking participants in diversion programs. These studies suggest that diversion programs yield recidivism rates that are equal to or lower than those of comparison or control groups who did not receive alternative sentences. The exception is the research on boot camps that indicates that recidivism may be higher (in some but not all studies) and that participants may face unacceptable risk and insult in these programs.

It is certainly important to know whether people who enter diversion programs continue to use drugs, maintain jobs, seek family contact, and so on; all of these fit squarely with the goal of rehabilitation. Equally important is whether the diversion programs provide coherent and consistent models of service delivery. But because everything other than recidivism is difficult to measure, there is almost no information about the efficacy of programs that seek to rehabilitate offenders, even though that goal is central to most diversion programs. A significant body of literature examines whether diversions can be successful as coerced treatment and explores the question of internal versus external motivation to abstain from drug use. It generally concludes that even without internal motivation, coerced treatment can be effective (Farabee, Prendergast, & Anglin, 1998).

Table 6.1 Recidivism Findings From Key Studies of Diversion Impact

Study	Location	Main Finding
Porter (2001)	New York	Coordinated city-wide ATI initiative showed little evidence of reduced recidivism but no increased risk to public safety and mixed results for other outcomes.
Anglin et al. (1996)	National	Monitored treatment is more likely to reduce recidivism and drug use among serious offenders than among those facing less legal jeopardy.
Belenko et al. (2004)	New York	Prosecutor-controlled diversion for serious, repeat felony offenders showed significant reduction in recidivism.
GAO (2005)	National	Drug courts show strong evidence of reduced recidivism during program participation and mixed results for other outcomes and post-program.
Harrel & Roman (2001)	Washington, DC	Alternative sentencing was found to significantly reduce recidivism and drug use both during and after program participation for serious felony offenders.
MacKenzie & Armstrong (2004)	National	Boot camps fail to reduce recidivism or demonstrate positive outcomes when not coupled with therapeutic aftercare.

POLICY ISSUES IN DIVERSION PROGRAMS

Diversion programs present several challenges to policymakers interested in expanding alternatives to incarceration. To conclude, we address three of the most salient challenges. First, how can diversion programs be used at sentencing to greatest effect? Second, what contradictions arise when treatment is used as punishment? Third, what are reasonable expectations by which to evaluate the performance of these alternatives in terms of rehabilitation and public safety?

Systemic Implementation

The United States maintains a decentralized criminal justice system that is rife with contradictions. Although crimes are nationally specified—for example, it is illegal to sell cocaine anywhere in the country—the severity of each crime varies by state. Consequently, punishments are not consistent across states, so the crime that leads to incarceration in Indiana may result in straight probation in Illinois. In addition to this fundamental challenge to our conception of justice, most states do not have centralized court systems, so each county and even each judge may apply the law differently. In this context diversion programs may be destined to remain boutique options, never able to reach the number of cases that would make them sustainable for all eligible cases.

To maximize the number of cases sentenced to alternatives, policymakers behind the drug court movement realized that they would have to develop sustained cooperation between court stakeholders. These stakeholders include the judiciary, defense and prosecuting attorney agencies, clinicians and other service providers, government, and other funders and political operatives. Because drug courts gain widespread collaboration in how cases are processed, they can reasonably attempt to screen all eligible cases for program entry. An independent ATI or even a state-run boot camp has much less assurance that all eligible cases will be screened for diversion because unlike drug courts these diversion programs maintain no central screening, so the mechanisms of case placement and management do not exist.

But drug courts run into another problem that limits their impact. With drug courts the weakest link in the collaboration has been public defenders, who remain skeptical about the value of treatment programs that make significant demands on their clients, threaten severe punishments if their clients fail to complete the program, and may be more onerous over time for clients than sentences that do not include diversion, even when those sentences would be brief jail terms. If defense attorneys or prosecutors do not want serious criminal offenders in their programs, they will tend toward net widening.

In order to understand why the concerns of the defense attorney undermine diversion goals, it is important to recognize the central role of plea bargaining in disposing of criminal cases in this country. More than 95% of all criminal cases are disposed of through plea bargaining, an astounding number given that the right to trial (which is waived in plea negotiations) is protected in the Bill of Rights of the Constitution. In plea negotiations the prosecutor offers the defendant a specific sentence if the defendant is willing to plead guilty. The plea negotiations may continue right up to trial, but the sentence first offered by the prosecutor is generally the most lenient. As the defendant refuses plea offers, they typically become more severe. In other words, the prosecution has more control in the plea process unless the defense decides to go to trial. Diversion programs, especially drug courts, attempt to circumvent the plea process by offering treatment programs as close to arraignment as possible. Before they will agree to pleas into diversion programs, defense attorneys must believe that their clients will not be punished excessively for failure. Defense attorneys may reasonably anticipate failure in a diversion program because the programs have such a strong monitoring component (also known as intensive supervision), so the same unwise or illegal behavior is more likely to be detected during the program than if the offender is on probation alone, has served a brief jail sentence, or has been released from prison. For people accused of lower-level crimes with less at stake in terms of legal jeopardy (the sentence upon a finding of guilt) this risk is not great; for people accused of more serious crimes who face more incarceration, defense attorneys may be more motivated to go to trial and less willing to take a diversion program that they think their client is likely to fail.

Treatment as Punishment

Many diversion programs respond to the perception that drug abuse or other chronic problems lead to offending. This perception is based largely on a desire to fix the problem of crime by finding the source of crime. Therefore, it is perfectly suited to the interventionist inclination of policymakers who support diversion. At the same time, treatment satisfies the mandate to punish by requiring the offender to participate. There is some consensus that mandated treatment may be as effective as—and perhaps more effective than—voluntary treatment (Young, 2002). But the mechanisms of treatment remain poorly researched and poorly understood. There is little accountability regarding the content of treatment (predictably, because courts are not run by clinicians), so rigorous examination of treatment content and coherence is unlikely. There is also the chance that mandated treatment is helpful only to those who want treatment. If motivation is central, then linking treatment to the criminal justice system becomes a way to get people who want treatment and are arrested into treatment that they could not get if they had not been arrested. In that case, court-mandated treatment becomes a segregated form of health care in which some people (who obey the law or who can afford it) get treatment through civilian channels and others (who cannot afford care and break the law) get it through threat of imprisonment. Logistically this opposition may not present a significant obstacle to treatment as diversion, but ethically and within our moral political philosophy it may.

Some treatment, such as treatment for batterers sentenced in domestic violence courts, is used primarily for its monitoring capacity, with little or no expectation that it will change behavior (Davis, Taylor, & Maxwell, 2000; National Institute of Justice, 2003). In this case the content and quality of treatment are secondary at best, usurped in primacy by the responsiveness of the treatment provider to the court. Without a clear understanding of the purpose of treatment, diversion programs may attempt to serve different goals for different stakeholders and end up not meeting anyone's expectations. Specifically, treatment programs that focus on responding to the court's ideas of participant accountability and clinical progress may be pressured toward a treatment model that does not make clinical sense, sets unreasonable expectations, or just doesn't work over time. The larger threat associated with these concerns is that the cultural understanding of treatment is distorted and weakened.

Perhaps most at risk for this type of confusion are the drug courts and other problem-solving courts for two reasons. First, judges and other court staff are encouraged to make decisions about clinical matters by keeping a participant in specific programming and, more overtly, by speaking to and often lecturing a participant about the therapeutic process. Second, these programs provide a market for treatment, with a steady demand and stable funding. Because some treatment is provided as a for-profit endeavor, and even nonprofit programs are pushed to maintain or increase their budgetary obligations, there is a powerful incentive to approach the partnership between treatment and the courts as a relationship between business partners in which the court is a client of the treatment program. This relationship could be benign or beneficial, but it also diverts the focus from program participants. In using treatment as a punishment, judges, prosecutors, and policymakers run the risk that the image of rehabilitation overwhelms its practice.

Evaluation Standards and Public Safety

Finally, policymakers considering diversion programs must carefully assess expectations for these programs and their interventionist goals. It is critical that courts using diversion sentences measure the results of their efforts, but how those results are conceptualized in large parts determines whether these programs are considered successful and whether they are expanded and replicated. There are several ways to measure the impact of diversion programs. From a noninterventionist perspective they can be measured using standard indicators of court processing:

- How many cases are disposed using diversions?
- What are the arrest (or arraignment) and conviction charges of people found eligible for program entry? Of those who actually enter the program (compared with those found eligible who choose not to enter the program)?

- How long does case disposition take from arrest to case end? This can be broken down to look at arrest to arraignment time, total time incarcerated (detention plus all jail or prison time), time in program, and so on.
- How many offenders are deemed ineligible?
- How many participants complete their programs?
- How many participants are arrested while in diversion programs? (This indicator is noninterventionist as a measure of a program's capacity to monitor and control participant behavior.)

All of these are useful indicators to reveal whether diversion programs are reducing jail and prison use and to assess their impact on case processing.

But these indicators do not assess program success in meeting interventionist goals for diversion. Broadly, there are two goals of intervention, rehabilitation and public safety, each of which can be assessed too leniently or too severely. Offender rehabilitation seeks improvement in social functioning, measured primarily as a decrease in offending and drug use. But there is a difference between compliance with prohibitions against crime and rehabilitation of the impulse to commit crimes. It may be that simply changing behavior during the program (including through threat of sanction alone) is sufficient to change long-term behavior by developing a law-abiding pattern that stays with participants after they leave a program. It may also be that once the threat of sanctions is removed, along with the supports associated with a program (e.g., counseling, resources, peers), the motivation to avoid old habits of drug use and crime wanes. Then, if the opportunities to offend are still around the ex-offender, that person may have little reason to decide not to offend or take drugs. Advocates of a diversion initiative may be willing to accept that long-term gains are significantly less than in-program rehabilitative effects, but it is often difficult to convince policymakers and others in search of demonstrable progress that realistic goals should carry the day. Policymakers' views and expectations are important because they are the ones who come up with the will, the funding, and other resources to implement diversion programs in the first place. If they are not happy with results, diversion programs will not survive.

The same argument applies to public safety, but the stakes for policymakers are higher because a crime, especially a violent crime, could provoke public outcry that a diversion program is soft on crime and leaves communities vulnerable. In evaluating the impact of a diversion program on public safety, policymakers will look first for assurances that the diversion yields no worse a reoffending rate than traditional sentencing. The impulse is surely to look for rates of reoffending that are lower than those of traditionally sentenced offenders, but program administrators should resist this impulse because it is unrealistic. This is not to say that some offenders will not change their attitudes fundamentally and go on to lead law-abiding lives. Certainly that happens, probably in every diversion program. But for diversion programs to really work at the systemic level, they cannot be reserved for the most likely to succeed. In order to attract and retain large numbers of jail-bound offenders, diversion programs must be designed to work for the least likely to succeed.

Finally, it is critical that policymakers hold diversion programs accountable for their implementation. Evaluation of a program model and the integrity of its application help program administrators and their policymaking partners understand where key program elements are succeeding and where they are not. Evaluators interview program participants, staff, and court actors, review program materials and files, and analyze program intake and service delivery data. Taken together, these data provide the foundation for a rigorous, analytic, and applied understanding of program implementation that can be communicated to program and court staff alike. Diversion programs have the potential to provide community-based treatment and other services designed to keep people from reoffending by strengthening their resources. Therefore, they are the precursor to the reentry efforts that have swept across the country.

DISCUSSION QUESTIONS

1. How can public safety and rehabilitation be balanced in alternative sentences for serious offenders?

2. In what ways does monitoring enhance diversion programs? How does it detract from the same programs?

3. What are the policy implications of straight (not interventionist) diversion?

4. Why do you think the interventionist model of diversion is so dominant?

5. Why should we care about net widening? Is it still important in the age of drug courts?

NOTES

1. For a very different analysis of the nature of diversion programs, see Cullen (2005).

2. Prison is a state or federal incarceration facility, typically reserved for more serious offenders. Jail is a local incarceration facility and is typically used for detention before conviction and sentences for less serious offenses, generally less than 1 year. In some cases this distinction does not hold, such as in Rhode Island, which maintains a single incarceration system, or in jails that rent out space to incarcerate state or federal prisoners.

SUGGESTED READINGS

Belenko, S., Schiff, M., Phillips, M., & Winterfield, L. (1994). Modelling the displacement effects of alternative sanctions programs: A case study. *Prison Journal, 74*(2), 167–197.

Benda, B. (Ed.). (2005). Boot camps special issue. *Journal of Offender Rehabilitation, 40*(3/4), 1–207.

Government Accountability Office. (2005). *Adult drug courts: Evidence indicates recidivism reductions and mixed results for other outcomes.* Washington, DC: Author.

MacKenzie, D. (2006). *What works in corrections: Reducing the criminal activities of offenders and delinquents.* New York: Cambridge University Press.

Mears, D., Winterfield, L., Hunsake, J., Moore, G., & White, R. (2003). *Drug treatment in the criminal justice system: The current state of knowledge.* Washington, DC: Urban Institute.

Morris, N., & Tonry, M. (1990). *Between prison and probation.* New York: Oxford University Press.

Petersilia, J. (1999). A decade of experimenting with intermediate sanctions: What have we learned? *Corrections Management Quarterly, 3*(3), 9–23.

Tonry, M., & Lynch, M. (1996). Intermediate sanctions. In *Crime and justice: A review of the research* (Vol. 20, pp. 99–144). Chicago: University of Chicago Press.

Vera Institute of Justice. (1996). *The unintended consequences of incarceration.* New York: Author.

REFERENCES

American Bar Association & National Bar Association. (2001). *Justice by gender: The lack of appropriate prevention, diversion and treatment alternatives for girls in the juvenile justice system.* Washington, DC: American Bar Association.

Andrews, D., Zinger, I., Hoge, R., Bonta, J., Gendreau, P., & Cullen, F. (1990). Does correctional treatment work? A clinically relevant and psychologically informed meta-analysis. *Criminology, 28*(3), 369–404.

Anglin, M., Longshore, D., Turner, S., McBride, D., Inciardi, J., & Prendergast, M. (1996). *Study of the functioning and effectiveness of Treatment Alternatives to Street Crime (TASC) programs: Final report.* Los Angeles: UCLA Drug Abuse Research Center.

Austin, J., & Irwin, J. (1993). *Does imprisonment reduce crime? A critique of voodoo criminology.* San Francisco: National Council on Crime and Delinquency.

Belenko, S., Foltz, C., Lang, M., & Sung, H.-E. (2004). Recidivism among high-risk drug felons: A longitudinal analysis following residential treatment. *Journal of Offender Rehabilitation, 40*(1/2), 105–132.

Belenko, S., Schiff, M., Phillips, M., & Winterfield, L. (1994). Modelling the displacement effects of alternative sanctions programs: A case study. *Prison Journal, 74*(2), 167–197.

Casey, P., & Rottman, D. (2000). Therapeutic jurisprudence in the courts. *Behavioral Science and the Law, 18,* 445–457.

Chesney-Lind, M., & Sheldon, R. (1998). *Girls, delinquency and juvenile justice.* Thousand Oaks, CA: Sage.

Clear, T. (2007). *Imprisoning communities: How mass incarceration makes disadvantaged neighborhoods worse.* New York: Oxford University Press.

Cullen, F. T. (2005). The twelve people who saved rehabilitation: How the science of criminology made a difference. *Criminology, 43,* 1–42.

Davis, R., Taylor, B., & Maxwell, C. (2000). *Does batterer treatment reduce violence? A randomized experiment in Brooklyn.* Washington, DC: National Institute of Justice.

Drug Courts Program Office. (1997). *Defining drug courts: The key components.* Washington, DC: Office of Justice Programs.

Duwe, G., & Kerschner, D. (2008). Removing a nail from the boot camp coffin: An outcome evaluation of the Minnesota's Challenge Incarceration Program. *Crime and Delinquency, 54*(4), 614–643.

Dynia, P., & Sung, H.-E. (2000). The safety and effectiveness of diverting felony drug offenders into residential treatment as measured by recidivism. *Criminal Justice Policy Review, 11,* 299–311.

Fagan, J., & Malkin, V. (2003). Theorizing community justice through community courts. *Fordham Urban Law Journal, 30,* 101–150.

Farabee, D., Prendergast, M., & Anglin, D. (1998). The effectiveness of coerced treatment for drug abusing offenders. *Federal Probation, 62*(1), 3–11.

Farrell, A. (2001). *Effect of gender and family status on downward departures in federal criminal sentences.* Dissertation, Northeastern University, Boston.

Feld, B. (1998). *Bad kids: Race and the transformation of the juvenile court.* New York: Oxford University Press.

Garland, D. (1990). *Punishment and modern society: A study in social theory.* Chicago: University of Chicago Press.

Gibson, J. (2006). The contributions of truth to reconciliation. *Journal of Conflict Resolution, 50*(3), 409–432.

Government Accountability Office. (2005). *Adult drug courts: Evidence indicates recidivism reductions and mixed results for other outcomes.* Washington, DC: Author.

Harrel, A., & Roman, J. (2001). Reducing drug use and crime among offenders: The impact of graduated sanctions. *Journal of Drug Issues, 31*(1), 207–231.

Harris, K. (1985). Reducing prison crowding and nonprison penalties. *Annals of the American Academy of Political and Social Science, 478,* 150–160.

Huddleston, W., Freeman-Wilson, K., Marlowe, D., & Roussell, A. (2005). *Painting the current picture: A national report card on drug courts and other problem solving court programs in the United States.* Washington, DC: Bureau of Justice Assistance.

Ignatieff, M. (1981). State, civil society, and total institutions: A critique of recent social histories of punishment. In M. Tonry & N. Morris (Eds.), *Crime and justice: An annual review of research* (Vol. 3, pp. 153–192). Chicago: University of Chicago Press.

Koons-Witt, B. (2002). Effect of gender on the decision to incarcerate before and after the introduction of sentencing guidelines. *Criminology, 40*(2), 297–328.

Kurlycheck, M., & Kempinen, C. (2006). Beyond boot camp: The impact of aftercare on offenders' reentry. *Criminology and Public Policy, 5*(2), 363–388.

Longshore, D., Turner, S., Wenzel, S., Morral, A., Harrell, A., McBride, D., et al. (2001). Drug courts: A conceptual framework. *Journal of Drug Issues, 31*(1), 7–26.

Loveland, D., & Boyle, M. (2007). Intensive case management as a jail diversion program for people with a serious mental illness: A review of the literature. *International Journal of Offender Therapy and Comparative Criminology, 51,* 130–150.

Macallair, D., & Roche, T. (2001). *Widening the net in juvenile justice and the dangers of prevention and early intervention.* San Francisco: Justice Policy Institute.

MacKenzie, D. (2006). *What works in corrections: Reducing the criminal activities of offenders and delinquents.* New York: Cambridge University Press.

MacKenzie, D., & Armstrong, G. S. (2004). *Correctional boot camps: Studies examining military basic training as a model for corrections.* Thousand Oaks, CA: Sage.

MacKenzie, D. L., Bierie, D., & Mitchell, O. (2007). An experimental study of a therapeutic boot camp: Impact on impulses, attitudes and recidivism. *Journal of Experimental Criminology, 3*(3), 221–246.

Martinson, R. (1974, Spring). What works? Questions and answers about prison reform. *Public Interest,* pp. 22–45.

Mears, D., Winterfield, L., Hunsake, J., Moore, G., & White, R. (2003). *Drug treatment in the criminal justice system: The current state of knowledge.* Washington, DC: Urban Institute.

Natarajan, M., & Falkin, G. P. (1997). Can corrections operate therapeutic communities for inmates? The impact on the social environment of jails. *Journal of Correctional Health Care, 4,* 19–36.

National Institute of Justice. (2003). *Do batterer intervention programs work? Two studies.* Washington, DC: Author.

National Institute of Justice. (2006). *Drug courts: The second decade.* Washington, DC: Author.

Pager, D. (2007). *Marked: Race, crime, and finding work in an era of mass incarceration.* Chicago: University of Chicago Press.

Parent, D. (2003). Correctional boot camps: Lessons from a decade of research. *Research for Practice,* NIJ 197018.

Petersilia, J. (1999). A decade of experimenting with intermediate sanctions: What have we learned? *Corrections Management Quarterly, 3*(3), 9–23.

Porter, R. (2001). *Treatment alternatives in the criminal court: A process evaluation of the Bronx County Drug Court. Report to the Criminal Court of the City of New York.* New York: Vera Institute of Justice.

Porter, R. (2002). *Supervised treatment in the criminal court: A process evaluation of the Manhattan misdemeanor drug court.* New York: Vera Institute of Justice.

Porter, R. (in press). *Performance indicators for problem solving courts.* New York: Center for Court Innovation.

Porter, R., Lee, S., & Lutz, M. (2002). *Balancing punishment and treatment: Alternatives to incarceration in New York City.* New York: Vera Institute of Justice.

Rempel, M. (2005). *Recidivism 101: Evaluating the impact of your drug court.* New York: Center for Court Innovation.

Rossman, S. B., Zweig, J., & Roman, J. (2008). *A portrait of adult drug courts.* Washington, DC: The Urban Institute.

SEARCH. (2003). *Drug court monitoring, evaluation, and management information systems: National scope needs assessment.* Washington, DC: Bureau of Justice Assistance.

Sherman, L., Gottfredson, D., MacKenzie, D., Eck, J., Reuter, P., & Bushway, P. (1998). *Preventing crime: What works, what doesn't, what's promising*. Research in Brief. Washington, DC: National Institute of Justice.

Simon, J. (1995). They died with their boots on: The boot camp and the limits of modern penality. *Social Justice, 22*(2), 25–48.

Skelton, A. (2002). Restorative justice as a framework for juvenile justice reform: A South African perspective. *British Journal of Criminology, 42*, 496–513.

Svirdoff, M., Rottman, D., Weidner, R., & Curtis, R. (2000). *Dispensing justice locally: The impacts, cost and benefits of the midtown community court*. Washington, DC: National Institute of Justice.

Sykes, G., & Messinger, S. (1960). The inmate social system. In R. Cloward (Ed.), *Theoretical studies of the social organization of the prison* (pp. 5–19). New York: Social Science.

Taxman, F. (1999). Unraveling what works for offenders in substance abuse treatment services. *National Drug Court Review, 2*(2), 93–134.

Thompson, A. (2002). Courting disorder: Some thoughts on community courts. *Journal of Law and Policy, 10*(63), 63–99.

Tonry, M. (1996). *Sentencing matters*. New York: Oxford University Press.

Tonry, M., & Lynch, M. (1996). Intermediate sanctions. In *Crime and justice: A review of the research* (Vol. 20, pp. 99–144). Chicago: University of Chicago Press.

Ward, G. (2009). The "other" child savers: Racial politics of the parental state. In A. Platt (Ed.), *The child savers* (40th anniversary ed.). New Brunswick, NJ: Rutgers University Press.

Ward, T., Day, A., Howells, K., & Birgden, A. (2004). The multifactor offender readiness model. *Aggression and Violent Behavior, 9*, 645–673.

Wells, J. B., Minor, K. I., Angel, E., & Stearman, K. D. (2006). Quasi-experimental evaluation of a shock incarceration and aftercare program for juvenile offenders. *Youth Violence and Juvenile Justice, 4*, 219–233.

Wilson, D. B., MacKenzie, D. L., & Mitchell, F. N. (2005). *Effects of correctional boot camps on offending*. Available at http://db.c2admin.org/doc-pdf/Wilson_bootcamps_review+abstract.pdf

Young, D. (2002). Impacts of perceived legal pressure on retention in drug treatment. *Criminal Justice and Behavior, 29*, 27–55.

Young, D., Fluellen, R., & Belenko, S. (2004). Criminal recidivism in three models of mandatory drug treatment. *Journal of Substance Abuse Treatment, 27*, 313–323.

Zimmering, F. (1998). *American youth violence*. New York: Oxford University Press.

Zimmering, F. (2000). The common thread: Diversion in juvenile justice. *California Law Review, 88*(6), 2477–2495.

CHAPTER 7

*Prison-Based
Substance Abuse
Programs*

Wayne N. Welsh

As of December 31, 2007, a total of 2,293,157 inmates were in custody in state and federal prisons and in local jails (West & Sabol, 2009). Two thirds of inmates were held in state or federal prisons; the remaining third were held in local jails. In 2007, the incarceration rate rose to 756 inmates per 100,000 U.S. residents. Available estimates suggest that the number of offenders who committed drug-related offenses, were using drugs, or were drug dependent at the time of their arrest is very high.

The Center on Addiction and Substance Abuse (CASA; 1998) reports that 60–80% of all prison inmates (federal, state, and county) have been involved with drug use or drug-related crimes in some fashion. For chronic users, activities and behaviors surrounding drug acquisition and use pervade their lifestyle (Johnson et al., 1985; Walters, 1992). Many drug-dependent offenders are repeatedly incarcerated but untreated, with the result that many relapse into drug use and crime after release (Wexler, Lipton, & Johnson, 1988).

The Arrestee Drug Abuse Monitoring (ADAM) program tracks drug use among booked arrestees in 35 large urban areas. In 2000, the ADAM program conducted interviews and drug tests with more than 188,000 adult male arrestees in 35 metropolitan areas (National Institute of Justice, 2003). In half of the 35 ADAM sites, 64% or more of adult male arrestees had recently used at least one of five drugs: cocaine (undistinguished between crack and powder), marijuana, opiates, methamphetamine, and phencyclidine (PCP). Marijuana was the drug most commonly used (41%), followed by cocaine (31%).

Drug-involved offenders make up a large portion of local, state, and federal correctional populations. Drug offenses accounted for 53% of sentenced prisoners under federal jurisdiction at year end 2007 and 20% of sentenced prisoners under state jurisdiction at year end 2005 (West & Sabol, 2009). More than a quarter of all property and drug offenders in state prison or local jail said they committed their current offense to obtain money for drugs, compared with about 8–10% of violent offenders and 5–7% of public order offenders (Bureau of Justice Statistics, 2009).

Drug users in general may not commit violent crimes at high rates, but seriously addicted drug users commit both violent and property crimes at very high rates. The most predatory offenders (high-rate, addicted offenders) committed 15 times more robberies, 20 times more burglaries, and 10 times more thefts than offenders who did not use drugs (Chaiken, 1986). Studies of heroin users in Baltimore (Ball, Shaffer, & Nurco, 1983) and New York (Johnson et al., 1985) demonstrated that active drug use accelerated the users' crime rate by a factor of four to six and that the crimes committed while people were on drugs were at least as violent as those committed by people who did not use drugs. Rand Inmate Surveys (Petersilia, Greenwood, & Lavin, 1977) indicate that among robbers, drug users have an offense rate twice that of nonusers. Studies of crack users indicate that the robbery rate for this group is as high as or higher than that of heroin-related crime, and their crimes are more violent (Lipton, 1995).

The availability of correctional drug treatment is clearly inadequate. In the 1997 Survey of Inmates in State and Federal Correctional Facilities, about two out of three inmates admitted drug histories, but less than 15% received any professional treatment while in prison (Mumola, 1999). Belenko and Peugh (2005) estimate that about one third of male inmates and more than half of female inmates in this sample needed long-term residential treatment. Although inmates in the most severe drug use categories were more likely to receive treatment while incarcerated, only about one fifth received any clinical treatment services.

In the 2004 Survey of Inmates in State and Federal Correctional Facilities, the Bureau of Justice Statistics included for the first time measures of drug dependence and abuse based on criteria specified in the *Diagnostic and Statistical Manual of Mental Disorders,* fourth edition (*DSM-IV*) (Mumola & Karberg, 2006). Fifty-three percent of state and 45% of federal prisoners met *DSM-IV* criteria for drug dependence or abuse. Among drug-dependent prisoners, 40% of state and 49% of federal inmates took part in some type of drug abuse program including self-help groups, peer counseling, and drug education. However, the percentage who took part in treatment programs with a trained professional (15%)

remained unchanged from 1997. In short, a tremendous need for prison-based drug treatment remains largely unmet.

Intensive and well-structured prison-based drug treatment has been shown to be effective in breaking the cycle of relapse and recidivism among seriously drug-involved offenders (Gaes, Flanagan, Motiuk, & Stewart, 1999; Mitchell, MacKenzie, & Wilson, 2006; Mitchell, Wilson, & MacKenzie, 2007; Pearson & Lipton, 1999). This chapter examines what we know about the content and structure of different prison-based drug treatment modalities, their effectiveness, barriers to implementation, and implications for policy. There is strong evidence that drug treatment, when well implemented, can significantly reduce recidivism, relapse, and costs of incarceration.

CURRENT APPROACHES AND PRACTICES

Types of Programs

Description and Rationale. Correctional approaches to Alcohol or Other Drug (AOD) treatment are often informed by a holistic health model that treats substance abuse as a complex problem with physiological, psychological, emotional, behavioral, spiritual, and environmental dimensions. Long-term goals are to reduce recidivism, drug dealing, and drug use and to increase the prospects for successful reintegration into society.

Although prison-based treatment for drug abuse disorders tends to be eclectic (Welsh & Zajac, 2004a, 2004b), behavioral treatments are widely used. Effective interventions include cognitive therapies that teach coping and decision-making skills, contingency management therapies that reinforce behavioral changes associated with abstinence, motivational therapies that enhance the motivation to participate in treatment (Chandler, Fletcher, & Volkow, 2009; Prendergast, Podus, Chang, & Urada, 2002; Wormith et al., 2007), and residential therapeutic community (TC) programs based on social learning and psychodynamic principles (De Leon, 2000). Evidence also suggests that certain medications may be useful in the treatment of addiction. Methadone, buprenorphine, and naltrexone may facilitate the treatment of heroin addiction, and naltrexone and topiramate can help treat alcoholism (Cropsey, Villalobos, & St. Clair, 2005; Johnson et al., 2007; Volkow & Li, 2005). Self-help programs such as Alcoholics Anonymous and Narcotics Anonymous often supplement more formal treatment modalities in jails and prisons (Humphreys et al., 2004), although self-help methods are also essential components of an integrated treatment approach (DeLeon, 2004).

Prison-based AOD programming can be grouped into five major categories (Welsh & Zajac, 2004a, 2004b): AOD education, ancillary groups, outpatient or group counseling, TCs, and other residential drug treatment units. Each is briefly described here.

AOD education programs are typically offered to inmates identified as having minimal drug and alcohol involvement. Such programs are usually of low intensity and duration but offer wide coverage to the offender population. Services focus on developing insight about the causes and consequences of drug abuse, skills to manage drug-using behaviors, and prosocial (non–drug-using) social networks. AOD education provides participants with a fundamental overview of the social, physical, and behavioral effects of drug and alcohol addiction. Participants learn the benefits of a drug-free lifestyle. Education groups usually cover topics such as the disease concept; the pharmacology of drugs; the physical, psychological, social, and financial impacts of use; self-assessment treatment options; the role of self-help groups; and relapse prevention. AOD education groups often function as entry-level treatment for the general population. The information presented is intended to act as a motivator for continued treatment. Considering the depth of the typical inmate's addiction, stand-alone drug education programs are unlikely to effectively address the needs of the offender population (Belenko & Peugh, 2005; Taxman, Perdoni, & Harrison, 2007; Welsh & Zajac, 2004a, 2004b).

Ancillary groups such as self-help and peer counseling are often offered to inmates as supplements to formal treatment or when slots are not available in the more intensive treatment modalities. According to Humphreys et al. (2004), a self-help group is a nonprofessional, peer-operated group devoted to helping people with addiction-related problems. The term *mutual help group* is often used to reflect the fact that group members give and receive advice, encouragement, and support. Self-help groups do not charge fees and should not be equated with professional treatment services. *Twelve-step groups* are a specific type of self-help group that rely on a particular philosophy of recovery that emphasizes the importance of accepting addiction as a disease that can be arrested but never eliminated, enhancing individual maturity and spiritual growth, minimizing self-centeredness, and providing help to other addicted people (e.g., sharing recovery stories in group meetings, sponsoring new members). Alcoholics Anonymous and Narcotics Anonymous are the best known of the self-help organizations that rely on the 12 steps. These types of groups are widely available in prisons (Taxman, Young, Wiersema, Rhodes, & Mitchell, 2007), and the 12-step approach permeates most prison-based AOD services including TC (De Leon, 2004).

Outpatient or substance abuse group counseling programs are typically offered to moderate-risk inmates who need more intensive, intermediate levels of intervention. In contrast to education and self-help groups, certified treatment counselors work directly and intensively with inmates to help them recognize and address their dependency problems. Treatment can include 12-step approaches, individual and group intensive counseling, rational–emotive therapy, cognitive restructuring therapy, and other services rendered by treatment specialists. Where clinically indicated, detoxification services may also be offered. These programs are integrated into the other activities that make up the inmate's day, such as work, education, and recreational activities. An inmate in this phase of treatment typically receives treatment for at least 1 hour per day.

TCs are offered to inmates identified as needing intensive, residential substance abuse intervention. An in-prison TC is a residential treatment program that provides an intensive, highly structured prosocial environment for the treatment of substance abuse and addiction. It differs from other treatment approaches principally in its use of the community as the key agent of change, in which treatment staff and recovering clientele interact in both structured and unstructured ways to influence attitudes, perceptions, and behaviors associated with drug use (De Leon, 2000).

The TC uses a staged, hierarchical model in which treatment stages are related to increased levels of individual and social responsibility. Peer influence, mediated through a variety of group processes, is used to help residents learn and assimilate social norms and develop more effective social skills. The therapeutic approach generally focuses on changing negative patterns of thinking and behavior through individual and group therapy, group sessions with peers, and participation in a therapeutic milieu with hierarchical roles, privileges, and responsibilities. Strict and explicit behavioral norms are emphasized and reinforced with specific contingencies (rewards and punishments) directed toward developing self-control and responsibility.

The TC treatment continuum for drug-dependent offenders (e.g., TC treatment in prison, followed by transitional TC in a work release setting, followed by supervision and aftercare treatment in the community) has become the dominant paradigm for residential treatment for drug-dependent inmates (Grella et al., 2007; Rockholz, 2004). By the end of 2002, there were an estimated 289 prison TCs, with total inmate capacity of 40,362. Federal grants required states to give preference to programs that provided aftercare services (Pelissier, Jones, & Cadigan, 2007).

Other residential drug treatment units provide some combination of drug education and outpatient programming. The purpose of housing inmates together in a residential unit in a prison is primarily one of administrative convenience. Inmates can be assigned to drug and alcohol groups that meet nearby so as to minimize their movement through the institution. In stark contrast to a TC, however, a residential drug treatment unit in prison rarely has either a unifying treatment approach or a self-governing community structure.

Taxman, Perdoni, and Harrison (2007) report results of a national survey of prisons, jails, and community correctional agencies. One of the goals of the National Criminal Justice Treatment Practices Survey was to estimate the prevalence of entry into and accessibility of correctional programs and drug treatment services for adult offenders. Prevalence is the percentage of respondents reporting that their facility provides specific treatment programs or services. Access is the percentage of facility residents who could receive the services or participate in the programs on any given day.

The prison sample used the Bureau of Justice Statistics 2000 census of prisons, in which specialized drug and alcohol prisons were selected with certainty ($n = 58$) and a stratified sample of 92 prisons was chosen based on probabilities proportional to size and region. A response rate of 70% was achieved. Prison results reported by Taxman, Perdoni, et al. (2007) are summarized in Table 7.1.

Substance abuse education and awareness was the most common form of service, offered in 74% of prisons, 61% of jails, and 53% of community correctional agencies (Taxman, Perdoni, et al., 2007). Although agencies reported a high availability of services, less than a quarter of the offenders in prisons and jails had daily access to AOD services, and few clinical services were provided.

Specialized drug treatment prisons offered more services than traditional prisons. The median average daily population (ADP) in a specialized prison was 770. Low-intensity group counseling and case management were provided to nearly all offenders, in contrast to traditional prisons. The services provided in traditional prisons were less likely to meet the recommended 90-day minimum duration than specialized treatment facilities. Eighty-five percent of the services provided in specialized prison facilities were of at least 90 days' duration, whereas only 63% of the services offered in traditional facilities exceeded 90 days. The programs most likely to exceed 90 days were TCs (both segregated and nonsegregated) and group counseling (5–25 hours/week), followed by AOD education and relapse prevention groups.

Increasing the rates of AOD service delivery across different types of correctional facilities remains a challenge. Another challenge is to increase the intensity of services offered to offenders, including providing more counseling and therapeutic interventions for longer durations. Consensus is that cognitive–behavioral, TC, and other behavioral strategies are more likely to

Table 7.1   Prevalence of AOD Services in Prisons

Type of Program	Percentage of Prisons With a Program	Estimated Number of Offenders Participating per Day	Specialized AOD Prisons		Nonspecialized (Traditional) Prisons	
			Percentage of Average Daily Population	Percentage of Programs > 90 Days	Percentage of Average Daily Population	Percentage of Programs > 90 Days
Drug and alcohol education	74.1	75,543	8.8	92.1	9	65.3
AOD group counseling						
1–4 hr/week	54.6	34,509	76.9	73.9	10	58
5–25 hr/week	46	52,293	8.8	92.9	8	72.9
≥ 26 hr/week	11.2	12,182	11.3	78.9	18.6	24.3
TC						
Segregated	19.5	34,776	8.8	84.3	15.5	74.8
Nonsegregated	9.2	10,710	5.7	91.6	14.4	66
Relapse prevention groups	44.5	39,493	13.0	74.3	3.8	62
Case management	6.9	10,761	100.0	91.1	9.1	40.7

Source: Taxman, Perdoni, et al. (2007).

reduce recidivism and drug use (Chandler et al., 2009). Another question concerns the appropriateness of services provided to offenders. More studies are needed to explore the nature of treatment services offered to different types of offenders. Correctional agencies may make service delivery decisions based more on reducing costs and providing minimal services to as many offenders as possible rather than on providing effective services that are more likely to yield reductions in drug use and recidivism (Taxman, Perdoni, et al., 2007; Taxman, Young, et al., 2007).

Program Content and Structure. Individual programs, even within the same generic type (e.g., outpatient counseling), often differ a good deal in terms of program content, structure, and approach. Any one program typically provides some unique combination of treatment components (Harrison & Martin, 2003). Although meta-analyses attempt to account for methodological differences across studies (e.g., differences in sample size, sampling technique, construction of comparison groups), they rarely code program differences related to the development, implementation, and evaluation of effective correctional programs.

Recognizing that most agencies lack substantial in-house research and evaluation expertise and resources, the National Institute of Justice issued a targeted solicitation in 1998 that encouraged research partnerships between correctional agencies and research institutions that could provide expertise tailored to meet state and local needs. A research partnership between Temple University and the Pennsylvania Department of Corrections undertook a system-wide assessment of AOD services. A brief summary of results describing the content and structure of prison-based AOD services is provided here.

A census instrument was developed to collect descriptive information about 118 prison-based drug treatment programs across 24 state prisons (Welsh & Zajac, 2004a, 2004b). The census assessed program content and structure (e.g., program type, duration, primary treatment approach), program staff (e.g., duties, staffing ratios), and inmates (e.g., eligibility, intake procedures).

Prison-based AOD programs varied widely in program duration and intensity. Both the nature and quantity of treatment that an inmate receives depend a great deal on which type of program he or she is assigned to. On average, the TC programs lasted much longer (mean = 46 weeks) and provided many more total hours of programming per week (mean = 30 hours/week) than any other program type. Education programs lasted anywhere from 4 to 32 weeks (mean = 12 weeks), outpatient programs lasted anywhere from 4 to 36 weeks (mean = 13 weeks), and other residential treatment programs ranged from 8 to 52 weeks (mean = 22 weeks).

Differences in intensity (e.g., treatment hours per week) also distinguished these program types. Education programs provided 1–14 hours of programming per week (mean = 3 hours), outpatient programs provided 1–28 hours per week (mean = 3 hours), other residential programs ranged from 2 to 20 hours per week (mean = 8 hours), and TC programs provided 15–40 hours per week (mean = 30 hours).

TC was far more likely than other program types to address diverse inmate needs, including substance abuse (e.g., criminality and lifestyle issues). Education programs were least likely to address inmates' needs. Outpatient programs tended to emphasize certain areas (thinking errors, problem-solving skills, and relapse prevention) but neglect others (AIDS, models of addiction). Individualized treatment plans were developed for inmates in all six TC programs (100%) but in only 5 (12%) education programs, 19 (34%) outpatient programs, and 5 (50%) other residential programs. Counselors were assigned to work with individual inmates in 5 (83%) TC programs and 7 (70%) other residential programs but in only 29 (50%) outpatient and only 10 (23%) education programs.

Although prison-based drug treatment is eclectic, drawing on various treatment approaches, cognitive–behavioral and rational–emotive therapy were frequently cited as primary treatment approaches. Each provides a structured approach to identifying and analyzing thoughts, values, and beliefs associated with drug use and criminal behavior (e.g., triggers for relapse). TC was much more likely than any other program type to emphasize a primary treatment approach of any sort.

Substantial variability was observed within program types other than TC. For example, 31 (53%) outpatient programs reported cognitive–behavioral therapy as the primary approach, 20 (35%) reported it as a secondary approach, and 7 (12%) claimed that it was not used at all. Similarly, psychotherapy was reported as a primary approach for 10 outpatient programs (17%), and a secondary approach for 12 programs (21%), but 36 programs (62%) did not use psychotherapy at all. Nineteen education programs (45%) reported cognitive–behavioral therapy as a primary approach, 15 (36%) reported it as a secondary approach, and 8 (19%) stated it was not used at all.

Substantial variability in program content was reported for education programs. For example, 12 (27%) education programs reported spending a great deal of time on problem-solving skills, 16 (36%) spent a moderate amount of time, and 16 (36%) spent very little or no time. Eleven (25%) programs reported spending a great deal of time on life skills, 17 (39%) reported spending a moderate amount of time, 14 (32%) spent very little time, and 2 (5%) spent no time at all on this topic. Twelve (27%) education programs reported spending a great deal of time on stress management, 14 (32%) reported spending a moderate amount of time, 13 (30%) spent very little time, and 5 (11%) spent no time at all on this topic. Outpatient programs evidenced similar variability.

Staffing varied substantially within program types. TC was the most consistent (9:1–16:1), other residential the least (8:1–92:1), with education (5:1–64:1) and outpatient (7:1–60:1) in between. Different program types such as TC place unique demands on treatment staff, and adequate numbers of well-trained, experienced staff are critical to the success of any treatment program (DeLeon, 2000). TC and outpatient had the lowest mean inmate/staff ratios (17:1), other residential had the highest (30:1), and education (20:1) was in between.

Except for TC, where very specific tasks, skills, and other indicators of progress must be demonstrated at each phase (DeLeon, 2000), most programs required completion of only a specific number of hours for successful program completion. There was little difference between education (mean = 14 hours) and outpatient (mean = 18 hours) in this regard; other residential programs required about twice as many hours (mean = 38 hours).

The importance of other criteria for program completion varied substantially. A drug and alcohol knowledge test was rated as more important by education than by outpatient programs (means = 1.7 vs. 2.5) but as very important by only 22 educational programs (51%). For the other three program types, measures of attitudinal and behavioral change and case progress review were more often rated as very important. Case progress review tended to be rated as very important for TC (100%) and other residential (70%) programs but rarely for outpatient (27%) or education (14%) programs.

Overall, results identified a number of critical issues regarding prison-based drug treatment programming and policies. Within certain program types (TC), we found high levels of consistency (e.g., primary treatment approach, program content). Within other program types, we found wide variation (e.g., program duration, intensity, and staffing; target selection criteria; and program placement decisions). It is highly unlikely that the within-program variation in drug and alcohol programming reported in this study is unique to any one state. Process evaluations of prison-based drug and alcohol treatment in other states have reported numerous implementation difficulties, including inadequate numbers of trained and experienced counseling staff and lack of standardized screening, assessment, and selection processes (e.g., Inciardi et al., 1992; Martin, Butzin, & Inciardi, 1995).

Barriers to Implementation

Evaluations of prison-based drug treatment only rarely provide detailed program descriptions or information about implementation (Taxman & Bouffard, 2002; Welsh & Zajac, 2004b). However, evaluators tend to find weaknesses as well as strengths when they look for them. Barriers to successful implementation often include staff recruitment, experience, and training; client screening, assessment, and selection; quality of interactions between inmates, correctional officers, and treatment staff; and use of appropriate sanctions (Farabee et al., 1999; Harrison & Martin, 2003; Inciardi et al., 1992; Linhorst, Knight, Johnston, & Trickey, 2001; Martin, Butzin, & Inciardi, 1995). Successful implementation of correctional treatment requires continuous adaptation over time. Correctional agencies and their partners should spend more time in house on program planning and development, not only at the outset but continuously throughout the life of a program (Welsh, 2006b; Welsh & Harris, 2008).

Prison treatment can begin a process of therapeutic change, but continuing treatment in the community is essential for sustaining these gains. Standards of care for TCs specify that community-based aftercare must continue for at least 6 months after prison release (Council of State Governments, 2003). Similarly, Principle #9 of the National Institute on Drug Abuse (NIDA; 2006) *Principles of Drug Abuse Treatment for Criminal Justice Populations* states, "Continuity of care is essential for drug abusers re-entering the community" (p. 5).

Aftercare treatment seeks to provide continuity of care to maintain behavioral changes made during in-prison treatment and to reduce the costs of more intensive services (McKay, 2001). Researchers argue that the effects of aftercare are additive to the benefits of in-prison treatment (Simpson, Wexler, & Inciardi, 1999), and aftercare services are a crucial element in reducing substance abuse and recidivism (De Leon, 2000; Harrison & Martin, 2003).

However, general research on community aftercare programs for released offenders is limited, and there is no standardized conceptualization of what constitutes aftercare (McKay, 2001). Neither the core intervention components nor the core implementation components associated with the aftercare phase of the continuum of care are well understood (Haggerty et al., 2003). Also, aftercare programs vary in modality (e.g., residential, outpatient), theoretical approach (TC, cognitive–behavioral, 12-step approach), setting (work release facility, community correctional center, halfway house, contractor-provided aftercare), and duration (3, 6, 9, or 12 months). Pelissier et al. (2007) conclude that claims about aftercare effectiveness are not well substantiated and that the precise nature of aftercare services needed is not well understood. Issues include self-selection bias and the need to disentangle offender behavior from the effects of criminal justice policies (e.g., parole supervision and revocation) and to identify the most effective types of aftercare for different offenders.

Unexamined variations in TC implementation practices (e.g., staff selection, training, and evaluation) and implementation outcomes (e.g., fidelity) probably influence client outcomes (Chou, Hser, & Anglin, 1998; Etheridge & Hubbard, 2000; Etheridge, Hubbard, Anderson, Craddock, & Flynn, 1997; Hiller, Knight, Broome, & Simpson, 1998; Inciardi et al., 1992; Melnick,

De Leon, Hiller, & Knight, 2000; Melnick, Hawke, & Wexler, 2004; Schildhaus, Gerstein, Dugoni, Brittingham, & Cerbone, 2000; Strauss & Falkin, 2000; Wexler, Melnick, Lowe, & Peters, 1999). Despite recommendations that treatment researchers need to more systematically measure implementation processes as predictors of treatment outcomes, researchers have been slow to assess such factors (Palmer, 1992, 1995; Welsh & Zajac, 2004a, 2004b).

Evidence from meta-analyses and systematic reviews suggests that many unique implementation practices (alone and in combination with one another) influence implementation outcomes (Andrews et al., 1990; Latessa, Cullen, & Gendreau, 2002; Pearson & Lipton, 1999; Prendergast, Podus, & Chang, 2000; Rogers, 1995; Welsh, 2006a). Between-program, between-unit, and between-agency differences in implementation practices and outcomes may seriously threaten the internal validity of many multisite outcome studies. Policy-relevant research would benefit greatly from more careful attention to mapping critical dimensions of implementation associated with outcomes such as recidivism.

Organizational and implementation research suggests that identifying evidence-based practices and programs (EBPPs) that yield positive client outcomes is only the first stage in improving health services for drug-involved offenders. Despite designation of many drug treatment and HIV interventions as "evidence-based," such interventions are slow to be disseminated (Kilbourne, Neumann, Pincus, Bauer, & Stall, 2007) and are often poorly implemented (Bourgon & Armstrong, 2005) or difficult to sustain (Brown & Flynn, 2002; Miller, Sorensen, Selzer, & Brigham, 2006).

There are particular challenges in introducing EBPPs into criminal justice agencies (Farabee et al., 1999; Linhorst et al., 2001), which are slow to be exposed to EBPPs and often isolated from practice and research. Significant system barriers relate to cyclical funding, vacillating support for offender programs, and a focus on security and punishment rather than treatment.

Current practice in criminal justice drug treatment often hinders effective implementation of AOD services. Target populations are often inappropriate, non–performance-based staff evaluations are used, and there is little organizational accountability for outcomes, high staff turnover, no reimbursement for implementation activities, and few incentives to enhance program effectiveness (Welsh & Harris, 2008).

The impact of prison-based drug treatment will be greatest if it leads to fully implemented and sustainable interventions (Fixsen, Naoom, Blase, Friedman, & Wallace, 2005; Schoenwald & Hoagwood, 2001) involving organizational and systems collaborations. Research and practice suggest that the best approach is to develop self-sustaining implementation sites. Similar to the "communities of practice" concept (Rosenheck, 2001), sites should follow systematic and scientifically based principles of program implementation and share innovative ideas and information to achieve positive organizational change.

Of key importance is the effective implementation of effective programs, encompassing both EBPPs and an implementation process. Without both the EBPP intervention and a systematic implementation process, positive client outcomes are unlikely to be achieved. Ineffective programs can be implemented well, and effective programs can be implemented poorly (Fixsen et al., 2005). Positive client outcomes are achieved only when both the intervention and implementation practices are effective. Another important lesson from implementation of research is that traditional dissemination, training, and implementation strategies (e.g., one-time training, dissemination of information only, implementation without changing staff roles, no assessment of organizational readiness) are often ineffective (Joyce & Showers, 2002).

NIDA's (2006) *Principles of Drug Abuse Treatment for Criminal Justice Populations: A Research-Based Guide* was based on drug abuse treatment research supported by NIDA (Table 7.2). Although scientific investigations spanning nearly four decades show that drug abuse treatment can be an effective intervention for many substance-abusing offenders, 13 evidence-based principles are offered to help improve drug treatment implementation and effectiveness.

Effectiveness: What Works?

The TC treatment continuum for drug-dependent offenders (TC treatment in prison, followed by transitional TC in a work release setting, followed by supervision and aftercare treatment in the community) is associated with significant reductions in drug use and crime after prison release (Gaes et al., 1999; Hiller, Knight, & Simpson, 1999a; Inciardi, Martin, & Butzin, 2004; Mitchell et al., 2006, 2007; Pearson & Lipton, 1999). However, important questions remain about the magnitude and generalizability of treatment effects and about relationships between inmate responses to treatment and postrelease outcomes (Farabee et al., 1999; Fletcher & Tims, 1992; Office of National Drug Control Policy, 1996, 1999; Pearson & Lipton, 1999; Welsh & Zajac, 2004a, 2004b).

Conclusions about the impact of in-prison TC treatment and aftercare on postrelease drug abuse and criminal behavior are based largely on the intensive evaluation of three model programs: KEY/CREST in Delaware, the Amity prison in California, and Kyle New Vision in Texas. The three studies all used extended follow-up periods for tracking outcomes (5 years in Delaware and

Table 7.2   NIDA Principles of Drug Abuse Treatment for Criminal Justice Populations

1. Drug addiction is a chronic brain disease that affects behavior.

2. Recovery from drug addiction requires effective treatment, followed by continued care.

3. Duration of treatment should be sufficiently long to produce stable behavioral changes.

4. Assessment is the first step in treatment.

5. Tailoring services to fit the needs of the individual is an important part of effective drug abuse treatment for criminal justice populations.

6. Drug use during treatment should be carefully monitored.

7. Treatment should target factors associated with criminal behavior.

8. Criminal justice supervision should incorporate treatment planning for drug abusing offenders, and treatment providers should be aware of correctional supervision requirements.

9. Continuity of care is essential for drug abusers reentering the community.

10. A balance of rewards and sanctions encourages prosocial behavior and treatment participation.

11. Offenders with co-occurring drug abuse and mental health problems often require an integrated treatment approach.

12. Medications are an important part of treatment for many drug-abusing offenders.

13. Treatment planning for drug-abusing offenders living in or reentering the community should include strategies to prevent and treat serious, chronic medical conditions such as HIV/AIDS, hepatitis B and C, and tuberculosis.

Source: NIDA (2006).

California; 3 in Texas). Each found that graduates of prison TC had lower rates of recidivism than comparison samples, especially when prison TC was combined with structured aftercare following release from prison.

The KEY/CREST program in Delaware represents a continuum of care that mirrors the offenders' custody status (Inciardi, Martin, Butzin, Hooper, & Harrison, 1997). Prisoners with a history of drug-related problems are identified and referred to the KEY TC program, and after prison release, these people go to the CREST program, a TC-based work release program for transitional aftercare (Inciardi et al., 1997; Lockwood, Inciardi, & Surratt,

1997; Nielsen, Scarpitti, & Inciardi, 1996). Finally, after release from residential aftercare, the clients receive supervised outpatient-based aftercare.

After 3 years elapsed between prison-based treatment and release to the community, significantly more of the clients who completed the in-prison program and the transitional aftercare program remained arrest-free (55%) than an untreated comparison group (29%) (Martin, Butzin, Saum, & Inciardi, 1999). Those who also received outpatient aftercare following the transitional residential treatment had the best outcomes (69% arrest free after 3 years). Results for relapse to drug use were similar, with 17% of those who completed only the in-prison TC, 27% who had the in-prison treatment and the transitional residential treatment, and 35% who also had outpatient aftercare remaining drug free during the follow-up period, compared with only 5% of the comparison group.

Five-year outcomes were similar to those reported at 3 years, with those who went through both KEY and CREST or through CREST alone having significantly lower recidivism rates. Participation in KEY in-prison TC treatment only did not significantly improve 5-year outcomes, although it was associated with higher rates of aftercare retention (Inciardi et al., 2004).

Although it is one of the strongest studies of prison TC to date, the Delaware study faced limitations. First, only a partial randomized research design was used. Random assignment was used only for one cohort of inmates randomly assigned to work release (CREST) or not. No random assignment was used to assign subjects to the experimental treatment (KEY, the TC program) or control group. Second, no pre-service assessment of need for drug treatment guided the creation of comparison groups (Martin et al., 1999, p. 300). Third, earlier analyses of outcomes (drug relapse, rearrest) relied on inmate self-reports (Inciardi et al., 1997), although later analyses incorporated criminal records for part of the sample (Inciardi et al., 2004; Martin et al., 1999). Arrestees' self-reports underestimate drug use detected by urinalysis by magnitudes of 40–60% (Taylor, Fitzgerald, Hunt, Reardon, & Brownstein, 2001), and limitations of self-report measures of criminal behavior are well known (Cantor & Lynch, 2000; Thornberry & Krohn, 2000).

In the Amity, California, prison study (Wexler et al., 1999), researchers used randomization to assign inmates who volunteered for treatment to either TC or a wait-listed, intent-to-treat comparison group. Volunteers were deemed eligible for TC if they had a drug problem and had 9 to 14 months remaining in their sentence before parole eligibility. Inmates remained in the TC-eligible pool until they had less than 9 months to serve, then they were removed from the pool and designated as members of the no-treatment control group.

Inmates in the no-treatment comparison group may have received some unknown mix of drug education, self-help, or outpatient services: "The control group did not receive any formal substance abuse treatment during their prison stay, although limited drug education and 12-step groups were available" (Wexler et al., 1999, p. 325).

Upon release from prison, parolees could volunteer for aftercare in a 40-bed community-based TC, so not all those who received in-prison treatment also received aftercare upon return to the community. Three-year post-parole outcome data showed that only 27% of those who received both in-prison and aftercare treatment were reincarcerated during the follow-up interval, compared with a 75% reincarceration rate for those in the comparison group, 79% for those who completed only the in-prison treatment, and 82% for those who dropped out of in-prison treatment (Wexler et al., 1999). However, when the entire "treatment" group (i.e., before dropouts from TC or aftercare were removed) was considered together (as it should be, to avoid biased outcomes in favor of the treatment group), the reincarceration rate for the treatment group increased to 69%, a difference that was no longer statistically significant. Interestingly, the 5-year outcome results for this sample suggested a rebound effect: The in-prison TC treatment group had a significantly lower reincarceration rate (76%) than the no-treatment control group (83.4%).

It is difficult to interpret the stability of these findings, the authors acknowledge, because "the unbiased assignment of randomization no longer operates, and selection bias becomes a possible (although by no means exclusive) explanation for the findings" (Prendergast, Hall, Wexler, Melnick, & Cao, 2004, p. 53). In addition, multivariate analyses of treatment subgroups were limited by small sample sizes ($ns < 100$ in three out of four subgroups) and low statistical power.

The Kyle New Vision program is a 500-bed facility that provides treatment to Texas inmates during the final 9 months of their prison term (Eisenberg & Fabelo, 1996). After release, parolees were required to attend 3 months of residential aftercare in a transitional TC, followed by up to another year of supervised outpatient aftercare. Authors constructed a matched comparison sample ($n = 103$) based on TC-eligible inmates who were rejected by the parole board or who had too little time remaining on their sentences (Knight, Simpson, & Hiller, 1999). TC-eligible parolees were rejected because the parole board judged them as unlikely to benefit from the program or inappropriate for the program (Knight, Simpson, Chatham, & Camacho, 1997, p. 82), introducing potential selection bias into the research design. Researchers separated treatment admissions into aftercare completers (TC + aftercare; $n = 169$) and aftercare dropouts (TC only; $n = 122$).

Analysis of 3-year outcome data showed that in-prison treatment followed by aftercare was most effective for high-risk, high-need offenders (Griffith, Hiller, Knight, & Simpson, 1999; Knight et al., 1999). Aftercare completers had a 3-year reincarceration rate of only 25%, significantly better than the 42% reincarceration rate of the comparison group and the 64% reincarceration rate of the aftercare dropouts. Because the treatment and comparison groups differed significantly on prior offense and problem severity (and perhaps other unmeasured characteristics), researchers further broke down the three groups into low-risk and high-risk subgroups (six comparisons overall, with sample sizes of less than 100 in four of the six groups). Treatment effects were greatest for high-risk inmates who completed both TC and aftercare (3-year rearrest rate of 26%) (see also Hiller et al., 1999a).

A quasi-experimental study in Pennsylvania examined postrelease outcomes for inmates participating in TC drug treatment (n = 217) or a minimal treatment comparison group (n = 491) at five state prisons (Welsh, 2007). The follow-up period extended to 26 months. Controlling for the influence of other predictors (e.g., drug dependency, criminal history), TC significantly reduced reincarceration (30% vs. 41%) and rearrest rates (24% vs. 33%) in contrast to the comparison group, but not drug relapse rates (35% vs. 39%). In addition, postrelease employment significantly reduced the likelihood of drug relapse, rearrest, and reincarceration.

Additional conclusions about prison-based drug treatment outcomes are based on systematic reviews and meta-analyses that estimate the effect sizes of treatment and examine the influence of factors that may increase or decrease effect size (including characteristics of the sample, the research design, and the intervention). Three reviews are summarized here.

In a recent meta-analysis of prison-based drug treatment programs (boot camp, narcotic maintenance, group counseling, and TC programs), Mitchell et al. (2006, 2007) found that TCs exhibited the strongest and most consistent reductions in drug relapse and recidivism. Although prison TC alone (without mandatory aftercare) resulted in a significant mean effect size for reincarceration and rearrest, it did so for drug relapse only when mandatory aftercare was provided. However, the authors cautioned that many of the studies they examined were methodologically weak, and many analyses were limited by low statistical power.

In one of the largest meta-analyses of correctional treatment to date, the Correctional Drug Abuse Treatment Project identified 1,606 distinct studies conducted between 1968 and 1996 (Pearson & Lipton, 1999). Pearson and Lipton used a four-point quality-of-methods scale (1 = *poor, very low confidence,* 2 = *fair, low confidence,* 3 = *good, midlevel of confidence,* and 4 = *excellent, high level of confidence*) in their analyses. The meta-analysis verified that prison TC was effective in reducing recidivism, finding a significant, weighted mean effect size of .133. However, of the seven TC studies examined, none was rated as excellent; only one was rated as good, three were rated as fair, and three were rated as poor.

Pearson and Lipton (1999) found only seven independent research comparisons of prison-based outpatient or group counseling programs. Although methodological weaknesses limited the conclusions that could be drawn, group counseling programs focused on substance abuse were not verified as effective in reducing recidivism. The mean effect size ($r = +.036$) was small and statistically nonsignificant, although the five fair-quality studies had a higher effect size ($r = +.052$). Two other studies were rated as poor in quality; no group-counseling studies were rated as good or excellent.

Gaes et al. (1999) reached similar conclusions in a review of adult correctional treatment. They particularly noted the persistence of bias caused by subject selection and attrition. In many studies, inmates were allowed to self-select into treatment, they were selected on criteria unrelated to their assessed level of need for treatment, or they dropped out of treatment. Dropouts have often been incorrectly analyzed as if they were a valid, independent comparison group. In each case, outcomes may be biased by selection or attrition processes (see also Austin, 1998; Pearson & Lipton, 1999).

Although Gaes et al. (1999) found evidence of positive prison drug treatment effects, especially prison TC, they offered four warnings: Few studies provided detailed descriptions of the treatment delivered, few studies monitored the quality or integrity of program implementation, subject selection and attrition bias were persistent problems, and few studies used "strong inference" designs (i.e., studies that not only detected a treatment effect but were able to detect a reduction in clients' needs or deficits that was statistically related to observed outcomes).

This approach is similar to what Bonta and Andrews (2003) and Andrews and Bonta (2006) call "dynamic" risk factors, which require measurement of intermediate treatment goals: "Successful programs are those that reduce relevant needs, which in turn are associated with reductions in criminal recidivism" (p. 68). Similarly, Farrington (2005) argues that studies of interventions should compare within-individual changes in risk factors with within-individual changes in offending and test hypotheses about causal processes intervening between risk factors and offending.

Empirical studies have identified important variables that mediate the effects of treatment on outcomes. Significant mediating variables include offender motivation and attributes, therapeutic relationships, program participation, behavioral compliance, therapeutic relationships with program staff and peers, psychosocial change, and length of stay (Simpson, 2001). However, most empirical research examining relationships suggested by this model has been conducted on community-based samples.

Where studies have been conducted with criminal justice populations, researchers have often focused on probation or parole settings. In a sample of 279 probationers assigned to a residential, 12-month TC, Broome, Knight, Joe, and Simpson (1996) found that variables predicting rearrest included self-esteem, counselor competence, and peer support. In a sample of 500 probationers randomly assigned to readiness training or a typical treatment program (Sia, Dansereau, & Czuchry, 2000), variables predicting therapeutic engagement and retention included the motivational measure of treatment readiness. In a sample of 429 probationers in a 6-month TC, Hiller, Knight, Leukefeld, and Simpson (2002) found that offender motivation and background characteristics predicted therapeutic engagement and inmate satisfaction, which in turn were related to retention. Researchers also found significant improvements in response to treatment over time, including improved self-esteem and decision making and decreased depression and risk taking.

The effects of observed changes in inmates' responses to treatment on outcomes such as recidivism remain largely unknown (Rosen, Hiller, Webster, Staton, & Leukefeld, 2004). Even the best studies of prison TCs to date in Delaware, Texas, and California have not examined relationships between in-treatment changes (e.g., changes in psychosocial functioning) and postrelease outcomes such as relapse and recidivism.

Many analysts argue that the effectiveness of prison-based TC drug treatment is less clear than commonly assumed, because of methodological deficiencies including selection or attrition biases, inadequate statistical controls, and low statistical power (Gaes et al., 1999; Mitchell et al., 2006, 2007; Pearson & Lipton, 1999). Other issues include unmeasured or compromised program implementation and insufficient attention to interactions between treatment process and outcome (Austin, 1998; Fletcher & Tims, 1992; Pearson & Lipton, 1999).

Major conclusions about the effectiveness of prison TCs are based largely on samples from three states (Delaware, California, and Texas), all of which received extensive program development and research funding from the National Institutes of Health (Melnick et al., 2004). The degree to which results from these three states represent the typical prison TC programs so widely implemented in the 1990s remains unknown (Harrison & Martin, 2003). At a minimum, replication across a greater number of sites is needed.

Relationships between inmate characteristics, treatment processes, and outcomes remain only partially understood (Farabee et al., 1999; Fletcher & Tims,

1992; Office of National Drug Control Policy, 1996; Pearson & Lipton, 1999; Welsh & McGrain, 2008). What are the independent and interactive effects of typically unmeasured individual and program characteristics (Welsh, 2006a; Welsh & Zajac, 2004a, 2004b)? How much does it cost to achieve a specific reduction in recidivism?

Economic Analyses of Prison-Based Drug Treatment

Economic studies across settings, populations, methods, and time periods consistently find positive net economic benefits of community-based alcohol and other drug treatment. By far, the majority of economic benefits stem from reduced crime, including reduced incarceration and victimization costs (Belenko, Patapis, & French, 2005; McCollister & French, 2003; Rajkumar & French, 1997).

Surprisingly few studies have conducted cost-effectiveness analyses (CEAs) or benefit–cost analyses (BCAs) of different *prison-based* treatment modalities. In the sections that follow, we briefly review estimated costs of different treatment modalities, CEAs, and BCAs.

Building on an earlier comprehensive review by Harwood et al. (2002), Belenko et al. (2005) conducted a meticulous review of published and unpublished articles, books, and reports on the economic analysis of substance abuse treatment. The authors reviewed 109 economic evaluations of substance abuse treatment published between 1990 and 2004. In addition, 17 unpublished reports and studies were included. It is important to note that Belenko et al. standardized all costs to 2004 dollars to allow for comparisons across studies; we use their figures in the studies summarized here.

As in other systematic reviews (e.g., Pearson & Lipton, 1999; Sherman et al., 1997), Belenko et al. (2005) rated each article on a five-point scale (1 = *high*, 5 = *low*) based on quality of research design (e.g., use of randomization, comparison sample, control variables, appropriateness or quality of economic measures, outcome measures) and a three-point scale (1 = *high*, 3 = *low*) of relevance (e.g., generalizability, sample size, recency). The authors added the design quality and relevance scores to get an overall score. Few studies evidenced high design quality. Of 47 published studies, only 4 (9%) achieved a score of 2 (highest-quality design and relevance), and 4 (9%) had scores of 3. Only 15 studies (32%) were rated as having high or high-medium quality for design or measurement rigor (and none of these studies with high-quality designs were conducted on prison-based treatment programs). Findings in three main areas were examined: costs of substance abuse treatment, CEAs of treatment, and BCAs of treatment.

Costs of Treatment. Compared with community-based treatment, prison treatment costs are low. Across four states, the incremental costs of treatment (i.e., above and beyond the costs of incarceration) ranged from $41 to $77 per week per inmate or from $1,120 to $3,624 per treatment episode (McCollister & French, 2002). In the Amity, California, prison TC, treatment costs were estimated at $77 per week per client (McCollister, French, Prendergast, et al., 2003). In Delaware, aftercare treatment costs after prison TC were estimated at only $21 per week (McCollister, French, Inciardi, et al., 2003). In Texas, Griffith et al. (1999) estimated the average cost of prison TC at $384 per week, substantially higher than for California or Delaware, but unlike other studies their estimates included incarceration costs for the stand-alone prison treatment facility and did not analyze the incremental costs of treatment above the prison costs.

In Connecticut, where the only economic study of nonresidential prison treatment was conducted, Daley et al. (2004) estimated the average cost per inmate of a 1-week in-prison drug education program at $199. The average cost per participant for a 10-week outpatient prison program (three group counseling sessions per week) was $791, and the cost for an intensive day treatment program (four group sessions per week for 4 months) was $3,139.

These findings highlight the need for more in-depth studies of different treatment modalities in prison. Furthermore, studies comparing community-based residential and outpatient treatment have found higher costs for residential treatment (Belenko et al., 2005). The higher costs of residential programs are attributable to clients being in the program 24 hours per day, lower caseloads, and higher costs associated with facilities and staffing. However, cost estimates for these two modalities vary a great deal because of differences in program structure, duration, frequency and type of services delivered, staffing, and cost of methods used. Variations for each type of program are summarized next.

Community outpatient treatment costs ranged from $77 per week (French, Salomé, Sindelar, & McLellan, 2002) to $166 per week for standard outpatient services (French, McCollister, Alexandre, Chitwood, & McCoy, 2004). Harwood, Kallinas, and Liu (2001) estimated costs of nine intensive outpatient programs at $272 per week, and Roebuck, French, and McLellan (2003) estimated costs at $493 per week across six intensive outpatient programs.

Estimated costs for community residential treatment ranged from $199 to $1,939 per week (Roebuck et al., 2003). One study found an average weekly cost of $626 across five TC programs (Roebuck et al., 2003). Another found a higher weekly cost for short-term residential ($642 per week per client) than for long-term residential treatment ($491 per week per client) (Koenig, Denmead, Nguyen, Harrison, & Harwood, 1999).

Cost-Effectiveness Analyses. CEA compares the costs of interventions for achieving specific health outcomes. Generally, one divides the incremental cost by the incremental outcome and compares this ratio for two or more interventions. The intervention with the lower cost per unit outcome is usually preferred. This ratio is interpreted as the additional treatment cost needed to achieve a one-unit improvement in the designated outcome (e.g., rearrest or reincarceration). Because CEAs may depend on the outcome measure used (Belenko et al., 2005), multiple outcome measures and multiple cost-effectiveness ratios should be incorporated into analyses of treatment programs (Sindelar, Jofre-Bonet, French, & McLellan, 2004).

Consistent with Harwood et al. (2002), Belenko et al. (2005) concluded that outpatient programs are generally more cost-effective than residential programs. Across 99 programs (Mojtabai & Zivin, 2003), the costs per abstinent case ($6,300) and per reduced drug use case ($2,400) were lowest for outpatient clients and highest for residential ($14,900 and $6,700, respectively) and inpatient clients ($15,600 and $6,100, respectively). Enhanced outpatient services were more cost-effective than standard services.

Using the number of days incarcerated during the follow-up as an outcome measure, researchers have examined the cost-effectiveness of prison TC treatment, work release treatment, and aftercare treatment. In general, residential prison treatment was cost-effective only if aftercare treatment was completed (Griffith et al., 1999; McCollister, French, Inciardi, et al., 2003; McCollister, French, Prendergast, Hall, & Sacks, 2004; McCollister, French, Prendergast, et al., 2003), and cost-effectiveness was greater for high-risk than for low-risk inmates (Griffith et al., 1999).

In Delaware, which operates a work release TC and an aftercare program for released inmates, McCollister, French, Inciardi, et al. (2003) reported that the incremental cost-effectiveness ratio (ICER) for all treatment clients (work release or aftercare) compared to the comparison group was $65 per incarceration day saved. Comparing clients who received aftercare to those who were only in the work release program, the ICER was $19 per incarceration day saved. Given the cost of incarceration in Delaware of $57 per day, McCollister et al. concluded that it is more cost-effective to add aftercare. However, because they examined only the costs of the program to the Department of Corrections, and the follow-up period was only 18 months (a number of offenders were still incarcerated at the end of the follow-up period), estimates of costs and the number of incarceration days saved may be underestimated.

In a 5-year follow-up to the Amity prison TC study, McCollister et al. (2004) found that the ICER for any treatment compared with controls was $65 per incarceration day saved, but only $45 per incarceration day was saved in a comparison of aftercare recipients with the control group. At a daily incarceration cost of $72, McCollister et al. concluded that prison treatment was cost-effective, and it was more cost effective if aftercare was received. In both the Delaware and Amity studies, however, clients self-selected into aftercare, and results must be replicated in better-controlled studies (Belenko et al., 2005).

In Texas, the cost-effectiveness of a 9-month prison TC was examined in a comparison of the 1- and 3-year outcomes of TC graduates with a matched group of general population inmates with substance abuse problems (Griffith et al., 1999). In-prison treatment when followed by aftercare realized substantial economic benefits, primarily through reduced criminal justice costs associated with significantly fewer treatment group participants being reincarcerated after their release on parole to the community. More in-depth examinations showed that the cost-effectiveness of in-prison TC treatment varied across groups of clients; those with the highest levels of risk produced the best cost-effectiveness ratios. Calculating the cost per 1% reduction in reincarceration, researchers found that treatment proved most cost-effective for high-risk parolees who completed treatment and aftercare relative to three other groups: high-risk and low-risk noncompleters, low-risk parolees who completed treatment and aftercare, and an untreated comparison group.

Benefit–Cost Analyses. BCAs typically focus on determining whether a program's benefits outweigh its costs (Aos, Phipps, Barnoski, & Lieb, 2001; Cohen, 2000; Farrington, Petrosino, & Welsh, 2001; Gaes & Kendig, 2002; Welsh & Farrington, 2000a, 2000b). By enumerating and converting costs and benefits to one dimension (dollars), we can examine whether there is a net benefit relative to the cost of a specific intervention. Major costs include capital (e.g., facilities) and operating costs (e.g., staffing, treatment materials) for a program (Aos et al., 2001; McCollister, French, Inciardi, et al., 2003; McCollister, French, Prendergast, Hall, & Sacks, 2004; McCollister, French, Prendergast, et al., 2003). Results can be expressed as either net economic benefits (total program benefits minus total program costs) or more typically as a benefit–cost ratio (BCR; total benefits divided by total costs). Programs that achieve a positive net benefit (i.e., a BCR greater than 1) may be considered economically beneficial, although the higher the BCR, the greater the return on the treatment investment.

Belenko et al. (2005) offer several cautions in regard to findings from BCAs in their review of the literature. First, the quality of the research designs used in these studies varied widely. Only one recent study used a randomized experimental design; many were methodologically weak pre–post studies of treatment clients only. Second, although all the studies found BCRs greater than 1, the ratios varied widely across studies, from 1.33 to 39.0. It is not possible at this time to generalize across studies and present an average BCR for particular types of treatment.

The largest share of economic benefits clearly accrues from reduced crime. The two primary cost components of crime reduction are incarceration costs and victimization costs (Aos et al., 2001; Cohen, 2000; Miller, Cohen, & Wierseman, 1996; Rajkumar & French, 1997). Although treatment outcome studies generally find reductions in post-program crime rates, the economic benefits can vary substantially depending on whether victimization costs are included. For example, Miller et al. (1996) estimated the intangible costs (i.e., effects on quality of life) of a victim of robbery to be $5,700 and for an assault victim $7,800, and the total victimization costs at $8,000 and $9,400 per crime, respectively (estimates in 1993 dollars). Rajkumar and French (1997) estimated the total social costs of victimization at $23,122 for robbery and $53,600 for assault (estimates in 1994 dollars). Depending on the crime categories used, the cost perspective, and the type of enumeration of victim costs chosen, the net economic benefits can vary widely.

Focusing on reduced criminality, Aos et al. (2001) compared the costs and benefits of adult offender programs. Among the different treatment modalities surveyed, the authors examined 16 adult in-prison TCs, 11 of which had aftercare programs. On average, the economic return from these programs ranged from $1.91 to $2.69 per dollar invested.

In a study of prison treatment in Connecticut, the largest return on investment was for less intensive outpatient treatment. The four levels of treatment received were Tier 1 (1 week of drug education classes), Tier 2 (three outpatient group counseling sessions per week for 10 weeks), Tier 3 (intensive day treatment including four group sessions per week for 4 months), and Tier 4 (residential TC treatment for 6 months). Researchers examined program costs and economic benefits from reduced rearrest for a sample of inmates released from prison (N = 831). All inmates who received any level of treatment before release (n = 358) were compared with a random sample of inmates who had been screened as having a substance abuse problem but did not receive any treatment (n = 473). Program costs included personnel time for delivering treatment services but excluded the costs of incarceration.

Using logistic regression to control for baseline differences between the samples, Daley et al. (2004) found significant reductions in rearrests 1 year after release for treatment participants overall (33% rearrested compared with 46% for the no-treatment comparison sample). There was no significant effect for inmates who received Tier 1 services compared with those receiving no treatment. Assuming that each rearrest resulted in reincarceration for 1 year, the calculated BCRs were 1.79 for the 6-month residential TC program (Tier 4), 3.16 for the intensive 4-month day treatment program (Tier 3), and 5.74 for the 10-week, low-intensity outpatient program (Tier 2). Thus, although three of the four prison treatment programs yielded net economic benefits, the largest BCR was for one of the less intensive treatments (outpatient), reflecting its low cost.

Because Daley et al. (2004) did not randomly assign inmates to the different treatment levels, caution is warranted (Belenko et al., 2005). We cannot yet conclude that low-intensity outpatient treatment is preferable to long-term residential treatment. Although Daley et al. controlled for baseline differences in risk, including a need for drug treatment score and an overall risk score, the quasi-experimental design did not allow them to rule out possible selection differences. These intriguing findings clearly show the need for more research on the relative economic benefits and cost-effectiveness of prison-based AOD treatment programs.

POLICY IMPLICATIONS

Prison-based drug treatment can be highly effective in breaking the cycle of relapse and recidivism among drug-involved offenders (Gaes et al., 1999; Mitchell et al., 2006, 2007; Pearson & Lipton, 1999). However, little research to date has examined the diverse individual and program factors that influence inmate responsiveness to treatment, relapse, and recidivism (Farabee et al., 1999; Fletcher & Tims, 1992; Hiller et al., 2002; Office of National Drug Control Policy, 1996, 1999; Pearson & Lipton, 1999; Rosen et al., 2004; Simpson, 2001; Welsh & Zajac, 2004a, 2004b).

The provision of drug treatment in corrections presents several challenges (Taxman et al., 2007). In addition to budgetary considerations, there are often issues of treatment availability, quality of services, and staff training. Other structural issues that treatment providers typically wrestle with include selection criteria for placement in drug treatment programs, the use of reinforcement techniques to encourage treatment retention, the use of support mechanisms to increase offenders' participation, the use of compliance measures to enforce requirements, and the time allocated for treatment within the correctional program (Farabee et al., 1999; Taxman & Bouffard, 2002). In this section we summarize four major research-based recommendations to strengthen prison-based AOD treatment (Welsh & Zajac, 2004a, 2004b).

Recommendation #1. Correctional agencies should make greater use of standardized instruments for screening inmates' need for treatment, readiness for treatment, and psychological functioning to improve program selection and placement decisions, inform treatment planning, and construct comparison groups in valid evaluation research designs. Research results consistently point out the importance of placing the right inmates into the right program types for the right reasons, and a more structured approach to inmate screening and assessment is needed.

Recommendation #2. The mission of AOD education and outpatient treatment programs within the full spectrum of AOD programming offered by correctional agencies deserves careful consideration and review. Substantial within-program variations in drug education and outpatient treatment programs indicate a need for more standardized procedures. For example, we recommend development of a program rating system that reflects the intensity of each AOD program offered to inmates at each institution. Written policies and procedures for different types of programs also need to be more clear, complete, and consistent across institutions. Although research has improved standardization in prison-based treatment, greater standardization could promote more consistent delivery of services and facilitate the development of a more cohesive, consistent treatment system.

Recommendation #3. Correctional agencies should develop overall information system capacities for offender program participation. Data should provide correctional agencies with useful information for program management and monitoring, and such information is vital for informing the research design of outcome evaluations (e.g., designing appropriate treatment and comparison groups). We need more reliable, current information about programs and offenders in order to understand how offender characteristics interact with program processes (e.g., program duration, treatment approach) to influence outcomes. Correctional administrators often lack the basic information needed to formulate new policies or to defend existing practices (U.S. Department of Justice, 1998).

Recommendation #4. Correctional agencies should carefully examine programming priorities and resources needed for prison-based drug treatment programs. Based on research findings illustrating substantial between-program differences, programming priorities (e.g., the extensive use of low-intensity education and outpatient programs) should be reevaluated. Nationwide, it is unlikely that a majority of inmates with serious substance abuse problems receive intensive treatment. In some states, research findings and recommendations have been used to revise drug treatment programming, policies, and priorities.

Efforts to design, monitor, and evaluate drug treatment programs in local and state correctional systems would benefit greatly from more careful attention to mapping of critical dimensions of program structure, content, and process than has been done so far (Welsh & Zajac, 2001). In order to demonstrate that a given program produces any specific outcome, such as lowered recidivism, we must be able to specify what the program was in the first place. Otherwise, the program becomes a "black box" that defies description (Simpson, 2001). How do we know what treatment components were delivered, or to what degree implementation varied across different sites? How can we form valid comparison groups for outcome evaluation absent a rigorous mapping of program characteristics?

This descriptive approach should precede and inform meaningful research designs examining drug treatment effects (Welsh & Harris, 2008). Although we have made progress toward identifying critical features of effective prison-based drug treatment, future analyses of this sort can further inform evidence-based programming and improve outcomes for drug-involved offenders and the communities they return to.

DISCUSSION QUESTIONS

1. Describe the different approaches used to provide drug treatment to incarcerated offenders.

2. What kinds of treatment or services are most commonly provided to incarcerated offenders? Do you see any incompatibility between the different approaches?

3. Which of the approaches discussed above works best? Describe evidence to support your argument.

4. Why is it that so many drug-addicted inmates do not receive drug treatment in prison?

5. Describe some of the major barriers in implementing prison-based drug treatment programs. What are the biggest barriers in need of attention?

6. How can programs and policies for drug-involved offenders be better designed to reduce recidivism and protect public safety?

7. How can we tell whether an inmate has truly benefited from treatment? What types of short-term and long-term changes should occur if treatment is effective?

8. Why do experts think that community aftercare, in addition to prison drug treatment, is so important to reduce drug abuse and recidivism?

9. Why should we be interested in the costs of drug treatment? What does the evidence tell us?

SUGGESTED READINGS

Belenko, S., Patapis, N., & French, M. T. (2005). *Economic benefits of drug treatment: A critical review of the evidence for policy makers.* Philadelphia: Treatment Research Institute at the University of Pennsylvania.

Chandler, R. K., Fletcher, B. W., & Volkow, N. D. (2009). Treating drug abuse and addiction in the criminal justice system: Improving public health and safety. *Journal of the American Medical Association, 301,* 183–190.

De Leon, G. (2000). *The therapeutic community: Theory, model and method.* New York: Springer-Verlag.

Gaes, G. G., Flanagan, T. J., Motiuk, L. L., & Stewart, L. (1999). Adult correctional treatment. In M. Tonry & J. Petersilia (Eds.), *Prisons. Crime and justice, a review of research* (Vol. 26, pp. 361–426). Chicago: University of Chicago Press.

Mitchell, O., Wilson, D. B., & MacKenzie, D. L. (2007). Does incarceration-based drug treatment reduce recidivism? A meta-analytic synthesis of the research. *Journal of Experimental Criminology, 3*(4), 353–375.

Mumola, C. J., & Karberg, J. C. (2006). *Drug use and dependence, state and federal prisoners, 2004* (NCJ 213530). Washington, DC: U.S. Department of Justice, Bureau of Justice Statistics.

National Institute on Drug Abuse. (2006). *Principles of drug abuse treatment for criminal justice populations: A research based guide.* Rockville, MD: Author.

Office of National Drug Control Policy. (1999). *Therapeutic communities in correctional settings: The Prison Based TC Standards Development Project. Final report of Phase II* (NCJ-179365). Washington, DC: Executive Office of the President, Office of National Drug Control Policy.

Pearson, F., & Lipton, D. (1999). A meta-analytic review of the effectiveness of corrections-based treatments for drug abuse. *The Prison Journal, 79,* 384–410.

Taxman, F. S., Perdoni, M. L., & Harrison, L. D. (2007). Drug treatment services for adult offenders: The state of the state. *Journal of Substance Abuse Treatment, 32,* 239–254.

REFERENCES

Andrews, D. A., & Bonta, J. (2006). *The psychology of criminal conduct* (4th ed.). Cincinnati, OH: Anderson.

Andrews, D., Zinger, I., Hoge, R. D., Bonta, J., Gendreau, P., & Cullen, F. T. (1990). Does correctional treatment work? A clinically relevant and psychologically informed meta-analysis. *Criminology, 28,* 369–404.

Aos, S., Phipps, P., Barnoski, R., & Lieb, R. (2001). *The comparative costs and benefits of programs to reduce crime.* Olympia: Washington State Institute for Public Policy. Retrieved September 11, 2009, from http://www.wsipp.wa.gov/rptfiles/costbenefit.pdf

Austin, J. (1998). The limits of prison drug treatment. *Corrections Management Quarterly, 2,* 66–74.

Ball, J. C., Shaffer, J. W., & Nurco, D. N. (1983). Day-to-day criminality of heroin addicts in Baltimore: A study in the continuity of offense rates. *Drug and Alcohol Dependence, 12,* 119–142.

Belenko, S., Patapis, N., & French, M. T. (2005). *Economic benefits of drug treatment: A critical review of the evidence for policy makers.* Philadelphia: Treatment Research Institute at the University of Pennsylvania.

Belenko, S., & Peugh, J. (2005). Estimating drug treatment needs among state prison inmates. *Drug and Alcohol Dependence, 77,* 269–281.

Bonta, J., & Andrews, D. A. (2003). A commentary on Ward and Stewart's model of human needs. *Psychology, Crime & Law, 9*(3), 215–218.

Bourgon, G., & Armstrong, B. (2005). Transferring the principles of effective treatment into a "real world" prison setting. *Criminal Justice and Behavior, 32,* 3–25.

Broome, K. M., Knight, K., Joe, G. W., & Simpson, D. D. (1996). Evaluating the drug-abusing probationer: Clinical interview versus self-administered assessment. *Criminal Justice and Behavior, 23*(4), 593–606.

Brown, B. S., & Flynn, P. M. (2002). The federal role in drug abuse technology transfer: A history and perspective. *Journal of Substance Abuse Treatment, 22,* 245–257.

Bureau of Justice Statistics. (2009). *Drugs and crime facts.* Retrieved March 6, 2009, from http://www.ojp.usdoj.gov/bjs/dcf/duc.htm

Cantor, D., & Lynch, J. P. (2000). Self-report surveys as measures of crime and criminal victimization. In D. Duffee (Ed.), *Criminal justice 2000* (NCJ-182411, Vol. 4, pp. 85–138). Washington, DC: U.S. Department of Justice, Office of Justice Programs, National Institute of Justice.

Center on Addiction and Substance Abuse. (1998). *Behind bars: Substance abuse and America's prison population.* New York: Columbia University.

Chaiken, M. R. (1986). Crime rates and substance abuse among types of offenders. In B. D. Johnson & E. D. Wish (Eds.), *Crime rates among drug-abusing offenders: Final report to the National Institute of Justice.* New York: Narcotic and Drug Research, Inc.

Chandler, R. K., Fletcher, B. W., & Volkow, N. D. (2009). Treating drug abuse and addiction in the criminal justice system: Improving public health and safety. *Journal of the American Medical Association, 301,* 183–190.

Chou, C. P., Hser, Y. I., & Anglin, M. D. (1998). Interaction effects of client and treatment program characteristics on retention: An exploratory analysis using hierarchical linear models. *Substance Use and Misuse, 33*(11), 2281–2301.

Cohen, M. A. (2000). Measuring the costs and benefits of crime and justice. In D. Duffee (Ed.), *Criminal justice 2000* (NCJ-182411, Vol. 4, pp. 263–314). Washington, DC: U.S. Department of Justice, National Institute of Justice.

Council of State Governments. (2003). *Report of the Re-Entry Policy Council: Charting the safe and successful return of prisoners to the community.* New York: Re-Entry Policy Council.

Cropsey, K. L., Villalobos, G. C., & St. Clair, C. L. (2005). Pharmacotherapy treatment in substance-dependent correctional populations: A review. *Substance Use and Misuse, 40,* 1983–1999.

Daley, M., Love, C. T., Shepard, D. S., Petersen, C. B., White, K. L., & Hall, F. B. (2004). Cost effectiveness of Connecticut's in-prison substance abuse treatment. *Journal of Offender Rehabilitation, 39,* 69–92.

De Leon, G. (1997). Therapeutic communities: Is there an essential model? In G. De Leon (Ed.), *Community as method: Therapeutic communities for special populations and special settings* (pp. 3–18). Westport, CT: Praeger.

De Leon, G. (2000). *The therapeutic community: Theory, model and method.* New York: Springer-Verlag.

De Leon, G. (2004). Commentary on "Self-help organizations for alcohol and drug problems: Toward evidence-based practice and policy." *Journal of Substance Abuse Treatment, 26,* 163–165.

Eisenberg, M., & Fabelo, T. (1996). Evaluation of the Texas correctional substance abuse treatment initiative: The impact of policy research. *Crime and Delinquency, 42,* 296–308.

Etheridge, R. M., & Hubbard, R. L. (2000). Conceptualizing and assessing treatment structure and process in community-based drug dependency treatment programs. *Substance Use and Misuse, 35,* 1757–1795.

Etheridge, R. M., Hubbard, R. L., Anderson, J., Craddock, S. G., & Flynn, P. M. (1997). Treatment structure and program services in the Drug Abuse Treatment Outcome Study (DATOS). *Psychology of Addictive Behaviors, 11*(4), 244–260.

Farabee, D., Prendergast, M., Cartier, J., Wexler, H., Knight, K., & Anglin, M. D. (1999). Barriers to implementing effective correctional drug treatment programs. *Prison Journal, 79*(2), 150–162.

Farrington, D. P. (2005). The integrated cognitive antisocial potential (ICAP) theory. In D. P. Farrington (Ed.), *Integrated developmental & life-course theories of offending. advances in criminological theory* (Vol. 14, pp. 73–92). New Brunswick, NJ: Transaction.

Farrington, D. P., Petrosino, A., & Welsh, B. C. (2001). Systematic reviews and cost–benefit analyses of correctional interventions. *The Prison Journal, 81,* 339–359.

Fixsen, D. L., Naoom, S. F., Blase, K. A., Friedman, R. M., & Wallace, F. (2005). *Implementation research: A synthesis of the literature.* Tampa: University of South Florida, Louis de la Parte Florida Mental Health Institute, The National Implementation Research Network (FMHI Publication #231).

Fletcher, B. W., & Tims, F. M. (1992). Methodological issues: Drug abuse treatment in prisons and jails. In C. G. Leukefeld & F. M. Tims (Eds.), *Drug abuse treatment in prisons and jails* (pp. 246–260). Washington, DC: U.S. Government Printing Office.

French, M. T., McCollister, K. E., Alexandre, P. D., Chitwood, D. D., & McCoy, C. B. (2004). Revolving roles in drug-related crime: The cost of chronic drug users as victims and perpetrators. *Journal of Quantitative Criminology, 20,* 217–241.

French, M. T., Salomé, H. J., Sindelar, J. L., & McLellan, A. T. (2002). Benefit–cost analysis of addiction treatment: Methodological guidelines and empirical application using DATCAP and ASI. *Health Services Research, 37,* 433–455.

Gaes, G. G., Flanagan, T. J., Motiuk, L. L., & Stewart, L. (1999). Adult correctional treatment. In M. Tonry & J. Petersilia (Eds.), *Prisons. Crime and justice, a review of research* (Vol. 26, pp. 361–426). Chicago: University of Chicago Press.

Gaes, G. G., & Kendig, N. (2002). *The skill sets and health care needs of released offenders.* Paper presented at the National Policy Conference, "From Prison to Home: The Effect of Incarceration and Reentry on Children, Families and Communities," January 30–31, 2002,

Washington, DC. Sponsored by the U.S. Department of Health and Human Services and the Urban Institute. Retrieved September 11, 2009, from http://www.urban.org/uploadedpdf/410629_ReleasedOffenders.pdf

Grella, C. E., Greenwell, L., Prendergast, M., Farabee, D., Hall, E., Cartier, J., et al. (2007). Organizational characteristics of drug abuse treatment programs for offenders. *Journal of Substance Abuse Treatment, 32,* 291–300.

Griffith, J. D., Hiller, M. L., Knight, K., & Simpson, D. D. (1999). A cost-effectiveness analysis of in-prison therapeutic community treatment and risk classification. *The Prison Journal, 79,* 352–368.

Haggerty, J. L., Reid, R. J., Freeman, G. K., Starfield, B. H., Adair, C. E., & McKendry, R. (2003). Continuity of care: A multidisciplinary review. *British Medical Journal, 327,* 1219–1221.

Harrison, L. D., & Martin, S. S. (2003). *Residential substance abuse treatment for state prisoners: Implementation lessons learned* (NCJ 195738). Washington, DC: Office of Justice Programs, National Institute of Justice. Retrieved September 11, 2009, from http://www.ncjrs.gov/pdffiles1/nij/195738.pdf

Harwood, H. J., Kallinas, S., & Liu, C. (2001). *The costs and components of substance abuse treatment.* Rockville, MD: Substance Abuse and Mental Health Services Administration, Center for Substance Abuse Treatment.

Harwood, H. J., Malhotra, D., Villarivera, C., Liu, C., Chong, U., & Gilani, J. (2002). *Cost effectiveness and cost benefit analysis of substance abuse treatment: A literature review.* Rockville, MD: Substance Abuse and Mental Health Services Administration, Center for Substance Abuse Treatment.

Hiller, M. L., Knight, K., Broome, K. M., & Simpson, D. D. (1998). Legal pressure and treatment retention in a national sample of long-term residential programs. *Criminal Justice and Behavior, 25*(4), 463–481.

Hiller, M. L., Knight, K., Leukefeld, C. G., & Simpson, D. D. (2002). Motivation as a predictor of engagement in mandated residential substance abuse treatment. *Criminal Justice and Behavior, 29,* 56–75.

Hiller, M. L., Knight, K., & Simpson, D. D. (1999a). Prison-based substance abuse treatment, residential aftercare, and recidivism. *Addiction, 94*(6), 833–842.

Hiller, M., Knight, K., & Simpson, D. (1999b). Risk factors that predict dropout from corrections-based treatment for drug abuse. *The Prison Journal, 79,* 411–430.

Humphreys, K., Wing, S., McCarty, D., Chappel, J., Gallant, L., Haberle, B., et al. (2004). Self-help organizations for alcohol and drug problems: Toward evidence-based practice and policy. *Journal of Substance Abuse Treatment, 26,* 151–158.

Inciardi, J. A., Martin, S. S., & Butzin, C. A. (2004). Five-year outcomes of therapeutic community treatment of drug-involved offenders after release from prison. *Crime and Delinquency, 50*(1), 88–107.

Inciardi, J., Martin, S., Butzin, C., Hooper, R., & Harrison, L. (1997). An effective model of prison-based treatment for drug-involved offenders. *Journal of Drug Issues, 27,* 261–278.

Inciardi, J. A., Martin, S. S., Lockwood, D., Hooper, R. M., & Wald, B. M. (1992). Obstacles to the implementation and evaluation of drug treatment programs in correctional settings: Reviewing the Delaware KEY experience. In C. G. Leukefeld & F. M. Tims (Eds.), *Drug abuse treatment in prisons and jails* (pp. 176–191). NIDA monograph no. 118 HHS. Rockville, MD: U.S. Government Printing Office.

Johnson, B., Goldstein, P. J., Preble, E., Schmeidler, J., Lipton, D. S., Spunt, B., et al. (1985). *Taking care of business: The economics of crime by heroin abusers.* Lexington, MA: Lexington Books.

Johnson, B. A., Rosenthal, N., Capece, J. A., Wiegand, F., Mao, L., Beyers, K., et al. (2007). Topiramate for treating alcohol dependence: A randomized controlled trial. *Journal of the American Medical Association 298,* 1641–1651.

Joyce, B., & Showers, B. (2002). *Student achievement through staff development* (3rd ed.). Alexandria, VA: Association for Supervision and Curriculum Development.

Kilbourne, A. M., Neumann, M. S., Pincus, H. A., Bauer, M. S., & Stall, R. (2007). Implementing evidence-based interventions in health care: Application of the replicating effective programs framework. *Implementation Science, 2,* 42.

Knight, K., Simpson, D., Chatham, L., & Camacho, L. (1997). An assessment of prison-based drug treatment: Texas' in-prison therapeutic community program. *Journal of Offender Rehabilitation, 24,* 75–100.

Knight, K., Simpson, D., & Hiller, M. (1999). Three-year reincarceration outcomes in-prison therapeutic community treatment in Texas. *The Prison Journal, 79,* 321–333.

Koenig, L., Denmead, G., Nguyen, R., Harrison, M., & Harwood, H. (1999). *The costs and benefits of substance abuse treatment: Findings from the National Treatment Improvement Evaluation Study (NTIES).* Prepared under contract no. 270977016 for the Center for Substance Abuse Treatment.

Latessa, E. J., Cullen, F. T., & Gendreau, P. (2002, September). Beyond correctional quackery: Professionalism and the possibility of effective treatment. *Federal Probation,* Special Issue, pp. 43–49.

Linhorst, D. M., Knight, K., Johnston, J. S., & Trickey, M. (2001). Situational influences on the implementation of a prison-based therapeutic community. *Prison Journal, 81*(4), 436–453.

Lipton, D. S. (1995). *The effectiveness of treatment for drug abusers under criminal justice supervision* (NCJ 157642). Washington, DC: U.S. Department of Justice, Office of Justice Programs, National Institute of Justice.

Lockwood, D., Inciardi, J. A., & Surratt, H. L. (1997). Crest Outreach Center: A model for blending treatment and corrections. In F. M. Tims, J. A. Inciardi, B. W. Fletcher, & A. M. Horton Jr. (Eds.), *The effectiveness of innovative approaches in the treatment of drug abuse* (pp. 70–82). Westport, CT: Greenwood.

Martin, S. S., Butzin, C. A., & Inciardi, J. A. (1995). Assessment of a multistage therapeutic community for drug-involved offenders. *Journal of Psychoactive Drugs, 27,* 109–116.

Martin, S. S., Butzin, C. A., Saum, C. A., & Inciardi, J. A. (1999). Three-year outcomes of therapeutic community treatment for drug-involved offenders in Delaware: From prison to work release to aftercare. *The Prison Journal, 79,* 294–320.

McCollister, K. E., & French, M. T. (2002). The economic cost of substance abuse treatment in criminal justice settings. In C. G. Leukefeld, F. Tims, & D. Farabee (Eds.), *Treatment of drug offenders: Policies and issues* (pp. 22–37). New York: Springer.

McCollister, K. E., & French, M. T. (2003). The relative contributions of outcome domains in the total economic benefit of addiction interventions: A review of first findings. *Addiction, 89,* 1647–1659.

McCollister, K. E., French, M. T., Inciardi, J. A., Butzin, C. A., Martin, S. S., & Hooper, R. M. (2003). Post-release substance abuse treatment for criminal offenders: A cost-effectiveness analysis. *Journal of Quantitative Criminology, 19,* 389–407.

McCollister, K. E., French, M. T., Prendergast, M., Hall, E., & Sacks, S. (2004). Long-term cost effectiveness of addiction treatment for criminal offenders. *Justice Quarterly, 21,* 659–679.

McCollister, K. E., French, M. T., Prendergast, M., Wexler, H., Sacks, S., & Hall, E. (2003). Is in-prison treatment enough? A cost-effectiveness analysis of prison-based treatment and aftercare services for substance-abusing offenders. *Law and Policy, 25,* 63–82.

McKay, J. R. (2001). Effectiveness of continuing care interventions for substance abusers: Implications for the study of long-term treatment effects. *Evaluation Review, 25,* 211–232.

Melnick, G., De Leon, G., Hiller, M. L., & Knight, K. (2000). Therapeutic communities: Diversity in treatment elements. *Substance Use and Misuse, 35*(12–14), 1819–1847.

Melnick, G., Hawke, J., & Wexler, H. K. (2004). Client perceptions of prison-based therapeutic community drug treatment programs. *The Prison Journal, 84,* 121–138.

Miller, T. R., Cohen, M. A., & Wierseman, B. (1996). *Victim costs and consequences: A new look* (NCJ 155282). Washington, DC: U.S. Department of Justice, National Institute of Justice.

Miller, W. R., Sorensen, J. L., Selzer, J. A., & Brigham, G. S. (2006). Disseminating evidence-based practices in substance abuse treatment: A review with suggestions. *Journal of Substance Abuse Treatment, 31,* 25–39.

Mitchell, O., MacKenzie, D. L., & Wilson, D. B. (2006, September). *The effectiveness of incarceration-based drug treatment on criminal behavior.* Paper approved by the Campbell Collaboration, Criminal Justice Review Group. Retrieved September 11, 2009, from http://db .c2admin.org/doc-pdf/Mitchell_Incarceration_DrugTx_review.pdf

Mitchell, O., Wilson, D. B., & MacKenzie, D. L. (2007). Does incarceration-based drug treatment reduce recidivism? A meta-analytic synthesis of the research. *Journal of Experimental Criminology, 3*(4), 353–375.

Mojtabai, R., & Zivin, J. G. (2003). Effectiveness and cost-effectiveness of four treatment modalities for substance abuse disorders: A propensity score analysis. *Health Services Review, 38,* 233–259.

Mumola, C. J. (1999). *Substance abuse and treatment, state and federal prisoners, 1997.* Bureau of Justice Statistics Special Report. Washington, DC: U.S. Department of Justice, Office of Justice Programs.

Mumola, C. J., & Karberg, J. C. (2006). *Drug use and dependence, state and federal prisoners, 2004* (NCJ 213530). Washington, DC: U.S. Department of Justice, Bureau of Justice Statistics.

National Institute of Justice. (2003). *2000 arrestee drug abuse monitoring: Annual report* (NCJ 193013). Washington, DC: U.S. Department of Justice, Office of Justice Programs, National Institute of Justice.

National Institute on Drug Abuse. (2006). *Principles of drug abuse treatment for criminal justice populations: A research-based guide.* Rockville, MD: Author.

Nielsen, A. L., Scarpitti, F. R., & Inciardi, J. A. (1996). Integrating the therapeutic community and work release for drug-involved offenders: The CREST program. *Journal of Substance Abuse Treatment, 13,* 349–358.

Office of National Drug Control Policy. (1996). *Treatment protocol effectiveness study.* Washington, DC: Executive Office of the President, Office of National Drug Control Policy.

Office of National Drug Control Policy. (1999). *Therapeutic communities in correctional settings: The Prison Based TC Standards Development Project. Final report of Phase II* (NCJ-179365). Washington, DC: Executive Office of the President, Office of National Drug Control Policy.

Palmer, T. (1992). *The re-emergence of correctional intervention.* Newbury Park, CA: Sage.

Palmer, T. (1995). Programmatic and nonprogrammatic aspects of successful intervention: New directions for research. *Crime and Delinquency, 41,* 100–131.

Pearson, F., & Lipton, D. (1999). A meta-analytic review of the effectiveness of corrections-based treatments for drug abuse. *The Prison Journal, 79,* 384–410.

Pelissier, B., Jones, N., & Cadigan, T. (2007). Drug treatment aftercare in the criminal justice system: A systematic review. *Journal of Substance Abuse Treatment, 32,* 311–320.

Petersilia, J., Greenwood, P., & Lavin, M. (1977). *Criminal careers of habitual felons.* Santa Monica, CA: Rand.

Prendergast, M. L., Hall, E. A., Wexler, H. K., Melnick, G., & Cao, Y. (2004). Amity prison-based therapeutic community: 5-year outcomes. *The Prison Journal, 84,* 36–60.

Prendergast, M. L., Podus, D., & Chang, E. (2000). Program factors and treatment outcomes in drug dependence treatment: An examination using meta-analysis. *Substance Use and Misuse, 35*(12–14), 1931–1965.

Prendergast, M. L., Podus, D., Chang, E., & Urada, D. (2002). The effectiveness of drug abuse treatment: A metaanalysis of comparison group studies. *Drug and Alcohol Dependence, 67,* 53–72.

Rajkumar, A. S., & French, M. T. (1997). Drug use, crime costs, and the economic benefits of treatment. *Journal of Quantitative Criminology, 13,* 291–323.

Rockholz, P. B. (2004). National update on therapeutic community programs for substance abusing offenders in state prisons. In K. Knight & D. Farabee (Eds.), *Treating addicted offenders: A continuum of effective practices* (pp. 14-1–14-10). Kingston, NJ: Civic Research Institute.

Roebuck, M. C., French, M. T., & McLellan, A. T. (2003). DATStats: Summary results from 85 completed drug abuse treatment cost analysis programs (DATCAPs). *Journal of Substance Abuse Treatment, 25,* 51–57.

Rogers, E. M. (1995). *Diffusion of innovations* (5th ed.). New York: The Free Press.

Rosen, P. J., Hiller, M. L., Webster, J. M., Staton, M. S., & Leukefeld, C. (2004). Treatment motivation and therapeutic engagement in prison-based substance use treatment. *Journal of Psychoactive Drugs, 36*(3), 387–396.

Rosenheck, R. A. (2001). Organizational process: A missing link between research and practice. *Psychiatric Services, 52,* 1607–1612.

Schildhaus, S., Gerstein, D., Dugoni, B., Brittingham, A., & Cerbone, F. (2000). Services research outcomes study: Explanation of treatment effectiveness, using individual-level and programmatic variables. *Substance Use and Misuse, 35*(12–14), 1879–1910.

Schoenwald, K. S., & Hoagwood, K. (2001). Effectiveness, transportability, and dissemination of interventions: What matters when? *Psychiatric Services, 52,* 1190–1197.

Sherman, L. W., Gottfredson, D. C., MacKenzie, D., Eck, J., Reuter, P., & Bushway, S. (Eds.). (1997). *What works, what doesn't, what's promising: A report to the United States Congress* (NCJ 165366). Prepared for the National Institute of Justice. Retrieved March 12, 2004, from http://www.ncjrs.org/docfiles/wholedoc.doc

Sia, T. L., Dansereau, D. F., & Czuchry, M. L. (2000). Treatment readiness training and proba-tioners' evaluation of substance abuse treatment in a criminal justice setting. *Journal of Substance Abuse Treatment, 19*, 459–467.

Simpson, D. D. (2001). Modeling treatment process and outcome. *Addiction, 96*, 207–211.

Simpson, D. D., Wexler, H. K., & Inciardi, J. A. (Eds.). (1999, September/December). Special issue on drug treatment outcomes for correctional settings, parts 1 & 2. *The Prison Journal, 79*(3/4), 291–293.

Sindelar, J. L., Jofre-Bonet, M., French, M. T., & McLellan, A. T. (2004). Cost-effectiveness analysis of addiction treatment: Paradoxes of multiple outcomes. *Drug and Alcohol Dependence, 73*, 41–50.

Strauss, S. M., & Falkin, G. P. (2000). The relationship between the quality of drug user treatment and program completion: Understanding the perceptions of women in a prison-based program. *Substance Use and Misuse, 35*(12–14), 2127–2159.

Taxman, F., & Bouffard, J. (2002). Assessing therapeutic integrity in modified therapeutic commu-nities for drug-involved offenders. *The Prison Journal, 82*, 189–212.

Taxman, F. S., Perdoni, M. L., & Harrison, L. D. (2007). Drug treatment services for adult offend-ers: The state of the state. *Journal of Substance Abuse Treatment, 32*(3), 239–254.

Taxman, F. S., Young, D. W., Wiersema, B., Rhodes, A., & Mitchell, S. (2007). The National Criminal Justice Treatment Practices Survey: Multilevel survey methods and procedures. *Journal of Substance Abuse Treatment, 32*(3), 225–238.

Taylor, B. G., Fitzgerald, N., Hunt, D., Reardon, J. A., & Brownstein, H. H. (2001). *ADAM pre-liminary 2000 findings on drug use and drug markets: Adult male arrestees* (NCJ 189101). Washington, DC: U.S. Department of Justice, National Institute of Justice.

Thornberry, T. P., & Krohn, M. D. (2000). The self-report method for measuring delinquency and crime. In D. Duffee (Ed.), *Criminal justice 2000* (NCJ-182411, Vol. 4, pp. 33–84). Washington, DC: U.S. Department of Justice, Office of Justice Programs, National Institute of Justice.

U.S. Department of Justice. (1998). *State and federal corrections information systems: An inventory of data elements and an assessment of reporting capabilities* (NCJ 171686). Washington, DC: U.S. Department of Justice, Office of Justice Programs, Bureau of Justice Statistics.

Volkow, N. D., & Li, T. K. (2005). Drugs and alcohol: Treating and preventing abuse, addiction and their medical consequences. *Pharmacological Therapy, 108*, 3–17.

Walters, G. (1992). Drug-seeking behavior: Disease or lifestyle. *Professional Psychology: Research and Practice, 23*(2), 139–145.

Welsh, B. C., & Farrington, D. P. (2000a). Correctional intervention programs and cost–benefit analysis. *Criminal Justice and Behavior, 27*, 115–133.

Welsh, B. C., & Farrington, D. P. (2000b). Monetary costs and benefits of crime prevention pro-grams. In M. Tonry (Ed.), *Crime and justice* (Vol. 27, pp. 305–361). Chicago: University of Chicago Press.

Welsh, W. N. (2006a). *Evaluation of drug treatment programs at the State Correctional Institution (SCI) at Chester: A partnership between the Pennsylvania Department of Corrections, Gaudenzia Inc., and Temple University*. Final report to the National Institute of Justice (2002-RT-BX-1002). Retrieved September 11, 2009, from http://www.cor.state.pa.us/stats/lib/stats/ ChesterReporttoNIJ-Final-November2006.pdf

Welsh, W. N. (2006b). The need for a comprehensive approach to program planning, development and evaluation. *Criminology and Public Policy, 5,* 603–614.

Welsh, W. N. (2007). A multi-site evaluation of prison-based TC drug treatment. *Criminal Justice and Behavior, 34,* 1481–1498.

Welsh, W. N., & Harris, P. W. (2008). *Criminal justice policy and planning* (3rd ed.). Cincinnati: LexisNexis, Anderson.

Welsh, W. N., & McGrain, P. N. (2008). Predictors of therapeutic engagement in prison-based drug treatment. *Drug and Alcohol Dependence, 96,* 271–280.

Welsh, W. N., & Zajac, G. (2001). Assessing prison-based drug and alcohol treatment: Pennsylvania's ongoing review has improved programming. *Offender Substance Abuse Report, 1*(6), 83–84, 90–93.

Welsh, W. N., & Zajac, G. (2004a). Building an effective research partnership between a university and a state correctional agency: Assessment of drug treatment in Pennsylvania prisons. *The Prison Journal, 84,* 143–170.

Welsh, W. N., & Zajac, G. (2004b). A census of prison-based drug treatment programs: Implications for programming, policy and evaluation. *Crime and Delinquency, 50,* 108–133.

West, H. C., & Sabol, W. J. (2009). *Prisoners in 2007.* Washington, DC: U.S. Department of Justice, Bureau of Justice Statistics.

Wexler, H. K., Lipton, D. S., & Johnson, B. D. (1988, March). *A criminal justice system strategy for treating cocaine–heroin abusing offenders in custody.* Issues and Practices Paper in Criminal Justice (U.S. GPO no. 1988-202-045:8-0082). Washington, DC: National Institute of Justice.

Wexler, H., Melnick, G., Lowe, L., & Peters, J. (1999). Three-year reincarceration outcomes for Amity in-prison therapeutic community and aftercare in California. *The Prison Journal, 79,* 321–333.

Wormith, J. S., Althouse, R., Simpson, M., Reitzel, L. R., Fagan, T. J., & Morgan, R. D. (2007). The rehabilitation and reintegration of offenders: The current landscape and some future directions for correctional psychology. *Criminal Justice and Behavior, 34,* 879–892.

CHAPTER 8

Prison-Based Educational and Vocational Training Programs

Georgen Guerrero

Prison educational programs are designed primarily to help inmates reach minimal state and federal education standards. Collectively, inmates are among the least educated members of society. Inmates report lower educational levels than the general population (Harlow, 2003). Forty-one percent of state and federal prisoners have not completed the requirements for a high school diploma or received a General Equivalency Diploma (GED) (Harlow, 2003). Sixty-eight percent of state inmates do not have a high school diploma (Harlow, 2003; Pollock, 2004). Inmates as a whole average a ninth-grade education level (Stone, 1997). Only 11% of inmates have attended some college, compared with 48% of the general population (Harlow, 2003). As a result of these deficiencies, educational programs are among the most important programs offered to inmates.

People who are incarcerated not only suffer from academic deficiencies but also routinely lack the vocational skills needed to obtain and perform adequately in the workforce (see chapter 13). Just as academic skills are needed to succeed in life, vocational skills are a must for inmates wanting to provide for themselves and their families. Vocational skills allow inmates to compete for entry-level positions in society once released. As inmates age in prison and are released back into society, much of their success depends on obtaining and maintaining meaningful employment. Harlow (2003) found that during the month of their arrest, 45% of inmates were unemployed or were maintaining only part-time employment.

THE HISTORY OF PRISON EDUCATION

Educational programs have been a part of American corrections since the first prison school was opened at the Walnut Street Jail in 1798 (Bosworth, 2002). Walnut Street Jail tried to reform inmates' behavior through religious contemplation; however, over time, education was emphasized over Bible reading. The school at Walnut Street Jail had a library with 110 books (Bosworth, 2002) and helped inmates learn basic reading, writing, and arithmetic (Roberts, 1971).

In 1825, the Boston Prison Discipline Society was founded; this society was led by Louis Dwight, who believed that inmates could be changed from their evil ways through Sabbath schools, where inmates were taught how to read Bible scriptures with the assistance of part-time chaplains. Even though Dwight's intentions were to create stronger religious convictions, he was instrumental in offering inmates a rudimentary education through the Sabbath schools, which helped them to become more productive members of society (Roberts, 1971).

In 1826, Auburn Prison implemented an instructional program with the assistance of Auburn's first resident chaplain, Jared Curtis, and 20 theological students who taught illiterate inmates to read (Sutherland, Cressey, & Luckenbill, 1992; Taft, 1956). Over the next few years, educational instruction for inmates was adopted by other prisons; these programs were instructed by prison chaplains. Prison chaplains were responsible for all inmate instruction until 1847, when New York State law provided for the appointment of two instructors at Auburn and Sing Sing state prisons (McKelvey, 1936).

Elmira Reformatory

In 1876, Elmira Reformatory set the standard for educational development (Stone, 1997). Elmira offered high school and college courses to its residents and hired full-time faculty to instruct these courses. Zebulon Brockway, the father of prison reform and superintendent at Elmira Reformatory, hired Dr. D. R. Ford to instruct courses to the youthful offenders at Elmira. After teaching for 1 year, Dr. Ford was given six school principals and three lawyers for elementary instruction (Roberts, 1971).

Elmira had a library with approximately 4,000 books and 650 magazines. Elmira also published a prison newspaper, *The Summary*, which allowed inmates to keep up with current events locally, nationally, and internationally (Johnson & Wolfe, 1996). The reformatory offered 36 different trades through industrial and agricultural learning (Roberts, 1971). Brockway implemented educational courses in geometry, bookkeeping, human physiology, sanitary science (McKelvey, 1936), biblical teachings, ethics, and psychology (Roberts, 1971). In 1883, Brockway hired Syracuse professor N. A. Wells to instruct courses in industrial arts for inmates who were not interested in obtaining an education; the courses included plumbing, tailoring, telegraphy, and printing (Roberts, 1971).

For all its grandeur, the Elmira Reformatory eventually fell victim to many of the standard prison problems we see today, such as lack of funding, lack of high-quality personnel, and overpopulation (Johnson & Wolfe, 1996; Stone, 1997). For example, toward the end of its tenure Elmira was found to have housed more than 1,500 inmates, even though it was designed to hold only 500 inmates (Johnson & Wolfe, 1996). However, even with all its problems it was still duplicated in various forms in at least 15 different states (Roberts, 1971).

Austin MacCormick

In 1927, Austin MacCormick conducted a nationwide survey of 60 prisons. Surprisingly, he found that 13 of the 60 prisons he examined did not have any type of academic instruction. Even more shocking, MacCormick (1931) reported that not a single prison surveyed was offering any type of vocational education for its inmates. According to MacCormick, correctional education had failed primarily because of a lack of funds but also because prisons lacked clear goals, followed rigid public school methods, had no individualized programs, and lacked high-quality teachers. He outlined very specific academic, vocational, social, and cultural education for institutions to follow, which would allow for the best possible learning environment (Roberts, 1971). MacCormick argued for providing individualized instruction, avoiding mass instruction, avoiding routine and stereotyped programs, and using a broad curriculum to meet the needs of all inmates (Barnes & Teeters, 1959).

MODERN CORRECTIONAL EDUCATION

The Correctional Education Association was formed in 1945 out of a subcommittee of the American Prison Association. In 1949, the *Journal of Correctional Education* was established, which allowed the exchange of ideas in prison education. The development of these two entities marked the beginning of modern correctional education (Stone, 1997).

The Higher Education Act

In 1965, Congress passed Title IV of the Higher Education Act, which included Basic Education Opportunity Grants (renamed Pell Grants after Claiborne Pell, the senator who sponsored the bill). Inmates, who usually qualified for maximum funding as a result of their minimum income, were allowed to apply for federal grants that would allow them to pay for college tuition in prison classrooms or correspondence courses (Ross & Richards, 2002). The implementation of Pell Grants led to 43 states offering associate degrees, 31 states offering bachelor's degrees, and 9 states offering master's degrees (Pollock, 2004). In 1977, 66% of federal and state institutions offered postsecondary education to inmates (Bell, 1977).

Funding for prison education programs was strong for the next 20 years. The passage of the Higher Education Act assisted in the development of other areas of prison education. The act provided funding to acquire more professional staff and better teaching materials for instructors (Silverman, 2001). Unfortunately, despite all the opportunities that were established with the use of Pell Grants, inmates were specifically banned from taking advantage of them in the mid-1990s (Tewksbury, Erickson, & Taylor, 2000).

Current Educational Practices

The prison population boom of the 1980s resulted in severe overcrowding, a lack of resources and staff to teach effectively, staggering levels of inmate illiteracy, and a societal demand for a more punitive and less rehabilitative prison system (Silverman, 2001). At present, all state and federal systems offer some type of educational program for inmates; however, most are enrolled in adult basic education or GED programs (Bureau of Justice Statistics, 1992). Many states have mandatory testing of inmates, and if inmates do not reach a certain satisfactory level, they will be required to enroll in the prison's educational program and remain there until they surpass the state's requirement (Thomas, 1995).

In 1982, the Federal Bureau of Prisons initiated a mandatory literacy program for all inmates who could not demonstrate a sixth-grade reading and writing level; the standard was then raised to an eighth-grade level in 1986 (Box 8.1). In 1991, the Federal Bureau of Prisons raised the standards again, requiring all inmates to have a high school diploma or GED. Currently, the courses required for federal inmates include basic literacy, English as a second language, and classes that are needed to obtain a high school diploma or GED (Bosworth, 2002).

Box 8.1	The Bureau of Prisons: Leading the Way in Prison Education

The Federal Bureau of Prisons has always had a strong commitment to the education of inmates through basic literacy and vocational training (Bosworth, 2002). Beginning in 1930, the federal prison system, under the leadership of Sanford Bates, set a new standard for states to follow in prison education. The U.S. Bureau of Prisons had a trained supervisor of education in each of its facilities (Roberts, 1971). Each facility had new classrooms, libraries were established, new textbooks and library books were purchased, and cell study correspondence courses were established to minimize classroom overcrowding (Roberts, 1971).

The number of inmates receiving academic instruction in the 1930s and 1940s symbolized the commitment the Bureau of Prisons had toward inmate education. In the early 1930s approximately 4,000 federal inmates were attending educational classes (U.S. Department of Justice, 1933). McNeil Island Federal Penitentiary had 70% of inmates voluntarily enrolled in classes (Roberts, 1971).

In 1982, the Bureau of Prisons initiated a mandatory literacy program for all inmates who could not demonstrate a sixth-grade reading and writing level. The reading and writing standards were raised to an eighth-grade level in 1986. In 1991, the Bureau of Prisons raised the standards again, requiring all inmates to have a high school diploma or GED (Bosworth, 2002).

The vocational and apprenticeship system in the Bureau of Prisons is also committed to academic excellence and recommends a variety of classes for inmates. Any inmate who wants to work in the federal prison system beyond entry-level positions is required to possess a GED. Vocational courses and apprenticeships are offered to federal inmates to help them prepare for their reintegration into society upon their release (Bosworth, 2002). Depending on the facility, vocational courses may include basic construction, electronic wiring, plumbing, culinary arts, horticulture, greenhouse management, dog handling, barbering, computer-assisted engraving, computer operations, masonry, carpentry, customized picture framing, and many more. Apprenticeships in the Bureau of Prisons are also restricted by each facility and include carpentry, cooking, baking, dental assistance, data entry, furniture making, upholstery, electrical science, horticulture, landscaping, tailoring, fish hatchery, industrial housekeeping, quality assurance, book binding, customer service, floor laying, painting, shoe repair, and many more (U.S. Department of Justice, 2006).

The federal system also offers courses that are mandatory and not just recommended. Mandatory courses include basic literacy, English as a second language, and classes that are needed to obtain a high school diploma or GED (Bosworth, 2002).

TYPES OF EDUCATIONAL PROGRAMS

Life Skills Programs

Life skills programs are aimed at developing the inmate's ability to function properly in society. These programs focus not on academic deficiencies but rather on deficiencies in practical knowledge. They are designed to help the inmates to adapt to life outside prison.

Life skills programs include a variety of topics such as money management, in which inmates learn about balancing personal budgets, paying rent, and shopping for necessities. Inmates can enroll in family development courses such as anger management, child-rearing practices, and resolving family conflicts. One of the most immediate areas of concern for inmates upon their release is job-seeking skills such as filling out application forms, developing a résumé, and interviewing.

Adult Basic Education and General Educational Development

Adult basic education programs have been the primary form of education in prisons. They focus on developing basic math, science, reading, and writing skills to establish a foundation that will allow inmates to pursue other educational options.

GED programs in prison are designed to encourage inmates to take and pass the GED test (also known as the General Equivalency Diploma test); the diploma is considered to be equivalent to a high school diploma (Stone, 1997). Inmates routinely choose GED programs rather than high school programs in order to finish before their release. Many inmates understand the importance of obtaining an education while in prison. Inmates understand that parole review boards will take their activities while in prison into account, and there is an advantage to having completed their education. GED programs have higher enrollments and produce more graduates than any other prison academic program.

Although enrollment is at an all-time high, it has been questioned whether GEDs reduce recidivism after release (Cecil, Drapkin, MacKenzie, & Hickman, 2000). As society becomes more educated, the GED may not help inmates reach the level of achievement they desire. Their inability to keep up with society's demands creates frustration and a poor self-image, leading the inmate to return to criminal activity (Stone, 1997). If the GED does not reduce recidivism, then prison administrations and legislatures will have to consider offering or mandating higher levels of education for inmates (Box 8.2).

Box 8.2   The Windham School District: Making Education a Priority in Texas Prisons

The largest prison education program is probably the Windham School District in Texas. The Windham School District was created by the Texas legislature to help Texas inmates obtain their GEDs (Renaud, 2002). Inmates who have educational achievement (EA) scores less than 6.0 (on a 12.9 scale) are automatically enrolled in the Windham School District and are not allowed to leave until they attain an EA score above 6.0, earn their GED, or are removed as a result of disciplinary infractions. Students are assigned to courses according to their EA scores, and special education courses are available for those who are illiterate or receive low EA scores (Renaud, 2002). Inmates can participate in adult basic education, secondary education, or postsecondary education programs at Windham (Martinez & Eisenberg, 2000). All postsecondary education programs must be paid for by the inmate (Martinez & Eisenberg, 2000).

Windham School District offers more than 30 vocational courses, including auto mechanics, culinary arts, carpentry, welding, bricklaying, barbering, radio and television repair, air-conditioning repair, truck driving, graphic arts, painting and decorating, and plumbing, through its vocational department, also known as Career and Technical Education. Many of the skills obtained are intended for use upon release from prison; however, the Texas prison system allows inmates to use their acquired skills while still in prison as on-the-job training. For example, graduates from the barbering school are allowed to cut hair at the prison barber shop, auto and diesel mechanic graduates are allowed to work in the numerous transportation and maintenance departments, and so on (Renaud, 2002).

Windham School District serves about 24,000 inmates at any given time, or about 18% of the Texas prison population. Therefore, inmates are admitted in accordance to priority. Inmates with EA scores under 6.0 within 2 years of release are given top priority. Career and Technical Education courses are assigned according to EA scores, disciplinary record, approval by the state classification committee (if a transfer is needed to enroll in the course at another facility), time left to serve, and ability to pay or promise to pay for all college vocational courses (Renaud, 2002). In accordance with House Bill 1 (1997), inmates who are in administrative segregation are prohibited from participating in the Windham School District (Martinez & Eisenberg, 2000).

(Continued)

(Continued)

Educational achievement at Windham is measured through standards established by the Texas legislature. The Texas legislature performance measures are expressed as the percentage of learners who complete the level in which they are enrolled (Martinez & Eisenberg, 2000, p. 19). In the 1997–1998 academic year, 46% of nonreaders became readers, 40% of functionally illiterate inmates became literate, 59% earned a GED or attended college, and 12% of all college-eligible inmates participated in college. Additionally, in the same year more than 5,000 inmates earned GEDs, 99 earned associate degrees, 4 earned bachelor's degrees, and 3 earned master's degrees (Martinez & Eisenberg, 2000).

College Education

Of all the different educational offerings in prisons, college education is the most debated by politicians, the public, the media, professors, and students. Society generally does not have a problem offering basic adult education, GEDs, or high school diplomas to inmates, largely because they are offered to the rest of society (Silverman, 2001). However, as a result of the high costs associated with obtaining a college education, many people are not able to afford a college education. As a direct result of this lack of opportunity, some think inmates should not be given these opportunities.

The elimination of Pell Grants for inmates in 1994, through the Violent Crime Control and Law Enforcement Act, nearly eliminated all prison college programs in the United States (Shuler, 2004). Pell Grants provided approximately $1,500 per year for each inmate (Silverman, 2001). Without federal assistance, many inmates were not able to take advantage of college education programs. As a direct result of the elimination of the federal Pell Grants, most college programs for inmates have been dissolved (Silverman, 2001). Academic institutions were not willing to continue prison programs when inmates were not able to pay tuition (Ross, 2008).

Although college education programs have become scarce (Ross, 2008; Ross & Richards, 2002) they are still offered in some prisons. College programs allow inmates to focus on obtaining college degrees or taking steps toward obtaining a degree while in prison. Completing a college education while in prison can have the same positive effect as completing a high school education or obtaining a GED; however, a college degree also allows the inmate to compete for jobs that require a higher education.

University courses are the single best mechanism available to increase inmates' post-prison success (Ross & Richards, 2002). The inmates can compete for higher-paying jobs and reduce the frustration of having to compete in a society that seeks college-educated workers. In addition, college-level curricula include ethical problem solving; college education has been found to improve not only analytical skills but also moral development (Parlett, 1981).

Even if an inmate does not earn a college degree, he or she may be able to take college courses while in prison and finish the degree requirements after his or her release. This gives the inmate something to look forward to (Ross & Richards, 2002).

There are three main methods of providing college education to inmates: distance education, on-site education, and on-campus education (Lawrence, 1994). Distance education allows inmates to take courses through the use of a host of different teaching methods including televised instructional services, correspondence courses, and Internet or Web-based courses. One of the benefits of distance education is that courses can be offered to inmates as well as staff.

The time it takes to complete a course depends on a variety of factors, such as time restrictions for the course, the inmate's ability to pay, the inmate's academic ability, the inmate's motivation, and all the distractions that the inmate will encounter while in prison (Ross, 2008). Security concerns complicate the process of obtaining college credits through correspondence courses (Ross, 2008; Ross & Richards, 2002). Obstacles include the need to screen mail entering or leaving the facility, limitations on the number of typewriters and copiers available and the number of books allowed in a cell, and the need to remove the outside covers of books to minimize the risk of contraband entering the facility (Ross & Richards, 2002).

On-site education is by far the most popular method of offering college education to inmates. Instructors are sent to the facilities from local colleges or universities and teach in a classroom setting much like that of a university campus. Instructors are paid not by the prison system but by the university that is offering the course. This setting allows the normal college learning process to occur, as ideas are presented and dissected by classmates and the instructor. In addition, the instructors act as role models for the inmates through their daily interactions, which is an invaluable service to inmates (Lawrence, 1994).

The last delivery method, on-campus education, is the least used by prison systems. This type of delivery allows inmates to leave their facilities, supervised by a prison official, and attend classes at local colleges or universities, much like a work release program. Inmates must abide by a variety of rules and regulations in addition to college or university rules; they are not allowed to conduct other business during their leave or visit with friends or family members, and they must report back to their facilities immediately (Lawrence, 1994).

Although college programs do exist in prison, inmate participation levels are not as high as the public might think. In a national study of state and federal prisons it was found that only 10% of inmates engaged in college pursuits, although more than 50% of inmates reported some educational activities in prison (Harlow, 2003).

Vocational Education Programs

Vocational education programs allow inmates to learn a trade or job skills under real work conditions, under the supervision of officers or other highly skilled inmates. They are able to develop a sense of self-worth and often, for the first time, take pride in their work. They may develop positive work habits that can help them once they are released. Inmates may be able to use the job skills they acquired in prison to obtain meaningful employment. However, many of the skills inmates learn are not directly transferable to jobs in society and are not as useful as prison officials might want people to believe.

There are several different types of vocational programs, and assignment to these programs depends on availability, need, and ability to pay (Gerber & Fritsch, 2001). Vocational programs include specialized and nonspecialized assignments. Nonspecialized assignments include types of work that allow the institution to operate from day to day, including washing dishes, sweeping and mopping floors, doing laundry for inmates and staff, preparing meals, mowing lawns, trimming hedges, and any other number of monotonous jobs. However, prisons also have many specialized job assignments such as plumbing, carpentry, air-conditioning repair, painting, construction, small and large engine repair, agriculture, and hair cutting. These assignments are also vital to the daily operations of any facility. Inmates can use many of the skills learned in these positions to obtain jobs after release.

Prison industries also provide inmates with opportunities to work in factories that manufacture mattresses, shoes, clothing, purses, bags, belts, furniture, and many more items. Prison industries can contract out inmate labor to private businesses. Businesses must pay market wages but are not required to provide the inmates with benefits (Hallinan, 2003). Because they allow inmates to compete for jobs with non-inmates, prison industries have received a great deal of negative attention from the media. States are able to avoid negative publicity by restricting inmate labor to state-funded labor such as road maintenance and litter cleanup.

Recreational Programs

Recreational programs encompass a range of activities that are invaluable to the safety and security of the prison facility. These programs give inmates opportunities to release tension that arises from the unhealthy nature of the prison environment and the monotony of prison life. Inmates engage in activities such as weight lifting, jogging, exercising, foosball, table tennis, music, drama, chess, checkers, and dominoes. Inmate teams can compete with teams outside prison in baseball, basketball, football, and other sports.

Recreational activities can provide vigorous exercise and reduce the time inmates spend on threatening activities while incarcerated (Silverman, 2001). Inmates are able to learn the rules and regulations of various sports. Recreational contests in prison allow inmates to interact with other inmates socially in the spirit of athletic competition.

Recreational programs that focus on health and fitness can help inmates build self-esteem and healthy life habits that can reduce future criminal activity. The time needed to develop and maintain a physically fit lifestyle after release can minimize the amount of time spent pursuing criminal activities (Silverman, 2001).

Prison Libraries and Law Libraries

Prison libraries offer inmates a stress-free alternative to education. Inmates can increase their knowledge through self-development without having to endure the rigors of a prison education. The inmate is not limited to the courses or programs being offered at the facility. The inmate does not have to be concerned with being transferred or relocated to a different facility during his or her prison term. Inmates are not limited by available seating or budgets. They can use the prison library for study or research on their own time.

Prison libraries generally offer inmates reading materials that include fiction and nonfiction books, magazines, journals, and newspapers. In an environment where privacy is limited, an inmate can engage in a very private activity: reading. The inmate can escape from the harsh reality of confinement through the characters he or she reads about in novels (Stevens, 1994). Prison libraries generally restrict access only to materials or topics that threaten the safety of the facility.

Law libraries are also available. Inmates can use these libraries to educate themselves on the law and perhaps fight for their release. Those who become very familiar with the law are often called jailhouse lawyers. Working in the law libraries, such inmates help other inmates fight for their release. Jailhouse lawyers are generally paid with commissary items, cash, or any other prison service that the client is able to provide (Silverman, 2001).

RECIDIVISM

The positive effects of educational and vocational programs in prison cannot be ignored. Numerous studies have found positive correlations between inmate education and reductions in recidivism (Batiuk, 1997; Batiuk, Moke, & Rountree, 1997; Duguid, Hawkey, & Knight, 1998; Gerber & Fritsch, 1993; Jensen & Reed, 2006; Ross, 2008; Ross & Richards, 2002; Stevens & Ward, 1997; Thomas & Thomas, 2008; Wilson, Gallagher, & MacKenzie, 2000).

This is not to say that educated people do not commit crimes, but as their educational status rises they are able to attain better and higher-paying jobs. As a direct result, they are less likely to sell drugs for money, steal for money, assault someone for money, or engage in any number of criminal activities for money. Simply having a job that provides the money for basic human necessities such as food, clothing, and shelter reduces the incentive to commit criminal acts. Obtaining an education in prison promotes responsibility and independence (McCollum, 1994), which allows former inmates to adapt more appropriately to society. By gaining worthwhile employment, former inmates are able to provide for themselves and their families.

However, many question whether programs are actually reducing recidivism. Studies that have shown reductions in recidivism have been criticized for being too methodologically weak to substantiate reductions in recidivism. One explanation for the lack of success of prison education programs might be the lack of social skills necessary for employment. Inmates' achievements in the academic arena do not necessarily mean that their social adaptability is improving (Stone, 1997). Additionally, the effects of inmate education on recidivism depend on the type of education the inmate receives.

Life Skills Program Evaluations

Evaluations of recidivism rates of inmates who participate in life skills programs have been found to be consistently poor. Numerous studies have found no significant differences between program participants and nonparticipants.

Phipps, Korinek, Aos, and Lieb (1999) examined a methodologically rigorous program, which included random assignment, from San Diego and found no significant differences between the program participants and the control group. Jolin et al. (1997) found no significant differences between the treatment and control groups in a community life skills program for women that instructed inmates on time management, budget management, personal safety, and reentering the workforce. Cecil et al. (2000) examined five life skills programs that varied in methodological rigor and were not able to draw any conclusions as to the programs' effectiveness in reducing recidivism.

Adult Basic Education and GED Program Evaluations

Studies evaluating for recidivism in adult basic education, GED, and high school programs have produced mixed results. Harlow (2003) found that inmates who did not have a high school diploma or a GED were more likely to recidivate when released. Cecil et al. (2000) examined 12 basic education studies from 1985 to 1995. From their findings they were able to conclude that the basic education programs did offer some positive results, but as a result of various factors including the lack of well-designed studies they were not able to claim that adult basic education and GED programs were the lone factors in reducing recidivism. In another study that was ranked below average on methodological rigor, in which Jensen and Reed (2006) evaluated correctional programs using evaluation guidelines established by University of Maryland researchers, Nuttall, Hollmen, and Staley (2003) found that inmates who earned a GED in prison were less likely to return to prison than those who did not.

In a more rigorous study, Wilson et al. (2000) found that inmates who participated in adult basic education and GED programs were less likely to recidivate than inmates who did not participate in such programs. Aos, Phipps, Barnoski, and Lieb (2001) examined three different studies on adult basic education that qualified as methodologically rigorous and found that program participants had an 11% lower rate of recidivism. In one of the more methodologically rigorous studies, Steuer and Smith (2003) found recidivism to be statistically significant for educational program participants on measures of rearrest, reconviction, and reincarceration.

Even if inmates do not complete their education in prison, there have been some other promising results of educational programs. For example, the Texas Criminal Justice Policy Council found property criminals were 37% less likely to recidivate when they learned to read while incarcerated (Pollock, 2004).

Vocational Program Evaluations

Evidence that vocational educational programs reduce recidivism is mixed. Some researchers argue that vocational educational programs are better at reducing recidivism than other prison programs (Barton & Coley, 1996; Simms, Farley, & Littlefield, 1987). According to one study, inmates who completed a vocational training program during their stay in a federal institution were 33% less likely to recidivate than inmates who did not complete the vocational training (Saylor & Gaes, 1997). Bouffard, MacKenzie, and Hickman (2000) examined nine different vocational programs with similar levels of methodological rigor and found that six did reduce recidivism, whereas three studies did not. Wilson et al. (2000) examined 17 vocational programs and found that program participants were less likely to recidivate.

College Program Evaluations

Of all the educational programs available to inmates, college programs are the most successful in reducing recidivism. Ironically, the college education is also the least available in prison, as discussed earlier. Regardless of the methodological rigor applied to studies examining college programs, prisoners who are able to complete at least 1 year of college education while imprisoned are less likely to violate their parole or return on a new conviction (Ross, 2008; Ross & Richards, 2002).

In a fairly rigorous methodological study, Batiuk and Moke (1996) examined the recidivism rates of approximately 1,200 Ohio inmates released from 1990 to 1992. The researchers found that the inmates had statistically significant reductions in their reincarceration rates if they earned college credits before their release. In a later study, Batiuk et al. (1997) examined recidivism rates of 318 Ohio inmates who were released from 1982 to 1983. In their study they found that inmates who had earned associate degrees while incarcerated had 58% lower recidivism rates.

Stevens and Ward (1997) examined 60 inmates who had completed an associate or a bachelor's degree while imprisoned and compared them with another group of inmates from the general population as a control group. The researchers found that after 3 years not one of the inmates who earned a bachelor's degree and only 5% of the inmates who had earned an associate's degree had returned to prison, whereas 40% of the control group had been reincarcerated (Stevens & Ward, 1997).

Wilson et al. (2000) examined 13 different postsecondary educational programs and found that program participants were less likely to recidivate than nonparticipants. In a study of 3,200 inmates in Maryland, Minnesota, and Ohio, researchers found 29% lower reincarceration rates for inmates who had received an education while imprisoned (Thomas & Thomas, 2008). The Open Society Institute reports that prisoners had a 50% rearrest rate; however, that number was only 10% if the inmate had completed at least 2 years of college (Thomas & Thomas, 2008).

SHOULD WE EDUCATE THE INCARCERATED?

For many years prison administrators, scholars, and politicians have all debated whether we should be educating inmates. This debate stems from different philosophical approaches about incarceration. What is the purpose of incarceration? Some believe that the purpose of the prison system is to punish the offender for wrongdoing, and others believe that the prison system is designed to rehabilitate the offender and change his or her way of thinking. These opposing viewpoints are at the very heart of a person's belief system, and they are merely the tip of the iceberg in the debate over prison education programs, which may be seen by their opponents as a reward for wrongdoing.

In order to fully appreciate the complexity of this issue, one needs to understand the possible consequences of educating inmates while in prison. The purpose of a prison education is not to have more educated criminals (Duguid, 1981). In combining different philosophical approaches, we are educating inmates to help them become more productive members of society while allowing them to pay their debt to society through their incarceration. The United States is not alone in addressing the inmate education debate through a mixture of philosophical methods. China has accepted a slightly different meaning of educational and vocational programs for its offenders, as presented in Box 8.3.

Box 8.3   Different Perspectives for Correctional Education: Reform and Reeducation Through Labor in China

Yuhsu (Gail) Hsiao

Unlike Western countries, China has its own unique philosophy and means for educating offenders. According to the seriousness of crimes, the Chinese correction system can be divided into two major components: a reform-through-labor system (Laogai) and reeducation-through-labor institutions (Laojiao).

(Continued)

(Continued)

The reform-through-labor system is used for people who have committed crimes that are subject to punishment by the Chinese Criminal Law, such as murder, robbery, rape, and arson. In the reform-through-labor camps, supervision and control, education, and labor are forced onto the offenders. Supervision and control force offenders to accept control and obey the regulations of the labor camp and the laws, ideological and cultural education helps offenders raise their moral and cultural standards, and labor cultivates offenders' work habits, teaches them production skills, and prepares them to support themselves upon release. The Chinese believe that combining punishment with reform and education with labor transforms offenders into law-abiding citizens (Ministry of Justice, 2004).

Unlike the reform-through-labor system, reeducation-through-labor institutions detain people who commit minor offenses, such as petty theft, prostitution, fraud, counterrevolutionary crimes, and other behaviors that are considered to disrupt social order. Reeducation through labor is not a judicial punishment but a form of administrative discipline, and these offenders are not legally considered criminals. Therefore, there is no trial for these offenders; the police are responsible for arresting and determining reeducation terms (Human Rights Watch, 1998). In the reeducation-through-labor institutions, detainees receive education in law, morality, and cultural norms for at least 3 hours a day. Also, detainees are put to work in order to develop stable work habits and obtain job skills. With education and labor, detainees are transformed into law-abiding citizens with sufficient job skills to be productive members of society (Ministry of Justice, 2002).

Despite their idealistic principles and goals, the reform-through-labor and reeducation-through-labor systems are often criticized for their violations of human rights. First, in these systems detainees work for 10 to 14 hours a day for little or no money. The administrators are concerned only with productivity and ignore the health of the offenders. Second, physical and mental torture is often used for control and thought reform. Third, administrators are usually the same authorities who determine whether a detainee has been reformed after serving his or her term. If not, officials have the power to extend the detainee's reeducation term for another year or to relocate the prisoner to a forced labor camp indefinitely. In response to these accusations, the Chinese government renamed the reform-through-labor system (Laogai) as "the prison system" in 1994 and renamed reeducation-through-labor institutions (Laojiao) as "correctional centers" in 2007. However, in practice only a few regulations have been changed, and unjust treatment and brutal abuse persist (Laogai Research Foundation, 2006).

ARGUMENTS AGAINST PRISON EDUCATION

Some people believe that prisons are designed to punish and are not eager to offer education to convicted offenders. These people are not interested in offering rehabilitative tools to those who have offended society in such a manner that our judicial system has deemed them unworthy of living among the rest of society. Opponents of prison-based education initiatives argue against educating inmates on the grounds of just deserts and the idea that inmates are not actually learning.

Just Deserts

Just deserts is the idea that the offender is receiving the punishment he or she deserves. People who subscribe to the just deserts model of punishment do not want to better the lives of the people who have harmed society. They believe inmates should be punished for the pain and suffering they cause through their transgressions.

Just deserts is rooted in the ancient concept of *lex talionis,* which in its purest and adamant form argues the offender should receive the same punishment that he or she inflicted on the victim. In its archaic form *lex talionis* argued a life for a life, an eye for an eye, a tooth for a tooth, and so on. Obviously, *lex talionis* is not fitting for many crimes such as rape, forgery, fraud, drug smuggling, drug distribution, drug possession, and a host of other offenses (Thomas & Thomas, 2008).

A more modern version would argue that the offender should receive the same amount of pain, loss, and inconvenience that the victim suffered, even though the punishment is not identical to the original crime. The punishment received by the offender is to be calculated so that the offender receives enough pain to ensure that, once released, the offender does not violate the laws of society. If the offender commits a small crime such as simple assault, then a few months in jail is an appropriate punishment. However, if the offender commits murder, then a longer sentence is to be imposed. Under the just deserts model of punishment, education is seen as a reward and not punishment; therefore, it is not appropriate under this line of thinking to allow inmates educational opportunities (Thomas & Thomas, 2008).

Inmates Are Not Actually Learning

It has also been argued that despite high levels of inmate participation in prison education programs, prison administrators are not fully committed to the idea of rehabilitating inmates. The prison educational process is under the control of prison administrators. Mandating inmate enrollment allows prison administrators to appear to be concerned with inmate education and rehabilitation (Thomas, 1995); however, the inmate may see the educational process as just another prison process (Forster, 1981).

Even if prison administrators support prison education programs, it still does not mean that learning is actually taking place (Pollock, 2004). There are numerous obstacles in prison that can inhibit the learning process. Learning is hampered by a lack of basic reading skills, learning disabilities, and lack of available resources for inmates. The inmate is attempting to make progress under the harsh reality that he or she may get transferred to another prison, fall victim to prison disciplinary problems, or any other host of prison problems. The most threatening obstacle is the lockdown. Once a lockdown occurs, inmates are unable to attend classes (Thomas, 1995).

Unethical staff can also sabotage the learning environment by invoking their authority in a disruptive manner in the classroom and preventing access to necessary resources (Pollock, 2004; Thomas, 1995). Instructors may not be qualified or may not be that interested in teaching inmates (Pollock, 2004). The constant noise, chaos, and stress in prison also are not conducive to learning (Thomas, 1995).

Obtaining an education in prison does not develop the mind in the same manner as obtaining an education in free society. In society, people are able to expand on the knowledge they gain in the classroom with others in society, at work, or at home (Forster, 1981). However, in prison inmates are unable to build on the ideas they learn in the classroom with other inmates who do not care about education.

ARGUMENTS IN FAVOR OF PRISON EDUCATION

Supporters of prison-based education programs believe that our prisons are intrinsically designed to rehabilitate offenders. These people argue for prison education for a variety of reasons, such as improving inmates' cognitive and analytical skills, helping them obtain meaningful employment after release, saving tax dollars, and increasing inmates' chances of being paroled.

Improving Cognitive and Analytical Skills

Offenders are sent to prison as a result of the errors in their thought processes. If the offender is not taught or given the tools needed to correct his or her behavior, he or she will return to prison soon after release. If the inmate is offered an education and is better prepared to face society's demands through improved cognitive and analytical skills, then he or she might be able to avoid returning to prison. It has been argued that prison education improves verbal, written, and analytical skills (Duguid, 1981).

An education also increases self-esteem. Inmates who have completed educational programs develop a more balanced view of life and help them to make more balanced and mature decisions when they are confronted with many of life's daily issues. Inmates are able to choose friends more wisely and avoid many of the pitfalls that may return them to prison (Duguid, 1981).

Supporting Meaningful Employment

In addition to improving cognitive and analytical skills, educated offenders are able to improve their chances of obtaining meaningful employment. More educated offenders may qualify for work opportunities that were previously unavailable to them.

Saving Tax Dollars

Incarceration can be quite costly. The average cost of incarceration in state prisons in 2001 was $22,650 per inmate, with a high of $44,379 in Maine and a low of $8,128 in Alabama. As various incarceration schemes are requiring inmates to serve longer sentences, inmates are getting older in prison. The cost of housing an inmate over the age of 55 is twice that of housing younger inmates (Thomas & Thomas, 2008).

Nationwide, about 95% of incarcerated offenders will leave prison, and a little more than half of them will return once released (Petersilia, 2003; Thomas & Thomas, 2008; Travis, 2005). However, millions of tax dollars can be saved if education reduces recidivism, and as discussed previously, the consensus among scholars and researchers is that education does reduce recidivism (Thomas & Thomas, 2008). In a study of the Bedford Hills Correctional Facility in New York, researchers found over a 2-year period that reduced reincarceration rates save approximately $900,000 per 100 students (Fine et al., 2001; Thomas & Thomas, 2008).

Increasing Likelihood of Parole

Some inmates quickly realize that their chances of being paroled increase greatly if they prove to the parole board that they have taken advantage of what the prison system has to offer and attempted to rehabilitate themselves while in prison. Because being employed is a requirement for parole, these inmates are able to argue to their parole boards that their educational achievements make them more marketable for employment once released. If they are able to obtain employment before their release, they can use that fact at their parole hearings to justify their release.

POLICY IMPLICATIONS

With 68% of state inmates not having a high school diploma and 41% of state and federal inmates not having a high school diploma or its equivalent (Harlow, 2003), policymakers and the public need to reexamine the impact of releasing uneducated offenders. The elimination of federal Pell Grants for inmates' postsecondary education has had profound consequences that are too costly for society to ignore (Ubah, 2004). Education is the vital link in bridging inmates from prison to the real world (Hershberger, 1987). By obtaining fundamental job and social skills, inmates are better equipped to succeed in life and decrease their chances of recidivating (Ubah, 2004).

The abolishment of Pell Grants for inmates in 1994, through the Violent Crime Control and Law Enforcement Act, resulted in decreased funding for state and federal prison education programs (Ubah, 2004). Politicians did this to appear tough on crime, despite the fact that only 0.1% of the annual budget of the Department of Education is assigned to correctional education (U.S. Department of Education, Office of Correctional Education, in Ubah, 2004) and despite the fact that repeated studies have found that obtaining a college education in prison drastically reduces the chances of returning to prison (Batiuk, 1997; Batiuk et al., 1997; Duguid et al., 1998; Gerber & Fritsch, 1993; Jensen & Reed, 2006; Ross, 2008; Ross & Richards, 2002; Stevens & Ward, 1997; Thomas & Thomas, 2008; Wilson et al., 2000).

Forty-one percent of correctional education administrators reported that the elimination of the Pell Grants had "completely changed" their educational programs, whereas only 18% of correctional administrators reported "no change" in their programs (Ubah, 2004). Many prison educational programs were eliminated completely (Petersilia, 2001; Tewksbury & Taylor, 1996). Within 1 year, all but 8 of the 350 prison college programs were eliminated nationwide (Torre & Fine, 2005). Inmates returning to society without an education are practically assured a return trip to prison after release.

Despite the elimination of Pell Grants for inmates, some states, such as Ohio, Maryland, Delaware, and New York, have found new sources of revenue for inmate education (Batiuk, 1997; Hobler, 1999; Tracy, Smith, & Steuer 1998).

Currently, inmates are able to pay for college education through the use of federal Perkins funds, private funds (the inmates' own funds or their families' funds), and state-based education grants (Tewksbury & Taylor, 1996).

If state and federal governments are not willing to educate inmates, we will be losing the war on crime. As uneducated inmates return to society, they will inevitably return to the only life they know: a life of crime. Although the evidence is mixed on the ability of educational and vocational programs to reduce recidivism, some programs have shown potential to fight criminality. Methodologically rigorous studies have found positive correlations between reduced recidivism and college education programs for inmates. College education programs should be considered as viable options for crime reduction. Politicians should fight to keep college programs in prison, not to dismantle them.

However, although many prisons still offer a wide variety of educational and vocational programs to inmates, the inmates themselves have to take the initiative to enroll in courses. Prison administrators can only offer the courses; the inmate must still take the first step (Lewis, 1981). Beyond the federal and state requirements for inmates who are functioning below acceptable academic standards, inmates still have to decide for themselves whether obtaining an education while in prison is worth their time. Many inmates who are eligible for prison education programs do not participate.

DISCUSSION QUESTIONS

1. If you were a prison administrator and were required to design an educational and vocational department for your facility with unlimited resources, what courses or trades would you include in your curriculum? Why?

2. Should inmates be required to participate in educational or vocational programs? Why or why not?

3. If empirical research demonstrated that postsecondary educational programming helped reduce recidivism, would you be willing to reinstate Pell Grants for inmates? Why or why not?

4. Which type of prison program is the most valuable: life skills, educational, vocational, or recreational? Why?

5. If you were an assistant warden and were responsible for the educational and vocational department in your prison, and you had to eliminate either the educational or the vocational program, which one would you eliminate? Why?

6. Should recreational programs be eliminated? Why or why not?

SUGGESTED READINGS

Barton, P., & Coley, R. (1998). *Captive students: Education and training in America's prisons.* Princeton, NJ: Educational Testing Service.

Bouffard, J., Mackenzie, D., & Hickman, L. (2000). Effectiveness of vocational education and employment programs for adult offenders: A methodology-based analysis of the literature. *Journal of Offender Rehabilitation, 31*(1/2), 1–41.

Davidson, H. S. (1995). *Schooling in a "total institution": Critical perspectives on prison education.* Westport, CT: Bergin & Garvey.

Haulard, E. (2001, December). Adult education: A must for our incarcerated population. *Journal of Correctional Education, 52*(4), 157–159.

Martinez, A. I., & Eisenberg, M. (2000). *Educational achievement of inmates in the Windham School District.* Austin, TX: Criminal Justice Policy Council.

Rankin, C. (2005, May). Illiterate prisoners? Myths and empirical realities. *Journal of Offender Rehabilitation, 41*(2), 43–55.

Schlossman, S., & Spillane, J. (1992). *Bright hopes, dim realities: Vocational innovation in American correctional education.* Santa Monica, CA: RAND.

Thomas, R. G., & Thomas, R. M. (2008). *Effective teaching in correctional settings: Prisons, jails, juvenile centers, and alternative schools.* Springfield, IL: Charles C Thomas.

Ubah, C., & Robinson, R. (2003, June). A grounded look at the debate over prison-based education: Optimistic theory versus pessimistic worldview. *The Prison Journal, 83*(2), 115–129.

Williford, M. (1994). *Higher education in prison.* Phoenix, AZ: American Council on Education and the Oryx Press.

REFERENCES

Aos, S., Phipps, P., Barnoski, R., & Lieb, R. (2001). *The comparative cost and benefits of programs to reduce crime, version 4.0.* Olympia: Washington State Institute for Public Policy.

Barnes, H. E., & Teeters, N. K. (1959). *New horizons in criminology* (3rd ed.). Englewood Cliffs, NJ: Prentice Hall.

Barton, P. E., & Coley, R. J. (1996). *Captive students: Education and training in America's prisons.* Princeton, NJ: Educational Testing Service.

Batiuk, M. E. (1997). The state of post-secondary correctional education in Ohio. *Journal of Correctional Education, 48,* 70–73.

Batiuk, M. E., & Moke, P. (1996). *Education in Ohio prisons: An analysis of recidivism rates.* Ohio Penal Education Consortium and the Ohio Department of Rehabilitation and Corrections. Wilmington, OH: Wilmington College.

Batiuk, M. E., Moke, P., & Rountree, P. W. (1997). Crime and rehabilitation: Correctional education as an agent of change—A research note. *Justice Quarterly, 14,* 167–178.

Bell, R. (1977). *Correctional education programs for inmates: Summary report.* Bethlehem, PA: School of Education, Lehigh University.

Bosworth, M. (2002). *The U.S. federal prison system*. London: Sage.

Bouffard, J., MacKenzie, D., & Hickman, L. (2000). Effectiveness of vocational education and employment programs for adult offenders: A methodology-based analysis of the literature. *Journal of Offender Rehabilitation, 31*(1/2), 1–41.

Bureau of Justice Statistics. (1992). *Sourcebook of criminal justice statistics: 1991*. Washington, DC: U.S. Department of Justice.

Cecil, D. K., Drapkin, D. A., MacKenzie, D. L., & Hickman, L. J. (2000). The effectiveness of adult basic education and life-skills programs in reducing recidivism: A review and assessment of the research. *Journal of Correctional Education, 51*, 207–226.

Duguid, S. (1981). Prison education and criminal choice: The context of decision-making. In L. Morin (Ed.), *On prison education* (pp. 134–157). Ottawa: Canadian Government Publishing Centre.

Duguid, S., Hawkey, C., & Knight, W. (1998). Measuring the impact of post-secondary education in prison: A report from British Columbia. *Journal of Offender Rehabilitation, 27*, 87–106.

Fine, M., Torre, M. E., Boudin, K., Bowen, I., Clark, J., Hylton, D., et al. (2001). *Changing minds: The impact of college in a maximum security prison*. New York: Graduate Center, City College of New York.

Forster, W. (1981). Towards a prison curriculum. In L. Morin (Ed.), *On prison education* (pp. 55–70). Ottawa: Canadian Government Publishing Centre.

Gerber, J., & Fritsch, E. J. (1993, July). *Prison education and offender behavior: A review of the scientific literature*. Prison Education Research Project, Report 1. Huntsville, TX: Sam Houston State University.

Gerber, J., & Fritsch, E. J. (2001). Adult academic and vocational correctional programs: A review of recent research. In E. J. Latessa, A. Holsinger, J. W. Marquart, & J. R. Sorensen (Eds.), *Correctional contexts: Contemporary and classical readings* (2nd ed., pp. 268–290). Los Angeles: Roxbury.

Hallinan, J. T. (2003). *Going up the river*. New York: Random House.

Harlow, C. (2003). *Education and correctional populations*. Bureau of Justice Statistics Special Report. Washington, DC: U.S. Government Printing Office.

Hershberger, S. L. (1987). Vocational education: Preparing for life outside. *Corrections Today, 8*, 128–132.

Hobler, B. (1999). Correctional education: Now and in the future. *Journal of Correctional Education, 50*, 102–105.

Human Rights Watch. (1998). *Reeducation through labor in China*. Retrieved January 29, 2009, from http://www.hrw.org/legacy/campaigns/china-98/laojiao.htm

Jensen, E. L., & Reed, G. E. (2006). Adult correctional education programs: An update on current status based on recent studies. *Journal of Offender Rehabilitation, 44*(1), 81–98.

Johnson, H., & Wolfe, N. (1996). *History of criminal justice* (2nd ed.). Cincinnati, OH: Anderson.

Jolin, A., Day, M., Christophersen, K., Friedman, S., Newton, S., & Hooper, R. (1997). *An evaluation of the WICS lifeskills program for women at the Columbia River Correctional Institution: Preliminary results*. Portland, OR: Portland State University, College of Urban and Public Affairs.

Laogai Research Foundation. (2006). *Laogai handbook*. Retrieved September 15, 2009, from http://papers.ssrn.com/sol3/papers.cfm?abstract_id=1395552

Lawrence, D. W. (1994). The scope and diversity of prison higher education. In M. Williford (Ed.), *Higher education in prison* (pp. 51–68). Phoenix: American Council on Education and the Oryx Press.

Lewis, M. (1981). The humanities in prison: A case study. In L. Morin (Ed.), *On prison education* (pp. 112–133). Ottawa: Canadian Government Publishing Centre.

MacCormick, A. (1931). *The education of adult prisoners: A survey and a program.* New York: National Society of Penal Information.

Martinez, A. I., & Eisenberg, M. (2000). *Educational achievement of inmates in the Windham School District.* Austin, TX: Criminal Justice Policy Council.

McCollum, S. (1994). Mandatory literacy: Evaluating the Bureau of Prisons' long-standing commitment. *Federal Prisons Journal, 3*(2), 33–36.

McKelvey, B. (1936). *American prisons.* Chicago: University of Chicago Press.

Ministry of Justice, People's Republic of China. (2002). *Introduction to the Chinese Laojiao system.* Retrieved September 15, 2009, from http://www.legalinfo.gov.cn/moj/ldjyglj/2007-05/16/content_19622.htm

Ministry of Justice, People's Republic of China. (2004). *China legal publicity: The prison system.* Retrieved January 29, 2009, from http://www.legalinfo.gov.cn/english/LegalKnowledge/legal-knowledge2_5.htm

Nuttall, J., Hollmen, L., & Staley, E. M. (2003). The effect of earning a GED on recidivism rate. *Journal of Correctional Education, 54,* 90–94.

Parlett, T. A. A. (1981). The benefits of advanced education in prisons. In L. Morin (Ed.), *On prison education* (pp. 106–111). Ottawa: Canadian Government Publishing Centre.

Petersilia, J. (2001). When prisoners return to the community: Political, economic, and social consequences. *Sentencing and Corrections, 9*(11), 1–8.

Petersilia, J. (2003). *When prisoners come home: Parole and prisoner reentry.* New York: Oxford University Press.

Phipps, P., Korinek, K., Aos, S., & Lieb, R. (1999). *Research findings on adult corrections programs: A review.* Olympia: Washington State Institute for Public Policy.

Pollock, J. M. (2004). *Prisons and prison life: Cost and consequences.* Los Angeles: Roxbury.

Renaud, J. A. (2002). *Behind the walls: A guide for families and friends of Texas prison inmates.* Denton: University of North Texas Press.

Roberts, A. R. (1971). *Sourcebook on prison education: Past, present, and future.* Springfield, IL: Charles C Thomas.

Ross, I. R. (2008). *Special problems in corrections.* Upper Saddle River, NJ: Pearson.

Ross, J. J., & Richards, S. C. (2002). *Behind bars: Surviving prison.* Indianapolis: Alpha Books.

Saylor, W. G., & Gaes, G. G. (1997). Training inmates through industrial work participation and vocational and apprenticeship instruction. *Corrections Management Quarterly, 1*(2), 32–43.

Shuler, P. (2004, April 4). Educating prisoners is cheaper than locking them up again. *City Beat.* Retrieved April 4, 2004, from http://www.citybeat.com/2002-04-04/statehouse.shtml

Silverman, I. J. (2001). *Corrections: A comprehensive view* (2nd ed.). Belmont, CA: Wadsworth/Thomson Learning.

Simms, B. E., Farley, J., & Littlefield, J. F. (1987). *Colleges with fences: A handbook for improving corrections education programs.* Columbus, OH: National Center for Research in Vocational Education.

Steuer, S. J., & Smith, L. G. (2003). *Education reduces crime: Three-state recidivism study. Executive summary*. Lanham, MD: Correctional Education Association.

Stevens, D. J., & Ward, C. S. (1997). College education and recidivism: Educating criminals is meritorious. *Journal of Correctional Education, 48*, 106–111.

Stevens, S. (1994). A prison library. In M. Williford (Ed.), *Higher education in prison* (pp. 75–90). Phoenix: American Council on Education and the Oryx Press.

Stone, W. (1997). Industry, agriculture, and education. In J. M. Pollock (Ed.), *Prisons: Today and tomorrow* (pp. 116–150). Gaithersburg, MD: Aspen.

Sutherland, E. H., Cressey, D. R., & Luckenbill, D. (1992). *Principles of criminology* (11th ed.). Dixon Hills, NY: General Hall.

Taft, D. R. (1956). *Criminology* (3rd ed.). New York: Macmillan.

Tewksbury, R., Erickson, D. J., & Taylor, J. M. (2000). Opportunities lost: The consequences of eliminating Pell Grant eligibility for correctional education students. *Journal of Offender Rehabilitation, 31*(1/2), 43–56.

Tewksbury, R., & Taylor, J. M. (1996). The consequences of eliminating Pell Grants eligibility for students in post-secondary correctional education programs. *Federal Probation, 60*, 60–63.

Thomas, J. (1995). The ironies of prison education. In H. S. Davidson (Ed.), *Schooling in a "total institution": Critical perspectives on prison education* (pp. 573–574). Westport, CT: Bergin & Garvey.

Thomas, R. G., & Thomas, R. M. (2008). *Effective teaching in correctional settings: Prisons, jails, juvenile centers, and alternative schools*. Springfield, IL: Charles C Thomas.

Torre, M. E., & Fine, M. (2005). Bar none: Extending affirmative action to higher education in prison. *Journal of Social Issues, 61*(3), 569–594.

Tracy, A., Smith, L. G., & Steuer, S. J. (1998). Standing up for education. *Corrections Today, 4*, 144–156.

Travis, J. (2005). *But they all come back: Facing the challenges of prisoner reentry*. Washington, DC: The Urban Institute Press.

Ubah, C. (2004). Abolition of Pell Grants for higher education of prisoners: Examining antecedents and consequences. *Journal of Offender Rehabilitation, 39*(2), 73–85.

U.S. Department of Justice. (1933). *Annual report, 1932–1933: U.S. Bureau of Prisons*. Washington, DC: U.S. Government Printing Office.

Wilson, D. B., Gallagher, C. A., & MacKenzie, D. L. (2000). A meta-analysis of corrections-based education, vocation, and work programs for adult offenders. *Journal of Research in Crime and Delinquency, 37*, 347–368.

CHAPTER 9

Community Reintegration of Violent and Sexual Offenders

Issues and Challenges for Community Risk Management

Patrick Lussier, Melissa Dahabieh,
Nadine Deslauriers-Varin, and
Chris Thomson

About 20 years ago, a paradigm shift occurred in the criminal justice response to adult offenders. The "new penology" marked a systematic change in the main functions and objectives of the criminal justice system (Feeley & Simon, 1992). Rather than rehabilitation or punishment, correctional practices emphasized the identification and management of dangerous populations. People convicted of violent or sexual crimes have been regarded as high-risk populations for which legal and penal measures already in place were not considered sufficient to protect the community. The "community protection" model emerged as a result of a combination of factors: pressure from the victims' rights movement, the perceived inability to control violent and sexual crimes, and doubts regarding the impact of treatment programs for offenders committing these crimes. As a result, a series of risk management mechanisms emerged to deal with violent and sexual offenders. This chapter highlights issues and challenges in the application of the community risk management model of high-risk sex offenders.

POLICING VIOLENT AND SEXUAL OFFENDERS

The Specificity of Violent and Sexual Offenders

The criminal justice system's response to violent offenders and sexual offenders has taken several forms over recent years. In addition to traditional criminal justice measures already in place, policymakers have proposed a series of specific measures to facilitate the risk management of these offenders. The need to implement specific measures to address the risk of reoffending is based on one core assumption about violent and sexual offenders and three related assumptions about their offending. The assumption of an offender's specificity has been used by criminal justice system to propose, develop, and implement specific measures to deal with violent and sexual offenders. The assumption of *specificity* stipulates that the underlying mechanisms responsible for violent and sexual offending are different from those of other offenders, which explains the need for a differential approach. Interestingly, this crucial aspect of policy development has been largely ignored by researchers. Prospective longitudinal studies have failed to find empirical support suggesting that violent offenders are significantly different from nonviolent chronic offenders (Piquero, Farrington, & Blumstein, 2003). Therefore, the same mechanisms responsible for frequent, repetitive offending may also explain the tendency to commit a violent crime. To date, only one empirical study has tested this assumption for sex offenders and did not find strong empirical support for the assumption of offender specificity (Lussier, LeBlanc, & Proulx, 2005), suggesting that the mechanisms responsible for their sexual offending are not different from those responsible for nonsexual, chronic offending (Lussier & Cortoni, 2008; Lussier, Proulx, & LeBlanc, 2005).

The Underlying Assumptions of Criminal Justice Policies

Three other assumptions about violent and sexual offending are pivotal for policymakers in developing measures aiming specifically at people involved in those offenses: high risk to reoffend, crime specialization, and the stable propensity of offending. The assumption of high risk stipulates that violent and sexual offenders have a high likelihood of reoffending. The assumption of crime specialization implies that violent and sexual offenders tend to repeat the same crime over their criminal careers. Finally, the assumption of stable propensity to reoffend stipulates that violent and sexual offenders' tendency to commit crimes remains stable over their adult life, making them at high risk to reoffend over long period. By implementing measures targeting specifically violent and sexual offenders, the criminal justice system is assuming that these measures will prevent a future violent and sexual crime. Thus, violent and sexual offenders are described as being at high risk, specialized in their offending, at risk for a long period of time to repeat the same crime type, and needing specific interventions to control their behavior. Those assumptions are at odds with current empirical findings.

Understanding the Risk. Although establishment of the base rate of violent and sexual reoffending has been plagued by methodological problems (e.g., relying on official data), empirical studies conducted in different countries and different jurisdictions with samples of adult offenders show that violent and sexual offenders are not more likely to reoffend than other offenders, and only a minority of violent and sexual offenders repeat the same crime after their prison release (Langan, Schmitt, & Durose, 2003; Lussier, 2005; Sample & Bray, 2003). Clearly, most of them do not reoffend after their prison release, and their recidivism rates tend to decrease as they get older. Recidivism studies and the analysis of base rates have shown that the risk of reoffending decreases linearly as the offender's age increases (Barbaree, Langton, & Blanchard, 2007; Lussier & Healey, in press; Thornton, 2006). For example, the risk of sexual reoffending is highest for 18- to 25-year-olds, and the risk of reoffending is close to 0 past age 60 (Wollert, 2006). Therefore, the likelihood of reoffending must be considered in light of the offender's age at the time of prison release. If they do reoffend, only a small proportion of violent and sexual offenders will repeat the same crime type.

Crime Switching and Criminal Justice Policies. There is a long tradition of empirical studies using different methods showing that crime switching rather than crime specialization is the general rule for offenders who persist their offending in adulthood (Britt, 1996; Lussier, 2005; McGloin, Sullivan, Piquero, & Pratt, 2007; Piquero et al., 2003; Simon, 1997). In other words, if violent or sexual offenders do reoffend, they are more likely to reoffend for another crime type. Some evidence of specialization in violent and sexual crimes has been reported after a pattern of crime switching, but this pattern characterizes a small proportion of criminal careers (Lussier, 2005). In fact, if offenders do reoffend, it tends to be for a less serious offense. This can be explained by the fact that the base rate of violent crimes is generally low in adult offenders, even more so for sexual crimes. More specifically, these findings challenge the conceptualization of violent offenders and sexual offenders as distinct groups of offenders. Although there is a small subgroup of high-risk, persistent violent and sexual offenders who remain at risk for longer periods, this pattern is not the norm among adult offenders (Hanson & Thornton, 2000; Quinsey, Harris, Rice, & Cormier, 2005). These findings are in sharp contrast with the proliferation of measures that have been implemented in recent years in the United States to manage the risk that violent and sexual offenders represent.

POLICY DEVELOPMENT IN THE UNITED STATES

Violent Offenders

For the last two decades in the United States, policy development targeting violent offenders has been characterized mainly by a series of "get-tough" measures to keep violent offenders in prison and increase public safety. For example, following the 1994 Crime Act, the Violent Offender Incarceration Program and the Truth-in-Sentencing Incentive Grants Program were implemented to reduce the gap between the sentence imposed and the actual time served in prison. Truth-in-sentencing laws require offenders to serve a substantial portion of their prison sentence before being released (MacKenzie, 2006). To qualify for the grants, states had to require that people convicted of a crime serve at least 85% of their prison sentence. Before the enactment of the truth-in-sentencing laws, violent offenders released from state prison were serving about 50% of their prison sentence (Ditton & Wilson, 1999). Most states specifically target violent offenders under the truth-in-sentencing laws. The costs associated with prison expansion and longer and more determinate sentences for violent offenders have led to a decline in preparation for return to the community by decreasing opportunities for treatment and rehabilitation (Travis & Petersilia, 2001). In fact, specific rehabilitation efforts for violent offenders have been directed mainly at one subgroup of offenders: male perpetrators of intimate partner violence. Court-mandated batterer treatment programs have been the most widely used method, but this policy and its associated guidelines have not been well supported by empirical evidence. Recent reviews and quantitative meta-analyses indicate that batterer treatment programs for violent male partners have minimal impact (Babcock, Green, & Robie, 2004; Feder & Wilson, 2005). It has been argued that the lack of a significant treatment effect might be attributable to methodological shortcomings of evaluative studies and variations in the quality of research designs found in the scientific literature (Gondolf, 2004). These general conclusions may also mask the presence of differential treatment impacts. It is possible that treatment program providers did not pay enough attention to the possibility that different treatment strategies might be necessary for offenders with different characteristics (MacKenzie, 2006).

Violent Offenders and Community Reentry

These changes in philosophy and practices have influenced the role of parole in the community reintegration and rehabilitation of violent offenders. Truth-in-sentencing laws have reduced the possibilities for violent offenders to benefit from legal supervision in the community, an important component of the transition from prison to the community. However, only recently were initiatives proposed and implemented to facilitate the community reentry and reintegration of violent offenders. The Serious and Violent Offender Re-entry Initiative (Lattimore & Visher, 2008) was implemented in 2003–2004 to facilitate the community reentry of serious and violent offenders 35 years or younger (adults and juvenile). This $110-million federal initiative provided grants to 69 state agencies across the country aiming to improve the offender's quality of life by facilitating employment opportunities, housing, and family and community involvement; improve the offender's health by addressing substance abuse and physical and mental health problems; decrease criminal activity through supervision and monitoring; and promote multiagency collaboration and case management strategies. Furthermore, the grantees were encouraged to include in their reentry program several components ranging from risk assessment and individual reentry plans to graduated levels of supervision. The people targeted by this initiative included offenders with lengthy criminal records (adult men had 13 arrests on average) and with multiple needs, as shown by their poor educational achievement, poor employment skills, drug and alcohol problems, and mental illness. Preliminary findings showed that participation in the Serious and Violent Offender Re-entry Initiative increased the likelihood of receiving a wide range of services addressing these multiple needs.

Sexual Offenders

Despite positive findings reported in the scientific literature (Hanson et al., 2002; Losel & Schmucker, 2005; MacKenzie, 2006), doubts and concerns over the impact of treatment programs for sex offenders have led to the implementation of a series of legal and penal measures since the early 1990s. Gradually, civil commitment, sex offender registration, community notification, and residence restrictions have been introduced by the criminal justice system to manage the risk of sexual offenders. These measures are in line with the new penology ideology in that they are aimed not to punish or rehabilitate but to increase public safety by assisting the criminal justice system in supervising and managing the risk of sex offenders. First, the policy responses aimed to identify and neutralize the most dangerous sex offenders for indeterminate periods through civil commitment laws. More specifically, civil commitment laws aim to incapacitate through long-term civil commitment sexual recidivists characterized by either a mental abnormality or a personality disorder that makes them likely to repeat sexual violent crimes (Janus, 2003; Winick, 1998). Second, the policy responses aimed to facilitate law enforcement agencies' work by implementing a Sex Offender Registry that allowed the identification of suspects and the monitoring of the whereabouts of convicted sex offenders in the community. The Sex Offender Registry, which was made possible through the passage of the Jacob Wetterling Act in 1994, requires sex offenders to provide their addresses to the local law enforcement agencies periodically (Lees & Tewksbury, 2006; Lieb, Quinsey, & Berliner, 1998).

Sexual Offenders and Community Reentry

The policy responses also were intended to help the criminal justice system in supervising sex offenders released in the community by increasing the public's awareness about the presence of a sex offender in their neighborhood. Community notification was initiated in 1996 after the passage of Megan's Law, which allowed the criminal justice system to disseminate personal information about sex offenders to the public (Simon, 1998). Some states chose to notify the public according to the offender's level of risk (i.e., low, medium, or high), and other states simply chose to notify the public about all sex offenders, regardless of risk level (Levenson, D'Amora, & Hern, 2007). In response to concerns about the proximity of offenders' residences to the residences of potential victims, residence restriction laws have been enacted gradually (Tewksbury, 2005). These laws require specific distances (typically 500 to 2,500 feet) between the offender's residence and specific locations where potential victims may be found, such as daycare centers, schools, parks, and bus stops. These measures are all based on assumptions about sexual offenders and their offending rather than on empirical evidence about the efficacy of those measures to decrease the risk of sexual reoffending.

Consequences of Policies on Sex Offenders' Reintegration

The evaluation of the policy measures implemented to deal with sex offenders has been the focus of several empirical analyses. The first goal of those policy analyses has been to determine the impact of these measures on the recidivism rates of sex offenders. Most of those studies have looked at comparisons of recidivism rates before and after the implementation of those measures in various states. Using different methods and using samples from various states, empirical studies that have looked at the recidivism rates of high-risk offenders subject to community notification have not shown significantly higher recidivism rates than those not subject to it (Adkins, Huff, & Stageberg, 2000; Schram & Milloy, 1995; Zevitz, 2006). In other words, these policy evaluation studies have not found strong empirical evidence that community notification reduces the risk of reoffending. On the other hand, criminologists have been quick to point out that these measures have several unintended consequences. Vigilantism has been reported in rare instances (3–16%) (Levenson et al., 2007; Tewksbury, 2005; Zevitz, Crim, & Farkas, 2000), and other consequences for the offender's ability to reintegrate have been reported. Although there is much heterogeneity in the prevalence rate across studies (and states where the studies took place), the findings do suggest that a substantial proportion of offenders experienced problems such as job loss (21–57%), eviction (10–83%), threats or harassment (21–77%), vandalism (18–21%), and ostracism by neighbors or acquaintances (54–77%) (Levenson & Cotter, 2005; Levenson et al., 2007; Tewksbury, 2005; Zevitz et al., 2000). Perhaps as a result of community notification and residency requirements, a substantial minority of sex offenders reside in disorganized neighborhoods (Tewksbury & Mustaine, 2006). These studies suggest that as a result of the unintended negative consequences of community notification, sex offenders might have difficulty finding a job, finding a residence, earning income, and so on. Furthermore, research has shown that the more citizens give importance to community notification, the more they tend to fear crime (Caputo & Brodsky, 2004). Thus, although previous studies have shown that recent policies implemented in the United States do not seem to attain their goal of reducing crime, they have several negative consequences for offenders and the public.

POLICING SEX OFFENDERS: A CANADIAN PERSPECTIVE

The Risk and Needs Perspective

The Canadian experience in dealing with sex offenders provides an interesting contrast to the policies implemented in the United States for the past two decades. Since the mid-1990s, the Canadian government has taken a series of legal measures to increase security aimed at protecting children and women from violence and sexual abuse (Lieb et al., 1998; Petrunik, 2002). In contrast to the more aggressive approach taken by the U.S. government, Canada's response to sex offenders has been more cautious, influenced in part by a correctional model focusing on the offender's risk and treatment needs (Petrunik,

2003).[1] The correctional model implemented in Canada relies heavily on risk assessment and risk prediction of sexual recidivism. Historically, risk assessment has been concerned mainly with the identification of static (i.e., historical) risk factors that have been shown to be linked to sexual recidivism, such as the number of previous sexual crimes, male victim, extrafamilial victim, and treatment dropout (Hanson & Bussière, 1998; Hanson & Thornton, 2000; Proulx, Tardif, Lamoureux, & Lussier, 2000). In recent years, the focus has been on identifying dynamic risk factors (i.e., those that can be changed by treatment) associated with sexual recidivism, such as deviant sexual arousal, cognitions supporting sexual assault, and emotional identification with children (Hanson & Harris, 2000; Hanson & Morton-Bourgon, 2005). This change of focus has been reinforced by the observation that dynamic risk factors provide incremental predictive accuracy of sexual recidivism over static risk factors and guide treatment interventions (Beech, Fisher, & Thornton, 2003). Canada's correctional model is also concerned with identifying treatment needs and providing sex offender treatment programs according to the offender's level of risk (Lussier & Proulx, 2001).

The Relapse Prevention Model

The most influential treatment approach has been based on the relapse prevention model (Laws, Hudson, & Ward, 2002; Pithers, 1990). The relapse prevention model has two major components: a therapeutic approach and a model of supervision. This model aims to guide practitioners in tailoring the treatment needs of offenders according to their individual dynamic risk factors. Therefore, this therapeutic approach is designed to help sex offenders understand their cycle of offending and learn appropriate coping skills in order to break it (Lussier, Proulx, & McKibben, 2001; McKibben, Proulx, & Lussier, 2001). The second component of the model, external supervision, provides guidelines for community correction workers in tailoring the supervision and the case management plan according to risk factors that are relevant to each offender. This model is not concerned with rehabilitation but is designed to help monitor and stabilize dynamic risk factors that may increase the risk of reoffending in the community. The therapeutic approach has been the subject of empirical examination, with different conclusions about its efficacy: the lack of an overall significant impact; the lack of methodologically sound studies, preventing firm conclusions about the impact; or the presence of a small effect on recidivism with much heterogeneity across treatment settings

(Hanson et al., 2002; Losel & Schmucker, 2005; Marques, Wiederanders, Day, Nelson, & Ommeren, 2005). Although there are still debates about the impact of the treatment approach on recidivism rates, the supervision model and its impact have been largely ignored by researchers. In line with the supervision model of the relapse prevention approach, legal modifications were made to the Criminal Code of Canada to monitor high-risk sex offenders returning to the community.

810 Order or Peace Bonds

In recent years, a distinctive measure was implemented in Canada to deal with high-risk sex offenders returning to the community and having shown a lack of collaboration with treatment during their incarceration (e.g., treatment dropout or refusal). In 1995, the federal government introduced Bill C-42 by making amendments to Section 810 of the Criminal Code of Canada. The amendments aimed at making 810 orders easier to obtain while increasing, from 6 months to 2 years, the maximum penalty for a breach.[2] Section 810 allows the court to restrict the liberty of people considered to be at risk of committing a crime. A person can receive an 810 order if there are "reasonable grounds" that the person will commit a crime. Therefore, the court can enforce a preventive order by imposing a set of conditions (e.g., no alcohol or drug use, staying away from a particular location or person, curfew, no weapons, reporting to a probation officer) that forces a person to avoid breaking the law. Section 810.1 of the Criminal Code of Canada focuses on people at risk of committing a sex crime against someone 14 years old or younger, and Section 810.2 deals with people at risk of committing a serious personal injury offense. Although Section 810.2 does not refer to specific types of victims, it does refer specifically to sexual assault and aggravated sexual assault. If the 810 order is granted by the court, it takes effect for a period of up to 12 months, after which it may be renewed upon application to the court. Therefore, 810 orders impose a series of conditions on sex offenders who are at risk of reoffending and who would otherwise be under no other legal dispositions. A breach of conditions specified by an 810 order is considered a criminal offense under Section 811 of the Criminal Code of Canada. Section 810 orders have been used mainly with offenders returning to the community after a period of incarceration of at least 2 years. These offenders are typically subject to community notification upon their prison release and subject to intensive supervision for the duration of the order.

Empirical Studies

To date, only one study has been conducted on this group of high-risk sex offenders. Lussier, Deslauriers, and Ratel (2008) analyzed a small group of sex offenders subject to this order. These offenders are typically Caucasian men in their 40s, have poor educational and professional backgrounds, are sexual recidivists with a substantial general criminal history, and are at risk of committing a sex crime against a child. Importantly, the study reported a substantial recidivism rate (about 30%) for a brief follow-up period (about 6 months on average). The reoffenses were mainly for breaching the conditions of their 810 order (e.g., curfew, substance use), with only one offender having committed a sex crime while under the order. Overall, these rates are much higher than what is typically reported for sex offenders but in line with those found in recidivism studies looking at the impact of intensive supervision programs (Petersilia & Turner, 1990, 1993).

AIM OF THIS STUDY

In the United States, sex offenders have been depicted as a specific group of offenders with a high risk to reoffend and a tendency to specialize in sex crimes despite contrary empirical evidence. The term *sex offender* has become synonymous with *high-risk offender*. Recent policy responses have been aimed at managing the threat that this high-risk group represents. In Canada, the focus of recent policy developments has been influenced by the ongoing tradition of risk assessment, risk prediction, and treatment in its correctional model. In that respect, the criminal justice response has been more cautious by focusing on a segment of this population, targeting high-risk violent and high-risk sexual offenders. Peace bonds, or 810 orders, exemplify this trend of facilitating the risk management of high-risk sex offenders returning to the community after their incarceration to prevent a future violent or sexual crime. However, not much is known about the main challenges criminal justice practitioners face when supervising high-risk sex offenders under an 810 order. The current study departs from previous studies by using a qualitative approach to better understand challenges faced by criminal justice practitioners involved in the supervision of high-risk sex offenders under an 810 order. This study is intended to inform policymakers about the impact of risk management techniques for high-risk populations. The findings provide baseline information on community risk management of sex offenders as perceived by criminal justice practitioners.

METHOD

Sample

Typically, in the province of British Columbia, Canada, 40–50 sex offenders per year are under an 810.1 or 810.2 order (Lussier, Leclerc, Cale, & Proulx, 2007). Because 810 orders fall under provincial jurisdiction, British Columbia Community Corrections has the mandate to supervise these offenders. The current study is based on a sample of criminal justice professionals involved in the case management of those sex offenders in British Columbia. Three types of criminal justice professionals were considered for the current study: British Columbia Community Corrections staff, outreach workers, and police investigators. British Columbia Community Corrections includes probation officers and local managers involved in the case management of sex offenders under an 810 order. From 2006 and 2007, 25 community corrections officers were involved in the supervision of these offenders across the province. For the purpose of the study, we included only those who took part in the case management of at least three sex offenders under an 810 order. In total, 11 community corrections officers met this criterion and were asked to participate in the study. The outreach workers are professionals who facilitate the reintegration of offenders into the community by addressing immediate needs (e.g., residence, food, income, transportation, support). All outreach workers ($n = 5$) involved in the management of high-risk offenders since 2006 were asked to participate in the study.[3] Finally, investigators working for various police departments were asked to participate in the study. The inclusion criteria for those professionals specified that they should be working in special units dealing with the supervision and investigation of high-risk offenders. In total, 20 people were contacted to participate in the study. Three people were excluded from the study for two main reasons: They could not be contacted, or they did not meet the inclusion criteria. Therefore, the study is based on a sample of 17 criminal justice professionals, including 9 British Columbia Community Corrections staff (participation rate = 82%), 4 outreach workers (participation rate = 80%), and 4 police investigators (participation rate = 100%). The mean age of the sample at the time of the study was 40.9 years ($SD = 7.5$), with an average of 9.3 years ($SD = 7.1$) of experience in their respective positions and an average of 5.6 years ($SD = 5.7$) of experience working with sex offenders. The majority were male (58%), were Caucasian (59%), had a bachelor's degree (59%), and had a graduate university degree (29%).

Procedure

Participants were informed that the study aimed to investigate their perceptions of risk management in the community for sex offenders under an 810 order. Participants were also advised that information was being collected for research purposes only and would remain confidential and anonymous, and that the study was not intended to assess their job performance. No incentives were given for their involvement in the study. Participants were interviewed once by a trained research assistant, all of whom ($n = 3$) were criminology graduate students. Interviews were conducted either in person ($n = 9$) or by telephone ($n = 8$). Some interviews were conducted by telephone because of the geographic distance between the interviewer and the interviewee. All interviews were conducted between May and November 2007, and on average they lasted between 60 and 90 minutes.

Interview Protocol

The interview protocol consisted of a semistructured questionnaire measuring six aspects relevant to the case management of sex offenders under a section 810 order. The semistructured interview included questions about perceptions of criminal justice professionals on issues relevant to the case management of those offenders. Most questions were open ended to allow the interviewees to talk freely about issues and about their experiences with the case management of high-risk sex offenders under an 810 order. First, the role of criminal justice practitioners working with this specific offender population was discussed. Most importantly, participants were asked to identify their own roles and responsibilities in the case management of high-risk sex offenders under an 810 order. Second, questions were asked about the level of collaboration between criminal justice professionals and the sharing of information. Third, the questionnaire included items related to the risk assessment of sexual reoffending and whether risk factors that characterize high-risk sex offenders under an 810 order are accurately assessed with existing risk assessment tools. Fourth, questions were asked about the risk management of sex offenders under an 810 order. More specifically, participants were asked to identify the most significant risk factors of reoffending and the strategies, if any, they had used to stabilize those risk factors and whether those strategies had been effective. Fifth, the interview protocol included aspects relevant to the process of community reintegration. Participants were asked to identify the most significant issues with regard to the community reintegration of sex offenders under an 810 order; the strategies, if any, that they had used to overcome problems they encountered; the level of offender collaboration in applying those strategies and the level of efficacy of the strategies used; and possible recommendations for facilitating the reintegration of those offenders. Whenever strategies for dealing with risk factors were mentioned, the interviewer probed the participant in order to evaluate the efficacy of strategies.

Analytical Strategy

A qualitative method of analyzing the narratives of semistructured interviews was used in order to gain insight about the case management of sex offenders under an 810 order.[4] Therefore, content analysis was used according to the guidelines for phenomenological studies that involve in-depth interviews with research participants (Noaks & Wincup, 2004). Participants' narratives were typed and analyzed, and for the current study only the information relevant to the following four risk management issues is presented and analyzed: perceptions of the risk factors that characterize sex offenders under an 810 order (e.g., "What are the most important factors that could lead to a sexual re-offence?"), perceptions of risk management and the strategies used to stabilize risks (e.g., "What do you do in order to deal with this factor to minimize the risk of reoffending?"), perceptions of criminal justice professionals with regard to the offender's needs when reintegrating the community (e.g., "What are the most important issues faced by offenders under an 810 order when reintegrating the community?"), and the most important constraints in providing support and assistance to offenders (e.g., "What are the significant constraints you've faced so far when working on the case management of 810 offenders?"). For each of these four risk management issues, we identified the main themes discussed by participants. The data collection and the analytic process were guided by the grounded theory approach (Strauss & Corbin, 1990). In line with the grounded theory approach, data collection and data analysis were done simultaneously. Notes were taken during and after each interview with criminal justice practitioners. The notes were then analyzed to highlight the themes emerging from the interview. This process allowed the identification of areas that needed to be discussed in subsequent interviews. Once these themes were identified, the prevalence of each was assessed and reported. When appropriate, the interviewer asked participants to determine the most important issue mentioned during the interview (e.g., "What do you consider to be the most important risk factor?"). This information was compiled across the 17 interviews conducted, allowing for analyses of the prevalence and the importance of issues raised by participants. Also, in order to examine the efficacy of strategies used in risk management of high-risk offenders, strategies were categorized as follows: what works (i.e., only very successful reports), what is promising (i.e., only successful or somewhat successful reports), what we are not sure about (i.e., mix of successful and unsuccessful reports), what is not working (i.e., only unsuccessful reports), and what is unknown (i.e., the participant can't determine the efficacy yet).

RESULTS

Principal Issues in Reintegration

We then analyzed the most important issues and challenges that characterize community reintegration of offenders. Inadequate or unsuitable residence was the most common theme reported by criminal justice professionals (53%). It was also reported by 29% of our sample as the single most important issue in community reintegration. Research participants raised four main concerns: the general lack of housing and shelters for clients, problems in finding affordable housing, difficulties in finding a residence meeting the conditions of the order (e.g., away from parks and schoolyards, with no children in the building) because most housing is close to elementary schools, and the location of offenders' residences.

The restriction on the offender's freedom was the second most prevalent issue in providing assistance and support (41%). It was also reported as the single most important issue by 35% of our sample. More specifically, criminal justice professionals raised the issue of community notification and the conditions of the 810 order impeding the offender's community reintegration. Criminal justice professionals expressed concerns that community notification led to discrimination in setting up community services because of the offenders' status. The main issue at play here is that these offenders are being depicted as multiple recidivists with a history of having refused treatment or dropped out of their treatment programs while incarcerated. Therefore, concern over the ability to rehabilitate this group of high-risk sex offenders was pivotal in the denial of access to treatment. It was reported that such hurdles to reentry led to negative emotional reactions that may prove difficult to overcome or inadequate behavioral reactions. In certain cases, it was pointed out that community notification could be counterproductive to the community reintegration process:

"The offender may experience significant stress as part of the process . . . and may go underground or be destabilized."

One interviewer reported that a support worker had to pick up groceries from a charity center because the client was not welcome there because of his status as a sex offender. It was also noted that community notification led to increasing workload (e.g., "Community will report all client activity even if it's allowed," "Clients are contacting probation officers more often"). Others used the community notification as a motivational tool by telling the client, "Let's do something about this so the poster doesn't go up next time."

Inadequate treatment program support was the third most important theme discussed by criminal justice professionals (35%), and it was ranked as the single most important issue by 12% of our sample. The lack of access to treatment and, to a lesser extent, the unavailability of treatment programs were cited as important limitations in the case management of sex offenders (e.g., "At the same time programming is available, seasonal jobs open up for clients, so there is a conflict between getting treatment and employment"). This issue was most important for offenders residing in rural areas in British Columbia because of the cost of transportation needed to attend treatment programs offered only outside the offender's community (e.g., "Majority of clients do not have cars. . . . Probation finds (and pays) driver to take clients to treatment").

The socioeconomic circumstance of the offender was the next most prevalent theme cited by research participants (29%). Of concern here were the difficulties offenders encountered in finding a job after release from prison, their lack of technical and professional skills, and their low income. Many noted the offenders' lack of the very skills that limited their ability to reintegrate into society (e.g., "Many lack basic skills, like how to apply for welfare, open a bank account"). This was important because several practitioners noted that the offenders had to deal with the aftermath of several incarcerations or lengthy periods of incarceration: "They are helpless and institutionalized. . . . Did not have life skills. . . . Did not know how to obtain a bank card."

These issues suggest that some offenders experienced difficulties in becoming financially self-sufficient in the community. Three other issues were reported as significant challenges faced by both offenders and criminal justice professionals during reintegration: the presence of substance abuse and health problems (18%) (e.g., "Clients are able to identify and acknowledge that substance use is a factor in their offending. . . . Abstinence might not be the client's ultimate goal"); the fact that offenders are often resistant or lack motivation (18%) (e.g., "Clients are generally good at identifying risk, but ability to follow through and overcome it is lacking"; "It's difficult to change [their] overall opinion of Corrections"); and the absence of an adequate social support network to facilitate the offender's reintegration (12%).

Strategies Used to Facilitate Community Reintegration

Different strategies, with varying levels of success, were reported by criminal justice professionals for dealing with the most important challenges faced by offenders during reintegration (i.e., inadequate or unsuitable residence, restrictions on offender's freedom, and inadequate treatment support). The most promising strategies used include identifying the needs of offenders in order to facilitate setting up community resources in advance (e.g., "helping the client prepare a concrete plan for community re-entry," "providing help in finding a job that is less risky in terms of reoffending").

Second, practitioners stressed the importance of adopting a proactive attitude and initiative (e.g., "establishing a good rapport with hotel/rooming houses in order to secure a bed space for high risk offenders," "using online resources and personal contacts," "accompanying client to residence," and trying to "sell the client to the manager, service provider"). Not only do criminal justice practitioners have to be proactive, but at times they have to put pressure on service providers: "I made phone calls for 2 to 3 weeks and threatened the clinic with public action."

Furthermore, working in close collaboration with community resource providers to meet the offenders' needs was emphasized (e.g., "advise housing management that local police will conduct routine checks"), as was the use of external community resources. Interestingly, criminal justice practitioners also reported that an effective strategy was to encourage offenders to be honest and realistic about their current situation (e.g., "encourage client to disclose their history to prospective employer"; "helping, motivating the client in having a concrete plan"). In that regard, one interviewer added, "Talk honestly with clients; . . . encourage them to disclose to prospective employers their history or help them find other employment that is less risky in terms of potential to be around children, females."

Planning was also mentioned, because the strategies and the resources used are often unstable because of the client's status as a high-risk offender (e.g., "Plan ahead and be prepared to move offenders to different places subject to public notification," "Starts foot work for places to live about a week before [the offender gets released from prison] for certain cases"). At the same time, criminal justice professionals also reported strategies that were difficult to apply (e.g., "finding housing with no children"). The next two community reintegration issues raised by criminal justice professionals were socioeconomic situations and substance-related problems. Although none of the strategies used were perceived as very successful, some were described as promising: "contacting job placement agencies," "assisting client in applying for income assistance," "helping offenders in using vocational resources, although these are lacking," and "connecting offenders with appropriate programs to address substance use problems."

No significant strategies were reported for dealing with offenders' lack of motivation and resistance and the lack of adequate social support for offenders, which suggests some problems and limitations in assisting them with these complex issues.

Perceptions of Significant Risk Factors for Reoffending

First, we reported criminal justice professionals' perceptions of significant risk factors that characterize high-risk sex offenders under an 810 order. However, criminal justice practitioners were quick to point out that "it's very subjective, for different offenders, you have different risk factors."

Taking that into account, our analysis led to the identification of eight main themes, or eight significant sets of risk factors. These risk factors are presented in order of prevalence. Substance use problems were reported as a significant risk factor by 71% of participants. In fact, substance use problems were rated as the single most important risk factor by 35% of our sample of criminal justice professionals. Looking more closely at the narratives, we found that substance use (53%) was more frequently reported than "substance abuse," "dependence to a substance," or "addiction to a substance" (24%), suggesting that this aspect might reflect more of an antisocial lifestyle than a clinical condition.

Inadequate social network was reported by 41% of our sample and is the second most prevalent risk factor reported by criminal justice professionals. An inadequate social network was rated by 12% of our sample as the single most important risk factor. Some participants commented on the lack of prosocial influences (e.g., "lack of social support," "loneliness," "isolation"), some commented on the presence of negative social influences (e.g., "negative associates," "negative peer influences," and "hanging out with other sex offenders"), and other participants commented on offenders' inability to form healthy relationships (e.g., "being manipulative with others," "tendency to portray women as sexual objects," "desire to form inappropriate relationships with children"). Criminal justice professionals reported characteristics generally associated with an antisocial tendency as the next most prevalent risk factor (35%). Furthermore, 12% of the sample reported characteristics typically associated with an antisocial tendency as the single most important risk factor of high-risk sex offenders under an 810 order. Participants also reported "historical animosity toward authority," "hostility and anger," "procriminal attitudes," "criminality," and "attitudes supporting criminal activity." All those themes are in line with the presence of antisocial personality traits or a propensity for antisocial criminal behaviors.

Characteristics typically associated with sexual deviance were reported as a significant risk factor by 29% of the sample, but only 6% considered sexual deviance to be the single most important risk factor in terms of sexual reoffense. Participants reported "sexual preoccupations," "sexual impulses," "attitudes supportive of sexual offending," and "deviant sexual desires" as significant factors in those men. Furthermore, problems associated with difficulties in finding a residence were reported by 29% of the sample of criminal justice professionals. Although it was rarely reported as the most significant risk factor, participants mentioned being concerned by a "lack of appropriate residence," "unstable housing," and problems with "access to housing" as significant precursors to reoffending. Surprisingly perhaps, only 24% of the sample reported criminal opportunity or lifestyle as a significant risk factor, whereas 6% reported this risk factor as the single most significant one. Factors such as "living arrangements near schools and playgrounds" and "access to de-stabilizers, such as women, drugs and children" were reported as significant risk factors that needed to be monitored in the community. Finally, the presence of employment difficulties (18%) after community reentry (e.g., "lack of job training," "inaccessible employment," and "lack of employment") and the psychological distress and mental illness of the offenders (18%) (e.g., "emotional instability") were the last two themes emerging from the analyses. Six percent of the sample considered employment difficulties to be the single most important risk factor for reoffending.

Strategies Used to Stabilize Risk Factors in the Community

Different strategies, with varying levels of success, have been used by criminal justice professionals in dealing with the most prevalent risk factors (e.g., substance use problems, inadequate social influences, and antisociality). First, strategies used to address the most prevalent risk factors included methods that highlight the importance of facilitating the collaboration of the offender. One interviewer pointed out that crucial step was to make sure they understood well in advance, before getting out of prison, that they would be under an 810 order: "Most of them accept it because they've been advised. . . . They know it's coming (the 810 order). . . . It's not a big surprise. . . . It's a big part of the success."

The strategies described to facilitate that collaboration included "encouraging active involvement of the client with outreach workers," "ensuring that outreach workers and probation officers can establish a good rapport with the client early on in the reintegration process," "advise probation officers as it is the probation officer's job to monitor risk," and "using the services of law enforcement resources for intensive supervision and monitoring." The importance of having outreach workers to provide support was also emphasized:

> The impact of outreach workers is significant. . . . Once the client is released, they are very scared and uncomfortable. . . . Outreach workers are the initial people they spend most time with. . . . Outreach workers help clients with frustration of long line-ups, . . . educate clients on free resources they are not aware of.

Strategies that were perceived as the most promising in dealing with prevalent risk factors highlighted the need for a broad collaborative approach involving resources and services external to criminal justice professionals, including the use of community services such as Alcoholic Anonymous and Narcotics Anonymous. Other reported strategies considered to be promising stressed the need for external control mechanisms, especially with respect to the offender's cognitive emotional and behavioral state: "monitoring the offender's responses to direction and supervision," "encouraging the offender to introduce his peers to probation officers," "monitor the offender's level of anger, and particularly increases therein can be indicative of an increase in risk of reoffending," "addressing ways of coping with frustration and anger," and "supervise the offender's finances." Those strategies were particularly important for offenders with substance abuse problems, which were prevalent according to criminal justice practitioners. Most importantly, criminal justice practitioners are looking for situations that will put offenders in the same pattern as the one that led to their prior crime. By *pattern*, criminal justice practitioners understood situations and behaviors that preceded their previous sex crime. In that regard, the interviewees noted,

> We are looking for situations that might put them in the same pattern as before.

> As soon as the client is released, the outreach worker will help client get stabilized with rent, housing, and food, . . . make sure they have no extra money for drugs. . . . They [outreach worker] will be available by phone for support if the client does not call the next day, it is an indication they are using drugs.

The overlap between risk management and addressing the offenders' needs was also pointed out (e.g., "As soon as the client is released, outreach workers will help client get stabilized with rent/housing and food and make sure they have no extra money for drugs"). No strategies were reported as being clearly successful in dealing with negative social influences and antisociality of offenders in the community (e.g., "It is difficult to find new friends for the clients," "Very difficult to make new friends given the clients' offence history," "They have nothing else to fill that gap. . . . Everyone needs friends"). As one interviewee pointed out, "Sex offenders don't have many friends and tend to hang out with other sex offenders. . . . Is it a good or a bad thing? It's problematic when the offender is fixated."

Other strategies were reported that were unsuccessful or of mixed or unknown effectiveness. Motivational interviewing techniques, such as "talking to the client," "giving support and encouragement," and "brainstorming activities in group settings" were not perceived as having a significant impact on the most prevalent risk factors. It remained unclear to criminal justice professionals whether the identification of high-risk situations for reoffense and the identification of crime patterns were successful or unsuccessful in addressing the offenders' antisociality. One interviewer noted that although offenders were able to recognize the factors in their offending process, they lacked the motivation to deal with those problems: "Clients are generally good at identifying this [drug use] as a risk factor, but the ability to follow through and overcome it is lacking."

Four other risk factors were discussed in terms of the strategies participants used to deal with risk factors in the community: crime opportunity and lifestyle, sexual deviance, unsuitable or inadequate residence, and limited employment possibilities. Constraints associated with the last two risk factors overlap with important issues in the reintegration process and were not discussed further here. Therefore, we focus here on the strategies used to deal with crime opportunities and lifestyle and sexual deviance. All strategies for dealing with crime opportunities and lifestyle that were reported by criminal justice professionals were perceived as either successful or promising. Strategies reported were in line with the relapse prevention rationale in that they reflected means of helping offenders avoid situations that could increase the risks of reoffending. These means included "monitoring the whereabouts of the offenders" and "discuss[ing] the offender's leisure time, employment, and other situations or changes to circumstances which may facilitate contact with potential victims."

Similar strategies in line with the relapse prevention model were reported: "making sure the offender is busy and is free from negative thoughts or negative moods" and "staying in touch with former victims to ensure that the offender is staying away." The efficacy of strategies reported to deal with sexual deviance was somewhat unclear. Strategies were not aimed at changing sexually deviant behaviors, thoughts, and urges but rather at helping offenders control them if present. For example, motivational interviews emphasizing the "avoidance of sexual thoughts" and "discussing deviant and non-deviant sexual patterns" have been reported to monitor offenders' sexual deviance. Other strategies used by criminal justice professionals included being familiar with the case (e.g., "knowing details about previous offences") and paying attention, during home visits, to details indicating sexual activity: "I look at the types of magazines on client's table. . . . If I see a condom, I will joke as if it is bubble gum, . . . then I'll share the information with the probation officer."

Based on the narratives, it was unclear how criminal justice professionals were monitoring sexual deviance and the signs indicating an aggravating situation. The difficulties in monitoring and changing sexually deviant attitudes were noted (e.g., "Clients' attitudes are very entrenched," "Clients do not want to address this issue. . . . Push it too much and the client shuts down"). As one interviewee pointed out, "They attend group programming because they have to, but they will hide their sexual deviancy to the bitter end."

This is important because its manifestations are not as explicit as other risk factors. As a result, the monitoring of sexual deviance as a dynamic risk factor for sexual recidivism becomes very difficult, something pointed out by one interviewee: "You can't. . . . A lot of it is in their head."

Perceptions of Risk Management Constraints

Next, we looked at the most prevalent constraints impeding the risk management of high-risk sex offenders under an 810 order. Several themes emerged from the narratives of criminal justice professionals. The most prevalent constraint was the overall lack of resources for dealing with the risks and needs of these offenders (69%). It seemed to be a very significant issue: 46% of the sample reported it as the single most important issue. Three related issues were also important here. First, many criminal justice professionals complained about the lack of treatment programs to stabilize risk factors in the community, such as substance abuse and mental health problems. Second, criminal justice professionals also pointed out the "lack of collaboration from resource providers" in setting up resources and providing needed services because of the clients' status as high-risk sex offenders: "Client would be denied services because of females in treatment group or a female staff."

Third, criminal justice professionals cited the need for a specialized treatment program to deal specifically with this population of high-risk sex offenders, something that is not currently available in the community (e.g., "So many clients with a history of head trauma, [fetal alcohol spectrum disorder], brain injury. . . . Needed a trained person to deal with these clients"). The next most prevalent constraint in the risk management of offenders under an 810 order was inadequate housing (38%). Not only was this a significant issue in the case management of these offenders, but inadequate housing also impeded the ability of criminal justice professionals to stabilize risk factors in the community (e.g., "After a public notification, it is extremely difficult to secure residence for a client," "Most shelters or housing do not take anyone with a history of sex offences"). Practitioners were quick to point out that high-risk sex offenders were more likely to move to certain neighborhoods: "Housing in [Neighborhood A] is difficult because there is no tolerance of sex offenders. . . . In [Neighborhood B] no one really cares because of the mainly criminal population."

The important fact here is that many criminal justice professionals cited the lack of adequate housing as having led to the displacement of offenders to specific geographic areas considered criminogenic and disorganized social environments (e.g., "Terrible housing, . . . crack addicts and prostitutes in front of client's face"; "Places where clients resided were substandard accommodations; . . . third world like conditions with feces, vomit and rats").

Legal restrictions (31%) were the next significant issue raised by criminal justice professionals. Importantly, most professionals who reported legal restrictions as an important factor also acknowledged that they were the single most important issue limiting the ability to address risk factors. For example, it was reported that conditions of the order made it more difficult and sometimes impeded reintegration: "Refer to alcohol and drug counsellor, . . . but clients must meet counsellor outside of the building because it is close to a school."

A demanding caseload (31%) was the next most important issue raised by interviewees (e.g., "Police often receive calls, complaints that are not so serious," "Probation officers should be able to spend more time with outreach workers and clients to assist in stabilizing client upon release," "Lack of time to prepare release plan"). The next three most prevalent themes that emerged from the narratives were the absence of a specialized intervention for high-risk sex offenders (23%), the lack of collaboration from service providers (23%), and the difficulties encountered when trying to obtain reliable and valid information about the offender from collaterals (23%). Employment difficulties (15%) and client resistance (8%) in supervision were also reported by criminal justice professionals (e.g., "Client does not want help," "Some clients did not want help; most of the guys were grateful because they were helpless").

DISCUSSION

The analysis of these narratives by criminal justice practitioners revealed that community risk management of high-risk sex offenders involved a combination of supervision and monitoring as well as assistance and support. Both supervision and assistance were challenged by many constraints: the characteristics of the offenders, a community hostile to those offenders, and the general lack of services helping criminal justice practitioners address the risk and needs of the offenders. The findings suggest that high-risk sex offenders should be considered to have multiple risk factors that could lead to reoffending, with multiple needs requiring multiple interventions from criminal justice professionals. These findings have important implications for the supervision, support, and assistance provided by criminal justice professionals to high-risk sex offenders. In the following sections we review how those implications affect surveillance, assistance, and support for high-risk offenders in the community.

High-Risk Sex Offenders Returning to the Community

High-Risk Sex Offenders With Multiple Risk Factors

In line with previous empirical investigations (Beech et al., 2003; Hanson & Bussière, 1998; Hanson & Harris, 2000; Hanson, Morton, & Harris, 2003; Lussier & Cortoni, 2008; Quinsey et al., 2005), the findings of this study suggest that high-risk sex offenders are characterized by multiple risk factors that can lead to sexual reoffending. They are described as having many problems in various aspects of their personality (e.g., antisocial traits), attitudes (e.g., resistance, lack of collaboration), behavior (e.g., sexually deviant fantasizing), social network (e.g., antisocial peers), lifestyle (e.g., substance use), and environment (e.g., living in an unsuitable neighborhood). The multifaceted nature of these problems presents a challenge to criminal justice practitioners assigned to the case management of these high-risk sex offenders. The risk factors reported by criminal justice professionals have not been emphasized in the scientific literature (Beech et al., 2003; Hanson & Bussière, 1998; Hanson & Morton-Bourgon, 2005; Lussier & Cortoni, 2008; Quinsey et al., 2005). Sexual deviance and sexual crime opportunities were not the main risk factors considered by criminal justice professionals. In fact, according to our findings, the single most prevalent and most important risk factor characterizing this population was the presence of substance use problems, followed by the offender's inadequate social network and general antisociality. This result could reflect the following limitations. First, assessment tools designed specifically for sex offenders might be insufficient in assessing the multifaceted problems of high-risk offenders. Second, offenders for whom an 810 order was issued come mostly from federal penitentiaries and may share many of the characteristics typically associated with the general prison population (Lussier, Proulx, & LeBlanc, 2005). Third, because of the preventive nature of the order, these findings might reflect the fact that criminal justice professionals are preoccupied with factors leading to a high risk of reoffending (i.e., negative peer influence, drug and alcohol use) rather than a high-risk situation per se (e.g., a child molester interacting with a child). Finally, criminal justice professionals may lack training in assessment, identification, and recognition of the aspects of the offender's sexuality that can play a role in reoffending. The current findings do not allow us to determine the causes of such inconsistencies. However, the risk factors stated by criminal justice professionals are important and have been shown to increase the risk of reoffending, especially among the general prison population (Gendreau, Little, & Coggin, 1996).

High-Risk Sex Offenders With Multiple Needs

High-risk sex offenders are described by criminal justice professionals as having multiple needs during community reentry and throughout community reintegration. These needs, in order of importance, are finding a residence, getting access to treatment and services, securing a source of income, and getting a job. It was not possible to determine whether they reflected the continuation of prior deficits or the consequences of the offender's high-risk status. More specifically, it is possible that these needs reflected characteristics of the offenders before the 810 order was issued, consequences of the conditions of the 810 order and community notification, or the interplay of the two. This point is important and has not really been addressed by criminologists looking at the negative impact of community notification (Levenson & Cotter, 2005; Levenson et al., 2007; Tewksbury, 2005; Zevitz et al., 2000). Inadequate social networks, difficulties finding a residence, and limited employment opportunities might reflect preexisting offender characteristics (e.g., antisocial family members and peers, limited financial resources, limited professional skills), the negative consequences of the conditions of the 810 order, and the stigma associated with the label of high-risk sex offender (e.g., restrictions on the location of residence, disorganized neighborhoods, unwelcoming employers or building managers). Although our study could not clarify the exact nature of those dynamic risk factors, it revealed that many of the significant offender needs cited by criminal justice professionals are also integral parts of community reentry and community reintegration processes. These needs probably represent both the continuation of offender characteristics that can be destabilized as a result of the unintended consequences of community notification and the offender's legal status. Only a longitudinal study could disentangle those processes and their impact on reoffending.

Community Risk Management of High-Risk Sex Offenders

Risk Management as Supervision and Assistance

The risk management model put in place in British Columbia emphasizes the importance of both supervision of and assistance to high-risk sex offenders returning to the community. On one hand, the management of dynamic risk factors highlights the importance of information sharing and collaboration between criminal justice practitioners. In fact, the most promising strategies used to manage the risk factors were securing the collaboration of the offender, especially for outreach workers who can have a positive influence on this offender population; facilitating collaboration between various criminal justice professionals (e.g., police officers, outreach workers, probation officers) involved in offender case management; extending the collaborative approach to other services and agencies (e.g., treatment resources) in order to address relevant risk factors; and stressing the need for external means of supervision and surveillance. On the other hand, management of the offenders' needs was addressed through a combination of strategies to facilitate community reentry and community reintegration with monitoring offenders' risk factors. The type of assistance that has been used and reported as promising in helping offenders meet those needs involved a combination of offender advocacy, networking, proactive actions and attitudes of criminal justice professionals, and external supervision. Therefore, the strategies used by criminal justice professionals do not emphasize transformation or modification of the offender's personality, behavior, or lifestyle. Criminal justice professionals acknowledged the importance of treatment, and their role was to assist offenders by facilitating access to treatment programs. However, they also mentioned that treatment programs are often unavailable or difficult to access, offenders are denied access because of their status, or offenders refuse treatment. The situation is made more difficult by the multifaceted characteristics of this group of sex offenders, who need specialized treatment intervention. Although these four aspects of assistance and support (i.e., offender advocacy, networking, proactive attitudes, and external supervision) are perceived as facilitating community reintegration, there is no empirical evidence that they significantly decrease the risk of reoffending.

Constraints on the Risk Management Process

It is obvious from these findings that the risk management model put in place by the criminal justice system is challenged by a series of constraints, often working in combination. Criminal justice professionals cite four main areas of challenges and constraints that can hinder the offender's community reintegration: preexisting characteristics of the offenders; an unwelcoming, uncollaborative community; a lack of resources to address the offenders' multiple needs; and legal restrictions on the offenders' freedom. As a group, high-risk sex offenders have been described by criminal justice professionals as antisocial, with substantial criminal histories, often characterized by substance use problems, subject to negative social influences, and, to a lesser extent, showing a pattern of resistance or a general lack of motivation to change, a lack of professional skills, and mental health problems. Criminal justice professionals report that these offenders need specialized treatment while in the community. On the other hand, the absence of a specialized treatment program to address the dynamic risk factors that could modify the offender's risk status has been mentioned as one of the most important constraint during community reintegration, often resulting from the offender's status as a high-risk sex offender. For similar reasons, and also because of the conditions of their order (e.g., staying away from children and parks), finding suitable housing has been reported as the most important constraint experienced by offenders during community reintegration. As a result, it was reported that a displacement effect might be in place, whereby some offenders had to move to inadequate residences, characterized by poor housing conditions, often located in disorganized neighborhoods. As Tewksbury (2005) points out, although this may characterize a substantial minority of cases, it does not necessarily mean that all offenders end up in disorganized, criminogenic neighborhoods. On the other hand, when present, this situation can increase the negative social influences of those offenders while also facilitating access to illicit substances, both of which are considered by criminal justice professionals to be important dynamic risk factors. This further complicates the case management process, as more time and resources become necessary to ensure that the conditions of the 810 order are met and as the information obtained from collaterals might be unreliable. The role and the impact of neighborhood factors in triggering a reoffense has been a neglected aspect of the recidivism process and warrants more scrutiny in future empirical studies (Kubrin & Stewart, 2006).

POLICY IMPLICATIONS

The risk management model put in place in British Columbia contrasts with the risk management model in the United States. Several measures have been implemented in the United States to manage the risk that all sexual offenders face, such as sex offender registry, public notification, and, more recently, residency restrictions. The Canadian model is concerned with the risk management not of all sex offenders returning to the community but of those considered to be at high risk to sexually reoffend. In line with the community protection ideology (Lieb et al., 1998; Petrunik, 2002, 2003), the Canadian risk management of high-risk sex offenders is tailored so that individualized risk factors and needs are monitored and addressed. In that regard, the risk management model implemented in the United States is more concerned with monitoring the offender's whereabouts and geographic location (Lees & Tewksbury, 2006; Levenson et al., 2007; Tewksbury, 2005). In doing so, this model focuses on limiting the number of criminal opportunities, which is only one of the several dynamic risk factors associated with sexual reoffending (Hanson & Harris, 2000). This is a limited approach, however, because sexual reoffending is multidetermined and the risk factors may vary across offenders (Hanson & Bussière, 1998; Hanson & Harris, 2000; Lussier & Cortoni, 2008). Furthermore, the criminal opportunities that can trigger a sex crime can vary from one offender to another, something not accounted for by the U.S. model. In that regard, the Canadian model emphasizes the monitoring of the offender's dynamic risk factors that have been shown to be empirically linked to reoffending. This approach is more individualized in that it deals with the specific risk factors that may lead an offender to sexually reoffend. This individualized approach has the advantage of allowing criminal justice professionals to monitor the risk of reoffending but also any changes in the risk of reoffending (Hanson & Harris, 2000; Lussier & Cortoni, 2008; Proulx et al., 2000). The current study suggests that the main risk factors characterizing the population of high-risk sex offenders are those typically associated with general reoffending, and the risk management model attempts to stabilize those risk factors in the community.

The U.S. risk management model is concerned mainly with the formal and informal supervision of sex offenders returning to the community to prevent future crimes. With the emphasis on public safety, specific aspects linked to the offender's risk of reoffending have been neglected. Although these measures are well intended, they can have serious negative consequences for the reintegration of these offenders. Successful community reintegration is key in decreasing the risk of reoffending by sexual offenders (Kruttschnitt, Uggen, & Shelton, 2000). Previous studies have shown that recent U.S. policies have several negative consequences for the offender's ability to reintegrate into the community (Levenson & Cotter, 2005; Levenson et al., 2007; Tewksbury, 2005; Zevitz, 2006; Zevitz et al., 2000; Zevitz & Farkas, 2000). More specifically, these measures have been shown to significantly and negatively affect the offender's ability to find a residence, secure employment, and develop or maintain positive relationships. Therefore, the U.S. model therefore provides no assistance to sex offenders returning to the community, nor does it provide support to mitigate the negative impact that public notification or residency restrictions may have on them. The Canadian risk management model is not limited to the external supervision of offenders but also involves the provision of assistance and support to facilitate the offender's community reentry and reintegration. In doing so, this risk management model is also concerned with the offender's needs (e.g., housing, employment, income, health) during community reentry in order to reduce the risk of reoffending. The Canadian model is not without its limitations; several constraints on the offender's ability to reintegrate the community noted in U.S. studies (e.g., Levenson & Cotter, 2005) were also reported by Canadian criminal justice professionals. Our study also found that the risk management model implemented in Canada might also impose several constraints on criminal justice professionals' ability to monitor and manage the offender's risk factors and needs. Although there are no empirical data showing the superiority of one model over the other, the Canadian model provides a more focused and individualized perspective on the risk management of high-risk sex offenders.

LIMITATIONS OF THE STUDY

This study has several methodological limitations, and the findings should be interpreted accordingly. First, it is exploratory and aimed at measuring the perceptions of criminal justice professionals with regard to offenders' community reentry and community reintegration. Therefore, there might be a gap between the perceptions of criminal justice professionals and empirical reality. On the other hand, to our knowledge this is the first study that describes the challenges faced by both sex offenders and criminal justice professionals who are involved in case management in the community. Furthermore, it is the first study to document the reintegration process of high-risk sex offenders in the community. Second, although the level of participation was high and we were able to include most criminal justice professionals, our findings are based on a small sample. However, one of the strengths of this study is that we included different types of criminal justice professionals (police investigators, outreach workers, and probation officers). Third, this study did not include offenders' perceptions about community reentry and community reintegration; these would have provided valuable complementary information. Furthermore, although our study documented themes that are relevant to community reintegration, the interviewer did not probe research participants about the various stages of reintegration (e.g., first week, first month, first 6 months). Different issues and challenges might be important at different stages of the offender's community reintegration. Finally, it was not possible to determine whether some of the findings were specific to sex offenders under an 810 order or whether they applied to sex offenders in general or to sex offenders under other forms of supervision (e.g., parole, probation, long-term supervision order).

CONCLUSIONS

The current study provides valuable information about the most important issues and challenges that criminal justice professionals face in providing support and assistance and in supervising high-risk sex offenders in the community. The findings from this qualitative study suggest that sex offenders under an 810 order have multiple risk factors, have multiple needs during community reentry and reintegration, and need multiple interventions to ensure that they do not reoffend in the community. The study provides some insights about the most significant risk factors of supervision and the most important needs of these offenders. It also reveals criminal justice professionals' perceptions about the most promising strategies for addressing these risk factors and needs. Our findings suggest that a complex interplay takes place between preexisting dynamic risk factors that characterize these high-risk offenders; their need for assistance, support, and interventions; and the constraints faced by both offenders and criminal justice officials during community reentry and reintegration. This complex interplay might explain the high proportion of sex offenders breaching the conditions of their 810 orders. The results of this study are based on the perceptions of criminal justice professionals, and the findings should be interpreted as such. Further studies are needed to investigate the link between preexisting dynamic risk factors, constraints faced during community reentry, and the role of criminal justice professionals in increasing or decreasing the risk of reoffending and, most importantly, the risk of committing another sexual crime.

DISCUSSION QUESTIONS

1. Compare U.S. and Canadian criminal justice policies for the risk management of high-risk violent and sexual offenders.

2. What are the key problems faced by high-risk violent and sexual offenders returning to the community, and how can those problems affect their community reentry and reintegration?

3. What are the main challenges criminal justice practitioners face when supervising high-risk violent and sexual offenders in the community?

4. Do you think criminal justice practitioners' role in the case management of high-risk offenders should be limited to monitoring the risk of violent or sexual reoffending in the community?

NOTES

1. In Canada, there are no provisions for civil commitment for dangerous sex offenders after their prison sentences. Dangerous offender (DO) legislation and the long-term supervision (LTS) legislation have been implemented to deal with offenders identified as posing a higher risk of sexual reoffending (Lieb et al., 1998; Petrunik, 2002, 2003). As part of the DO legislation, sex offenders who commit serious personal injury offenses and who show a failure to control sexual impulses can be sentenced to an indeterminate period of incarceration. Similarly, the LTS legislation allows the criminal justice system to impose a determinate prison sentence followed by community supervision (up to 10 years) on the assumption that there is a reasonable possibility that the risk can be managed through treatment and intensive supervision. This legislation lacks clarity in many respects. For example, it is not specific as to what a reasonable risk management is and how it should be determined in court.

2. In order for an 810 order to be issued, evidence that supports the likelihood of sexual recidivism must be brought to a provincial court judge. Whereas peace bonds first appeared in the Criminal Code of Canada in 1892, Sections 810.1 and 810.2 were introduced in the 1990s. Generally speaking, provincial crown attorneys or police services apply for an 810 order.

3. At the time of the study, it was not standard practice for outreach workers to assist in the community risk management of high-risk sex offenders. Their presence was unique to two geographic

locations in BC where the Co-ordinated High-Risk Offender Management Team (CHROME) pilot project was implemented. The CHROME pilot project is run by the BC Corrections Branch in partnership with different police departments, a psychologist, a team of outreach workers, the Forensic Psychiatric Services, and the Correctional Service of Canada. The key objectives are to enhance supervision through a collaborative, team-based approach; to ensure that risk factors are stabilized in the community; and to determine which aspects of the CHROME program are most effective. The program is a 3-year pilot project that was implemented in April 2006, when funding became available through the National Crime Prevention Centre (Ministry Public Safety and Emergency Preparedness, Canada). The funding allowed the pilot project to establish itself in two geographic locations in BC. Sex offenders under an 810 order who lived within the prescribed geographic location were offered CHROME services, which were not mandatory. One of the key features of the services was reliance on outreach workers to help stabilize risk factors in the community, thus promoting reintegration (e.g., help in finding a job, a place of residence, transportation to appointments).

4. It was not part of this study to look for different patterns between probation officers, outreach workers, and police investigators but simply to find common themes.

REFERENCES

Adkins, G., Huff, D., & Stageberg, P. (2000). *The Iowa sex offender registry and recidivism*. Des Moines: Iowa Department of Human Rights.

Babcock, J. C., Green, C. E., & Robie, C. (2004). Does batterers' treatment work? A meta-analytic review of domestic violence treatment. *Clinical Psychology Review, 23*, 1023–1053.

Barbaree, H. E., Langton, C. M., & Blanchard, R. (2007). Predicting recidivism in sex offenders using the VRAG and SORAG: The contribution of age-at-release. *International Journal of Forensic Mental Health, 6*, 29–46.

Beech, A. R., Fisher, D. D., & Thornton, D. (2003). Risk assessment of sex offenders. *Professional Psychology: Research and Practice, 34*, 339–352.

Britt, C. L. (1996). The measurement of specialization and escalation in the criminal career: An alternative modeling strategy. *Journal of Quantitative Criminology, 12*, 193–222.

Caputo, A. A., & Brodsky, S. L. (2004). Citizen coping with community notification of released sex offenders. *Behavioral Sciences and the Law, 22*, 239–252.

Ditton, P. M., & Wilson, D. J. (1999). *Truth in sentencing in state prisons*. Washington, DC: Bureau of Justice Statistics.

Feder, L., & Wilson, D. B. (2005). A meta-analytic review of court-mandated batterer intervention programs: Can courts affect abusers' behavior? *Journal of Experimental Criminology, 1*, 239–262.

Feeley, M., & Simon, J. (1992). The new penology: Notes on the emerging strategy of corrections and its implications. *Criminology, 30*, 449–474.

Gendreau, P., Little, T., & Coggin, C. (1996). A meta-analysis of the predictors of adult offender recidivism: What works. *Criminology, 34*, 575–607.

Gondolf, E. W. (2004). Evaluating batterer counseling programs: A difficult task showing some effects and implications. *Aggression and Violent Behavior, 9*, 605–631.

Hanson, R. K., & Bussière, M. T. (1998). Predicting relapse: A meta-analysis of sexual offender recidivism studies. *Journal of Consulting and Clinical Psychology, 66,* 348–362.

Hanson, R. K., Gordon, A., Harris, A. J. R., Marques, J. K., Murphy, W., Quinsey, V. L., et al. (2002). First report of the collaborative outcome data project on the effectiveness of psychological treatment for sex offenders. *Sexual Abuse: A Journal of Research and Treatment, 14,* 169–194.

Hanson, R. K., & Harris, A. J. R. (2000). Where should we intervene? Dynamic predictors of sexual offense recidivism. *Criminal Justice and Behavior, 27,* 6–35.

Hanson, R. K., Morton, K. E., & Harris, A. J. R. (2003). Sexual offender recidivism risk: What we know and what we need to know. *Annals of the New York Academy of Sciences, 989,* 154–166.

Hanson, R. K., & Morton-Bourgon, K. E. (2005). The characteristics of persistent sexual offenders: A meta-analysis of recidivism studies. *Journal of Consulting and Clinical Psychology, 73,* 1154–1163.

Hanson, R. K., & Thornton, D. (2000). Improving risk assessments for sex offenders: A comparison of three actuarial scales. *Law and Human Behavior, 24,* 119–136.

Janus, E. S. (2003). Legislative responses to sexual violence: An overview. *Annals of the New York Academy of Sciences, 989,* 247–264.

Kruttschnitt, C., Uggen, C., & Shelton, K. (2000). Predictors of desistance among sex offenders: The interaction of formal and informal social controls. *Justice Quarterly, 17,* 61–87.

Kubrin, C. E., & Stewart, E. A. (2006). Predicting who reoffends: The neglected role of neighborhood context in recidivism studies. *Criminology, 44,* 165–197.

Langan, P. A., Schmitt, E. L., & Durose, M. R. (2003). *Recidivism of sex offenders released from prison in 1994.* Washington, DC: U.S. Department of Justice.

Lattimore, P. K., & Visher, C. (2008). *Prisoner reentry policy and practice: Lessons from the SVORI multi-site evaluation.* Presented at the annual meeting of the American Society of Criminology, St. Louis, MO.

Laws, D. R., Hudson, S. M., & Ward, T. (2002). *Remaking relapse prevention with sex offenders: A sourcebook.* Thousand Oaks, CA: Sage.

Lees, M., & Tewksbury, R. (2006). Understanding policy and programmatic issues regarding sex offender registries. *Corrections Today, 68,* 54–57.

Levenson, J. S., & Cotter, L. P. (2005). Effect of Megan's Law on sex offender reintegration. *Journal of Contemporary Criminal Justice, 21,* 49–66.

Levenson, J. S., D'Amora, D. A., & Hern, A. L. (2007). Megan's Law and its impact on community re-entry for sex offenders. *Behavioral Sciences and the Law, 25,* 587–602.

Lieb, R., Quinsey, V., & Berliner, L. (1998). Sexual predators and social policy. In M. Tonry (Ed.), *Crime and justice: A review of research* (Vol. 23, pp. 43–114). Chicago: University of Chicago Press.

Losel, F., & Schmucker, M. (2005). Effectiveness of treatment for sexual offenders: A comprehensive meta-analysis. *Journal of Experimental Criminology, 1,* 117–146.

Lussier, P. (2005). The criminal activity of sexual offenders in adulthood: Revisiting the specialization debate. *Sexual Abuse: Journal of Research and Treatment, 17,* 269–292.

Lussier, P., & Cortoni, F. (2008). The development of antisocial behavior and sexual aggression: Theoretical, empirical and clinical implications. In B. Schwartz (Ed.), *Sex offenders* (Vol. 6). New York: Civic Research Institute.

Lussier, P., Deslauriers, N., & Ratel, T. (2008). A descriptive profile of high-risk sex offenders in British Columbia, Canada. *International Journal of Offender Therapy and Comparative Criminology.*

Lussier, P., & Healey, J. (In press). Rediscovering Quetelet, again: The "aging" offender and the prediction of reoffending in a sample of adult sex offenders. *Justice Quarterly.*

Lussier, P., LeBlanc, M., & Proulx, J. (2005). The generality of criminal behavior: A confirmatory factor analysis of the criminal activity of sex offenders in adulthood. *Journal of Criminal Justice, 33,* 177–189.

Lussier, P., Leclerc, B., Cale, J., & Proulx, J. (2007). Development pathways of deviance in sexual aggressors. *Criminal Justice and Behavior, 34,* 1441–1462.

Lussier, P., & Proulx, J. (2001). Le traitement et l'évaluation des agresseurs sexuels: Perspectives nord-américaines et européennes [Treatment and evaluation of sex offenders: North American and European perspectives]. *Revue Internationale de Criminologie et de Police Technique et Scientifique, 54,* 69–87.

Lussier, P., Proulx, J., & LeBlanc, M. (2005). Criminal propensity, deviant sexual interests and criminal activity of sexual aggressors against women: A comparison of explanatory models. *Criminology, 43,* 247–279.

Lussier, P., Proulx, J., & McKibben, A. (2001). Personality characteristics and adaptive strategies to cope with negative emotional states and deviant sexual fantasies in sexual aggressors. *International Journal of Offender Therapy and Comparative Criminology, 45,* 159–170.

MacKenzie, D. L. (2006). *What works in corrections: Reducing the criminal activities of offenders and delinquents.* Cambridge: Cambridge University Press.

Marques, J. K., Wiederanders, M., Day, D. M., Nelson, C., & Ommeren, A. V. (2005). Effects of a relapse prevention program on sexual recidivism: Final results from California's Sex Offender Treatment and Evaluation Project (SOTEP). *Sexual Abuse: A Journal of Research and Treatment, 17,* 79–107.

McGloin, J. M., Sullivan, C. J., Piquero, A. R., & Pratt, T. C. (2007). Local life circumstances and offending specialization/versatility: Comparing opportunity and propensity models. *Journal of Research in Crime and Delinquency, 44,* 321–346.

McKibben, A., Proulx, J., & Lussier, P. (2001). Sexual aggressors' perceptions of effectiveness of strategies to cope with negative emotions and deviant sexual fantasies. *Sexual Abuse: Journal of Research and Treatment, 13,* 257–273.

Noaks, L., & Wincup, E. (2004). *Criminological research: Understanding qualitative methods.* London: Sage.

Petersilia, J., & Turner, S. (1990). Comparing intensive and regular supervision for high-risk probationers: Early results from an experiment in California. *Crime & Delinquency, 36,* 87–111.

Petersilia, J., & Turner, S. (1993). Intensive probation and parole. *Crime and Justice, 17,* 281–335.

Petrunik, M. (2002). Managing unacceptable risk: Sex offenders, community response, and social policy in the United States and Canada. *International Journal of Offender Therapy and Comparative Criminology, 46,* 483–511.

Petrunik, M. (2003). Hare and the tortoise: Dangerousness and sex offender policy in the United States and Canada. *Canadian Journal of Criminology and Criminal Justice, 45,* 43–72.

Piquero, A., Farrington, D. P., & Blumstein, A. (2003). The criminal career paradigm. In M. Tonry (Ed.), *Crime and justice: A review of research* (Vol. 30, pp. 359–506). Chicago: University of Chicago Press.

Pithers, W. D. (1990). Relapse prevention with sexual aggressors: A method for maintaining therapeutic gain and enhancing external supervision. In W. L. Marshall & H. Barbaree (Ed.),

Handbook of sexual assault: Issues, theories, and treatment of the offender (pp. 343–361). New York: Plenum.

Proulx, J., Tardif, M., Lamoureux, B., & Lussier, P. (2000). How does recidivism risk assessment predict survival? In D. R. Laws, S. M. Hudson, & T. Ward (Eds.), *Remaking relapse prevention with sex offenders: A sourcebook* (pp. 466–484). Thousand Oaks, CA: Sage.

Quinsey, V. L., Harris, G. T., Rice, M. E., & Cormier, C. A. (2005). *Violent offenders: Appraising and managing risk* (2nd ed.). Washington, DC: American Psychological Association.

Sample, L. L., & Bray, T. M. (2003). Are sex offenders dangerous? *Criminology & Public Policy, 3*, 59–82.

Schram, D., & Milloy, C. D. (1995). *Community notification: A study of offender characteristics and recidivism.* Olympia: Washington Institute for Public Policy.

Simon, J. (1998). Managing the monstrous: Sex offenders and the new penology. *Psychology, Public Policy, and Law, 4*, 452–467.

Simon, L. M. J. (1997). Do offenders specialize in crime types? *Applied & Preventive Psychology, 6*, 35–53.

Strauss, A., & Corbin, J. (1990). *Basics of qualitative research: Grounded theory procedures and techniques.* London: Sage.

Tewksbury, R. (2005). Collateral consequences of sex offender registration. *Journal of Contemporary Criminal Justice, 21*, 67–82.

Tewksbury, R., & Mustaine, E. E. (2006). Where to find sex offenders: An examination of residential locations and neighbourhood conditions. *Criminal Justice Studies, 19*, 61–75.

Thornton, D. (2006). Age and sexual recidivism: A variable connection. *Sexual Abuse: Journal of Research and Treatment, 18*, 123–135.

Travis, J., & Petersilia, J. (2001). Reentry reconsidered: A new look at an old question. *Crime and Delinquency, 47*, 291–313.

Winick, B. J. (1998). Sex offender law in the 1990s: A therapeutic jurisprudence analysis. *Psychology, Public Policy, and Law, 4*, 505–570.

Wollert, R. (2006). Low base rates limit expert certainty when current actuarials are used to identify sexually-violent predators. *Psychology, Public Policy, and Law, 12*, 56–85.

Zevitz, R. G. (2006). Sex offender community notification: Its role in recidivism and offender reintegration. *Criminal Justice Studies, 19*, 193–208.

Zevitz, R. G., Crim, D., & Farkas, M. A. (2000). Sex offender community notification: Managing high risk criminals or exacting further vengeance? *Behavioral Sciences and the Law, 18*, 375–391.

Zevitz, R. G., & Farkas, M. A. (2000). Impact of sex-offender community notification on probation/parole in Wisconsin. *International Journal of Offender Therapy and Comparative Criminology, 44*, 8–21.

CHAPTER 10

Seeking Medical and Psychiatric Attention

Elizabeth Corzine McMullan

As early as 1929 it was recognized that the health care services provided to inmates were woefully inadequate (Rector, 1929). Recommendations for minimum standards were provided to address the inadequacies and largely ignored. These recommendations included the provision of two physical exams by a medical professional for all inmates, daily clinic hours, and complete dental and optometric care (Rector, 1929). The issues surrounding the inferior care inmates received during incarceration began to gain public attention and subsequently led to a shift in public thinking around the 1960s. This shift in public thinking is said to have sparked a change in the judicial approach.

Until 1962, the judiciary adopted a hands-off approach to corrections. The justifications for this approach were based on the beliefs that members of the court lacked the proper expertise in correctional matters to determine whether actions taken by prison and jail officials were warranted, and interference by the courts could undermine the authority of those officials. Another rationale for the hands-off doctrine was a belief that interfering in matters of the state and local governments would constitute a violation of federalism. The 1970s ended the hands-off approach and saw significant health care reform for prisoners. It was not until 1962 (*Robinson v. California*) that the federal courts were able to review state court decisions. Only then would there be a legal mechanism to enforce the recommendations for improving health care for inmates nationwide.

Several important court cases provided significant change and specifically addressed the health care needs of inmates. *Cooper v. Pate* (1964) was the landmark Supreme Court case that recognized prisoners' rights to seek protections provided by the Civil Rights Act (Alexander, 1972). *Newman v. Alabama* (1972) signaled an end to the hands-off era of medical care for inmates (American Bar Association, 1974). This decision held the entire Alabama correctional system in violation of the 8th and 14th Amendments for failing to provide inmates with adequate and sufficient medical care. *Estelle v. Gamble* (1976) was the first Supreme Court case that set forth specific standards concerning medical care in U.S. prisons. The Court ruled that when the government deprives a person of liberty (i.e., through incarceration) it must provide adequate medical care for this person. Incarceration denies a person the freedom to seek medical treatment outside the facility and subsequently forces the inmate to rely on the government to meet his or her needs. This decision states that "deliberate indifference to serious medical needs" constitutes "unnecessary and wanton infliction of pain" and is therefore a violation of a person's 8th Amendment right. A later Supreme Court decision, *Farmer v. Brennan* (1994), clarified the Court's definition of "deliberate indifference" and requires that a prison official know of and disregard a serious medical need before he or she can be held liable.

These court decisions provided inmates with three basic rights: the right to basic access to care, a right to the care that is ordered for them, and a right to a professional medical judgment (National Commission on Correctional Health Care, 2001). Inmates are now guaranteed access to proper medical care under Section 1983 of the U.S. Code (USC), and denial of these rights is remedied by litigation. This section of the U.S. Code permits prisoners to sue correctional officials in federal court when the conditions of confinement fail to meet constitutional standards. According to two federal court decisions, *West v. Atkins* (1988) and *Ort v. Pinchback* (1986), a physician who contracts with the state to provide medical care to inmates acts under the color of state law and is also liable for violations under 42 USC 1983. This not only pertains to the provision of basic health care but also includes mental health care.

The President's Commission on Law Enforcement and Administration of Justice published three reports in 1967 identifying some of the major health problems faced by incoming prisoners. Three of the major conditions addressed were alcoholism, drug abuse, and mental illness (Clark, 1971). Each of these problems presented unique health care concerns. Those suffering from alcoholism were prone to seizures, delirium tremens, malnutrition, and chronic liver ailments. Substance abuse presented similar problems but also carried the risk of hepatitis infections when certain types of drugs were used. Mental illness was thought to contribute to the high rates of suicide and the physical and sexual assaults that occurred in these facilities (National Commission on Correctional Health Care, 2001). Crimes such as prostitution were also thought to contribute to significant health risks (e.g., sexually transmitted diseases). Today we know there are many other problems associated with alcoholism, substance abuse, and mental illness and the Commission's findings uncovered only the tip of the iceberg.

National data concerning the number of correctional institutions that provided medical facilities were nonexistent until the 1970s, although it was assumed that most did not provide such services. What little we do know about the type and amount of health care services that existed during this time period is limited to state studies or evidence presented in court cases (National Commission on Correctional Health Care, 2001). Before the 1970s there were no formal intake procedures used to assess the health of incoming prisoners. It was merely assumed that those coming to prison were in poorer health than their unincarcerated counterparts. These assumptions were based on the theoretical correlations between criminal activity, poverty, and poor health (Clark, 1971). Correctional facilities were considered to have the worst health care system in the United States (Shervington, 1974), but there was little empirical evidence to support these claims. Instead, the literature provided assumptions about the overall status of health care and focused on specific conditions that contributed to poor health among people in correctional facilities.

The Office of Health and Medical Affairs (1975) provided a list of unacceptable living conditions that probably contributed to poor health of inmates incarcerated during this time period. Poor living conditions included overcrowding, lack of sanitary conditions, poor diet, and absence of exercise or recreational outlets (National Commission on Correctional Health Care, 2001). Correctional buildings at this time were often old and in disrepair. The documentation of these conditions led to recommendations for correcting them.

The first national standards for health care specifically written for correctional institutions were published by the American Public Health Association in 1976. Unfortunately, these standards lacked any avenue for enforcement, and the only tangible reward for adherence to these standards came in the form of accreditation. The first correctional institution to receive accreditation for its health system was the Georgia State Prison (in Reidsville) in 1982 (National Commission on Correctional Health Care, 2001).

Today most correctional institutions, jails, and prisons require some form of screening for preexisting mental and medical conditions that may necessitate special care at the time of intake. This may be as simple as having the inmate or detainee answer questions about his or her medical needs on an intake form or may consist of a medical evaluation by a health care professional. Once preexisting medical conditions are identified, health care professionals design a treatment plan. Every institution adopts its own operating procedures that specify how an inmate must seek mental health or medical attention after intake. In some institutions this consists of completing a request form that specifies his or her complaints and results in an appointment with a medical professional. The manner in which medical emergencies are handled also varies greatly depending on the type of treatment needed and the facilities available at the institution. Some prisons have their own hospitals and medical professionals on site; others contract with local hospitals and provide transportation and security in the event of medical emergencies.

MEDICAL NEEDS FOR SPECIAL POPULATIONS

Inmates who are considered disabled under the Americans with Disabilities Act (ADA) are entitled to adequate accommodations during incarceration. This includes access to buildings, adequate transportation accommodations, and communication devices. Correctional facilities may be required to make architectural changes to their facilities to ensure that accommodations are suitable. The U.S. Supreme Court ruled in *Ruiz v. Estelle* (1980) that adequate accommodations, regardless of how unusual, must be provided to inmates in order to satisfy the provisions set forth by the court. Specific accommodations were outlined in *Cummings v. Roberts* (1980) and *Johnson v. Hardin County* (1990). These included wheelchairs and prosthetic devices for inmates unable to walk and assistance for inmates with hearing or vision impairments. States are protected from monetary damages by the 11th Amendment on grounds of sovereign immunity (National Commission on Correctional Health Care, 2001), but they are required to adhere to the standards set forth by the ADA and may be forced to comply to these standards through an injunction.

The incarceration of a pregnant woman presents unique problems for correctional institutions. Failure to seek prenatal care during this period of gestation could result in a serious medical emergency. The potential complications associated with pregnancy make this a serious health care need, and failure to provide care during this time could constitute a violation of the 8th Amendment (*Boswell v. Sherburne County,* 1988). Most pregnant women entering a correctional facility are considered to be at high risk because of their habits and lifestyle before admission. Literature (Fogel, 1995; Goldkuhle, 1999; Hufft, Fawkes, & Lawson, 1993) indicates that these women are more likely to experience complications during pregnancy because of a variety of health factors such as being HIV positive; having another sexually transmitted disease; being obese, malnourished, or in poor physical condition; and experiencing some form of emotional distress such as anxiety or depression.

According to the Bureau of Justice Statistics (Greenfeld & Snell, 1999), 6% of women admitted to local jails and 5% sent to state prison were pregnant at the time of their arrival. Correctional institutions must provide the option for an incarcerated woman to terminate an unwanted pregnancy even if she is unable to pay for the procedure herself (*Monmouth County Correctional Institution Inmates v. Lanzaro*, 1987). Women who do decide to carry their pregnancies to term while incarcerated do not have the right to keep the children with them after birth. However, they do have the right to breastfeed their children during visitation (*Berrios-Berrios v. Thornburg*, 1989). Seven of every 10 women incarcerated have minor children (under the age of 18) at the time of their incarceration. About 64% of female inmates resided with their minor children before incarceration (Greenfeld & Snell, 1999).

Women are also susceptible to gender-specific ailments related to their reproductive systems and should be evaluated for such conditions on a regular basis. These ailments include menstrual irregularities, gynecological disorders, and pregnancy. Survey results (Greenfeld & Snell, 1999) indicate that 90% of women admitted to state prison and 22% of those admitted to jail had a gynecological exam performed since their arrival to the facility. These exams are important for diagnostic and treatment purposes.

Women in state prisons report higher levels of drug use than men. Approximately 40% of women were under the influence of drugs or alcohol at the time they committed the crime for which they were sentenced. Forty-eight percent of women detained in local jails reported being the victim of physical or sexual abuse. Fifty-seven percent of those incarcerated in state prison reported abuse of this nature. Drug and alcohol use and prior abuse histories are important factors that contribute to overall mental health (Greenfeld & Snell, 1999).

HIV-Positive Inmates

In 2006, 1.6% of the male prison population and 2.4% of the female prison population were either HIV positive or confirmed to have AIDS (Maruschak, 2006). Despite the belief that prisons are breeding grounds for the spread of HIV, most inmates were infected in the community before their incarceration (Hammett, 2006). Those most likely to contract HIV during incarceration are younger, non-White men serving time for sex crimes (Krebs in Hammett, 2006).

The 1998 *Bragdon v. Abbott* Supreme Court decision established that the ADA protects people with HIV from the moment of infection. This case established that services could not be denied to people because the practitioner was afraid of contracting HIV. The Court held that under the ADA, policies and procedures must rely on objective, scientific evidence regarding the statistical likelihood of transmission. The dentist who denied services to patients with HIV was in direct violation of this ruling because there was a lack of empirical evidence supporting the statistical likelihood that treating patients with HIV would result in transmission of the virus.

The U.S. Supreme Court has refused to hear cases involving segregation and mandatory testing of inmates for HIV. In 2000, the U.S. Supreme Court denied certiorari in *Davis v. Hopper* (1984). This was an appeal from an 11th Circuit Court of Appeals ruling that held that the segregation of prisoners with HIV from other inmates residentially and in classrooms, workplaces, and all other programs did not violate the ADA. The decision to deny certiorari for this case without comment indicates that the Supreme Court is not yet ready to rule on the issues raised by the case. Although the ruling of the 11th Circuit Court of Appeals to allow segregation of inmates with HIV has been upheld by the denial of certiorari, many oppose this practice. The practice of segregating inmates with HIV from the general prison population has been condemned by the National Commission on AIDS, the National Commission on Correctional Health Care, and the Federal Bureau of Prisons as having no legitimate basis in public health.

Absent further clarification or guidance from the U.S. Supreme Court, some correctional facilities require testing of all inmates upon arrival for HIV, and others refuse to test inmates at all. According to a 2006 Bureau of Justice Statistics report (Maruschak, 2006), only 21 states required testing of all inmates for HIV upon admission or during their custody. Forty-seven states will provide testing if the inmate requests it or if he or she shows signs or symptoms of the disease while incarcerated. These states also test inmates who are exposed to the virus during an incident while incarcerated. Five states test inmates before release from incarceration, three state correctional systems test all inmates at some point during custody, and four states and the federal system test inmates at random.

The denial of certiorari has led to the continuation of segregating inmates who are HIV positive from the general population in some correctional facilities at this time. This has resulted in HIV-positive inmates being denied access to educational and religious programs because of their segregation. Inmates infected with HIV often attempt to enroll in clinical drug trials. This provides them with access to drugs they otherwise might not receive and care from outside medical professionals. The top three states with the most inmates with HIV or confirmed AIDS were New York, Florida, and Texas (Maruschak, 2006).

Older Adults

The population of incarcerated older adults has grown substantially over the past two decades because of mandatory minimum sentencing guidelines, an increase in determinate sentencing, and truth-in-sentencing legislation (e.g., three strikes laws). This population presents unique medical considerations for the correctional institutions where they reside. These people may experience a higher rate of life-impairing and life-threatening conditions that prove costly to the institutions where they reside. Many older inmates die in prison because of the length of their sentences and will need some form of hospice or end-of-life care. It is estimated that the average prisoner under the age of 55 who is not HIV positive will need approximately $20,000 per year for care and custody, and an older inmate averages between $60,000 and $69,000 a year for care and custody (Ornduff, 1996).

Other Issues

More than $3.5 billion is spent on inmate health care each year (National Commission on Correctional Health Care, 2002). The proportion of inmates who suffer from communicable diseases tends to be higher than that of the larger population. People serving jail or prison sentences also seem to have higher rates of asthma, diabetes, and hypertension than their unincarcerated counterparts (National Commission on Correctional Health Care, 2002). Other diseases of concern in the correctional population are hepatitis B and C, tuberculosis, and sexually transmitted diseases.

According to Maruschak (2006), arthritis and hypertension were the most common ailments among state and federal prisoners. Older inmates are more likely to report hearing and vision impairments. Most state and federal inmates reported receiving some form of medical services after admission to the facility. Most inmates undergo a medical exam, blood test, tuberculosis test, and HIV test upon arrival at the correctional facility.

Suicide

Suicide was the number-one cause of death in American jails in 1983 but has since been surpassed by natural causes. Although the suicide rate has declined significantly since 1983, it still accounted for 32% of all deaths in jail (Figure 10.1). The potential for severe legal consequences from a suicide, recognition of suicide as a public health concern, and our increased focus on prevention have helped reduce these numbers.

Suicide in correctional settings is a public health issue that has been the subject of prevention efforts by several national associations, such as the American

Figure 10.1   Suicide Rates Since 1983

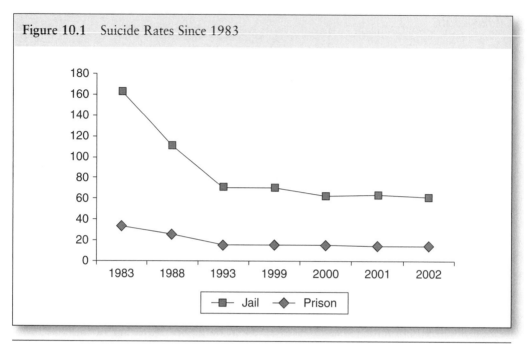

Source: Mumola (2005).

Correctional Association, American Psychiatric Association, and National Commission of Correctional Health Care. One of the most basic requirements for suicide prevention is the adoption and use of adequate screening techniques that properly identify those at risk for suicide immediately after admission.

Lawsuits are common after a jail or prison suicide. The issues in a suicide case often involve identifying possibly suicidal inmates, protecting and monitoring them once identified, and responding to suicide attempts. *Balla v. Idaho Board of Corrections* (1984) ruled that prisons and jails are legally obligated to provide a mental health screening at intake in order to identify potentially serious problems (e.g., suicidal tendencies). Simple screening procedures may help reduce the number of lawsuits and legal liability associated with suicides that occur in custody each year. One commonly used screening tool in correctional facilities is the Beck Hopelessness Scale. Most lawsuits focus on the lack of adequate screening for suicidal tendencies. Appropriate screening and training for staff members who come into regular contact with inmates may further reduce the suicide rates in correctional institutions. Prevention is the key for potential cases of suicide.

One quarter of all suicide deaths occur within 2 days after intake. Forty-eight percent of inmates who commit suicide do so within the first week of custody (Mumola, 2005). More than 80% of suicides in jails and prisons occur in the victim's cell (Figure 10.2).

Figure 10.2   Prison Suicide Locations

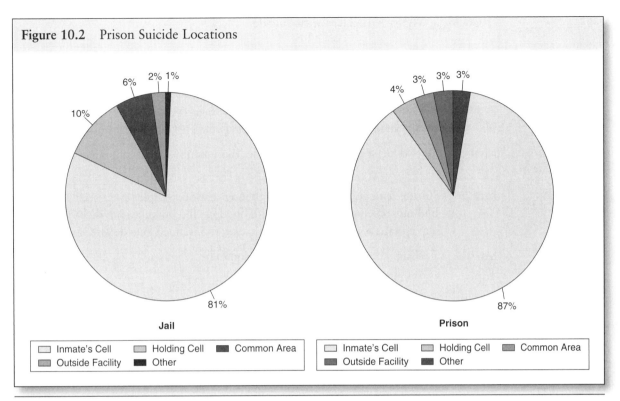

Source: Mumola (2005).

A number of factors make the rate of suicide in the correctional setting higher than that of the larger population. Those experiencing incarceration for the first time experience a variety of frightening and unfamiliar circumstances that can be heightened by the insensitivity of the arresting officers. Often detainees are subjected to a strictly regimented routine that limits their contact with the outside world. People in the midst of legal proceedings are also faced with uncertainty, which often breeds feelings of hopelessness and powerlessness.

Perhaps one of the most important tools for suicide prevention is training of correctional staff members. These professionals are often the first line of defense against suicide because they have the most contact with inmates and will be the first to notice changes in behavior or any warning signs exhibited by those in custody. Simon and Hales (2006) recommend at least 8 hours of training in suicide prevention for all correctional staff and an additional 2 hours in refresher courses each year. Dispelling common myths associated with suicide is an extremely important element of this educational process. All threats of suicide should be taken seriously and reported immediately to the mental health or medical professionals who are trained to handle these situations.

Common Myths Associated with Suicide

Myth 1:   People who threaten to kill themselves are merely seeking attention.

Fact 1:   Eight out of 10 people who commit suicide made direct or indirect statements of their intentions before their death. Any threat to commit suicide should be taken seriously regardless of how practical their intended method of suicide seems.

Myth 2:   Once a person is intent on suicide, there is no way of stopping him or her.

Fact 2:   Suicides can be prevented through intervention. Simple things such as finding someone to talk to suicidal people and encouraging them to make plans for their future can thwart an intended suicide attempt.

Myth 3:   Talking about suicide or asking someone whether he or she feels suicidal will encourage suicide attempts.

Fact 3:   Talking about suicide does not encourage a person to carry out the threat but instead provides the person with the opportunity to communicate his or her thoughts and fears.

Suicide Warning Signs

- Recent suicide or death of a friend or relative
- Previous suicide attempt or expression of suicidal thoughts
- Preoccupation with death or dying
- Depression, negative changes in behavior, or coping through substance abuse
- Serious changes in sleep patterns (too much or too little) or eating habits (weight loss or gain)
- Giving away prized possessions, putting final affairs in order (e.g., making a will or funeral arrangements)
- Withdrawing from friends or family, no longer participating in group activities, losing interest in the future
- Personality changes such as nervousness, outbursts of anger, impulsive or reckless behavior, or apathy about appearance or health
- Frequent irritability or unexplained crying, lingering expressions of unworthiness or failure

Psychiatric Needs

The Mentally Ill Offender Treatment and Crime Reduction Act (S. 1194) of 2004 (hereinafter the Mentally Ill Offender Act, 2004) was signed into law by

President George W. Bush on October 30, 2008. The goals of this legislation were to improve access to mental health services for adult and juvenile nonviolent offenders. This act was also designed to increase the amount of collaboration between the criminal justice, juvenile justice, mental health, and substance abuse treatment systems in an attempt to ensure that both adult and juvenile nonviolent offenders with mental health disorders are identified properly and receive the treatment they need from the point of arrest to reentry into the community and are not simply recycled into the system. Up to 40% of mentally ill Americans are expected to enter the criminal justice system within their lifetime (Mentally Ill Offender Act, 2004). Currently the three largest psychiatric facilities in the United States are county jails: the Los Angeles County Jail in California, Cook County Jail in Chicago, and the jail at Riker's Island in New York City (Lurigio & Swartz, 2006). As of July 2005, more than half of all jail and prison inmates had a mental health problem.

Female inmates have higher rates of mental illness than male inmates in all correctional settings (James & Glaze, 2006). Furthermore, White inmates were more likely to suffer from mental illness than Blacks or Hispanics. James and Glaze (2006) suggest that jails encounter larger numbers of mentally ill people than prisons because of their ability to serve as a temporary holding facility until a court order is obtained and delivery to an adequate treatment facility in the community can be arranged. Inmates with mental illness are more likely to report homelessness or residing in foster care before incarceration than those without mental illness. Co-occurring disorders, or a dual diagnosis of mental illness and substance abuse, are common in the correctional setting.

Factors that contribute to large numbers of mentally ill in prisons and jails include deinstitutionalization, stricter civil commitment laws, homelessness, public order policing, and the fragmentation of the mental health and drug treatment service systems (Human Rights Watch, 2003; Lurigio, 2005; Swartz & Lurigio, 2006). According to the latest statistics, more than half of the people in prison and jail in the United States have a mental health problem (James & Glaze, 2006). People who have undiagnosed or untreated mental illnesses while incarcerated are at a greater risk for committing suicide, being victimized, creating disturbances, and committing disciplinary infractions (Veysey & Bichler-Robertson, 2002).

Research over the past 20 years indicates that there is a disproportionate incidence of severe mental illnesses such as schizophrenia, bipolar disorder, and major depression in correctional institutions (Abram & Teplin, 1991; Abram, Teplin, & McClelland, 2003; Diamond, Wang, Holzer, Thomas, & des Anges, 2001; Ditton, 1999; Human Rights Watch, 2003; McLearen & Ryba, 2003). This figure ranges from 6 to 15% (Corrado, Cohen, Hart, & Roesch, 2000; Fisher, Packer, Simon, & Smith, 2000; Lamb & Weinberger, 1998; McLearen

& Ryba, 2003). Many see this as a demonstration of the Penrose effect, by which psychiatric patients often find themselves incarcerated in correctional facilities (Penrose, 1939). Although the incarceration of mentally ill people is not a new phenomenon, it has been exacerbated by deinstitutionalization.

Before the 1960s, people deemed mentally ill were involuntarily hospitalized to receive necessary treatment and care. In the early 1960s antipsychotic medications were made available for mental health treatment outside mental hospital settings. Substantial litigation led to more stringent requirements for involuntary commitment procedures and more liberal release procedures. This resulted in deinstitutionalization, which is defined as the downsizing and closure of many state public mental health hospitals. Government support for this process was demonstrated when President John F. Kennedy signed the Mental Retardation Facilities and Community Mental Health Centers Construction Act of 1963 (also known as the Mental Health Act of 1963), with the intention of reducing and even eliminating severe mental illness through early detection and treatment. Perhaps more importantly, this act provided funding for the provision of mental health treatment in the community.

The U.S. Supreme Court decided in *L.C. & E.W. v. Olmstead* (1999) that states must provide mental health services to people in the community. The number of people who reside in mental health hospitals today has declined approximately 84% from the numbers recorded in the 1950s (Human Rights Watch, 2003). The number of hospital beds allocated to mental illness in the United States dropped significantly from 1970 to 1998 (Figure 10.3) (McQuistion, Finnerty, Hirschowitz, & Susser, 2003).

Inmates with mental illnesses who are not properly identified and treated are more prone to victimization by other inmates and more likely to commit suicide, cause disturbances, and have disciplinary infractions (Veysey & Bichler-Robertson, 2002). Litigation is another potential risk of not properly identifying those in need of treatment or not providing treatment in a timely manner to those identified. Although correctional institutions are constitutionally required to provide adequate care to their incarcerated populations, these terms are open to interpretation.

The Mentally Ill Offender Act of 2004 also provides a significant amount of grant funding to states and counties that want to establish mental health courts, expand prisoners' access to mental health treatment while incarcerated and upon reentry into the community, provide additional resources for pretrial jail diversion programs and related initiatives, and fund cross-training for law enforcement officials and mental health personnel dealing with adult and juvenile offenders with mental health disorders.

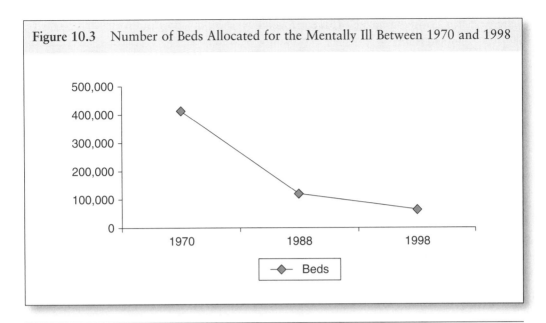

Figure 10.3   Number of Beds Allocated for the Mentally Ill Between 1970 and 1998

Source: McQuistion, Finnerty, Hirschowitz, & Susser (2003).

Mental Health Courts

A recent attempt to reduce the number of inmates with mental illness residing in local jails and prisons has been through the establishment of mental health courts. Like drug courts, they offer alternatives to incarceration, with an emphasis on treatment and reintegration. (Drug courts and specialized courts are discussed in Chapters 5 and 6.) One must be identified as having a mental illness or co-occurring disorder before participation. Aside from a history of treatment for a mental illness in the community before incarceration, screening, assessment, and evaluations are needed to identify those meeting the criteria. There are more than 100 mental health courts in operation throughout the United States and even more in planning phases (Bureau of Justice Assistance, 2008).

Screening, Assessment, and Evaluation

Detection of medical or mental health problems usually follows a three-pronged process. This process includes screening for all, assessment for those flagged during screening, and an additional evaluation by a trained professional for those in need. These procedures should occur immediately after the inmate's arrival.

Most jails do not have the time or financial resources to administer lengthy psychological assessments or evaluations to all incoming inmates but still need to ensure that they are able to provide mental health treatment to those who need it. This is where screening instruments are useful. An ideal screening tool should consist of 6–24 items, take no longer than 15 minutes to complete, and be available for little or no cost (Sacks, 2008). It is important to note that a screening tool does not necessarily determine the type or severity of a disorder, only the probability that this person might have a disorder and whether additional assessment is needed. The primary purpose of screening is to identify people who need further evaluation.

The National Commission on Correctional Health Care has set forth nationally recognized standards for medical and mental health screening of incarcerated people. These standards are required for accreditation purposes, but they are completely voluntary for agencies not seeking accreditation. Some facilities choose not to seek accreditation because of the costs associated with participation. However, the few thousand dollars spent on this process could result in significant long-term savings by preventing unnecessary and costly lawsuits. Inadequate health care is the second biggest reason for lawsuits in prison and jails in the United States (National Commission on Correctional Health Care, 2002).

Despite constitutional requirements for standard medical and mental health treatment for inmates (*Estelle v. Gamble*, 1976; *Ruiz v. Estelle*, 1980), a nationally standardized screening instrument currently does not exist (Steadman, Scott, Osher, Agnese, & Robins, 2005). Most jails administer some form of mental health screening for inmates during their initial booking (Steadman & Veysey, 1997; Veysey & Bichler-Robertson, 2002) but these screening instruments vary greatly from facility to facility and have questionable validity (Teplin, 1990). To date, there is no standardized tool used in all correctional facilities to test inmates for mental illness (Steadman et al., 2005).

The most commonly used screening techniques include the Brief Jail Mental Health Survey (BJMHS), the Symptom Checklist–90, the Brief Symptom Inventory (Steadman et al., 2005), and the Correctional Mental Health Screen (Goldberg & Higgins, 2006). The BJMHS has a high false-negative rate for female inmates (Steadman et al., 2005). The Correctional Mental Health Screen for Women (CMHS-W) yields better results when used in female populations.

The first mental health screening tool, the Referral Decision Scale, was developed by Teplin and Swartz (1989) as a way to quickly screen for schizophrenia and major mood disorders in jail populations. This instrument consisted of 14 items and was initially used as a means of identifying people who might need additional mental health assessments. The BJMHS is the most appropriate screening tool for men in a jail setting (Steadman et al., 2005). A recent validation study revealed that this screening tool can be administered within 2.5 minutes and correctly classified 73.5% of the male population. However, this tool is not as successful with female populations, and therefore the CMHS-W should be used for female detainees instead.

Screening for co-occurring mental and substance use disorders is becoming more common in criminal justice settings today. Although the BJMHS and CMHS-W have been identified as valid tools for mental health screening in jail and prison populations, they are not intended to identify people with dual diagnosis. The Criminal Justice Co-Occurring Disorders Screening Instrument was developed to provide professionals with a brief yet standardized screening instrument (Coen, Sacks, & Melnick, 2006). Co-occurring mental and drug dependency disorders complicate treatment goals by interfering with adherence to treatment plans and often contribute to patient relapse (Fletcher & Wexler, 2005).

An initial screening should be provided during booking by a correctional officer to identify people who may need more medical or psychological attention. Screening tools for mental health should include indicators for schizophrenia, bipolar disorder, and major depressive disorders (Lurigio et al., 2003). Medical screening should include questions about the existence of and current treatment for serious medical conditions and life-threatening ailments that warrant immediate treatment. Most correctional facilities do not allow inmates to retain their own medications, so it is essential to provide facility-issued insulin and asthma inhalers to those who need them in a timely manner.

The screening process should include not only information that the inmate reports experiencing from the checklist of indicators but also observations from the person screening the inmate. Many criminal justice agencies create their own screening tools that are not standardized or tested for reliability and validity (Swartz & Lurigio, 2006).

The screening process is useful in detecting a host of potential mental or physical health problems, but these techniques are also helpful for classification purposes when incoming inmates have special needs. Inmates may need special treatment or accommodations when incarcerated because of mental illness, youth or advanced age, disabilities, chronic or terminal illness, diabetes, or asthma.

Correctional staff members are in a unique position to provide information to mental health professionals based on their constant contact and observation of inmates. Training for correctional staff members should teach them some basic warning signs and tips for making appropriate and inappropriate observations. Our perceptions of events vary based on our personal experiences, also known as our frame of reference. When reporting observations it is extremely important to report the behavior of the person being observed, without making assumptions about the meaning of this behavior. Reporting an observation that "Jimmy was talking to himself and swaying back and forth in his cell today" is much more useful than reporting that "Jimmy was acting crazy." When in doubt, it is better to provide too much detail than not enough.

Assessments should be conducted by a mental health professional or medical professional. The *Diagnostic and Statistical Manual of Mental Disorders,* Fourth Edition, Text Revision (*DSM-IV-TR*), is used as the standard for mental health diagnoses. This manual was published by the American Psychiatric Association (2000) for the specific purpose of providing guidelines for assessment. Psychiatric assessments use diagnostic tools to determine whether a person meets the criteria for mental illness. This requires the person conducting the assessment to not have an educated understanding of the instrument being used and the criteria for serious mental illness. Counselors or those with a psychology background can perform mental health assessments. The assessment aims to answer questions about how the person in question is thinking, feeling, and functioning when he or she takes the test (Carbonell & Perkins, 2004).

There are 16 major diagnostic categories and "other conditions" covered by the *DSM-IV-TR*. Each disorder included in the manual is accompanied by a set of diagnostic criteria and text containing information about the disorder, such as associated features; prevalence; familial patterns; age-, culture-, and gender-specific features; and differential diagnosis. The *DSM-IV-TR* allows professionals to communicate a large amount of information about a person's symptoms by using a few words or diagnostic codes. The *DSM-IV-TR* does not provide explanations for what causes the specific mental disorders it describes because professional opinions and theories vary widely. There are five different levels (axes) of classification in the *DSM-IV-TR*. The first two describe clinical and personality disorders and mental retardation and are often consulted during the assessment phase of inmate intake. The other axes cover concepts such as medical conditions and social and environmental stressors.

The first axis consists of clinical disorders, including major mental disorders, as well as developmental and learning disorders. Some of the more common Axis I disorders are depression, anxiety disorders, bipolar disorders, attention deficit–hyperactivity disorder, phobias, and schizophrenia. The second axis consists of underlying pervasive or personality conditions and mental retardation. Paranoid personality disorder, schizoid personality disorder, borderline personality disorder, antisocial personality disorder, narcissistic personality disorder, histrionic personality disorder, avoidant personality disorder, dependent personality disorder, obsessive–compulsive personality disorder, and mental retardation are among the most common Axis II disorders. Axis III disorders consist of acute medical conditions and physical disorders and include brain injuries and other physical disorders that may aggravate existing diseases or present symptoms similar to those of other disorders. Psychosocial and environmental factors contributing to the disorder are discussed in Axis IV, and Axis V focuses on the assessment and functioning of children under the age of 18.

Affective disorders, also known as mood disorders, may be the most common mental health problem today. The severity of these disorders varies tremendously from person to person. Almost everyone experiences feelings of sadness or happiness from time to time, but for people with affective disorders these feelings are intensified to the point that they interfere with their daily life or routine. Depression is common in correctional facilities because of the nature of incarceration. Affective disorders are unique in that they can be prompted by or result from situational events. Inmates experience various forms of loss when subjected to incarceration (e.g., loss of freedom, loss of social support systems), which may exacerbate feelings of depression. These disorders are particularly problematic when depression leads to thoughts of suicide. Proper identification of affective disorders is necessary to provide appropriate treatment and prevent undue suffering.

Psychotic disorders are also of concern to correctional institutions. These disorders include a group of serious illnesses that affect the mind. These illnesses alter a person's ability to think clearly, make good judgments, respond emotionally, communicate effectively, understand reality, and behave appropriately. When symptoms are severe, people with psychotic disorders have difficulty staying in touch with reality and often are unable to meet the ordinary demands of daily life. However, even the most severe psychotic disorders can be treated after proper diagnosis. People with psychotic disorders should be identified as quickly as possible to ensure adequate treatment. In a recent report (James & Glaze, 2006), approximately 24% of jail inmates, 15% of state prisoners, and 10% of federal prisoners reported at least one symptom of psychotic disorder.

Mental retardation is assessed through the use of a two-pronged test. The first component is a measurement of the person's intelligence quotient (IQ). Typically this score must be below 70 in order for the person to be considered mentally retarded. However, it is no longer enough for a person to merely have an IQ of 70 or below; he or she must also lack the ability to meet normal life demands. These people are of concern to correctional administrators because their low IQ and inability to function make them ill equipped for the demands of prison life. These people may adopt socially unacceptable coping mechanisms (e.g., violence or aggression) that violate prison rules and result in disciplinary infractions. The prevalence of mental retardation is believed to be between 2% and 10% (Carbonell & Perkins, 2004; Smith, Schmid, & Hennly, 1990).

One approach to IQ testing is using a group test such as the Beta Examination for screening purposes. Those who score below a set minimum (e.g., 76) are referred for additional testing using a more in-depth standardized assessment tool such as the Wechsler Adult Intelligence Scales-III (WAIS-III). The Beta Examination can indicate potential deficiencies, but the WAIS-III provides a more in-depth explanation for a person's functioning capacity. It is important to note that intelligence tests such as the WAIS-III do not measure academic achievement, and if education is a goal, additional testing may be needed. The results of these assessments are useful in determining proper living accommodations and program assignments.

If it is determined that a person cannot understand English, he or she will be given a non-English assessment such as the Test of Nonverbal Intelligence. There are two basic types of assessments: dynamic and static. A dynamic assessment is one that has the ability to fluctuate over time and may be influenced by a multitude of factors (e.g., divorce, newly acquired prison sentence, diagnosis of a terminal illness). A person who is currently on trial for a crime and facing prison time may feel entirely different 6 months after the trial is over and he or she is acquitted. Dynamic assessments are useful in determining how a person is feeling at any given time. These assessments provide helpful insight into a person's immediate state of mind.

A static assessment measures factors that generally do not change much over time. Examples of static assessments include personality and intelligence testing. Unlike dynamic assessments, the results from static assessments should not fluctuate.

People who conduct medical assessments should also have adequate skill, training, and knowledge of the diagnostic tools being used and familiarity with the criteria for diagnosis. Registered nurses are typically needed for a physical health assessment. If the findings from the assessment are normal, a physician's assistant may sign off on the findings, but if there are any questionable findings, a physician must then evaluate them.

Most correctional officers do not have the educational background needed for assessments, so outside personnel are brought into the facility for this purpose. Correctional staff members who come into contact with inmates on a regular basis are needed to provide observations. The assessment process is very time consuming and costly. People conducting the assessments often are available only for specific periods of time and have extremely high caseloads. The time and costs associated with assessments make them impossible to carry out on the entire inmate population. This is why adequate screening is so important. The purpose of assessment is to properly identify those who are most likely to need treatment for psychiatric or medical conditions. Those identified as needing treatment are then referred to a doctor for an additional evaluation.

It is important to note that the *DSM-IV-TR* serves as a tool for the assessment and diagnosis of a condition but does not provide universal treatment plans for people afflicted with the condition described. This is why an evaluation is usually conducted by a medical doctor or psychiatrist who is able to write a prescription to the patient being evaluated, if need be. It is here that the diagnosis is officially documented and a treatment regimen is assigned.

Medical evaluations should be conducted by a competent medical doctor who can properly diagnose and recommend a treatment plan or prescribe medications for the patient. Psychological evaluations are also conducted by a competent mental health professional, usually a psychiatrist, who can prescribe medications or other treatment. Medications must be prescribed and dispensed by people licensed to do so.

Telemedicine is a new approach to correctional health care and provides interactive health care through the use of modern technology. It allows patients and physicians to communicate with each other live over video regardless of their physical distance from one another. This is similar to the manner in which Web cameras are used to communicate over the Internet, but the equipment used for telemedicine is far more powerful than a standard Webcam and is much clearer. Telemedicine also allows inmates to submit a list of their symptoms along with video recordings or digital photographs of their afflictions to a physician for documentation and diagnosis. This tool can also be used in conjunction with on-site medical personnel when a specialist's opinion is needed. The use of this technology in jails and prisons reduces the need to transfer inmates to other facilities for specialist care and reduces the safety risks posed to medical professionals working with inmates.

This approach is perhaps best suited for larger facilities that need significant numbers of specialty consultations or facilities that would incur significant travel expenses to bring such specialists to their facility on a regular basis. There are some costs associated with this practice, primarily during startup, which may prove too costly for smaller facilities. Facilities must pay for the equipment, installation, and other basic operational expenses. The equipment alone is estimated to cost somewhere between $80,000 and $100,000 (Gailiun, 1997). However, the benefits go far beyond financial savings and include reducing security risks by eliminating the need to transport inmates to specialty care providers' offices, decreasing the waiting periods for prisoners needing specialty care, and increasing inmates' access to specialty care providers who otherwise may not be available to them (McDonald et al., 1999). The Federal Bureau of Prisons was able to reduce specialty care costs by $100 per consultation by using telemedicine (McDonald et al., 1999).

Legally, medications must be dispensed every day of the year, up to four times a day. There are a variety of ways in which medications can be dispensed in a correctional facility. One involves a centralized distribution center where all inmates who need medicines must pick up their medications. Another option involves delivery of medications by an authorized medication aide or licensed or registered nurse to all inmates who need them. The third approach uses a combination of these techniques and allows members of the general population to pick their prescriptions up while requiring delivery of medications to inmates in segregation. Some facilities have created committees to oversee the amount and types of medications prescribed in an attempt to cut costs.

Sometimes medications can be distributed in multiple doses, reducing the need for inmates to return to a service counter or await delivery. One such approach is known as a keep-on-person program. Institutions that try these programs should have strict policy guidelines in place to ensure success. Key considerations that must be addressed before program implementation include the number and type of drugs eligible for this type of distribution, restrictions on inmate participation, and procedures for noncompliance or illegal use (e.g., selling or giving drugs to someone else).

POLICY IMPLICATIONS

In 1997 the U.S. Supreme Court ruled in *Kansas v. Hendricks* that use of the civil commitment process for the continued confinement of sexual predators is constitutional. Hendricks argued that civil commitment after a prison sentence constitutes double jeopardy and is an ex post facto law, both of which are prohibited by the Fifth Amendment of the U.S. Constitution. However, the Court ruled that civil commitment of sex offenders was not a violation of the Fifth Amendment because it was not a criminal proceeding. The civil commitment process targets sex offenders under the rationale that they possess a mental abnormality that creates a danger to society. It is this threat of danger that allows the civil commitment process to occur.

A diagnosable mental illness is not required as long as the threat to cause harm to others exists. Additionally, the courts gave full discretion to the states to determine what the term *mentally abnormal* means and how to determine whether a sexual offender still poses a threat to society after his or her prison sentence ends. The rationale for this decision was that those confined under civil commitment procedures were not serving a double sentence but were instead provided an environment where they could seek treatment for their abnormality.

Civil commitment has become a tool for the prevention of further acts of violence perpetrated by sexual predators on other members of society. The underlying assumption is that this process allows treatment of the people being committed. The problem is that some offenders refuse to take part in the treatment programs offered during their commitment, and some facilities simply do not provide the treatment program that would best meet the offender's needs.

The National Association of State Mental Health Program Directors objects to civil commitment of sexual predators on the grounds that these commitments have the potential to harm those with diagnosable mental illnesses who have been involuntarily committed to a mental health facility for genuine treatment purposes. Their primary objections are that this process will detract from the mission of state mental health agencies that provide treatment to people with diagnosed and treatable mental illnesses and will place these people, who have not committed a crime, in harm's way when others are housed with them.

According to a *New York Times* article published in 2007, there were more than 2,700 sexual predators being held in 17 states under civil commitment laws. These laws allowed the civil commitment of sex offenders indefinitely or until they no longer posed a threat to society. Although civil commitments appeal to the public's desire for safety, these commitments often cost taxpayers up to four times what it would cost to simply incarcerate them. Very few people confined to these facilities ever "graduate" from treatment, meaning that they do not participate in treatment programs available to them or they simply never reach the point where they would no longer be considered to pose a threat to society.

Perhaps a better solution would be to lengthen the prison sentences given to sexual predators and increase penalties for subsequent offenses. The current civil commitment programs are draining taxpayers' resources and not yielding tangible results. New York was the first state not only to provide a variety of mental health treatment programs for sexual predators during their civil commitment but also to include intensive supervision after release to further its overall mission of preventing recidivism among those being released. If this New York program is successful, it could influence other states' civil commitment policies and subsequently reduce the financial burden placed on taxpayers to support these programs.

LEGAL CASES AND SIGNIFICANT OBLIGATIONS

- *Estelle v. Gamble* (1976) held that the state must provide for basic human needs after depriving a person of his or her liberty (i.e., incarceration).
- *Ruiz v. Estelle* (1980) "established a state's obligation to provide medical care for those whom it is punishing by incarceration." This includes mental health care.

- Title 42, Section 1983, of the U.S. Code provides inmates with the opportunity to sue correctional officials who deny them proper medical treatment.
- *Balla v. Idaho Board of Corrections* (1984) obligated prisons and jails to provide a mental health screening at intake in order to identify potentially serious problems (e.g., suicidal tendencies).
- *Ort v. Pinchback* (1986) and *West v. Atkins* (1988) established that a physician who contracts with the state to provide medical care to inmates acts under the color of state law and is also liable for violations under Title 42, Section 1983, of the U.S. Code.
- *Washington v. Harper* (1990) granted inmates the same rights to refuse treatment as citizens not incarcerated, but the due process clause permits a state to treat an incarcerated inmate having a serious mental disorder with antipsychotic medication against his will, under the condition that he is dangerous to himself or others and the medication prescribed is in his best medical interest.
- *Casey v. Lewis* (1993) states that the rights of inmates under the 8th Amendment are violated when correctional facilities fail to provide them with psychiatric and psychological treatment.
- The Mentally Ill Offender Treatment and Crime Reduction Act of 2004, Public Law No. 108-414, was signed into law by President George W. Bush on October 30, 2004.

DISCUSSION QUESTIONS

1. What are some of the unique mental and physical health challenges that female inmates present for correctional administrators? What type of additional screening or assessments would you recommend for this population?

2. What are some of the potential risks and benefits associated with the implementation of a keep-on-person program? Would you recommend a keep-on-person program? Why or why not?

3. If you were told to create some basic policies and procedures to govern the keep-on-person program at your institution, what would they be?

4. As a correctional administrator, would you recommend a mandatory HIV testing policy? Why or why not? If so, when would this take place (e.g., during admission, sometime during incarceration, before release)?

5. Would you recommend segregating inmates who are HIV positive or have confirmed cases of AIDS? Why or why not? Do you believe this constitutes a violation of their constitutional rights? If so, which one and how?

SUGGESTED READINGS

Anno, B. J. (2001). *Correctional health care: Guidelines for the management of an adequate delivery system*. Washington, DC: U.S. Department of Justice. Retrieved February 12, 2009, from http://www.nicic.org/pubs/2001/017521.pdf

California Department of Corrections and Rehabilitation. (2005). *Minimum standards for local detention facilities: 2005 health guidelines*. Retrieved February 12, 2009, from http://www.cdcr.ca.gov/divisions_boards/CSA/fso/Docs/2005_Title_15_Health_Guidelines_FINAL.pdf

Collins, W. C. (2007). *Jails and the Constitution: An overview*. Washington, DC: U.S. Department of Justice. Retrieved February 12, 2009, from http://www.nicic.org/Downloads/PDF/Library/022570.pdf

Freudenberg, N. (2001). Jails, prisons, and the health of urban populations: A review of the impact of the correctional system on community health. *Journal of Urban Health, 78*(2), 214.

James, D. J., & Glaze, L. E. (2006). *Mental health problems of prison and jail inmates*. Bureau of Justice Statistics special report NCJ 213600. Washington, DC: Bureau of Justice Statistics.

National Association of State Mental Health Program Directors. (1997). *Position statement on the laws providing for the civil commitment of sexually violent criminal offenders*. Alexandria, VA: Author. Retrieved September 15, 2008, from http://www.nasmhpd.org/general_files/position_statement/sexpred.htm

Telemedicine.com. (2009). Frequently asked questions. Cameron Park, CA: Author. Retrieved April 15, 2009, from http://www.telemedicine.com/faqs.html

REFERENCES

Abram, K. M., & Teplin, L. A. (1991). Co-occurring disorders among mentally ill jail detainees: Implications for public policy. *American Psychologist, 46,* 1036–1045.

Abram, K. M., Teplin, L. A., & McClelland, G. M. (2003). Comorbidity of severe psychiatric disorders and substance use disorders among women in jail. *American Journal of Psychiatry, 160,* 1007–1010.

Alexander, S. (1972). The captive patient: The treatment of health problems in American prisons. *Clearinghouse Review, 1,* 16–27.

American Bar Association. (1974). *Survey of United States implementation of the United Nations standard minimum rules for the treatment of prisoners*. Washington, DC: ABA Commission on Correctional Facilities and Services.

American Psychiatric Association. (2000). *Diagnostic and statistical manual of mental disorders* (4th ed., text revision). Washington, DC: Author.

Bureau of Justice Assistance. (2008). *Mental health courts program*. Retrieved September 15, 2008, from http://www.ojp.usdoj.gov/BJA/grant/mentalhealth.html

Carbonell, J. L., & Perkins, R. (2004). Diagnosis and assessment of criminal offenders. In *Correctional counseling & rehabilitation* (5th ed., pp. 113–132). Cincinnati, OH: Anderson.

Clark, R. (1971). *Crime in America*. New York: Pocket Books.

Coen, C., Sacks, S., & Melnick, G. (2006). *Screening for co-occurring mental and substance use disorders in the criminal justice system*. American Society of Criminology 2006 annual meeting.

Corrado, R., Cohen, I., Hart, S., & Roesch, R. (2000). Diagnosing mental disorders in offenders: Conceptual and methodological issues. *Criminal Behaviour and Mental Health, 10,* 29–39.

Diamond, P. M., Wang, E. W., Holzer, C. E. III, Thomas, C., & des Anges, C. (2001). The prevalence of mental illness in prison. *Administration and Policy in Mental Health, 29,* 21–40.

Ditton, P. (1999). *Mental health and treatment for inmates and probationers.* Washington, DC: Bureau of Justice Statistics.

Fisher, W., Packer, I., Simon, L., & Smith, D. (2000). Community mental health services and the prevalence of severe mental illness in local jails: Are they related? *Administration and Policy in Mental Health, 27,* 371–382.

Fletcher, B. W., & Wexler, H. K. (2005). National Criminal Justice Drug Abuse Treatment Studies (CJ-DATS): Update and progress. *Justice Research and Statistics Association: The Forum, 23*(5), 1, 6–7.

Fogel, C. I. (1995). Pregnant prisoners: Impact of incarceration on health and health care. *Journal of Correctional Health Care, 2,* 169–190.

Gailiun, M. (1997). Telemedicine takes off. *Corrections Today, 4,* 68–70.

Goldberg, A. L., & Higgins, B. R. (2006). *Brief mental health screening for corrections intake.* Rockville, MD: National Institute of Justice.

Goldkuhle, U. (1999). Health service utilization by women in prison: Health needs indicators and response effects. *Journal of Correctional Health Care, 1,* 63–83.

Greenfeld, L. A., & Snell, T. L. (1999). *Women offenders.* Bureau of Justice Statistics special report. Washington, DC: Bureau of Justice Statistics.

Hammett, T. M. (2006). HIV in prisons. *Journal of Criminology and Public Policy, 5*(1), 109–112.

Hufft, A. G., Fawkes, L. S., & Lawson, W. T. (1993). Care of the pregnant offender. In *Female offenders: Meeting needs of a neglected population.* Lanham, MD: American Correctional Association.

Human Rights Watch. (2003). *Ill equipped: U.S. prisons and offenders with mental illness.* Retrieved April 15, 2009, from http://www.hrw.org/en/reports/2003/10/21/ill-equipped

James, D. J., & Glaze, L. E. (2006). *Mental health problems of prison and jail inmates.* Bureau of Justice Statistics special report. Washington, DC: Bureau of Justice Statistics.

Lamb, H. R., & Weinberger, L. E. (1998). Persons with severe mental illness in jails and prisons: A review. *Psychiatric Services, 49,* 483–492.

Lurigio, A. J. (2005). Taking stock of community corrections programs. *Criminology & Public Policy, 4*(2), 259–262.

Lurigio, A. J., Cho, Y. I., Swartz, J. A., Johnson, T. P., Graf, I., & Pickup, L. (2003). Standardized assessment of substance-related, other psychiatric, and comorbid disorders among probationers. *International Journal of Offender Therapy and Comparative Criminology, 47,* 630–653.

Lurigio, A. J., & Swartz, J. A. (2006). Mental illness in correctional populations: The use of standardized screening tools for further evaluation or treatment. *Federal Probation, 70*(2), 29–35.

Maruschak, L. M. (2006). *HIV in prisons, 2006.* Bureau of Justice Statistics. Retrieved September 4, 2008, from http://www.ojp.usdoj.gov/bjs/pub/html/hivp/2006/hivp06.htm

McDonald, D. C., Hassol, A., Carlson, K., McCullough, J., Fournier, E., & Yap, J. (1999). *Health care costs: An evaluation of a prison telemedicine network.* Washington, DC: U.S. Department of Justice, National Institute of Justice.

McLearen, A. M., & Ryba, N. L. (2003). Identifying severely mentally ill inmates: Can small jails comply with detection standards? *Journal of Offender Rehabilitation, 37,* 25–40.

McQuistion, H. L., Finnerty, M., Hirschowitz, J., & Susser, E. S. (2003). Challenges for psychiatry in serving homeless people with psychiatric disorders. *Psychiatric Services, 54*(5), 669–676.

Mumola, C. (2005). *Suicide and homicide in state prisons and local jails*. Washington, DC: U.S. Department of Justice.

National Commission on Correctional Health Care. (2001). *Correctional health care: Guidelines for the management of an adequate delivery system*. Chicago: National Commission on Correctional Health Care.

National Commission on Correctional Health Care. (2002). *The health status of soon-to-be-released inmates: A report to Congress* (Vol. 1). Chicago: National Commission on Correctional Health Care.

Office of Health and Medical Affairs. (1975). *Key to health for a padlocked society*. Lansing: Michigan Department of Corrections.

Ornduff, J. S. (1996). Releasing the elderly inmate: A solution to prison overcrowding. *Elder Law Journal, 4*, 173–200.

Penrose, L. S. (1939). Mental disease and crime: Outline of a comparative study of European statistics. *British Journal of Medical Psychology, 18*, 1–15.

The President's Commission on Law Enforcement and Administration of Justice. (1967a). *The challenge of crime in a free society*. Washington, DC: U.S. Department of Justice, Law Enforcement Assistance Administration.

The President's Commission on Law Enforcement and Administration of Justice. (1967b). *Task force report: Drunkenness*. Washington, DC: U.S. Department of Justice, Law Enforcement Assistance Administration.

The President's Commission on Law Enforcement and Administration of Justice. (1967c). *Task force report: Narcotics and drugs*. Washington, DC: U.S. Department of Justice, Law Enforcement Assistance Administration.

Rector, F. L. (1929). *Health and medical service in American prisons and reformatories*. New York: National Society of Penal Information.

Sacks, S. (2008). Brief overview of screening and assessment for co-occurring disorders. *International Journal of Mental Health and Addiction, 6*(1), 7–19.

Shervington, W. (1974). Prison, psychiatry and mental health. *Psychiatric Annals, 3*, 43–60.

Simon, R. I., & Hales, R. E. (2006). *The American Psychiatric Publishing textbook of suicide assessment and management*. Arlington, VA: American Psychiatric Publishing.

Smith, C. B., Schmid, A. R., & Hennly, T. (1990). Prison adjustment of youthful inmates with mental retardation. *Mental Retardation, 28*, 177–181.

Steadman, H. J., Scott, J. E., Osher, F., Agnese, T. K., & Robins, P. C. (2005). Validation of the brief jail mental health screen. *Psychiatric Services, 56*, 816–822.

Steadman, H. J., & Veysey, B. M. (1997). *Providing services for jail inmates with mental disorders* (Research in Brief, U.S. DOJ publication no. NCJ 162207). Washington, DC: National Institute of Justice.

Swartz, J., & Lurigio, A. J. (2006). Screening for serious mental illness in populations with co-occurring substance use disorders: Performance of the K6 scale. *Journal of Substance Abuse Treatment, 31*(3), 287–296.

Teplin, L. A. (1990). Detecting disorder: The treatment of mental illness among jail detainees. *Journal of Consulting and Clinical Psychology, 58*, 233–236.

Teplin, L. A., & Swartz, J. (1989). Screening for severe mental disorders in jail: The development of the referral decision scale. *Law and Human Behavior, 13*(1), 1–18.

Veysey, B. M., & Bichler-Robertson, G. (2002, April). Providing psychiatric services in correctional settings. In *The health status of soon-to-be-released inmates: A report to Congress* (Vol. 2, pp. 157–165). Chicago: National Commission on Correctional Health Care.

CHAPTER 11

Faith-Based Prisoner Reentry

Beverly D. Frazier

More than 2 million Americans are incarcerated in state and federal prisons. It is estimated that on any given day, at the turn of the century, one out of every 200 Americans was incarcerated. By the end of 2007, an estimated 7.3 million people were incarcerated, on probation, or on parole, equivalent to 1 in every 31 U.S. adult residents. Increasing numbers of ex-offenders (about 97% of those incarcerated)—more now than at any other time in our history—are leaving prisons across the country to return to their families and communities. In 2008, more than 700,000 people will be released from state and federal prisons throughout the nation, a fourfold increase over the past two decades. Another 10 million will be released from local jails. In many cases, however, these people are less prepared for their return to society and less connected to community-based social structures than their predecessors were 10 to 20 years ago. As in previous years, many prisoners are released with only a bus ticket and a small amount of money. In addition to this lack of economic or financial capital, most prisoners also have limited human capital, such as education and employment skills. Because of decreased funding, society's changed ideology of prison, and the skyrocketing number of people behind bars, fewer higher education and other programs are offered to prepare inmates for life outside prison walls. When those programs are offered, far fewer prisoners have the opportunity to take advantage of them because of limited space and steep eligibility guidelines.

Still, upon their release many ex-offenders must face the immediate challenges of obtaining food, clothing, housing, and health care. Their lack of sufficient human, social, economic, and spiritual capital puts many at a disadvantage as they attempt to manage the most basic ingredients for successful reintegration: reconnecting with their families and accessing substance abuse and health care treatment as needed. Longer-term reintegration needs of returning prisoners range from finding and maintaining employment to accessing other community services. Previous reports indicate that most ex-offenders will be rearrested within 3 years, and many will be returned to prison for new crimes or parole violations. This cycle of incarceration and reentry into society carries the potential for profound adverse consequences for prisoners, their families, and communities and translates into thousands of new victimizations each year and billions of dollars in correction expenditures. Therefore, there are enormous opportunities for programs and interventions that could improve public safety, public health, and cohesion of the communities at the center of this cycle. Community organizations are integral to ensuring successful and enduring reintegration outcomes among former prisoners and their families. The literature has shown that institutions of faith can also play an important role in easing the reentry process for ex-offenders.

FAITH-BASED ORGANIZATIONS

Some theorize that because faith-based and community-level organizations typically have close ties to the communities they serve, they can be more efficient than traditional government agencies in helping those in need and should therefore have greater access to federal social service funds. This rationale supported the federal government's establishment and expansion of the White House Office of Faith-Based and Community Initiatives, which created centers in five cabinet departments, including the U.S. Department of Justice, paving the way for faith-based organizations (FBOs) to provide prisoner reentry programming and services.

FBOs and other community groups have historically played a critical role in supporting incarcerated and paroled prisoner populations. Rossman (2002) states, "Currently, thousands of faith-based and community organizations provide emergency and long-term shelter, job training, substance abuse treatment, and mentoring for ex-offenders and their families, all of which may ease the former prisoner's reintegration into the community" (p. 164). Along with the recent emphasis on expanding the opportunities of churches, temples, mosques, and other faith institutions to provide a wide range of social services, there has been growing interest in the systematic study of the effectiveness of faith-based reentry programs and other services.

This chapter examines the literature on the problem of prisoner reentry in America: what is known, what is unknown, and the faith-based response to its various facets. *REST* Philly, a faith-based reentry program, is discussed in the context of the "stages of reentry" model, which specifically focuses on the key reentry challenges. The past and present reentry research is then examined and critiqued. Finally, the chapter discusses the policy implications of faith-based prisoner reentry. First, however, the definitions that frame the concept of faith-based prisoner reentry are provided.

FAITH-BASED PRISONER REENTRY DEFINED

Prisoner Reentry Defined

Prisoner reentry is a broad term used to refer to the transition of ex-prisoners from prison to their communities (Bureau of Justice Statistics, 2002) or the process of leaving prison or jail and returning to society. This includes prisoners who are released when they have served their maximum court-ordered sentence or who have not completed their maximum court-ordered sentence and have been granted release on the condition of a period of community supervision (parolees). It applies to people released from prisons, jails, federal institutions, juvenile facilities, or even pretrial detention. Although both adults and juveniles experience reentry, their experiences are significantly different. We limit our discussion of prisoner reentry here to adult reintegration.

Reentry entails planning for inmates' transition to free living, including how they spend their time during confinement, the process by which they are released, and how they are supervised after they are released. Although *reentry* in its most basic sense denotes a process, success is implied in its meaning. Reentry or reintegration is treated as "the concept of rejoining and becoming a productive member of society" (Taxman, 2004, p. 2), implying that reentry includes all activities and programming conducted to prepare ex-offenders to return safely to the community and to live as law-abiding citizens (Petersilia, 2003). Likewise, the U.S. Department of Justice posits that reentry entails the "use of programs targeted at promoting the effective reintegration of offenders back to communities upon release from prison and jail" (U.S. Department of Justice, n.d.). In this context, then, reentry can be viewed as the prosocial integration of ex-prisoners into the community.

Prosocial suggests behavior in accordance with the law, as opposed to *antisocial*, which can be described as "behavior in violation of the law," or deviance (Gottfredson & Hirschi, 1990). One might argue that what is now called reentry programming, such as parole or probation, previously fell under the title *community supervision*. However, explicit inclusion of prosocial community actors such as family members, block group presidents, community watch group organizers, community development corporation leaders, and clergy separates reentry programs from community supervision programs. Increasingly, reentry programming, planning, and policy are being addressed on many fronts, including a faith or spiritual perspective used in spiritually or faith-based interventions or by FBOs. An overview of the many complex issues surrounding the topic will help explain why this is so. First, however, it is necessary to get a better understanding of FBOs in general.

FBOs and Prisoner Reentry

Partnerships between government and FBOs in America are hardly new. In one form or another, such partnerships have existed for hundreds of years. However, broader participation of FBOs in the delivery of public service has been advancing over the past two decades by program devolution. Program devolution, a component of the New Federalism, is used to describe the shifting of responsibility for social programs from the federal government to the states. It reflects the view that placing program authority closer to the point of service will permit locally tailored, more effective services for poor families than standardized, uniform efforts controlled from Washington. As program administrators look outside the capitol for solutions, nongovernment organizations, such as community-based organizations and FBOs, are seen as valuable resources that can address a variety of social needs and should be financially supported in their work.

Probably the most significant political move toward this was the "charitable choice" provision of the Personal Responsibility and Work Opportunity Reconciliation Act of 1996. The 1996 statute that created Temporary Assistance to Needy Families also included a "charitable choice" provision, which encourages states to allow FBOs to be involved in creating work opportunities. This provision allows faith-based providers to compete on equal footing with other private entities for social service grants, contracts, and vouchers while protecting providers' autonomy, religious character, and Title VII religious employment exemption. It also forbids religious discrimination against clients and requires that an alternative be provided for those who do not want to be served by an FBO. For the last several years, the federal government has given grants to a variety of organizations in an effort to increase the number of FBOs providing social services, including reentry services.

FBOs and Interventions

To be considered an FBO, an organization must be connected with an organized faith community, such as an organized religion. The terms *faith-based* and *spiritually based* are used interchangeably in this chapter; they both refer to personal and public practice of religious activities and acts of worship, such as prayer, reading of sacred texts, and belief in religious dogma or theology. According to one school of thought, the connections of organizations to a faith community or organized religion occur when an FBO is based on a particular religious ideology and draws staff, volunteers, or leaders from a particular religious group. Other characteristics that qualify an organization as faith-based are its religiously oriented mission statement, receipt of substantial support from a religious organization, or initiation by a religious institution. Likewise, spiritually or faith-based interventions are also religiously oriented and usually involve some religious practices (e.g., prayer, meditation, reading of sacred texts, and other acts of worship). Such defining characteristics are valuable because they help to distinguish FBOs from secular organizations, yet they also mask the numerous distinctions that can be found between faith-based organizations. A small local congregation and the national Salvation Army, for example, are both FBOs that draw staff and volunteers from a particular religious group. However, these FBOs differ substantially in the scope and scale of their service provision.

FBOs can be distinguished from one another according to a number of factors, such as the size of the organization, the size of the organization's geographic service area, and the religious intensity of the organization. Of particular interest for this chapter is the level of religious activities offered by FBOs. Examples of religious activities include prayer at meetings, worship as a program activity, and the inclusion of religious teaching. Smith and Sosin (2001) suggest that FBOs directly sponsored by a denomination or other religious organizations are more closely connected to a faith tradition than those that are not.

Although these typologies help reveal how differentiated FBOs are based on a number of factors, the basic definition that binds them together and separates them from secular organizations is the presence of religion, in its organizational affiliation, funding source, or mission statement and in their provision of interventions. Recent studies have demonstrated that FBOs and religious congregations, which typically use spiritually or faith-based interventions, have already been an essential part of the social welfare net for decades, providing food and clothing pantries, financial aid, job referrals, tutoring, childcare, language classes, self-help programs, and services to prisoners.

The challenges of reentry are many, and so are the social implications. Therefore, there are enormous opportunities for programs and interventions to enhance the public safety, health, and cohesion of the communities that are at the center of this cycle by improving reentry outcomes for ex-prisoners. The literature has shown that institutions of faith can and do play a significant role in easing what proves to be a very complicated problem in America.

STATEMENT OF THE PROBLEM

The United States has a higher per capita incarceration rate than any other industrialized democratic nation. According to Lynch (2002), although there is no difference in the propensity to incarcerate violent criminals, no other nation treats people who commit nonviolent (especially drug) crimes as harshly as does the United States. With more than 4% of the population being incarcerated at least once in their life, the process of transitioning from prison or jail back into the community has become an epidemic social problem. The faith-based community is poised and called upon to respond to these problems. The problems of massive incarcerations and subsequent reentry can be understood in the context of two broad categories. The first is structural factors, such as legislation (e.g., harsh sentencing guidelines) and the lack of both prerelease and postrelease programming and supervision, which result in a cycling of men and women in and out of the criminal justice system. The second is cultural factors, such as those that create an environment for social disorganization and disorder by weakening family relationships and other social ties. A more systematic review of such structural factors is presented in chapter 14, and the following section addresses structural factors that deal with racial disparity as it pertains to FBOs.

STRUCTURAL FACTORS

It is estimated that nearly 10% of Black men and 3% of Hispanic men in their late 20s and early 30s were in prison at the end of 2001 (Beck, Karberg, & Harrison, 2002). More than 20% of Black men will experience a prison term before reaching the age of 35, compared with fewer than 3% of White men

(Petersilia, 2003). Furthermore, about 33% of parole entrants are White, 47% are Black, and 16% are Hispanic. Hence, about two thirds of all returning prisoners are racial or ethnic minorities, compared with less than one third in the general population (Petersilia, 2003). Many of these communities of color are those in which FBOs and congregations are active in the life of the community and in many cases called on to address issues such as reentry.

The United States has largely abandoned the religious-based rehabilitative model used by the first Quaker-instituted penitentiary in Philadelphia, a model based on the view that effective imprisonment disciplines a person while promoting healing and growth so that the ostracized person may reenter society and be welcomed as a productive citizen. A person who is able to understand and acknowledge his or her crime may choose to make restitution for it. However, rehabilitation was replaced as the core mission of corrections with programs designed to deter and incapacitate. Petersilia (2003) maintains that "even in states that continued treatment programs, many were retained primarily as a means of keeping inmates manageable rather than methods to reduce recidivism" (p. 13). Legislators looked more favorably on programs that could generate goods and services that the states needed than on education and work programs that might reform inmates. Logan (1993) conveys the sentiment of the changing ideology toward prisons: "It is the duty of prisons to govern fairly and well within their own walls. It is not their duty to reform, rehabilitate, or reintegrate offenders into society" (p. 13).

FAITH-BASED PRISONER REENTRY

Religious education and training programs have always been a part of state prison systems, which offer different levels of religious and rehabilitative services to offenders. Until recently, however, these rehabilitative programs received very little attention and resources because of constitutional restrictions concerning the separation of church and state and because of widely held perceptions of religion. Lukoff, Turner, and Lu (1992) point out that in theory, research, and practice, mental health professionals have tended to ignore or pathologize the religious and spiritual dimensions of life. This trend has begun to reverse somewhat with the deletion of "religiosity" as pathology in the fourth edition of the *Diagnostic and Statistical Manual of Mental Disorders (DSM)* and the move to increase the competence and sensitivity of mental health professionals in dealing with spiritual issues. Religious programs also did not receive much attention because of the lack of research evaluating such programs. Although there has been more scientific research over the past decade, policy changes at the federal level and federal funding to support state-level efforts require a closer examination of faith-based partnerships as they begin to serve as alternatives to traditional, secular efforts.

FBOs are increasingly given the opportunity to provide a variety of rehabilitative services to corrections facilities, either voluntarily or contractually. These services often include religious and moral teachings and incorporate religious practices, such as reading of sacred texts, meditation, and prayer, in addition to the more commonly offered anger management and substance abuse counseling, job and life skill education and training, and housing assistance. Religious practices, which research suggests may be associated with fewer in-prison disciplinary problems, may also be associated with better physical and mental health among prisoners. Many of those incarcerated, nearly one third, are reported to have serious physical or mental illnesses. Some studies show that prisoners who identify themselves as religious have fewer physical and mental health problems overall than those who do not identify themselves as religious (Johnson & Larson, 1998). Because mental and physical illnesses can prevent ex-offenders from successfully reintegrating into society after their release, the connection between religion and health is an important avenue for research. However, mental and physical challenges are only two of the primary obstacles for ex-prisoners, as discussed in chapter 10.

As a consequence of a growing trend that began with devolution and continued with the creation and expansion of "charitable choice" and the Office of Faith-Based and Community Initiatives, there are many examples of faith-based organizations providing and partnering with governments to provide reentry services. The effect of this trend can be seen as prisons and jails are increasingly looking at faith-based programs to cut costs, help reduce recidivism, and address the problems associated with the record number of offenders. This trend, coupled with the growing political and social demands to address the issues of prisoner reentry, has led many states and local governments, as well as the federal government, to consider faith-based providers for reentry programming. However, there are still many questions about the effectiveness of and processes used in faith-based interventions and service delivery.

The faith community has a long history of interaction with incarcerated populations. Prison inmates have a constitutional right to religious participation in prison, and prison chaplains have long been available to inmates for spiritual guidance. Researchers have found that religious or faith-based programming is extremely popular among prisoners. A Florida study found that 38% of inmates were interested in attending faith-based programs or activities, a proportion higher than that reported for other activities. Several theories may explain the popularity of spiritually or faith-based religious programming: It may be used to express true remorse for the crimes, time spent in chapel or reading religious texts can be a practical response to the monotony and lack of privacy in correctional institutions, and in some cases "finding religion" in prison may be motivated by a desire to present a more favorable case to the parole board for an early release. The federal government recently began exploring the use of faith-based programming in the Federal Bureau of Prisons. Programs differ between jurisdictions: Some focus on a particular faith, whereas others encompass various religious faiths. Many states and federal correctional systems have already implemented faith-based programs that use religious teachings and instruction to change inmate behavior and promote successful reentry into society.

A range of religious services and activities are offered in America's prisons and jails. At a minimum, every prison has at least one chaplain available for inmate counseling. At the other end of the spectrum, some states are experimenting with 24-hour, 7-day-a-week intensive Bible-based rehabilitation programs. It is important to note that Christianity is the dominant religion in American prisons, as in American society, but Islam and various Native American religions also have a strong presence. According to Read and Dohadwala (2003), although Muslims make up just 2% of the general population, they account for 20% of the prison population. In some areas, the proportion of Muslims is as much as half of the total prison population. Little is known about the rehabilitative effects of Christian-oriented incarceration programs, however, and even less information is available about the effects of other religion-based programs.

In 2002, the Serious and Violent Offender Initiative (SVORI), funded by the U.S. Departments of Education, Health and Human Services, Housing and Urban Development, Justice, and Labor, was launched as a comprehensive, collaborative federal effort to improve reentry outcomes in the areas of criminal justice, employment, education, health, and housing. SVORI programs target supervised populations, including juvenile and adult high-risk offenders, substance abusers, and those with mental illness or dual diagnoses, as well as serious and violent offenders, who were often excluded from previous programming efforts (Bureau of Justice Statistics, 2002). Through the initiative, federal funding is used to initiate or supplement existing programs (e.g., education, job and life skills, substance abuse) and to encourage partnerships between state and local agencies so that needed services are provided to prisoners returning to the community. Ultimately, the initiative ensures that funding will be provided to develop, implement, enhance, and evaluate reentry strategies that will ensure the safety of the community and the reduction of serious, violent crime. The states and the District of Columbia were given

$2 million each, which was disbursed to 69 state and local collaboratives, such as labor and education departments or programs. These collaboratives were selected to receive more than $100 million to develop or expand SVORI programs offering integrated supervision and services to offenders.

The Council of State Governments and the National Governors Association began major state-level policy initiatives around the issue of reentry years before this national initiative was under way, however. Many states began implementing faith-based efforts aimed specifically at rehabilitation and reentry in the late 1990s. Texas began a program at the Winfield Correctional Facility in 1997, which involved offering classes, such as Bible studies and life skill training, and providing prison jobs to offenders. Similarly, a partnership between Louisiana corrections officials and the New Orleans Baptist Theological Seminary in 2000 resulted in the creation of a program at the Angola prison that allows inmates to pursue an associate degree or a bachelor's degree in Christian ministry. Corrections officials allow inmates with such degrees to transfer to other prisons in the state in order to conduct counseling sessions and otherwise strengthen religious programming. More recently, state corrections officials in Florida have established faith-based prisons for men and women. A male-only facility at the Lawtey Correctional Institution became operational in 2003, and a female-only facility in the Hillsborough Correctional Institution opened in 2004. The female facility is equipped to house 300 prisoners and will provide instruction on such topics as character building, anger management, job skills, substance abuse, parenting, and strengthening marriages.

A FAITH-BASED REENTRY CASE STUDY: REST PHILLY

Although city and county jails are characterized by short terms of incarceration, officials at these institutions are increasingly becoming aware of the need to provide reentry programming and planning. The Philadelphia Prison System (PPS), for example, operates a number of programs for inmates. Some programs, such as Rational Emotive Spiritual Therapy (REST) Philly, actually recruit for enrollment, whereas others, such as the Options program, have court-ordered participants whose participation is a mandatory part of their sentence. Inmates who are awaiting trial or sentencing are entitled to participate, but sentenced inmates have priority in entering programs. In the most recent report available, about 35% of inmates in the PPS had been sentenced; the remainder were awaiting trial (Philadelphia Prison System, 2002). Inmates interested in participating in a program usually make a request through their assigned social worker, who might recommend a specific program, or through other prison staff. The social worker then does the necessary administrative paperwork to enroll the inmate. Through a series of interviews with PPS staff, Roman, Kane, Turner, and Frazier (2006) identified six main programs offered in the PPS: OPTIONS, Pennypack, PLATO, JEVS, PhilaCor, and REST.

Research shows that not all inmates are given the option to participate in such programs, however. In a report published by the Urban Institute in which 200 inmates were asked questions about reentry planning and preparedness, only 21–50% of those surveyed said they were given the opportunity to participate in some type of reentry program (Roman et al., 2006). Roman and colleagues attribute this low percentage to a number of reasons: the significant movement between facilities within the PPS; the short stay—about 80 days— for most inmates in the PPS; the selectivity of some programs, such as PhilaCor, which looks for inmates with specific vocational or trade skills; and the fact that some of those in the survey sample were housed in a neighboring facility outside Philadelphia, where the programs were not offered. Also, almost all programs have a waiting list if the program is full, which means the inmate may not be able to participate if he or she is released before an opening occurs. Of those given the opportunity to participate in a program, 63–82% said they accepted the offer. It is important to note that the participation rate was highest for those mandated to enter a program.

One of the programs administered through the volunteer services office at the PPS is REST Philly. REST Philly, a three-phase program with a faith-based or spiritually based cognitive–behavioral theoretical framework, has been well documented (see Billups, 2001; Cnaan, 2006; Cnaan & Sinha, 2002; Herndon, 2003; McKinney, 2004a, 2004b, 2004c, 2005; Roman et al., 2006). The fundamental purpose of REST is successful reentry for its participants. The REST program teaches cognitive–behavioral techniques to inmates to promote prosocial behavioral changes (Roman et al., 2006). The first phase of the REST program runs three cycles per year, with 200 to 300 inmates enrolling in each cycle; fewer inmates actually complete the prison-based 13-week, 90-minute group intervention (Roman et al., 2006). Upon completion of the 13-week course, those who have successfully fulfilled the requirements of attendance and homework receive a certificate at a graduation ceremony. Of those who complete the class, even fewer follow through with the next two phases of the program. Participants in Phases II and III are sponsored by an outside congregation (e.g., church, temple, synagogue). These ex-prisoners can be released to REST under community supervision under an early release program. However, they sometimes elect to "max out" or complete their full sentence rather than enroll in the next phase of REST program. REST Philly also offers

Ready4Work, a job training and placement program that includes social service referrals (Roman et al., 2006).

The Urban Institute survey indicated that the majority of respondents found REST to be useful and needed upon release (Roman et al., 2006). These responses referred to the prison-based portions of REST, which might have included the 13-week course, one-on-one sessions with a faith counselor, and some postrelease reentry planning. Although this was not an evaluative study and all programs are not equal (e.g., level of intensity and amount of exposure), the results reveal some level of satisfaction with this faith-based cognitive–behavioral intervention. REST Philly is an example of how FBOs provide spiritually or faith-based interventions. Yet little is known about these interventions, including how and if they work.

Stages of Reentry

REST Philly includes a three-phase reentry program, the Inmate Restoration and After-care Program (IRAP). REST Philly also provides spiritually based counseling in settings other than prison (e.g., there are programs to help people overcome substance abuse and other addictions, grief, and other emotional or psychological challenges) (McKinney, 2004b). IRAP is the three-phase program used in the PPS. Phase I of IRAP is an in-prison faith- or spiritual-based group counseling intervention that includes 13 weeks of 90-minute counseling sessions, as discussed previously. Phase II consists of aftercare orientation and preparation groups, and Phase III involves aftercare support services for released inmates (Figure 11.1). McKinney's IRAP reentry model is similar to the model created by the National Institutes of Justice to assess the federally funded SVORI. The goal of the model is to provide a roadmap for a successful reentry journey that begins when inmates are housed in jails and prisons and follows them upon their release, guiding them as they transition from correctional institutions to complete stabilization in the community. The model takes into account the issues that are common to most ex-prisoners reintegrating into society and seeks to incorporate that knowledge into its three phases. For example, the first two phases of IRAP usually begin while the inmate is still incarcerated. Phase I ends before release, and Phase II continues after release. In addition, sometimes Phase II begins after release.

Phase I—Protect and Prepare: Institution-Based Programs

These programs are designed to prepare inmates to reenter society. Services provided include education, mental health and substance abuse treatment, job

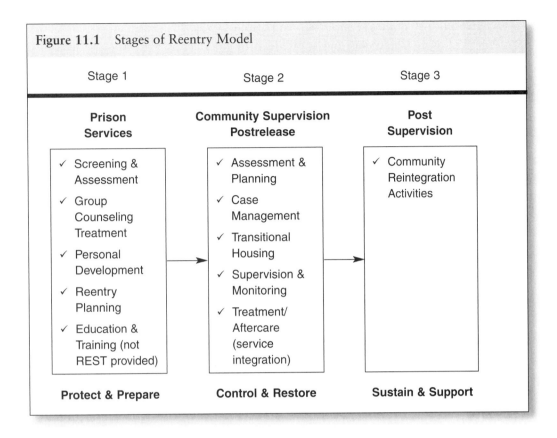

Figure 11.1   Stages of Reentry Model

Stage 1	Stage 2	Stage 3
Prison Services	**Community Supervision Postrelease**	**Post Supervision**
✓ Screening & Assessment ✓ Group Counseling Treatment ✓ Personal Development ✓ Reentry Planning ✓ Education & Training (not REST provided)	✓ Assessment & Planning ✓ Case Management ✓ Transitional Housing ✓ Supervision & Monitoring ✓ Treatment/ Aftercare (service integration)	✓ Community Reintegration Activities
Protect & Prepare	**Control & Restore**	**Sustain & Support**

training, mentoring, and full diagnostic and risk assessment. IRAP does not provide education and training directly but rather directs ex-prisoners to programs that provide such training. Screening and assessment are done with the help of level-one access to inmates' files and two primary instruments, the Karson Clinical Report and the Hare Psychopathy Checklist, Revised (PCL-R). The Karson Clinical Report, which contains sections describing basic areas of functioning, offers a narrative description of inmates, including information about their overall personalities and clinical patterns that can be used to identify areas in which counseling may be necessary. The PCL-R is used to determine the extent to which a given person matches the "prototypical psychopath." In addition, the IRAP administrators gather information on inmate placement and release-related issues when possible. Most demographic information is obtained from PPS administrative records. Inmates are asked about faith selection, family support systems, and entrance into the second phase of reentry. This information, along with the results of the Karson and Hare assessment tools, is used for tailored reentry planning. Treatment includes both one-on-one counseling and group therapy throughout the 13-week program. The counseling is provided by faith counselors, who are identified and trained by REST Philly to provide on-site services to inmates. These faith counselors, including members of local Philadelphia congregations and other volunteers, are required to successfully complete a week-long training session and a week-long internship before being assigned to an inmate.

Phase II—Control and Restore: Community-Based Transition Programs

In this phase, inmates or ex-prisoners work before and immediately after their release from correctional institutions. Services provided in this phase can include education, monitoring, mentoring, life skill training, assessment, job skill development, and mental health and substance abuse treatment. As mentioned earlier, these services may be provided in both Phase I and Phase II depending on when inmates are released. IRAP graduates of Phase I are prepared to reenter and reintegrate into society as a whole and into the faith community in particular. In many cases, this includes providing the Philadelphia Defender's Association with information to petition the court for an inmate's early release. Also, after an inmate selects a faith sponsor, that is, a member of a congregation (e.g., church, mosque, temple, or synagogue), REST Philly visits with the sponsor to make him or her aware of the inmate's request and to enroll the sponsor in the program. For each inmate, REST Philly also identifies a faith partner: a trained mentor of the same faith tradition as the ex-prisoner. The faith partner contacts the person selected by the inmate, usually a family member, who agrees to serve as the primary support system in Phase III.

Phase III—Sustain and Support: Community-Based Long-Term Support Program

In this phase, REST Philly seeks to connect ex-prisoners with a network of social service agencies and community-based organizations that will provide ongoing services and mentoring relationships and will help ex-prisoners acquire training and employment if needed. If an ex-prisoner enters Phase III as an early release client through the Philadelphia public defender's office, he or she is required to participate in 12 months of faith-based aftercare, which includes attending worship services, completing a religious educational program, and attending a Friday night support group. The goal at this stage is to provide inmates with a secondary support system while helping them build or restore their families as strong prosocial primary support systems. Faith sponsors collaborate with the former prisoner's sponsoring faith institution to build social and spiritual capital, create an aftercare program, and help ex-prisoners secure housing, employment or job training, and other fundamental reentry needs. These faith sponsors then continue to monitor the inmate's reentry progress through the eyes and ears of faith partners. Faith partners, many of whom are ex-prisoners, undergo a year-long training program and a subsequent internship via faith sponsors in order to serve as partners to other former inmates who have successfully completed the first year of reentry after release.

Theoretical Framework

The theoretical framework of the REST Philly model of prisoner reentry, IRAP, hinges on symbolic interactionism, social capital, and spiritual capital. Each of these theories can explain the process in each phase of the reentry model (Figure 11.2). However, in the first stage symbolic interaction is the primary theory. Likewise, social capital is dominant in Phase II, and spiritual capital in Phase III. The participation of local congregations of different faith traditions is paramount at each stage of the model. However, the focus of this

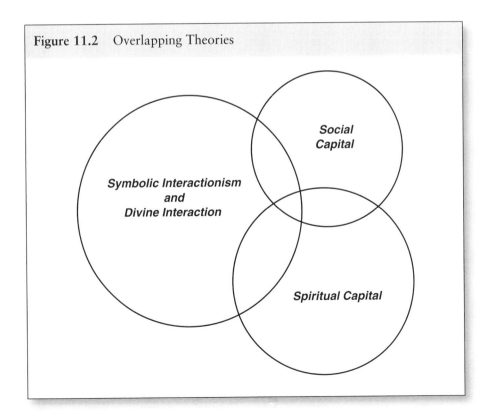

Figure 11.2 Overlapping Theories

Social Capital

Symbolic Interactionism
and
Divine Interaction

Spiritual Capital

case study is the theoretical process by which ex-prisoners use spirituality or faith to meet the challenges of reintegration, which is seen primarily in Phase I during the 13-week faith-based cognitive–behavioral intervention (see Ellis, 2000; Grimsrud & Zehr, 2002; Harris, Thorseen, McCullough, & Larson, 1999; Hatcher & McGuire, 2001; Johnson, Nielsen, & Ridley, 2000; Pipes & Ebaugh, 2002; Reed, Bergin, & Loftus, 1992).

Social Capital and Congregations

Churches, mosques, synagogues, and other faith-based institutions are often the single best source of volunteers in a community. These institutions are often considered the most comprehensive service provider—and the most credible, established, and respected institution—in underserved communities, where people released from prison and jail most often return. As of 2003, REST Philly had trained volunteers from 103 congregations in the Philadelphia area as faith counselors, mentors, and partners who have committed to supporting ex-prisoners. These volunteers provide a single point of contact through which released offenders may access a network of resources and role models. The structure of congregations can provide valuable efficiencies to corrections administrators. Corrections staff can train clergy to work in the prison setting and then trust those leaders to educate their parishioners and to support volunteers with their work in the institution and with prisoners released to the community.

Concepts of social networks, such as the ones found in REST Philly, are closely linked to those of social capital. Scholars generally understand social capital to be the quantity and quality of resources (individual, group, or community) that people can access through the various social networks in which they are embedded. Although the aim is for inmates to accumulate such social capital, it must be noted that more is involved than just the widening of social ties. It also involves "transforming contingent relations, such as those of the neighborhood, the workplace, or even kinship, into relationships that are at once necessary and elective, implying durable obligations subjectively felt (feelings of gratitude, respect, friendship, etc.)" (Bourdieu, 1983, p. 8).

Spiritual Capital

The concept of spiritual capital, assets, or equity builds on recent research on social capital, which shows that religion is a major factor in the formation of social networks and trust. There is a growing recognition in economics and other social sciences that religion is not epiphenomenal, nor is it fading from public significance in the 21st century, and that it has increasing importance to the social and economic dynamics of human economic intangibles. Recent developments in the social sciences suggest a growing openness to nonmaterial factors, such as the "radius of trust," behavioral norms, and religion, having profound economic, political, and social consequences. The development of the concept of spiritual capital is new, but social scientists increasingly attribute meaning to this broad concept. Some scholars define it as "the effects of spiritual and religious practices, beliefs, networks and institutions that have a measurable impact on individuals, communities and societies" (Spiritual Capital Research Program, 2005). Fogel (2000) defines it as a "sense of purpose, self-esteem, a sense of discipline, a vision of opportunity, and thirst for knowledge" (p. 4). Berger and Hefner (n.d.) view spiritual capital as a subset of social capital, "referring to the power, influence, knowledge, and dispositions created by participation in a particular religious tradition" (p. 3). Woodberry (n.d.) describes spiritual capital as "power, influence, knowledge, and dispositions created by participation in a particular religious tradition" (p. 6).

Spiritual capital differs from other forms of capital, but not because religious groups do not have material resources, skills, trusting relationships, and culturally valued knowledge—that is, financial, human, social, and cultural capital (Woodberry, n.d.). They do. But religious groups are concerned with more than these. Most religious groups purport to be more than mere social clubs. They often stress that their relationship with God is central and that the focus of group activity is precisely to emphasize and actualize that relationship. Moreover, participants often claim that people can access spiritual resources anywhere without respect to group solidarity. Woodberry (n.d.) suggests that what happens in religious groups is not fully encompassed by the concept of social capital.

SYMBOLIC INTERACTION AND A DIVINE OTHER

Symbolic interactionism, one of the major theoretical perspectives in sociology, has a long intellectual history and was used by Pollner (1989) to postulate an explanation of how religious involvement may work. Both Weber (1946) and Mead (1968) emphasized the subjective meaning of human behavior, the social process, and pragmatism. However, Blumer (1939), who studied with Mead at the University of Chicago, is responsible for coining the term *symbolic interactionism* and formulating the most prominent version of the theory. The theory focuses on the subjective aspects of social life rather than on objective, macrostructural aspects of social systems. The theory, which is based on the image of humans rather than on the image of society, postulates that humans are pragmatic actors who must continually adjust their behavior to the actions of other actors. We can adjust to these actions only because we are able to interpret them (i.e., to denote them symbolically and treat the actions and those who perform them as symbolic objects). This process of adjustment is aided by our ability to use our imagination to rehearse alternative lines of action before we act. The process is further aided by our ability to think about and react to our own actions and even ourselves as symbolic objects. Thus, humans are active, creative participants who construct their social world rather than passive, conforming objects of socialization.

Pollner (1989) points out that people may construct divine relationships much as they build social relationships, engaging a divine other in a quest for solace and guidance. A divine personification may be experienced through identification with various figures portrayed in religious texts. People may resolve problematic situations more easily by defining them in terms of a biblical figure's plight and by considering their own personal conditions from the vantage point of the God role. These emphases on symbols, negotiated reality, and the social construction of society lead to an interest in the roles people play. Goffman (1959) discusses roles dramaturgically, using an analogy to the theater, with human social behavior seen as scripted and with humans as role-taking actors. Role taking is a key mechanism of interaction, for it permits us to take the other's perspective, to see what our actions might mean to the other actors with whom we interact. Also emphasized in symbolic interaction is the improvisational quality of roles, with human social behavior seen as poorly scripted and with humans as role-making improvisers. Role-making, too, is a key mechanism of interaction, for all situations and roles are inherently ambiguous, thus requiring us to create those situations and roles to some extent before we can act.

Pollner (1989) proposes that this creation can be religious in nature and uses the term *divine interaction* to describe the engagement of a divine other in personal religious practices such as praying, meditation, and reading and studying sacred texts. He asserts that research has focused quite naturally on the support that derives from interaction with concrete others in "real" relationships. Yet reference group theory and the symbolic interaction perspective underscore that not all relations are concretely "real" (Rosenberg & Turner, 1981). Symbolic interactionism, for example, postulates that human interaction is mediated by the use of symbols, by interpretation, or by ascertaining the meaning of another's actions. There is evidence that people participate in "divine relations" as well as social relations and that divine relationships may approximate concrete social relationships in intensity. These divine relations or interactions are also linked to improvement of one's coping skills. People may feel that with the support or consent of a divine other they can control or manage life events (Pollner, 1989). Furthermore, in addition to providing a resource for resolving problematic situations, divine interaction may enhance well-being by shaping the sense of self and providing an emotional vehicle for change.

Divine interaction may bolster individual self-esteem and self-efficacy. A new awareness of one's self, as intimately known and valued by a divine other, could well increase one's sense of self-worth and create the perception of enduring significance beyond one's physical self and life. In addition, the perception of unconditional divine forgiveness of sins may mitigate personal guilt feelings and enhance the perception that life's challenges are manageable through personal partnership with a more powerful force. In addition to providing a resource for resolving problematic situations, divine interaction may enhance well-being by shaping the sense of self and providing a source of empowerment, creating a feeling "that with the support of a divine other they can control or manage life events" (Mirowsky & Ross, 1986, p. 25).

As a source of new cognitions in problematic situations, a source of empowerment and enhancement of the self, and a contributor to a sense of meaningfulness, interactions with a divine other may be expected to have a significant effect on psychological well-being. An analysis of artwork, poetry, and letters from inmates suggests that incarceration has a profoundly negative impact on psychological well-being and can be extremely dangerous. Like life on the playground, where the strongest child rules when there is no adult supervision, life in prison has a complex social hierarchy. Emotions must be carefully guarded and carefully expressed. Inmates lose their personal identities and are referred to by their ward addresses or intake numbers rather than by their given names. As documented in Goffman's (1961) study of asylums, these circumstances cause inmates to experience a cauldron of emotions, which can have deleterious effects on their psychological well-being, leading to weakened emotional stability, sociability, and sense of purpose as well as low self-esteem and confidence. Although these theories explain how a faith-based reentry intervention and aftercare program may work, there is little research on the efficacy and the process of these programs.

RESEARCH ON FAITH-BASED INTERVENTIONS AND PROGRAMS

Evidence suggests that participation in faith-based religious activities is correlated with personal and emotional well-being, especially with regard to coping with stress. Engagement in spiritually or faith-based religious practices could therefore play a positive role in a prisoner's ability to handle the stress associated with incarceration and reentry. In addition, evidence suggests that religious and spiritual beliefs are important sources of strength for many people, and research indicates that a person's well-being may be enhanced by certain dimensions of spirituality. Likewise, being a spiritual person might be beneficial for a prisoner facing the challenges of reentry. For example, a Fetzer Institute (1999) study contends that highly religious people are less likely to abuse drugs or alcohol than less religious people. And in a meta-analysis of the relationship between religion and crime, Baier and Wright (2001) found that religious beliefs and behaviors exert a moderate deterrent effect on criminal behavior. Bradley (1995) suggests that faith-based or religious groups can be important emotional and tangible support systems.

Studies have examined whether a person's religious involvement can reduce the likelihood that she or he will engage in crime. For example, Johnson and Larson (2002) examined the role of religious involvement in preventing crime among African American youth and found a negative relationship between church involvement and the perpetration of serious crime. In addition, McDaniel, Davis, and Neff (2005) conclude that "both anecdotal and statistical evidence do seem to demonstrate a negative relationship between crime/recidivism and 'moderate to high levels' of participation in religious programs" (p. 167). Yet the mechanism by which involvement reduces or eliminates criminal activity and the specific faith-based models used in criminal rehabilitation remain unclear.

Fewer Disciplinary Infractions

Some studies have found that prisoners who participate in religious or faith-based programming commit fewer disciplinary infractions than nonparticipants (e.g., Johnson, Larson, & Pitts, 1997). A study conducted by the Florida Department of Corrections revealed that attendance at religious services is linked to improved inmate behavior, as measured by the number of disciplinary infractions. Such services are also one of the least expensive of 163 types of potential programming for inmates. In another study, researchers found that the state spent an estimated $150–250 for each of the 779 inmates who attended religious services; only 11% of inmates with medium or high levels of religious participation had subsequent infractions, compared with 21% with low or no level of religious involvement. Yet another study found that "highly religious" inmates are less likely to be affected by depression and have fewer disciplinary problems during incarceration than other prisoners. Lastly, Clear et al. (1992) studied 20 correctional institutions across 12 states in different regions of the United States and reported that even after adjustments for variables such as age, race, and self-esteem, a statically significant inverse relationship existed between religious participation and offenses committed during incarceration. Despite such positive findings, much about the relationship between religious or faith-based programming and inmate behavior remains unclear. For example, it is not known whether attendance at religious services is directly correlated with fewer infractions or whether those more likely to attend services may simply be less likely to break prison rules in general. Also, it is not clear how this affects the inmate's ability to reintegrate into society. Therefore, the relationship between spiritually or faith-based programming, religious participation, and reentry outcomes warrants further study.

Lower Rates of Recidivism: Prison Fellowship Ministries

Prison Fellowship Ministries (PFM), a national nonprofit organization, has conducted a number of studies evaluating the effectiveness of its in-prison programs on postrelease recidivism outcomes (Johnson et al., 1997; Young, Gartner, O'Connor, Larson, & Wright, 1995). In one 1990 study, inmates who attended 10 or more PFM Bible study sessions in a year were less likely to be rearrested in the 12 months after release than a matched comparison group of inmates who did not participate in the PFM program. In another 1990 study, the researchers found that participants in heavily religious programs were less likely to be arrested for new crimes after release than those who were described as having little or no participation in religious or faith-based programs.

According to Maginnis (1996), additional studies by PFM in 1992 and 1996 reinforced the conclusion that high participation in faith-based programs, such as Bible study, lowered the likelihood of arrest after release. Using the same data but different statistical techniques, Johnson, Larson, and Pitts (2000) concluded that although significant differences in recidivism were not observed between participants and nonparticipants in prison fellowship (PF) programs as a whole, "after controlling for level of participation in PF-sponsored Bible studies, PF inmates in the high participation category (10 or more Bible studies) were significantly less likely than their non-PF counterparts (alpha = .05) to be arrested during the follow-up period (14% vs. 41%)" (p. 65).

Results from PFM's InnerChange Freedom Initiative (IFI), a comprehensive, Bible-centered rehabilitation program that has been implemented in various prisons in Texas, Iowa, Kansas, and Minnesota, are also promising. A study conducted among graduates of the IFI program revealed that these ex-offenders were less likely to be rearrested than a matched comparison group and to be reincarcerated. To summarize, the analysis yields the following recidivism findings:

> (1) There is no statistical difference between the total sample of IFI prisoners and the matched group on either measure of recidivism during the two year tracking period; (2) IFI program graduates were significantly less likely than the matched group to be arrested (17.3% vs. 35%) during the two-year post period release; (3) IFI program graduates were significantly less likely than the matched group to be incarcerated (8% vs. 20.3%) during the two year follow-up period; and (4) mentor contact is associated with lower rates of recidivism. (Johnson & Larson, 2003, p. 22)

Critique of Present Research

A critique of the faith-based reentry research highlights several important problematic issues. First, there is too little research. The number of faith-based reentry programs is growing, yet there is a paucity of studies on their effectiveness or on the processes they use. This could be partly because of the lack of research funding in the area. Second, of the research available, much is funded or conducted by the organization providing the service or intervention, thus raising questions of conflict of interest and bias. Third, there are few systematic and methodologically sound studies. The method in many of the studies does not adhere to rigorous research standards, such as adequate sample size in quantitative studies. Lastly, few studies look at both the process of reentry and the reentry experiences of ex-prisoners and examine outcomes (e.g., obtaining employment or housing and reconnecting with families) other than recidivism. In their examination of faith-based prisoner reentry programming and interventions, Solomon, Waul, Van Ness, and Travis (2005) concluded that longitudinal and ethnographic studies are needed to learn more about their longer-term prosocial impact and processes.

Classic Versus Alternative Reentry Research Model

Most research on prisoners or former prisoners examines the likelihood of continued involvement in criminal activity or recidivism. As mentioned earlier, recidivism is usually identified through officially recorded instances of rearrest, reconviction, or reincarceration (Langan & Levin, 2002; Wolfgang,

Thornberry, & Figlio, 1987). Recidivism studies typically focus on identifying the factors that predict the recurrence of criminal activity. Such research generally does not examine the process by which a person continues to be involved in crime or desists from crime, nor does it focus on an ex-prisoner's reintegration into society. Rather, it focuses on one outcome: arrest. Recently, scholars have recognized that the study of prisoner reentry and reintegration is similar to research on desistance, which requires a broader focus on a longitudinal process rather than on a discrete outcome. Such a broader focus would permit a more comprehensive understanding of the challenges of prisoner reentry and pathways to subsequent success or failure, which is critically important in reducing the costs associated with the high rates of reincarceration. Historically, few studies have examined the experiences of men and none of women released from prison or jail; however, that trend is changing as scholars and practitioners ask questions that can be answered only with in-depth qualitative research.

POLICY IMPLICATIONS

Before the 2008 election, FBOs experienced an unprecedented opportunity for funding under the Bush administration. Although there may not be abundant funding opportunities, this may be an opportune time for congregations and other FBOs to seek funding, which is the number-one barrier to provision of services according to the findings of a recent study. However, more research is needed to determine whether FBOs are as effective as non-FBOs in the delivery of reentry programming and services. FBOs have been the target of increased scrutiny with regard to their effectiveness in recent years. In addition, because FBOs are on the front lines of prisoner reentry service provision, more research is needed to form and defend policy and to inform the debate on the use of faith-based reentry programs.

Meanwhile, concerns about regulatory precision and transparency with regard to provision of faith-based programs and intervention are serious ones. Since the inception of the Office of Faith-Based and Community Initiatives, government funding of faith-based social services has generated a significant volume of litigation, and there has been an increase in the number of lawsuits and judicial decisions about publicly financed, faith-based social services in the past 6 years. Most of these lawsuits have been initiated by public interest groups that are committed to strong principles of church–state separation. Federal agencies, states, and localities take measures to ensure greater clarity, provide proper monitoring, and continue capacity-building efforts.

Lastly, FBOs should be leaders in collaborations, partnerships, networks, and outreach efforts. As community organizations, they are uniquely positioned to do so. Studies show that outreach is a critical issue in connecting ex-prisoners to services. It has also found that community justice and reentry partnerships and networks are important strategic tools in serving more ex-prisoners and providing them with more comprehensive services.

Some of the most salient comments providers made when asked about perceived barriers to reentry were in reference to "invisible sentencing," that is, restrictions that prohibit provision of services to ex-prisoners. For example, restrictions regarding public housing, occupational and vocational options, and guaranteed student loans for higher education create limitations for ex-prisoners, thereby making it more difficult to reintegrate into society. In addition to legal restrictions, ex-prisoners face invisible sentencing in the form of stigma and discrimination. Laws and policies may prohibit services to ex-prisoners, such as student loans, housing, access to certain professions, or cash assistance, if they have been convicted of certain types of crimes. On the other hand, there are few or no laws that protect ex-prisoners from the stigma of being incarcerated or from the discrimination they face. The most recent attempt to pass legislation that would assist ex-prisoners in reintegration resulted in the recently enacted Second Chance Act. In order to address the issue of reentry on all fronts, existing social welfare policies should be amended to address the needs of ex-prisoners and their families, and new ones that address the complexities of reintegration should be created.

DISCUSSION QUESTIONS

1. Public funding for faith-based prisoner reentry programs and interventions continues to be a controversial and litigious issue for federal, state, and local agencies. What are the areas of contention for those who support and oppose the use of public funds for faith-based services? What are the possibilities and dangers of each?

2. What are the advantages of community organizations in the provision of faith-based prisoner reentry programs? Are these advantages the same for national organizations? Compare the advantages and disadvantages of each.

3. How well does symbolic interaction explain how faith-based interventions may work? What are the questions raised by the theoretical framework suggested in this chapter?

SUGGESTED WEB SITES

- The Roundtable on Religion & Social Welfare Policy, the Rockefeller Institute of Government, State University of New York: http://www.religionandsocialpolicy.org
- Americans for Separation of Church and State: http://www.au.org
- Prison Fellowship International: http://www.pfi.org/

SUGGESTED READINGS

Cnaan, R. A., & Sinha, J. W. (2004). *Back to the fold: Helping ex-prisoners reconnect through faith.* Baltimore: The Annie E. Casey Foundation.

Dammer, H. R. (2002). The reasons for religious involvement in the correctional environment. *Journal of Offender Rehabilitation, 35,* 35–58.

Dilulio, J. (2007). *Godly republic: A centrist blueprint for America's faith-based future.* Los Angeles: University of California Press.

REFERENCES

Baier, C. J., & Wright, B. R. E. (2001). If you love me, keep my commandments: A meta-analysis of the effect of religion on crime. *Journal of Research in Crime and Delinquency, 38,* 3–21.

Beck, A. J., Karberg, J., & Harrison, P. M. (2002). *Prison and jail inmates at midyear 2001.* Washington, DC: U.S. Department of Justice, Bureau of Justice Statistics.

Berger, P. L., & Hefner, R. W. (n.d.). *Spiritual capital in comparative perspective.* Retrieved March 15, 2005, from http://www.metanexus.net/spiritual%5Fcapital/pdf/Berger.pdf

Billups, A. (2001, April 15). Keeping the faith, Philadelphia's mayor helps make a difference. *Washington Times,* p. A1.

Blumer, H. (1939). *Symbolic interactionism: Perspectives and method.* Englewood Cliffs, NJ: Prentice Hall.

Bourdieu, P. (1983). Forms of capital. In J. G. Richardson (Ed.), *Handbook of theory and research for the sociology of education* (pp. 241–258). New York: Greenwood.

Bradley, D. E. (1995). Religious involvement and social resources: Evidence from the data set "Americans' changing lives." *Journal of the Scientific Study of Religion, 34,* 259–267.

Bureau of Justice Statistics, U.S. Department of Justice. (2002). *Reentry trends in the United States, 2002.* Retrieved April 1, 2004, from http://www.ojp.usdoj.gov/bjs/pub/pdf/reentry.pdf

Clear, T. L., Stout, B. D., Dammer, H. R., Kelly, L., Hardyman, P. L., & Shapiro, C. (1992). *Does involvement in religion help prisoners adjust to prison?* National Institute of Justice no. NCJ 151513, pp. 1–7. Retrieved September 24, 2009, from http://www.ncjrs.gov/App/Publications/abstract.aspx?ID=151513

Cnaan, R. A. (2006). *The other Philadelphia story: How local congregations support quality of life in urban America.* Philadelphia: University of Pennsylvania Press.

Cnaan, R. A., & Sinha, J. W. (2002). *A preliminary investigation of a most urgent social issue: The faith-based community and ex-prisoner reentry.* Philadelphia: University of Pennsylvania, Program for the Study of Organized Religion and Social Work.

Ellis, A. (2000). Can rational emotive behavior therapy be effectively used with people who have devout beliefs in God and religion? *Professional Psychology, Research and Practice, 3,* 29–33.

Fetzer Institute, National Institute on Aging Work Group Report. (1999). *Multidimensional measurement of religiousness/spirituality for use in health research.* Kalamazoo, MI: Author.

Fogel, R. W. (2000). *The fourth great awakening.* Chicago: University of Chicago Press.

Gerth, H. H., & Mills, C. W. (Eds.). (1946). *From Max Weber: Essays in sociology.* New York: Oxford University Press.

Goffman, E. (1959). *The presentation of self in everyday life.* Garden City, NY: Doubleday.

Goffman, E. (1961). *Asylums: Essays on the social situation of mental patients and other inmates.* New York: Doubleday.

Gottfredson, M. R., & Hirschi, T. (1990). *A general theory of crime.* Stanford, CA: Stanford University Press.

Grimsrud, T., & Zehr, H. (2002). Rethinking God, justice and treatment of offenders. In T. O'Connor & N. J. Pallone (Eds.), *Religion, the community and the rehabilitation of criminal offenders* (pp. 215–230). New York: Haworth.

Harris, A. H., Thorseen, C. E., McCullough, M. E., & Larson, D. B. (1999). Spiritually and religiously oriented health interventions. *Journal of Health Psychology, 4,* 413–433.

Hatcher, R., & McGuire, J. (2001). Offense-focused problem solving: Preliminary evaluation of a cognitive skills program. *Criminal Justice Behavior, 28,* 564–567.

Herndon, L. (2003, August 24). Spiritual help for ex-prisoners. *The Philadelphia Inquirer,* p. D7.

Johnson, B. R., & Larson, D. B. (1998). The faith factor. *Corrections Today, 60,* 106–110.

Johnson, B. R., & Larson, D. B. (2002). *Assessing the role of faith-based organizations: A systematic review of the literature.* New York: Manhattan Institute, Center for Civil Innovation.

Johnson, B. R., & Larson, D. B. (2003). *The InnerChange Freedom Initiative.* Philadelphia: University of Pennsylvania, Center for Research on Religion and Urban Civil Society.

Johnson, B. R., Larson, D., & Pitts, T. (1997). Religious programming, institutional adjustment and recidivism among former inmates in prison fellowship programs. *Justice Quarterly, 14,* 145–166.

Johnson, B. R., Larson, D. B., & Pitts, T. A. (2000). Religious programming, institutional adjustment and recidivism among former inmates in prison fellowship programs. *Justice Quarterly, 14,* 145–166.

Johnson, B. W., Nielsen, S. L., & Ridley, C. R. (2000). Religiously sensitive rational emotive behavior therapy: Elegant solutions and ethical risks. *Professional Psychology, Research and Practice, 31,* 14–21.

Langan, P., & Levin, L. (2002). *Recidivism of prisoners released in 1994.* Washington, DC: U.S. Department of Justice, Bureau of Justice of Statistics.

Logan, C. (1993). Criminal justice performance measures for prisons. In J. J. Dilulio Jr. (Ed.), *Performance measure for the criminal justice system* (pp. 19–60). Washington, DC: U.S. Department of Justice, Bureau of Justice Statistics.

Lukoff, D., Turner, R., & Lu, F. (1992). Toward a more culturally sensitive *DSM-IV:* Psychoreligious and psychospiritual problems. *Journal of Nervous and Mental Disease, 180,* 673–682.

Lynch, J. P. (2002). Crime in international perspectives. In J. Q. Wilson & J. Petersilia (Eds.), *Crime: Public policies for crime control* (pp. 5–42). San Francisco: ICS Press.

Maginnis, R. L. (1996). *Faith-based prison programs cut costs and recidivism. Insight.* Washington, DC: Family Research Council.

McDaniel, C., Davis, D. H., & Neff, S. A. (2005). Charitable choice and prison ministries: Constitutional and institutional challenges to rehabilitating the American penal system. *Criminal Justice Policy Review, 16,* 164–189.

McKinney, R. (2004a). *The clinical Jesus.* Wilmington, DE: Shara.

McKinney, R. (2004b). *Introducing R.E.S.T. (Rational Emotive Spiritual Therapy): A 2000 year old healing paradigm.* Paper presented at the American Counseling Association World Conference, St. Louis, MO.

McKinney, R. (2004c). *The role of family in the reentry and reintegration of inmates into the community.* Unpublished manuscript.

McKinney, R. (2005). *The REST Philly project: REST early release aftercare (reentry) program.* Unpublished report.

Mead, G. H. (1968). *George Herbert Mead: Essays on his social philosophy.* New York: Teachers College Press.

Mirowsky, J., & Ross, C. E. (1986). Social patterns of distress. In R. H. S. Turner Jr. & James F. Short (Eds.), *Annual review of sociology* (Vol. 12, pp. 23–45). Palo Alto, CA: Annual Reviews.

Petersilia, J. (2003). *When prisoners come home: Parole and prisoner reentry.* New York: Oxford University Press.

Philadelphia Prison System. (2002). *Annual report.* Philadelphia: Author.

Pipes, P. F., & Ebaugh, H. R. (2002). Faith-based coalitions, social services, and government funding. *Sociology of Religion, 63,* 49–69.

Pollner, M. (1989). Devine relations, social relations, and well-being. *Journal of Health and Social Behavior, 30,* 92–104.

Read, J. G., & Dohadwala, B. A. (2003). *From the inside-out: Coming home from prison to the Islamic faith.* Baltimore: Annie E. Casey Foundation.

Reed, P. I., Bergin, A. E., & Loftus, P. E. (1992). A review of attempts to integrate spiritual and standard psychotherapy techniques. *Journal of Psychotherapy Integration, 2,* 171–192.

Roman, J., Kane, M., Turner, E., & Frazier, B. (2006). *An assessment of prisoner preparation for reentry in Philadelphia.* Washington, DC: The Urban Institute.

Rosenberg, M. T., & Turner, R. H. (Eds.). (1981). *Social psychology: Sociological perspectives.* New York: Basic Books.

Rossman, S. (2002). *Building partnerships to strengthen offenders, families and communities.* Washington, DC: The Urban Institute.

Smith, S. R., & Sosin, M. R. (2001). The varieties of faith-based agencies. *Public Administration Review, 61,* 651–670.

Solomon, A., Waul, M., Van Ness, A., & Travis, J. (2005). *Outside the walls: A national snapshot of community-based prisoner reentry programs.* Washington, DC: The Urban Institute.

Spiritual Capital Research Program. (2005). *What is spiritual capital?* Retrieved April 27, 2005, from http://www.metanexus.net/spiritual_capital/What_is.asp

Taxman, F. (2004). *Brick walls facing reentering offenders.* Paper presented at the Reentry Roundtable, Prisoner Reentry and Community Policing: Strategies for Enhancing Public Safety, Washington, DC, May 12–13, 2004.

U.S. Department of Justice, Office of Justice Programs. (n.d.). *Reentry.* Retrieved September 24, 2009, from http://www.reentry.gov/learn.html

Wolfgang, M., Thornberry, T., & Figlio, R. (1987). *From boy to man: From delinquency to crime.* Chicago: University of Chicago Press.

Woodberry, R. D. (n.d.). *Research spiritual capital: Promises and pitfalls.* Retrieved March 15, 2005, from http://www.metanexus.net/spiritual%5Fcapital/pdf/woodberry.pdf

Young, M. C., Gartner, J., O'Connor, T., Larson, D., & Wright, K. (1995). Long-term recidivism among federal inmates trained as volunteer prison ministers. *Journal of Offender Rehabilitation, 22,* 97–108.

CHAPTER 12

Parole

Moving the Field Forward Through a New Model of Behavioral Management

Faye S. Taxman

Although it is the arm of the correctional system that is most directly responsible for public safety, community supervision is just beginning to be recognized as a valued component of the criminal justice system. More than 6 million adults and 530,000 youth are supervised in the community, many on probation, but often these people have a short period of incarceration in jail or detention facilities; more than 700,000 are incarcerated in prison and then released. *Parole supervision* generally refers to people who are released from prison, but it can also refer to those released from jail (in some communities because of legislation to abolish parole, this is called supervised release).

Little attention has been given over the last several decades to community supervision. Although intensive supervision, boot camps, drug courts, and a few other innovations have occurred over the last two decades, the core function of supervision was not changed as part of this effort. Yet research over the same period of time has identified key structural components that, if used, would improve community supervision as a crime reduction strategy (Taxman, 2008; Taxman, Shepardson, & Byrne, 2004). This research is slowly being translated into new models for handling more than 6 million offenders under supervision. The transformation of supervision from a slap on the wrist to crime reduction strategy will evolve with the use of a principled, focused strategy to address criminogenic risk factors of the individual and related communities to make gains in reducing crime. Success will place supervision in the forefront of our criminal justice policy.

This chapter traces changes in the supervision model, with a focus on adopting evidence-based practices and incorporating treatment into the fold of supervision. The new models of supervision evolve from the "what works" research that grew out of Canada's experience (now called evidence-based practices) (Andrews & Bonta, 1998). Recent attention has been given to applying such evidence-based practices to reentry, which has renewed attention to community supervision. New models of community supervision are being piloted that change the focus of the supervision process from enforcing conditions to managing risky behaviors and from holding the offender accountable to facilitating offender change and holding the system accountable. This chapter reviews some of these models and outlines a new generation of probation and parole supervision programming that redefines the nuts and bolts of the core business function of supervision: face-to-face contacts and supervision levels. The challenge before us is whether supervision can be at the forefront of public policy.

MAJOR TRANSITIONS OF PAROLE

The First Generation: Parole Supervision

The Urban Institute paper "Does Parole Work?" raised a number of questions about the efficacy of parole supervision (Solomon, Kachnowski, & Bhati, 2005). (Although the discussion is focused on parole, it pertains to all community supervision.) Regardless of the data used in the study, which has been the subject of much discussion (e.g., the data reflected supervision in the early 1990s, they pertained to only 14 states, and they included California, which has unique patterns), the report illustrates that parole supervision based on monitoring and face-to-face contacts has little saliency. In other words, parole does not reduce the recycling of offenders through the criminal justice system and may even contribute to it. And the use of antiquated supervision technologies has little effect on offending behavior, specifically on recidivism.

The findings of this study come as no surprise. Parole supervision in the 14 states under study involved face-to-face contacts that were intensified to monitor the conditions of the offender. Few agencies used risk instruments to determine the supervision level or even to identify the criminogenic needs that affect criminal behavior. Conditions were assigned to hold the offender accountable. The numerous intensive supervision experiments in the 1990s basically found that the number of contacts did not reduce recidivism or technical violations and often did not increase access to services (MacKenzie, 2000; Taxman, 2002). In this type of monitoring or contact, offenders are given a number of conditions, the parole agent monitors the conditions, and the offender often fails to meet the expectations. These failures increase the number of revocations, resulting in increasing incarceration rates.

In an analysis of the caseload size and intensive supervision literature, it was observed that the monitoring and face-to-face contact supervision model is atheoretical (Taxman, 2002). Stated simply, the monitoring function focuses on compliance or external controls by formal institutions that place demands on offenders. Because negative behavior is likely to draw the attention of the criminal justice system, supervision agencies are responsible for responding to the negative behavior. In many ways, monitoring is an unforgiving process in which attention is drawn to what has *not* been done instead of any small gains that the offender makes.

The burden of the monitoring protocol is on the offender as the sole party responsible for meeting the assigned conditions. The offender is responsible for paying supervision fees (even if the offender is unemployed or underemployed or cannot afford basic life essentials such as rent and food), finding treatment (even if services are not readily available in the community), becoming sober immediately after a long period of alcohol or drug use, and finding a sober, crime-free place to live (even if other members are under community supervision or have substance abuse problems). All these scenarios illustrate how the supervision system can be unforgiving toward the offender and the communities that many offenders reside in. That is, monitoring generally provides the offender with little assistance in learning how to be responsible or accountable.

Adding conditions to the standard parole and probation orders in the late 1980s–1990s has had a number of unintended consequences. The first and most obvious is the increased potential for technical violations that might result in incarceration. With added conditions of drug testing, electronic monitoring, house arrest, curfews, or other new tools, offenders have more chances for not being compliant or failing to meet expectations. Most parole agencies recognize that the effectiveness of these new tools is likely to be tied to the ability for offenders to learn to change their ways. Unfortunately, funds are available for the monitoring tools but seldom for the accompanying behavioral interventions that would help offenders learn to change their ways.

Second, monitoring has translated into more parole agencies adopting an enforcer model, coupled with law enforcement technologies. Many parole and probation agencies assumed a law enforcement perspective that included arming their staff, with 41 states allowing parole officers to be armed (Fuller, 2002). For some organizations this raised the profile of the probation and parole staff, including access to benefits afforded law enforcement (e.g., retirement systems, which are usually better than those of other state employees, and salary enhancements for clothing). It also forced the organizations to participate in law enforcement–type training, particularly certification for gun use. And it reinforced the commitment to rigorous enforcement of conditions as a form of accountability for the offender. The graduated sanction movement in the early 1990s reinforced this mentality, with a focus on responding to violations and the importance of accountability.

Some parole officers subscribed to the law enforcement perspective, whereas others continued to straddle the gap between law enforcement and social work. Some rigorously enforced the conditions, whereas others did not. And some officers suggest that they become frustrated with offenders and their actions, contributing to an acrimonious climate for supervision. Parole officers and offenders often get into verbal tugs of war that generally have negative results. Sanction guidelines (Burke, 2001) were developed to assist the parole staff in working productively with offenders to sanction behavior before pursuing revocation. But, like other guidelines in the criminal justice system, these are difficult to implement because the staff resist the structure that the guidelines impose (e.g., it affects their professionalism, they want to individualize responses, they believe that the guidelines give the offender too many chances, and they do not agree with the premise of the guidelines).

A punitive tone, emphasizing individual accountability and responsibility, appears to be characteristic of parole agencies. Taxman and Thanner (2003) note that messages of accountability and the actions of the parole and probation systems can create scenarios in which some offenders are treated differently from others. That is, procedural justice cannot occur in parole settings because some parole officers respond vigorously to violations of conditions, whereas others ignore the conditions unless the offender is arrested, and others will reinforce some conditions but ignore others. Studies in law enforcement and psychology suggest that such an environment of unjust punishment that is doled out under varying conditions is likely to lead to more disobedience than compliance (Skogan & Frydl, 2004; Taxman & Thanner, 2003; Tyler, 2004).

Second-Generation Programming: Accountability Within the Framework of Treatment

The intermediate sanction experiments have generally found that increasing the intensity of supervision through a variety of external controls has not improved offender outcomes (Mackenzie, 2000; Taxman, 2002). In fact, similar results are likely to occur for enhanced technical violations because of the detection that results from increased visibility of the offender. In the early 1990s new programs were developed that included drug courts, "breaking the cycle" and other seamless efforts, diversion to treatment (both front-end and back-end), and enhanced programs that built on traditional community supervision. Most of these programs emphasized treatment, drug testing, and sanctions. Overall, research has found that the provision of high-quality treatment services reduces recidivism. The key programmatic components that have been tied to effective interventions are as follows:

- Participation in treatment programs, particularly those that involve multiple levels of care (more intensive followed by less intensive services) such as in-prison treatment services followed by aftercare, intensive outpatient services followed by less intensive services
- Appropriate placement of higher-risk offenders into treatment services
- Engagement in clinical treatment services for at least 90 days
- Participation in clinical treatment services that involve certain types of therapeutic interventions, such as cognitive–behavioral therapy, contingency management systems (reward systems), social learning–based therapies, and therapeutic communities
- Programs that use positive reinforcers, which are more likely to shape behaviors than sanctions (Festinger, personal communication, 2005)
- Programs that are well implemented and maintain some integrity

Most programs are constrained by the failure to assign offenders to appropriate programs based on their needs (Lowenkamp & Latessa, 2005; Lowenkamp, Latessa, & Hoslinger, 2006; Taxman & Marlowe, 2006), to implement programs that use more effective clinical strategies, or to manage compliance by offenders.

During this era, the focus of the criminal justice system was on finding the best avenue to facilitate offender participation in treatment programs. Drug courts, intensive supervision programs, "breaking the cycle," boot camps, and other criminal justice programs that incorporated some types of treatment services developed different techniques to link offenders with services:

- *Brokerage:* The parole officer refers the offender to another agency for assessment or services without having input into the assessment process or the services delivered.
- *Case management:* The parole officer monitors participation in the assessment and service participation of the offender. The emphasis is on compliance with the order.
- *Dedicated services:* The parole office offers services on site; assessment and services are provided at the same location. Sometimes these services are paid by the parole office, while at other times they are offered by community and other organizations.

Although few high-quality studies have assessed the merits of the different linkage approaches, a review of the literature suggests that dedicated staff using behavioral management techniques (e.g., assessment tools and clinical, client-centered interviewing techniques) are likely to yield greater participation in treatment services. It is unclear whether treatment services have an impact on overall outcomes. The major issue regarding treatment services is retention because 60% of the addicts who participate in treatment services do not complete their programs (McLellan, 2003).

The drawback to this era of programming is that the role of the supervision staff in acquiring treatment services and promoting retention has not been advanced. For the most part, the style of supervision was similar to those used in intensive supervision projects, where the emphasis was on more face-to-face contacts to fulfill requirements. The actual nature of the contact was focused on compliance, making sure that the offender meets the conditions of release. That is, the offender was primarily responsible for ensuring that conditions were fulfilled, regardless of the actions taken by the supervision staff. The research did not examine the role of the supervision staff in achieving public safety goals.

Third-Generation Advances in Supervision: A Behavioral Management Strategy

Although the research over the last three decades has many limitations, it provides guidance to improve criminal justice public policy and supervision practice. Much of the relevant research derives from studies in substance abuse treatment, education, and vocational training outside traditional correctional and criminal justice settings. The research identifies themes that should be incorporated into current policies and practices: The supervision period should be short, with clearly defined goals and objectives that speak to punishment and reparation of harms (for low-risk offenders) and habilitation (for moderate- to high-risk offenders); informal social controls (e.g., families, friends) are more effective in controlling behavior than formal government agencies; many external control tools (e.g., curfews, drug testing) merely fuel the churning process and have limited efficacy in improving offender outcomes (which suggests that it might be advisable to limit the use of such tools for most offenders); treatment-based interventions should be reserved for moderate- to high-risk offenders who have clearly addressable criminogenic needs for which clinical or pharmacological programming would be appropriate; and clarifying expectations to the offender, limiting the use of discretion, and developing rapport with offenders are key program components that can improve offender outcomes. All of this can be translated into a behavioral management approach that supervision staff can use with offenders, particularly for moderate- to high-risk offenders who are susceptible to the churning wheel.

Overall, the research suggests that efforts should be devoted to reducing the overarching umbrella of the correctional system for the clear purpose of focusing supervision resources on offenders and communities in the greatest need. Stated simply, core resources should be devoted to moderate- to high-risk offenders, particularly those who reside in highly disadvantaged geographic areas (e.g., high concentrations of poverty, higher levels of instability), as a means to improve public safety and community well-being. Such a policy would require the criminal justice system to diversify responses in a manner that concentrates efforts on offenders who are likely to return to the community (as are most) and who are likely to have problem behaviors. Other offenders would be handled in ways that benefit the community and that entail less intensive restrictions and interventions. This is particularly true of the low-risk offenders, for whom punishment and reparation goals might be more appropriate.

The core component is a behavioral contract that includes the conditions of release and short-term goals for the offender. The supervision plan should be included in the behavioral contract to create one guiding document for the offender and the parole officer. The behavioral contract is a negotiated agreement in which conditions are designed to ameliorate criminogenic risk and need factors. The process of developing and monitoring the contract should involve establishing agreed-upon milestones, providing feedback to the offender about progress on the contract, revisiting situations in which the offender struggles with a particular issue, using incentives and sanctions to shape offender behaviors, communicating with the offender to review progress on the case plan and achievement of supervision goals, and developing natural supports to provide the offender with a support system that offers assistance upon completion of supervision.

The role of the supervision agent in this model shifts significantly away from mere enforcement to a partnership. The officer can model prosocial behavior. There are four main goals of contacts:

- *Engagement:* Engagement helps offenders take ownership of their supervision contract and behavioral plan. Ownership derives from the offender's understanding of the rules of supervision (e.g., the criteria for being successful, the rewards for meeting expectations, the behaviors that will end in revocation), the offender's criminogenic drivers that affect the likelihood of involvement with the criminal justice system, the dynamic criminogenic factors that can be altered to affect the chance that the offender will be likely to change, and the prosocial behaviors that will be rewarded by the community and the criminal justice system.

- *Early change:* Early change helps the offender address dynamic criminogenic factors in a manner meaningful to both the offender and the criminal justice system. As part of the change process, all people have interests and needs that can motivate them to commit to a change process. The change process begins by allowing the offender to act on these interests and address one dynamic criminogenic driver (which will eventually lead to addressing other criminogenic traits). The trade-off in achieving this goal is that the offender's interests in being a parent or provider or addressing specific needs (e.g., religious, health) should be acted upon simultaneously with the needs identified in the standardized risk and needs tool as a means to help the offender take ownership of his or her own change process.
- *Sustained change:* The goal of supervision is to transfer external controls from the formal government institutions to informal social controls (e.g., parents, peers, community supports, employers). This is best achieved by assisting the offender as gains are made in the change process to stabilize in the community and to use informal social controls to maintain the changes. The supervision process should include identifying the offender's natural support systems or developing these natural support systems.
- *Reinforcers:* As part of each contact, the goal is to reinforce the change process. Formal contingency management systems assist with this goal by providing supervision staff with tools to reward positive behavior and address problems. The formal process of swift and certain responses supports the offender by showing that the supervision staff recognizes small incremental steps that facilitate change and sustain change.

SEAMLESS SYSTEMS OF CARE

Evaluations of drug treatment programs have consistently found that participation in such treatment reduces substance abuse and recidivism (Anglin & Hser, 1990; Hubbard et al., 1989). In various individual program evaluations and meta-analyses, therapeutic communities and cognitive–behavioral models have consistently shown more positive results than other approaches, such as counseling, reality therapy, or other services (Taxman, 1999). However, control-oriented interventions (e.g., electronic monitoring, house arrest) generally create short-term results in reducing recidivism (Petersilia, 1999). The two key variables of successful interventions are the type of intervention and the length of time in treatment. Both have been shown repeatedly to be critical factors affecting recidivism reduction potential.

Although drug treatment programs for offenders have been shown to be effective, such programs are generally threatened by system factors that dilute the impact of a single treatment program, and supervision can expect results that are more likely to occur over time. In community supervision, most often the supervision agency is a bridge to the treatment community through referrals to treatment programs or funding of treatment programs for offenders. In either case, it is recognized that community supervision agencies and public health agencies usually work together to achieve the best outcome from the offender's involvement in treatment programs. In fact, certain actions by the supervision agency can increase offenders' access to and retention in treatment programs (Taxman, Shepardson, & Byrne, 2004; Thanner & Taxman, 2003). The linkages support the need to develop boundaryless systems of care that engage public health and criminal justice agencies in efforts to reduce recidivism. For example, client selection is a common problem for correctional programs because it is important to identify offenders who will benefit from the services. Another typical problem is that the offender spends too little time in prison or jail to benefit from the full duration of a treatment program. Another important selection issue is the fact that program eligibility criteria are often ambiguous, making it difficult to identify the characteristics of offenders who are likely to benefit from the treatment program. Treatment programs need special correctional staff, which often places excessive demands on a correctional institution. Aftercare is often desired but seldom materializes because it entails crossing organizational boundaries to link offenders to treatment services in the community. Most of the issues raised by Farabee and his colleagues (1999) were also uncovered in the present process evaluation.

The concept of a boundaryless organization evolves from system theory, where the focus is on creating processes that contribute to desired outcomes instead of examining subsystem performance. As noted by Hammer (1996),

The problems that afflict modern organizations are not task problems. They are process problems. The reason we are slow to deliver results is not that personnel are performing individual tasks slowly and efficiently; fifty years of time-and-motion studies and automation have seen to that. We are slow because some of our personnel are performing tasks that need not be done at all to achieve the desired result and because we encounter agonizing delays in getting the work from the person who does one task to the person who does the next one. . . . We are inflexible not because individuals are locked into fixed ways of operating, but because no one has an understanding of how individual tasks combine to create a result, an understanding absolutely necessary for changing how the results are created. (pp. 5–6)

Figure 12.1 illustrates how these boundaryless processes must occur in order to allow the criminal justice and treatment systems to work together on key decision points. The implementation of both treatment and correctional services will be streamlined by the coordination of the treatment and criminal justice systems in regard to these key decision points. In their work with private sector companies, Ashkenas, Ulrich, Jick, and Kerr (1995) have shown that the creation of boundaryless (i.e., seamless) organizations requires a new focus that allows processes to function far better as a whole than their separate parts. Under this framework, the role and responsibilities for the processes are congruent with those of the employing organization. In fact,

> There are still leaders who have authority and accountability, there are still people with special functional skills, there are still distinctions between customers and suppliers, and work continues to be done in different places. (Ashkenas et al., 1995, p. 4)

If each organization is focused on the overall process and not simply on its own goals and responsibilities, services can be implemented in a manner that maximizes their efficiency and effectiveness.

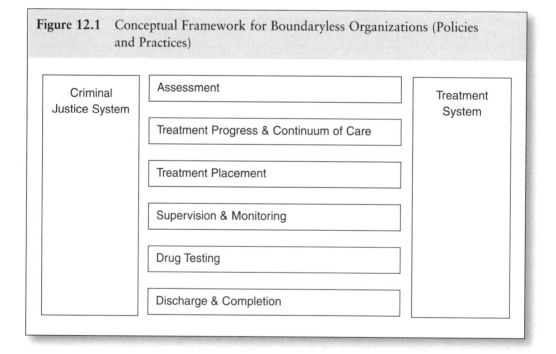

Figure 12.1   Conceptual Framework for Boundaryless Organizations (Policies and Practices)

The integrated system of service delivery is characterized by several distinct core components, including client-focused policies, delivery systems based on a continuum of care, and the use of coerced treatment, behavioral contracts, and graduated sanctions with clients, as well as the prioritization of system resources. Each of these core components is implemented with the cooperation of both criminal justice and relevant public health agencies.

The systemic approach to service delivery is designed to combine the roles and functions of different social systems, such as public health, criminal justice, social services, mental health, and other relevant agencies. In so doing, the seamless system approach expands the organizational boundaries of these participating agencies. For the criminal justice client, this involves treatment and criminal justice agencies functioning as a single agency rather than two separate units. In the traditional service delivery model these two entities would probably try to coordinate fragmented services, typically struggling over which agency ultimately controls decision making about the client. In a systemic or seamless organizational approach, the participating agencies would initially agree on certain guiding principles of care and then determine the appropriate roles and functions for each player in delivering that level of care. From this organizational perspective the emphasis is then on the system itself and its complementary parts rather than on the role of any one agency.

In his discussion of integrated services, Moore (1992) suggests that each agency would participate in key decisions about the client, including placement in appropriate services, modification of treatment plans based on client progress, the transition to other services when deemed appropriate, and eventual discharge from the system. Rather than mere coordination of services and efforts around these issues, there would be an integration and synthesis of both agency policies and operational practices. In the system approach to service delivery the initial focus must be on building the infrastructure needed to support the functions of each agency. In order to accomplish this, policy development must focus on such issues as client assessment, referral, placement, tracking, and monitoring; service planning; transition through services; and eventual discharge. In terms of the criminal justice and treatment system, such boundary-spanning activities, especially as related to the initial development of integrated policies, appear to be an essential next step in the evolution of effective treatment delivery systems.

Boundary spanning and organizational approaches are needed to ensure that offenders receive appropriate treatment and supervision services focused on long-term changes in behavior. The following is a list of the operational practices that are important for developing and implementing a seamless system of care:

Joint assessment and placement: Treatment and criminal justice (jail, probation or parole, and prison) staff should jointly determine the type of offenders eligible for the treatment services. Involvement in jail treatment should be premised on the expected length of stay and willingness to continue treatment in the community.

Information sharing between agencies: Agencies should share criminal history and substance abuse information to ensure that appropriate offenders are placed in treatment. Substance abuse staff can use the information to become better acquainted with their clients, particularly their criminal histories.

Specialized probation and parole agents: Probation and parole staff members are often passive players in relation to treatment programs. They are not active in providing case management, securing treatment slots for the offender after release, or addressing compliance problems. Specialized parole officers would allow the agents to develop discharge plans and establish a behavioral contract before release from jail, but they are usually not available. The behavioral management approach discussed in the next section includes new roles for the officer. The supervision plan must reinforce the understanding that treatment is a critical part of supervision.

Designated community treatment slots: To avoid gaps in services, designated slots are advisable. Often offenders have to be reassessed, and jail or prison records are not provided to community treatment providers. Often the programs are not selected to provide continuity of care between treatment in prison or jail and community programs.

Motivation for change: Recent research has found that treatment approaches focusing on contemplation (e.g., preparing to change one's behavior) or motivation to change behavior are uncommon in treatment programs (Roman & Johnson, 2002). Readiness-to-change curricula are especially useful as the first stage of treatment or for treatment programs of short duration (less than 60 days).

Structured curricula and closed groups: Most correctional programs do not have a curriculum underlying the treatment program. This often leads to inconsistent goals for the treatment sessions. Program phases are useful tools to structure the treatment program along a continuum consistent with the different stages of recovery. Phases are useful in a correctional setting because they can be geared to the expected length of time of the program. Closed groups of clients who progress through treatment together help build a sense of community and peer support.

In addition to changes in various agencies' operational practices, a focus on building and monitoring specific interagency policies would be useful to ensure that these implementation and policy issues are addressed adequately. A coordinated effort is needed between the state treatment agency and correctional agencies to ensure the long-term success of these treatment programs outcomes. A full commitment is needed from state agencies to ensure that the continuum of care is seamless (e.g., treatment behind the walls, treatment in the community, supervision and sanctions, and drug testing), supported by an integrated approach to major policy decision making. This would help to eliminate some of the difficulties that occur during the implementation of continuum-of-care models, such as prisons transferring offenders before they have completed jail-based programs or a lack of involvement by supervision agencies in transitional planning. Although they are labor intensive in the short term, in the long run this type of integrated treatment approach is likely to improve the quality of services delivered, which in turn will improve client retention and outcomes.

THE BEHAVIORAL MANAGEMENT APPROACH

Many supervision agencies recognize that putting behavioral management systems in place entails other organizational changes and enhancements. Change strategies are needed to facilitate behavioral management goals and to develop new resources in the criminal justice system to achieve these goals. And as part of efforts to improve reentry programs and change the nature of supervision, a need exists to ensure that the supervision system addresses behavioral management goals. For example, useful goals are to ensure that offender accountability includes officer responsibility to obtain recommended services, to use assessment tools to define supervision tools, and to ensure that officers and offenders are provided incentives to reduce recidivism.

   An important part of the behavioral management model is to recognize that the key element in offender change is the alliance with the supervision officer. Offenders' attitudes and behavioral outcomes can be influenced by their interactions with supervision officers and treatment providers. Interpersonal communication styles are often dismissed as factors that affect the correctional milieu. Palmer (1995) and Bonta and Gendreau (1990) state that nonprogram elements, such as agent decorum and interaction style with offenders, are critical to positive offender outcomes. Andrews and Kiessling (1980) determined that after receiving intensive training on strategies of interpersonal communication and anticriminal modeling and reinforcement, parole and probation officers were more effective in reducing recidivism than officers who did not use these techniques. In a recent review of audiotaped interviews of officers and offenders, researchers found poor adherence to some of the basic principles of using assessment tools to guide supervision conditions (Bonta, Rugge, Scott, Bourgon, & Yessine, 2008). Officers spent much of the time on enforcement issues such as complying with the conditions of probation; insufficient attention was given to the offender's progress in obtaining services and the offender's attitudes, including antisocial attitudes, and peer and social supports for crime. The officers did not use their face-to-face interactions with offenders to impart prosocial modeling, provide differential reinforcement, or attend to criminal thinking (Bonta et al., 2008). Many correctional agencies are moving toward adopting motivational interviewing as a tool to open communication lines and to assist officers in developing motivation-enhancing strategies in working with offenders (see Taxman et al., 2004; Walters, Clark, Gingerich, & Meltzer, 2007).

The importance of the relationship to outcomes is reported in a recent study by Skeem, Eno Louden, Polaschek, and Camp (2007). They used instruments to measure relationship components for probationers with mental health disorders on three dimensions: caring–fairness, trust (indicative of a behavioral management approach), and toughness–authoritarianism (law enforcement approach) and therapeutic alliance, and they found that treatment alliance was unrelated to offender outcomes. Behavioral management techniques predicted success and law enforcement approaches predicted failure, where every 1-point increase in an officer's toughness score increased the odds of revocation by 94%. Skeem and Manchak (2008, p. 228) comment:

> In surveillance-oriented relationships, officers used control in an indifferent or even belittling manner that often compromised probationers' functioning and engendered reactance to officers' directives. In synthetic relationships, officers used control in the "right way," that is, in a manner perceived as fair, respectful, and motivated by caring. Probationers were allowed to express their opinions, explain themselves, and participate actively in the problem solving process (see Cullen, Eck, & Lowenkamp, 2002; Skeem & Petrila, 2004; Taxman, 2002).

This "right way" is an interpersonal form of procedural justice (see MacCoun, 2005), which leaves individuals feeling less coerced, even if they do not agree with the ultimate decision reached by an authority figure (Lidz et al., 1995).

The working relationship between officers and offenders is often the unstated component of evidence-based corrections. Researchers have recognized that organizational attention must be given to addressing this milieu to facilitate the implementation of sound practices and to achieve gains in offender outcomes. These relationships are important in creating an environment where offenders feel they can trust the officer and to have some desire to comply with the conditions of release. Turning decades of enforcement-style supervision into a working hybrid that can change offender behavior cannot be ignored in this evolution of probation and parole.

Some examples of new approaches are as follows:

- Advancing the use of motivational interviewing and other strategies to help the staff communicate constructively with the offender. Many agencies are training their staff in motivational interviewing techniques and other strategies for the purpose of providing a technique to focus on client-centered approaches that build trust and rapport. Communication becomes the key strategy for the behavioral management approach because parole officers must provide consistent feedback to the offender and community to assist the offender in the change process. For the approach to be effective in shaping behavior, the offender needs to have timely and consistent information about performance under the case plan.

- Using supervision plans that incorporate behavioral contracts, targeted goals to address criminogenic needs, conditions of supervision, and incremental steps to achieve goals. The supervision plan is more than a piece of paper; it is a document that is subject to revision based on the progress of the offender and changing goals of supervision (e.g., engagement, change, sustained progress). The plan also incorporates contingency management agreements, which hold both the offender and the system actors accountable.

- Integrating natural supports as part of the reentry and supervision process. More agencies are developing programs and services that include the community in the supervision process. As part of some of the reentry efforts, community guardians (e.g., civic activists, community volunteers) are being assigned to offenders to assist them in the transition from prison to community; to assist offenders in retention efforts as part of employment, schooling, or treatment services; and to assist offenders in developing a network that does not involve criminal peers or associates.

These efforts are designed to address retention issues and lay the ground-work for building those natural support systems.

- Expanding the service options to accommodate both the offender's inter-ests and a broader array of services that can be used to address crimino-genic needs. Many parole agencies have expanded the range of service providers to include more natural supports in the community such as faith-based organizations, civic associations, educational institutions, employers, or local businesses. Opening the doors of the correctional sys-tem can assist the offender in the change and maintenance process.

- Using place-based strategies to adopt new innovations and affect the com-munity in which the offender resides and in which the parole office is located. Place-based strategies allow the parole office to achieve key bench-marks that affect the whole office, and the integration of community-based services is more likely to occur if the parole office draws on the community to be part of the supervision process. Place-based strategies can have col-lateral impact by improving community well-being, thereby helping super-vision agencies become a more valued component of the community.

- Using performance management systems to provide weekly feedback on progress. The old saying, "What gets measured gets done" is being trans-lated into strategic management sessions where supervision staff are held accountable for the gains in meeting supervision goals. In some offices these meetings are held weekly, in others monthly. But the goal is to use the performance management system to monitor outcomes (e.g., assess-ments and case plans completed, employment retention, treatment ses-sions attended, negative drug test results, rearrests, warrants for violations) and then to build the organization to achieve these outcomes.

POLICY DIRECTIONS TO ADVANCE PAROLE

Improving community supervision should be at the forefront of crime control policy. If community supervision were more effective, states could reduce their new prison intakes by 30% to 40% simply by reducing technical violations on parole. New models suggest that this can best be accomplished through seam-less systems of care in which parolees are provided needed services, and the role of the supervision officer is to facilitate behavioral change. That is, the super-vision officer should be required to be a partner with the offender in the change process, instead of the law enforcement model, which provides oversight to orchestrate change.

The following provides a prescription for moving toward this new generation of supervision that is focused on offender outcomes. It should be noted that this prescription provides the framework to achieve public safety goals within current resource constraints.

- Systems should have validated risk tools that help officers make decisions about the likelihood that an offender will present a public safety risk. Risk tools are critical in helping agencies sort offenders into categories that will determine the appropriate level of service. Low-risk offenders should be placed in more punishment- or reparation-oriented programming. The risk tool should be used to identify medium- to high-risk offenders who need assistance in managing their behaviors to increase public safety. These risk tools are vital to provide systematic decision making and will clarify how different offenders should be handled. They will also preserve the most expensive community-based options for offenders who are more likely to benefit. Studies document the importance of using risk level in determining appropriate placement in services and show that better outcomes can be achieved if offenders are assigned to appropriate levels of services (Lowencamp & Latessa, 2005; Lowencamp et al., 2006).
- Systems need to adopt policy-based contingency management systems to guide decisions about reinforcing positive behaviors and pursuing revocation. Discretionary decisions by parole officers contribute to problems in the supervision system by allowing some offenders with similar behavior to be treated differently from other offenders. This situation does not bode well for compliance to general conditions of supervision (Taxman & Thanner, 2003). Contingency management systems provide for swift and certain rewards (positive reinforcers) to facilitate prosocial behavior. They change the focus of the criminal justice system from acknowledging failures to recognizing gains. As part of the process, negative behaviors can be similarly handled in a swift and certain manner. Policy-based guidelines should include both incentives to shape positive behavior and sanctions for negative behaviors. Modeled after parole guidelines (Burke, 2001), contingency management systems can be delivered that provide a formula for focusing attention on improvements. (For a discussion of contingency management, see Petry et al., 2004; Taxman, Shepardson, & Byrne, 2004). Offenders should not be reincarcerated for failure to comply with violations that are not criminal behaviors, which should reduce reincarceration rates.

- Supervision should not be longer than 18 months for moderate- to high-risk offenders. Any longer period of supervision requires too many resources that are not likely to yield public benefits. Reducing the length of supervision will reduce the workload of supervision staff and focus their efforts on achievable goals. During the tenure of supervision, the goal should be to transfer the control from formal institutions to natural support systems.

- Pharmacological interventions (e.g., medications for drug use, alcohol use, and mental health) should become more common in habilitation efforts for moderate- to high-risk offenders. Advances in medications have made these tools useful in helping people learn to control their behavior and to become more productive citizens. Medications should be perceived not as a crutch but as a mechanism to improve the offender's cognitive capabilities. Some medications also can be used to treat addictions, and along with behavioral therapies, they have been shown to be effective in changing offender behavior.

- Parole staff should be certified in different skills as they advance through the organization. The development of staff should be toward client-centered skills such as interviewing and communication techniques, behavioral contracting, and problem solving. On the social work–law enforcement continuum of goals, these skills do not shift the officer in one direction or another but rather emphasize the tools that have been shown to be most effective in helping the offender move toward changing his or her own behavior.

- Low-risk offenders should be given swift and certain punishments that have reparative principles. For the most part, these offenders should not be under any form of supervision for more than a month. The goal should be to handle these punishments expeditiously and to have the offenders focus their efforts on reparation to communities. The model can replicate the fine experiments in the early 1990s or the community service (e.g., weekend service) concept, which minimizes the period of correctional control but is focused on clear outcomes. This could be part of the strategy of supervision agencies addressing some of the needs of communities or neighborhoods that are highly disadvantaged (e.g., high poverty levels, high degree of instability). Reinvesting in these communities, where many offenders happen to reside, would increase stability in the neighborhoods and contribute to healthier communities.

- Moderate- to high-risk offenders should be placed in supervision that is designed to facilitate offender change. The risk tool should guide the identification of the types of behaviors that contribute to criminal conduct such as violence and power or control issues, substance abuse or dependency, predatory sexual behavior, and detached or dissociated supervision. The core component is a behavioral contract that includes the conditions for release and short-term goals for the offender. The supervision plan should be encompassed in the behavioral contract to allow for one guiding document for the offender and the parole officer. The behavioral contract is a negotiated agreement in which the conditions are designed to ameliorate criminogenic risk and need factors.

As we focus our attention on behavioral management strategies for moderate- to high-risk offenders, the role of the supervision agent in this model shifts significantly. The supervision officer does not merely have enforcement responsibilities but also has responsibilities to instruct and model prosocial behavior. This changes the basic function of the supervision business to goal-directive face-to-face contacts. Goal-directive face-to-face contacts recognize that in each interaction (e.g., interviews, collateral contacts, phone contacts), the purpose of the contact must be clear.

CONCLUSION

Supervision and community corrections are the backbone of the correctional system, with more than 6 million adults under the control of these agencies. Although researchers, scholars, and policymakers focus on the need to change current policies to reduce the use of incarceration, this is not possible until the public has confidence that supervision and community corrections can be effective in protecting them. Prior efforts to improve correctional programs neglected one of the core functions: the role of parole or supervision officer. Research shows that the type of treatment programming is important, as is the type of offender who is placed in these programs, yet many prior efforts have not developed the role of the parole officer in achieving these goals.

This chapter highlights some of the core components that are necessary to move in the direction of a behavioral management approach. Efforts are under way to implement many components of a behavioral management approach in Maryland (the proactive community supervision model); the National Institute of Corrections' evidence-based practice cooperative agreement work in Maine and Illinois; Oklahoma; Virginia; New Jersey's parole system; Maricopa County, Arizona; Multnomah County, Oregon; and other jurisdictions. Findings from evaluation studies are also available on the Maryland proactive community supervision model, which demonstrates reductions in rearrests and requests for violation of parole or probation warrants.

Tools of the Trade: A Guide to Incorporating Science Into Practice (Taxman et al., 2004) describes the core components and can guide practitioners in the development of their own behavioral management approach. In her foreword to the manual, Judith Sachwald, director of Maryland's Division of Parole and Probation, reiterates that movement into this third generation of supervision programming requires a commitment of the organization. Her model consists of preparing the organization, clarifying the vision, establishing key benchmarks and meeting these benchmarks, building community supports, and implementing core components of the model in an incremental process (organizational change similar to individual change). Sachwald writes, "Without ongoing thoughtful professional development, supervision based on science and offender outcomes will become a fad and quickly extinguish the recent spark of interest in community supervision" (Taxman et al., 2004, p. viii).

The time has come for community supervision to step up and become the most critical component of the correctional and criminal justice system. Changing the role of the supervision officer and benefiting from the core function of contacts cannot be done without a commitment to a revised policy, vision, and program components. Supervision agencies must also make a commitment to use the key tools of the trade: communication, assessment tools, supervision plans, contingency management systems, effective treatment and service programs, and policies that focus efforts on moderate- to high-risk offenders and disadvantaged communities. This is where the most gains will occur, and this is how public safety goals will be achieved.

DISCUSSION QUESTIONS

1. Under a behavioral management approach, what are the main ways in which parole supervision differs from a control model?

2. Explain how an interagency approach can help offenders get into treatment services.

3. Describe how compliance management can help offenders stay in treatment.

SUGGESTED READING

Petersilia, J. (2003). *When prisoners come home: Parole and prisoner reentry*. New York: Oxford University Press.

REFERENCES

Andrews, D., & Bonta, J. (1998). *The psychology of criminal conduct* (2nd ed.). Cincinnati, OH: Anderson.

Andrews, D. A., & Kiessling, J. J. (1980). Program structure and effective correctional practices: A summary of the CaVIC research. In R. R. Ross & P. Gendreau (Eds.), *Effective correctional treatment* (pp. 441–463). Toronto: Butterworths.

Anglin, D. A., & Hser, Y. I. (1990). Treatment of drug abuse. In M. Tonry & J. Q. Wilson (Eds.), *Drugs and crime* (pp. 389–460). Thousand Oaks, CA: Sage.

Ashkenas, R., Ulrich, D., Jick, T., & Kerr, S. (1995). *The boundaryless organizations: Breaking the chains of organizational structure.* San Francisco: Jossey-Bass.

Bonta, J., & Gendreau, P. (1990). Reexamining the cruel and unusual punishment of prison life. *Law and Human Behavior, 14,* 347–366.

Bonta, J., Rugge, T., Scott, T., Bourgon, G., & Yessine, A. K. (2008). Exploring the black box of community supervision. *Journal of Offender Rehabilitation, 47,* 248–270.

Burke, P. (2001). *Responding to parole and probation violations: A guide to local policy development.* Washington, DC: National Institute of Corrections. Retrieved February 1, 2009, from http://www.nicic.org/Library/016858

Cullen, F. T., Eck, J. E.,& Lowenkamp, C. (2002). Environmental corrections: A new paradigm of effective probation and parole supervision. *Federal Probation, 66,* 28–37.

Farabee, D., Prendergast, M., Cartier, J., Wexler, H., Knight, K., & Anglin, M. D. (1999). Barriers to implementing effective correctional drug treatment programs. *Prison Journal, 79*(2), 150–163.

Fuller, K. (2002). *Adult and Juvenile Probation and Parole Firearm Survey.* Lexington, KY: American Probation and Parole Association.

Hammer, S. (1996). *Beyond reengineering: The process-centered organization is changing our work and our livings.* San Francisco: Jossey-Bass.

Hubbard, R. L., Marsden, M. E., Rachal, J. V., Harwood, H. J., Cavanaugh, E. R., & Ginzburg, H. M. (1989). *Drug abuse treatment: A national study of effectiveness.* Chapel Hill: University of North Carolina Press.

Lidz, C., Hoge, S., Gardner, W., Bennett, N., Monahan, J., Mulvey, E., et al. (1995). Perceived coercion in mental hospital admission: Pressures and process. *Archives of General Psychiatry, 52,* 1034–1039.

Lowenkamp, C. T., & Latessa, E. J. (2005). Increasing the effectiveness of correctional programming through the risk principle: Identifying offenders for residential placement. *Criminology and Public Policy, 4*(2), 291–310.

Lowenkamp, C. T., Latessa, E., & Hoslinger, A. (2006). Risk principle in action: What have we learned from 13,676 offenders and 97 correctional programs? *Crime and Delinquency, 52,* 77–93.

MacCoun, R. (2005). Voice, control, and belonging: The double-edged sword of procedural fairness. *Annual Review of Law and Social Science, 1,* 171–201.

MacKenzie, D. L. (2000). Evidence-based corrections: Identifying what works. *Crime and Delinquency, 46*(4), 457–461.

McLellan, T. (2003, September 15). *Myths about and the future of addiction treatment.* Washington, DC: National Association of Alcohol and Drug Directors.

Moore, S. T. (1992). Case management and the integration of services: How service delivery systems shape case management. *Social Work, 37,* 418–423.

Palmer, T. (1995). Programmatic and non-programmatic aspects of successful intervention: New directions for research. *Crime & Delinquency, 41,* 100–131.

Petersilia, J. (1999). A decade with experimenting with intermediate sanctions: What have we learned? *Perspectives, 23*(1), 39–44.

Petry, N. M., Tedford, J., Austin, M., Nich, C., Carroll, K. M., & Rounsaville, B. J. (2004). Prize reinforcement contingency management for treating cocaine users: How low can we go, and with whom? *Addiction, 99*(3), 349–360.

Roman, P. M., & Johnson, J. A. (2002). Adoption and implementation of new technologies in substance abuse treatment. *Journal of Substance Abuse Treatment, 22,* 211–218.

Skeem, J., Eno Louden, J., Polaschek, D., & Camp, J. (2007). Assessing relationship quality in mandated community treatment: Blending care with control. *Psychological Assessment, 19,* 397–410.

Skeem, J., & Manchak, S. (2008). Back to the future: From Klockars' model of effective supervision to evidence-based practice in probation. *Journal of Offender Rehabilitation, 47,* 220–247.

Skeem, J., & Petrila, J. (2004). Problem-solving supervision: Specialty probation for individuals with mental illness. *Court Review, 40,* 8–15.

Skogan, W., & Frydl, K. (2004). *Fairness and effectiveness in policing: The evidence.* Washington, DC: National Research Council.

Solomon, A., Kachnowski, V., & Bhati, A. (2005). *Does parole work? Analyzing the impact of post-prison supervision on rearrest outcomes.* Washington, DC: Urban Institute. Retrieved February 1, 2009, from http://www.urban.org/url.cfm?ID=311156

Taxman, F. S. (1999). Unraveling "What Works" for offenders in substance abuse treatment services. *National Drug Court Institute Review, 2,* 93–134.

Taxman, F. (2002). Supervision: Exploring the dimensions of effectiveness. *Federal Probation, 66*(2), 14–27.

Taxman, F. S. (2008). To be or not to be: Community supervision deja vu. *Journal of Offender Rehabilitation, 47,* 209–219.

Taxman, F. S., & Marlowe, D. (2006). Risk, needs, responsivity: In action or inaction? *Crime & Delinquency, 52,* 3–6.

Taxman, F. S., Shepardson, E. S., & Byrne, J. M. (2004). *Tools of the trade: A guide to incorporating science into practice.* Washington, DC: U.S. Department of Justice, National Institute of Corrections. Retrieved February 1, 2009, from http://www.nicic.org/Library/020095

Taxman, F. S., & Thanner, M. (2003). Probation from a therapeutic perspective: Results from the field. *Contemporary Issues in Law, 7*(1), 39–63.

Thanner, M., & Taxman, F. (2003). Responsivity: The value of providing intensive services to high-risk offenders. *Journal of Substance Abuse Treatment, 24,* 137–147.

Tyler, T. (2004). Enhancing police legitimacy. *The Annals of the American Academy of Political and Social Science, 593,* 84–99.

Walters, S. T., Clark, M. D., Gingerich, R., & Meltzer, M. L. (2007). *Motivating offenders to change: A guide for probation and parole.* Washington, DC: National Institute of Corrections.

CHAPTER 13

Employment Barriers to Reintegration

Mindy S. Tarlow

Most of us know what it's like to look for a job when you don't have one. But imagine doing that after being physically disconnected from your community, perhaps for years, with little education or work experience and with a felony conviction that you now have to explain to an employer. All this and more confronts formerly incarcerated people when they come home from prison and need a job.

Securing a job during the fragile period after release from prison (known in the criminal justice and workforce development arenas as employment reentry) is crucial, not just for these job-seekers but for their children, families, and communities. It also touches on some of the most pressing economic and public policy issues facing us as a country. A successful employment reentry strategy can improve public safety, help governments reduce correctional spending during tough economic times, and reduce poverty and joblessness for an exceptionally hard-to-employ population. Employment reentry can also promote family stability and a healthier future for millions of children in the United States who have parents in the criminal justice system.

There is a growing consensus that the issue needs more attention, most notably for young men of color (Pager, 2007; Uggen, Manza, & Thompson, 2006). This chapter first puts employment reentry into a broad public policy context, then examines the issue in depth with an emphasis on barriers to success, and finally highlights proven and promising practices, with a focus on what works, when, and for whom.

> ## What Formerly Incarcerated People Say About Finding Work
>
> *"I went to a few jobs, filled out a few applications.... They didn't call me back. Nothing.... My mother and my PO told me to stay away from the street and to stay working."*
>
> *"That's my biggest fear: not getting hired.... Sometimes I feel discouraged.... How am I supposed to advance myself?"*
>
> *"They always look at the blemish on my record. Always! I don't understand why if I have one felony, and it isn't even like I sold drugs or robbed. Why I am having such a hard time getting a job?"*
>
> *"I did a ten year bid. I actually did two five year bids. I'm only allowed one visit every two weeks to see my children. My daughter and I were close when I got out the first time, but she was upset after I got rearrested.... [Now]... I'm working for my kids."*

PUTTING EMPLOYMENT REENTRY IN CONTEXT

Overview

Practical experience and empirical research (Bloom, 2008; Mukamal, 2000; Solomon, 2004; Western & Jacobs, 2006) teach us that work and crime interconnect in complex ways, but there are things we know for sure: People leaving prison want to work (Bryan, Haldipur, & Williams, 2008). People leaving prison face significant barriers to work (Independent Committee on Reentry and Employment, 2006; Pager, 2007). Most important, people with jobs commit fewer crimes than people without jobs, and the sooner formerly incarcerated people start working, the better (Bloom, 2007; Solomon, Johnson, Travis, & McBride, 2004).

The issue can also be linked to national policy concerns, including a shrinking economy; joblessness and poverty; the welfare of young adults, children, and families; and of course public safety. Each of these is presented below and detailed in the sections that follow.

Employment Reentry and Public Safety: High unemployment rates, before incarceration and before violation of conditions of probation and parole, strongly suggest that unemployment contributes heavily to the cycle of incarceration experienced by so many involved in the criminal justice system. This phenomenon hurts not only former inmates but also their families and the communities to which they belong, creating neighborhood-wide crises in large urban centers such as New York City, areas where 30% of the adult male population may be incarcerated at any given time (Clear, Rose, & Ryder, 2001; Travis, 2005). Not surprisingly, these are the neighborhoods where unemployment rates are the highest. Finding employment can play a crucial role in breaking this cycle and reducing recidivism, creating more stable individuals and communities.

Employment Reentry, Joblessness, and Poverty. National workforce development strategy aims to help hard-to-employ people who are jobless and living in poverty. According to Harlow (as cited in Solomon, 2004), there is widespread unemployment among African American men, many of whom have criminal convictions, and among young people with limited education. Here employment reentry can play a vital role: More than 90% of prison inmates are male, 63% are Black or Hispanic, more than half are between the ages of 18 and 34, and approximately 40% have no GED or high school diploma according to Harlow (as cited in Solomon, 2004). Finally, there is an increasingly limited number of low- and middle-skill jobs that are open to people with criminal records, and employers are reluctant to hire people with convictions (Maxwell, 2006; Pager & Quillian, 2005).

Employment Reentry, Children, and Families: Focusing on Fathers. In some significant ways, welfare-to-work policies and programs are evolving into prison-to-work policies and programs (Travis, 2007). National policy efforts to improve the lives of children and reduce reliance on government funding started by focusing on helping mothers on welfare enter the labor market. Today, those efforts are focusing on helping formerly incarcerated fathers do the same (Husock, 2008). Seven million children in America currently have a father involved in the criminal justice system (in prison or jail, on parole, or on probation) (Mumola, 2006); meeting these fathers' employment needs also improves the well-being of their children.

Employment Reentry and Economic Policy. All states grapple with the rising costs of imprisonment. Employment can demonstrably reduce returns to prison, employment programs cost less per person than prison, and people with jobs add to the economic base. Investing in employment reentry programs can save tax dollars and benefit the economy.

Detailed Review

Employment Reentry and Public Safety: What the Research Tells Us

What do we know about the relationship between work and the cycle of crime? This much, at least: The absence of employment is a consistent factor in recidivism and parole or probation violations, and having a criminal history limits employment opportunities and depresses wages (Holzer, 1996). In New York State, labor statistics show that 89% of formerly incarcerated people who violate the terms of their probation or parole are unemployed at the time of violation (Mukamal, 2000). Further research suggests that 1 year after release, up to 60% of former inmates are not employed (Nightingale & Watts, 1996). Nationally, according to a study by Bushway and Reuter (as cited in Solomon, 2004), one in three incarcerated people reported being unemployed before entering state prison, and fewer than half had a job lined up before release.

A disproportionate share of inmates have health, mental health, and substance abuse problems that greatly complicate their chances of employment. Approximately 21% of prisoners report having some condition that limits their ability to work, compared with 11% of all people who report such a condition nationwide (Freeman, 2003). Employment rates among young men who had previously been incarcerated are estimated to be approximately 20 to 25 percentage points lower than those of their non–criminal justice involved counterparts (Freeman, 1992). After they enter the job market, former prisoners often earn less than other workers with comparable demographics (Western, 2002). Time spent in prison severs ties to employers, making it more difficult to make connections to work upon release (Solomon, 2004). Time in prison may strengthen ties to antisocial peer groups and thereby limit awareness of or access to legitimate work opportunities (Solomon, 2004).

Although a number of compelling findings support the claim that employment reduces recidivism, Petersilia (2004), one of the foremost experts in the field, cautions that some evaluations are not as rigorous as others. Some evaluations are limited by their focus on recidivism as the only outcome criterion (Petersilia, 2004) or are biased by selectivity (Uggen, 2000). Without a broader focus on other impacts such as employment (as measured by whether people are working, whether the work is full or part time, and whether income derived is supporting families), research may not be as relevant to practice as it could be (Petersilia, 2004).

Since Petersilia's review from 2004, more evidence has been collected, adding insight to what works in employment reentry. In particular, two independent studies of employment reentry programs highlighted later in this chapter— the Center for Employment Opportunities (CEO) and Community and Law

Enforcement Resources Together (ComALERT)—offer reputable research methods and show that employment significantly reduces recidivism. The CEO study uses a random assignment method, considered to be the most rigorous study design (Bloom, 2007, 2008); the ComALERT study uses a carefully matched comparison group (Western & Jacobs, 2006). Findings from both studies show statistically significant reductions in recidivism rates, including significantly lower rates of return to prison for a new crime (Bloom, 2007, 2008; Western & Jacobs, 2006).

A qualitative research study conducted by the CEO Learning Institute, the research and evaluation arm of CEO, relies on in-depth qualitative interviews and focus groups and quantitative analyses of program data to illustrate some of the most pressing challenges facing formerly incarcerated people as they try to remain employed (Bryan, Haldipur, & Williams, 2008). The study, using first-hand accounts of the reentry experience, finds common ground with the existing quantitative literature (Bloom, 2007, 2008; Holzer, 1996; Pager, Western, & Bonikowski, 2006; Western & Jacobs, 2006) and concludes that people coming home from prison want to work and support their families but face significant personal and structural barriers as they attempt a successful transition from prison to the workplace. Bryan, Haldipur, and Williams (2008) observe that "formerly incarcerated people want to work. They want to make a better life for their children and families. However, they lack the networks, skills, experience, and ultimately opportunities to do so—in part due to race, in part due to class, and in part due to their criminal conviction" (Bryan et al., 2008, p. 17). Researchers have studied the attitudes of employers toward people with criminal records (Holzer, 1996; Pager et al., 2006). Bryan et al.'s interviews complement these findings by revealing the attitude of the job seeker with a criminal record, noting that "one of the most difficult and often overlooked struggles formerly incarcerated people face is coming to terms with what they did in their past and understanding how much their conviction could affect their ability to get a job and earn a decent living" and pointing out that "nearly all of the participants who engaged in the study expressed a great deal of anxiety over how they would discuss their criminal background on a job interview, and who would hire them" (Bryan et al., 2008, p. 9). Finally, as Bloom and others note, Bryan et al.'s interviews support the importance of the nonprofit community's role in bridging gaps and developing employment opportunities to help formerly incarcerated people connect to the labor market.

Beyond adding to what we know about crime and work, Bryan et al.'s study presents a particularly interesting viewpoint from a director of research in a direct service organization that runs an employment reentry program. Bryan (personal communication, October 15, 2008) believes that in the United States, there has not been much work on how staff demeanors and staff interactions affect outcomes in workforce development and reentry programs. Bryan believes that without the first-hand experience and insider perspective that come from being a practitioner, it is difficult for outside evaluators to determine how personal styles, predispositions, and approaches of staff members affect service delivery and program models over time.

Employment Reentry, Joblessness, and Poverty

In 2006, Mayor Michael R. Bloomberg appointed a Commission for Economic Opportunity to address poverty in New York City. The Commission's report puts poverty into a historical context, noting that New York City and other large urban centers tend to have poverty rates above the national average but that New York and other cities' poverty levels are affected by the same macroeconomic factors that have contributed to poverty throughout the country (New York City Commission for Economic Opportunity, 2006).

The following is an example of how joblessness and poverty intersect with employment reentry. Using New York City as an example, it provides a clear picture as to how these issues are interrelated.

The Community Service Society (CSS), a nonprofit organization that engages in advocacy, research, and direct service to improve conditions among low-income New Yorkers, produces an annual report focusing on employment and job-holding rates of New Yorkers. The CSS reports use two specific measurements: the commonly used unemployment rate and another, arguably more accurate measurement, the employment–population ratio. There is an important distinction between the two. The unemployment rate captures only people who are jobless, seeking work, and unable to find it; the employment–population ratio includes those looking for work and those not looking. It provides a more accurate picture of who is jobless. In other words, the employment–population ratio directly measures the share of the working-age population that is actually holding a job (Levitan, 2005).

In early 2004, CSS made headlines with an annual report titled *A Crisis of Black Male Employment* (Levitan, 2004a). The report revealed a "crisis of joblessness facing the City's Black men, barely half of whom were employed in 2003" (p. 1), and found that "African American men have lost ground relative to other groups in the city" (p. 1). The *New York Times* reported that "it is well known that the unemployment rate in New York City rose sharply during the recent recession. It is also understood that the increase was worse for men than for women, and especially bad for black men. But a new study examining trends in joblessness in the city since 2000 suggests that by 2003, nearly one of every two black men between 16 and 64 was not working" (Scott, 2004, p. B1).

When the economy slows down, Blacks are more susceptible to job loss and have a greater difficulty finding employment (Figure 13.1) (Rogers, 2008). In 2003, the unemployment rate for New York City was 8.3%, the highest rate since 1997 (New York State Department of Labor, 2008). Examining gender and racial groups, about one half (51.8%) of New York's Black men were employed in 2003; by comparison, 57.1% of the city's Black women and 75.7% of New York's White men were working in that year (Levitan, 2005). This is further indicated by the Black unemployment rate jump, by 5.3 percentage points to 12.9%, in 2003. The unemployment rate for Whites, by contrast, rose 2.6 percentage points to 6.2%. The result of these changes was a widening of the Black–White disparity from 3.9 percentage points in 2000 to 6.7 percentage points in 2003. The employment–population ratio for Black men was the lowest for all periods ever studied by CSS, dating back to 1979.

Over the next 3 years, as the economy began a recovery, Black men started to fare better, but not nearly well enough to erase the damage of years of negative employment–population ratio trends. In 2004, a study looking at race,

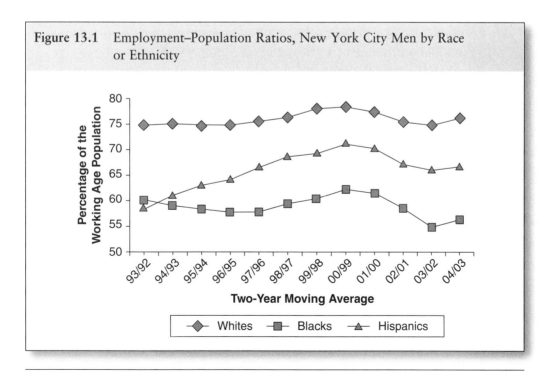

Figure 13.1 Employment–Population Ratios, New York City Men by Race or Ethnicity

Source: Levitan (2004b).

criminal history, and the New York City job market found Black job seekers were less likely to be hired for positions than Latinos or Whites, especially if they had a criminal conviction (Pager & Western, 2005). In addition to low job availability, low educational attainment and low skills further decrease job-holding prospects for this population (Maxwell, 2006).

Age and Education. To further investigate the relationship between employment, age, and education, it is helpful to compare changes in employment rates and ratios in two different years. In 2000, the unemployment rate in New York City was 5.8%; in 2006 the rate was 5% (New York State Department of Labor, 2008). In a report, the CSS compares 2000 to 2006 and notes that the employment–population ratio for young people, Black and Hispanic men, and less educated men declined during the period. While there was a decrease in overall unemployment in the city, there was a tremendous drop in the job-holding rate among young people ages 16–24 (from 44.1% in 2000 to 34.6% in 2006), largely attributable to a 7.9 percentage point drop in the employment–population ratio among young people disconnected from school (Levitan, 2007). Since 2006, teen unemployment rates have continued a steady decline, nationally, at a rate of more than 3% per year (Sum, McLaughlin, Khatiwada, & Palma, 2008). Unemployment rates for people with less than a high school diploma were 6.5%, compared with the citywide unemployment rate of 4.9% in 2006 (Levitan, 2007).

Most people in prison are male, Black or Hispanic, young, and undereducated; if we take into account the drops in employment suffered by these groups, a bigger picture takes shape.

Industries. The CSS points out that industries traditionally dominated by men, such as manufacturing, finance, and professional services, are particularly sensitive to economic cycles (Levitan, 2004). All these sectors suffered large declines in employment from 2000 to 2003 (Levitan, 2007). According to the New York State Department of Labor, manufacturing, construction, trade, and utilities—all traditionally male jobs—continued to experience some of the highest rates of job loss in later years (New York State Department of Labor, 2008). Nationally, the construction and manufacturing trades experienced steady declines in employment that remain today (U.S. Department of Labor, 2009).

Table 13.1 shows which industries were significant providers of employment to Black men in 2000, before the declines that occurred between 2000 and 2003. The table highlights the important role of the public sector, which provided a job to nearly one out of five Black men in 2000. Government, along with the next top four private sector industries, employed 60.4% of Black men in 2000 (Levitan, 2007). For the purposes of this chapter, it is vital to consider how these industries relate to those that have occupational or licensure restrictions on hiring people with criminal convictions. For example, in New York State, according to the Legal Action Center in New York City, more than 100 occupations require a license, registration, or certification; many of these have restrictions that prevent formerly incarcerated people from obtaining the licenses (Independent Committee on Reentry and Employment, 2006). An

Table 13.1 Industries Hiring Black Men in 2000		
Industrial Sector	**Percentage of Black Male Employment**	**Jobs Legally Closed to People with Felony Convictions**
Government	19	Firearm carrier, firefighter, police officer, private investigator, jobs requiring security clearance
Construction	11	None
Transportation and utilities	10.6	Bus driver, taxi driver (specific offenses), Transportation Security Administration security clearance restrictions (airport, railroads)
Wholesale and retail trade	10	None
Professional and business services	9.9	Real estate broker, insurance broker
Education and health services	9.8	Providing health care services paid through Medicare, childcare providers
Leisure and hospitality	9.2	None
Manufacturing	6.7	None
Financial activities	6.6	Blanket ban per Federal Deposit Insurance Corporation regulations
Other services	4.7	None
Information	2.6	None

Source: Levitan (2004a).

analysis of the industries that hire Black men and those that restrict hiring of those with criminal convictions taken together reveals that the industrial sectors most open to hiring Black men are among those most closed to hiring people with criminal convictions. In fact, 55.9% of the industries that employed Black men in 2000 have some legal barriers to employment for people with felony convictions (Independent Committee on Reentry and Employment, 2006; Levitan, 2007). Of the top five industries that employed Black men, almost two thirds have restrictions on hiring people with felony convictions (Independent Committee on Reentry and Employment, 2006). Although there are ways around such restrictions, such as by obtaining a Certificate of Relief from Disability, occupational and licensure bans are among the more intractable barriers to employment for people with convictions. Again, this illustrates the additional struggles and barriers faced by Black men involved in the criminal justice system on top of an already difficult employment environment.

In sum, the economic, racial, education, age, and gender job-holding trends captured in the CSS reports indicate a growing employment gap for formerly incarcerated people. Most people in prison have traits in common with those deemed to be most disadvantaged by current job-holding trends, and they face barriers imposed by criminal convictions. It can be expected that this problem will continue to grow without a concerted effort to reverse it.

Employment Reentry, Children, and Families: Focus on Fathers

Of the more than 6.6 million people in the United States under criminal justice supervision, more than 2.8 million are fathers (Mumola, 2006). Since 1991, the number of parents incarcerated in state or federal prisons has increased by 79% (Mason & Williams-Mbengue, 2008). This accounts for 7 million children who have a parent involved in the criminal justice system (Mumola, 2006). Children of incarcerated parents face many obstacles, including financial hardship and social and academic struggles (Mason & Williams-Mbengue, 2008). Possibly the most sobering statistic is that children of incarcerated parents are six times more likely than other youth to end up in prison at some point in their lives (Mumola, 2006). Helping parents returning home from prison reconnect with their children and support their families will help not only this generation of young people but generations to come.

In significant ways, the focus on employment reentry and efforts to help fathers with criminal convictions can be traced directly to the welfare reform efforts of the mid-1990s. The overwhelming numbers of children with a father involved in the criminal justice system, and the effect this has on multiple generations of young people, have led scholars and policymakers from a wide range of viewpoints to realize the relationship between welfare reform, prisoner reentry, and responsible parenthood. Howard Husock (2008), vice president of policy research at the Manhattan Institute, notes, "The welfare reform of the '90s was the most important social-policy change in the United States in recent decades. But it was, in a key way, narrow: It focused on women—that is, on getting welfare mothers into the workforce. But now a successor to 'welfare-to-work' is emerging—a reform mainly for men. Call it prison-to-work."

New York City's CEO (2006), appointed by Mayor Michael Bloomberg in 2006, noted in their report to the mayor, "Since welfare reform was mainly targeted to help single mothers with children find employment, there has been a gap in programs that target men in the same way" (p. 7). Similarly, Harry Holzer and Paul Offner (2002) of Georgetown University's Public Policy Institute emphasize that there are 1.9 million men behind bars, and 70% of Black children are growing up with a single parent. They further emphasize that the next big challenge for welfare reform is to try to reach these men.

The Economic Success Clearinghouse/WIN (formerly Welfare Information Network), a resource that helps low-income and working poor families, notes that states and localities have a vested interest in ensuring children's well-being, so they may want to consider helping parents with criminal records get the necessary resources to support their families (Haberkern, 2003).

Prisoner reentry has much to learn from welfare-to-work, and the welfare population has characteristics similar to the formerly incarcerated population that make them hard to employ: low educational attainment, sporadic work histories, and mental health and medical problems (Solomon, 2004). There is a similar debate about work policies and the need to balance a quick connection to the labor market (a work-first approach) with adequate training and preparation to enter the workforce (Solomon, 2004).

On the legislative side, the Personal Responsibility and Work Opportunity Reconciliation Act, or "Welfare Reform Act," of 1996 has served as a guide to current legislative approaches and policies surrounding prison-to-work efforts. Of particular relevance is the Second Chance Act (HR 1593, S1060), which became public law on April 9, 2008.

The purposes of the Second Chance Act are

to assist [people] reentering the community from incarceration to establish a self-sustaining and law-abiding life by providing sufficient transitional services for as short a period as practicable, not to exceed one year, unless a longer period is specifically determined to be necessary by a medical or other appropriate treatment professional; and to provide offenders in prisons, jails or juvenile facilities with educational, literacy, vocational, and job placement services to facilitate re-entry into the community. (U.S. Congress, 2007)

Specific provisions for employment reentry in the Second Chance Act include mentoring in the community and the workplace to address the challenges faced by formerly incarcerated people. The Second Chance Act also calls for providing job training and job placement services, including work readiness activities, job referrals, basic skill remediation, educational services, occupational skill training, on-the-job training, work experience, and post-placement support. The act will also provide outreach, orientation, intake, assessments, counseling, case management, and other transitional services, including prerelease outreach and orientation after release from incarceration (National Transitional Jobs Network, http://www.transitionaljobs.net).

The act was strongly supported by the public before it was supported by legislation. According to a survey of people in the New York City and Tri-State Region, approximately 80% of respondents supported the Second Chance Act (see chapter 2). The work activities of the Second Chance Act bear a remarkable resemblance to the Welfare Reform Act, as illustrated in Table 13.2.

Table 13.2   Comparison of the Second Chance Act With the Welfare Reform Act

Welfare Reform or Temporary Assistance for Needy Families	Second Chance Act
Unsubsidized or subsidized employment	Transitional job services
On-the-job training	On-the-job training
Work experience	Work experience
Community service	Mentoring programs
Job search, not to exceed 6 total weeks and no more than 4 consecutive weeks	Workforce development services
Vocational training, not to exceed 12 months	Occupational skill training
Job skill training related to work	Job training
Satisfactory secondary school attendance	Educational services
Providing childcare services to people who are participating in community service	Other reentry services

Sources: Nelson and Turetsky (2008); U.S. Department of Health and Human Services (2009).

A final important connection between welfare reform and prison reform is the issue of child support and the impact it has on fathers returning from prison and the children who rely on them financially. The Welfare Reform Act highlights the large number of children on welfare (1965, 3.3 million; 1992, 9.3 million) and recognizes the intergenerational poverty resulting from welfare and single-parent households in poverty. Among its key findings were the benefits of marriage and responsible fatherhood. In addition to the stringent work requirements for welfare recipients that resulted from the act, there was also a distinct toughening of child support laws (Zuckerman, 2000).

This act has had a profound impact on incarcerated and formerly incarcerated fathers. According to Holzer and Offner (2002), many fathers accumulate large child support arrears while in prison and are obligated to begin making payments the moment they get out, regardless of their employment status. And because the child support collections are not always passed through to low-income families who have been on public assistance, the incentives for the fathers to work in the formal economy and make these payments are very low if they can escape detection by the child support enforcement system (Holzer & Offner, 2002).

The child support enforcement system can act as a deterrent to entering the legitimate labor market, thereby taking away an opportunity for formerly incarcerated fathers to begin to support their dependent children financially and create a gateway to supporting them emotionally.

Employment Reentry and Fiscal Policy. Public safety is among the most visceral topics in politics. Most people in positions of power are reluctant to seem soft on crime or make decisions that reduce public safety spending, for fear that they will be blamed on future election days if something goes wrong (Campbell, 2003). So there was a boom in corrections spending throughout the country in the 1980s and 1990s as government and the public stood behind "tough-on-crime" policies. However, as corrections spending grew, other important public needs went unmet. In fact, between 1985 and 2000 the increase in state spending on corrections was nearly twice the increase in spending on higher education ($20 billion vs. $10.7 billion), and the total increase in spending on higher education by states was 24%, compared with 166% for corrections (Justice Policy Institute, 2002).

As economic times get bleaker, there is a growing public awareness that the budget is a zero-sum game, meaning that spending more in one place means spending less in another. Recent public opinion polls have shown increasing support for alternatives to prison, particularly in job training and employment. Among top priorities for dealing with prisoners after they break the law, 66% cited requiring education and job training, compared with 28% who cited longer prison sentences (Robert D. Hart Research Associates, 2002). Of those surveyed, 82% said job training is a very important barrier to successful reintegration into society after incarceration (Krisberg & Marchionna, 2006). When asked whether access to the following services is very important, somewhat important, or not important to a person's successful reintegration into society after incarceration, job training came out on top for respondents, followed by drug treatment, mental health services, family support, mentoring, and housing (Krisberg & Marchionna, 2006).

Budget crises can spur governments to take risks and implement policies they may otherwise have shied away from. Emboldened by public opinion and pushed by economic realities, officials talk less about being "tough" on crime and more about being "smart" on crime. Here employment reentry programs can emerge as socially and fiscally responsible alternatives to prison spending (Box 13.1).

Box 13.1   New York City's Center for Employment Opportunities

Independent evaluation shows that CEO's employment reentry program keeps 200 people from returning to state prison each year.

This saves the state of New York more than $12 million annually.

CEO costs the state $2.3 million annually, for a net savings to the state of $9.7 million each year.

Put another way, prison is more than five times as expensive as CEO.

BARRIERS TO IMPROVING EMPLOYMENT REENTRY OUTCOMES

Employment reentry is a significant policy issue that, if addressed, could have far-reaching implications for people with criminal convictions, their families, and the communities in which they live. So what is stopping us from tackling this issue on a broad scale? Part of the answer lies in the significant barriers public policymakers and practitioners face in their efforts to move formerly incarcerated people into the workforce. These barriers can be looked at from the supply side (i.e., addressing the limitations of the formerly incarcerated job seeker) and the demand side (i.e., meeting the needs of the employer). This chapter has looked at many of the supply-side barriers of most people with criminal convictions: limited employment skills and work experience, low educational attainment, high levels of health and substance abuse problems, and child support and other family obligations. On the demand side, there is widespread reluctance among employers to hire people with criminal records. This is the result of a severe lack of education in the employer community about the laws surrounding hiring people with criminal convictions, employer discrimination, and occupational and licensure bans in certain industries.

In a recent survey in the New York City area, 441 people were asked employment-specific questions to indicate attitudes and beliefs about employment for formerly incarcerated people. In response to the statement, "Convicted offenders should not have the opportunity to compete with non-convicted members of the community over jobs," 31.1% said they would somewhat agree, agree, or strongly agree. Approximately 48% of respondents disagreed. In a second question, participants were given the statement, "If I am an employer I would not mind hiring a released offender"; 34.1% somewhat agreed with this statement, and another 20.2% agreed with it, suggesting people do not automatically object to hiring the formerly incarcerated (see chapter 2). However, it is important to note that although some state they are willing to hire a person with a criminal conviction, it does not always happen (Pager & Western, 2005).

With respect to the statement, "Released offenders should receive assistance in finding employment from governmental agencies for the first few months after their release," 60.6% of respondents reported they will support employment assistance by the government to released offenders, reinforcing the notion that the Second Chance Act was called for by the public before it was drafted as legislation.

Employer Discrimination

Formerly incarcerated people, especially men of color, face widespread discrimination in the workplace because of their past convictions. Background checks have become a normal, established part of the hiring process; this is especially true for low-skilled jobs (Western, 2008). Various studies and focus groups have revealed a clear bias among employers against hiring people with criminal convictions. Some employers believe a person with a criminal history is less trustworthy, is more likely to cause trouble at the job, has a lower work ethic, and will be less productive than someone without a criminal conviction (Freeman, 2008). A study asked employers in four major cities whether they would accept an applicant with a criminal record. Just 12.5% of employers said that they would definitely accept such an application, and 25.9% said that they probably would. By contrast, employers had no problem accepting applications from workers in disadvantaged groups (Holzer, Raphael, & Stoll, 2003). Employer reluctance to hire those with criminal records might even cause them to engage broadly in "statistical discrimination against less-educated black males" (Holzer, 2007, p. 2).

The New York City Hiring Discrimination Study, conducted by Pager et al. (2006), revealed that Black ex-prisoners seeking employment in New York City were only one third as likely to receive a positive response to their inquiries as their White counterparts. A focus group of employers conducted by Global Strategy Group for the Independent Committee on Reentry and Employment in New York State found that "employers express serious reservations about hiring individuals with a criminal record, especially when it comes to notions of personal safety and professional liability" (Independent Committee on Reentry and Employment, 2006, p. 28).

Failure to Educate Employers

The Global Strategy Group focus sessions confirm what many in the employment reentry field have long known. Employers are unfamiliar with, or do not understand, the laws in their states that govern employment discrimination and negligent hiring standards. Furthermore, there is a lack of awareness of employment intermediaries that serve people with criminal records, the services they provide, and the tax and other hiring incentives they can offer. This lack of knowledge is one of the biggest barriers to employment for people with criminal convictions, strongly suggesting the need for a communication and information sharing strategy to educate employers (Independent Committee on Reentry and Employment, 2006).

Occupational and Licensure Bans

Many workers, including daycare workers, nurses, and even manicurists, need a professional license issued by the state. Employment opportunities are also limited by occupational and licensure bans for people with convictions, as seen earlier in our discussion of joblessness among Black men. Some of these bans are federally promulgated. For example, the Federal Deposit Insurance Corporation (FDIC) regulates the banking and insurance industries and bars people with felony convictions from any employment there. The Patriot Act, put in place after the events of September 11, 2001, places restrictions on employment in airports and railroads and any jobs involving transportation of hazardous materials. Other bans are set by state governments and can vary from state to state. In New York, one of the more progressive states with respect to these bans, there are 30 different occupations from which the formerly incarcerated either are barred or may be rejected by licensing authorities solely because of their conviction (Legal Action Center, personal communication, December 2, 2008).

Although some restrictions are sensible, as in situations where the job is directly related to an individual conviction (e.g., an embezzler working as a bank teller or a drug dealer working in a pharmacy), others are overly restrictive and limit employers' choices about whom they can hire.

EVIDENCE-BASED BEST POLICIES AND PRACTICES IN EMPLOYMENT REENTRY

Organizations and Programs

Myriad factors place people with criminal convictions at a disadvantage in the struggle to retain employment and build a better life. If these barriers are addressed, the accumulation of positive factors—such as basic work skills, sobriety, and connections to children and families—build on one another to promote the participants' steady advancement. So what approach is best suited to helping people overcome barriers to finding employment? To highlight best practices, four organizations or programs were chosen to take a complete approach to employment reentry, serving clients from enrollment through at least 1 year after job placement. Each of these organizations or programs has independent evidence of success. Although each organization offers services throughout the reentry process, specific approaches that best address the barriers to employment will be highlighted. Information about these programs, except where noted, comes from organization Web sites and the independent knowledge of the author. The organizations and programs are CEO, New York; ComALERT, New York; the Safer Foundation, Chicago; and Project Re-Integration of Offenders (RIO), Texas.

CEO

For more than 30 years CEO has offered immediate, effective, and comprehensive employment services exclusively to men and women with criminal records. CEO's vision is that anyone with a recent criminal history who wants to work should have the preparation and support needed to find a job and to stay connected to the labor force. CEO's programs help participants gain the workplace skills and confidence needed for a successful transition to a stable, productive life.

CEO's theory of change posits that if the employment needs of people with criminal convictions are addressed at their most vulnerable point—when they are first released from incarceration or soon after conviction—through transitional employment, job readiness training, and job development and retention services, they will be less likely to become reincarcerated and more likely to build a positive foundation for themselves and their families.

CEO began as a project of the Vera Institute of Justice in the late 1970s and became a free-standing nonprofit corporation in 1996. Today, CEO engages an average of 2,000 people each year. In the past 10 years, CEO has made 10,000 full-time job placements in hundreds of New York City businesses.

Evidence-Based Highlights. CEO participated in a national random assignment research study funded by the U.S. Department of Health and Human Services and conducted by the Michigan Disability Rights Coalition, one of the leading research organizations in the nation that uses random assignment, considered the most rigorous research design. Findings from this independent evaluation of CEO programs show that people who enroll in CEO have significantly lower rates of recidivism on a variety of measures—including a 40% reduction in reincarceration for a new crime—2 years after joining the program, an effect rarely seen in highly demanding studies such as the one CEO underwent (Bloom, 2008).

ComALERT

ComALERT was created in 1999 by Kings County (New York) district attorney Charles J. Hynes. ComALERT helps formerly incarcerated people to make a successful transition from prison to home by providing drug treatment and counseling, mental health treatment and counseling, GED classes, and employment. ComALERT coordinates these services through a structured partnership with community-based providers including the Counseling Service of the Eastern District of New York and the Doe Fund's Ready, Willing and Able workforce development program.

ComALERT's overall goal is to reduce criminal recidivism by providing the formerly incarcerated with the tools and support they need to remain drug-free, crime-free, and employed. As of October 1, 2007, ComALERT had served 991 participants in total.

Evidence-Based Highlights. ComALERT underwent an evaluation in October 2006 in which clients were carefully matched to a demographically similar comparison group. In their first 2 years after release, participants in the ComALERT program were rearrested at a rate of 29%, reconvicted at a rate of 19%, and reincarcerated for a new crime at a 3% rate. The matched comparison group of nonparticipating parolees were rearrested at a rate of 48%, reconvicted at a rate of 34%, and reincarcerated for a new crime at a 7% rate (Western & Jacobs, 2006).

The Safer Foundation

The Safer Foundation, based in Chicago, has been working for more than 30 years to reduce recidivism by helping people with criminal records obtain employment and social services. Safer provides a range of direct client services through an integrated strategic model that promotes employment retention. Today, Safer serves approximately 10,000 people per year.

The Safer Foundation offers educational programs designed specifically for people with criminal records, based on educational needs, learning styles, and past educational experiences. Safer offers programs both inside correctional facilities and in the community to help people with records increase their basic literacy and attain their GEDs.

Finally, the Safer Foundation is part of the Ready4Work faith-based initiative, which provides supportive programming to young men and women during their transition from prison. Ready4Work provides mentoring, supportive services such as housing, substance abuse treatment, mental health services, and job placement and retention services. Ready4Work is offered at four community sites throughout Chicago.

Evidence-Based Highlights. According to a study by Loyola University, the recidivism rate for released prisoners in the state of Illinois from 2003 to 2006 was 51.8%. For Safer participants who kept a job for 30 days, the rate was 22%, and for participants who kept a job for a year the recidivism rate dropped to 13%. Although the study does not use a control or carefully selected comparison group to detect the impact of Safer's programming, these findings reinforce the reentry literature on the inverse relationship between employment and recidivism.

Project RIO

Project RIO began as a two-city pilot program in Texas in 1984. Project RIO is a statewide program committed to reducing recidivism and helping those who have been incarcerated in Texas state facilities find employment. The project is a collaboration of two state agencies: the Texas Workforce Commission and the Texas Department of Criminal Justice. Each agency uses its own resources and strengths to address the different criminal justice and workforce needs of people coming out of prison. Participants are offered both prerelease and postrelease services. Many participants enter the RIO program through the Windham School District, an in-prison school that offers academic and vocational skill-building courses (see chapter 8, pp. 199–200). For participants who are not referred to post-placement services after training at Windham, RIO offers separate skill-building courses at its offices. RIO's full-service and regional offices provide placement services for participants, including skill assessment and matching to open jobs in the community. Project RIO provides placement services to roughly 16,000 clients each year.

Evidence-Based Highlights. Between 1985 and 1992, Project RIO placed 69% of more than 100,000 formerly incarcerated people in jobs. A comparison group matched by similarity to Project RIO participants was found to have an employment rate of 36% upon release. The evaluation of Project RIO also demonstrated that, the year after release, only 23% of high-risk RIO participants returned to prison, compared with 38% of non-RIO parolees (Buck, 2000).

Although the Project RIO study was conducted more than a decade ago, it remains one of the larger analyses performed on employment reentry and continues to stand the test of time as other studies are completed.

Best Practices for Overcoming Barriers to Employment

Improving Job Readiness: What Are Soft Skills, and How Do We Make Them Better?

Economic scholars, such as Holzer, Moss, and Tilly, note that over the past several decades the labor market has trended away from industrial work that requires manual labor and toward customer service work that requires a set of interpersonal and cognitive aptitudes. This is particularly true in urban centers and is changing the way employers assess their needs and the skills they seek from employees. These skills tend to be grouped together under the heading of "soft skills." *Soft skills* are defined in various ways, including effective communication, positive attitude, and a high level of motivation (Holzer, 1996; Moss & Tilly, 2003). Soft skills have also been defined as thinking and cognitive skills (including the ability to identify problems and evaluate alternative solutions, weighing their risks and benefits), communication skills (including the ability to understand and give instructions and the ability to communicate with messages appropriate to listeners and the situation), personal qualities and work ethic (including attributes such as self-esteem, motivation to work, and willingness to learn but excluding work habits such as punctuality and appropriate dress, which are a product of soft skills), and interpersonal and teamwork skills (including the ability to negotiate, to participate as a member of a team, to serve and satisfy the expectations of clients and customers, and to resolve conflicts maturely, all of which require elements of the other soft skill sets) (Conrad, 1999).

This shift has influenced employer attitudes toward race according to Pager et al. (2006), who observes that personal skills such as attitude and motivation are often "strongly race-coded by employers" and that "minority workers, especially young black men, are widely viewed by employers to be lacking these qualities compared to other low-skill workers" (p. 3). Personal attributes are judged subjectively and do not lend themselves to objective measurement, creating a tendency to stereotype job applicants (Pager et al., 2006).

On a more positive note, the Pager study found that many employer attitudes toward minority job applicants were based on cursory interaction rather than interviews of the applicants. In the New York City Hiring Discrimination Study, employers often made judgments after initial meetings and did not call back minority applicants. However, for those who did, personal interaction substantially reduced discrimination against non-White testers in the study. Pager et al. (2006) found that "the friendly, appealing qualities of the testers appear to mediate the effects of racial stereotypes, reducing the negative bias evident in more superficial reviews" (p. 13).

From this we can conclude that soft skill training in basics such as attitude, customer service, and motivation can influence hiring decisions. And if prepared job seekers can get their foot in the door for an interview and demonstrate their customer service skills, the discrimination gap can be narrowed. Therefore, if practitioners and policymakers can improve the customer service skills on the supply side, they can change attitudes and practice on the demand side.

Organizations that offer employment services to people with criminal convictions do just this: They improve the soft skills, and therefore the job readiness, of job seekers to better meet the demands of employers. Some provide this training in a supportive classroom setting; others provide on-the-job training with supervision and coaching (known as transitional employment). Some provide training while people are still in prison; others offer services immediately upon release. All are considered best practices and have proven effective at preparing people for the workplace.

Best Practice: Preparing for Jobs While Still in Prison

The Safer Foundation

Safer operates an in-prison program (Sheridan) and two Adult Transition Centers (ATCs) for the state of Illinois. Those clients who enter the ATCs go through a minimum 35-hour-a-week training program of vocational training, life skills training, community service work and/or employment, all while serving the last few months of their sentences. The ATCs emphasize ordering participants' time and giving them a sense of structure in their day-to-day lives. A similar program is found in Safer's Sheridan program. Safer's pre-employment offerings extend from the prison to the post-prison stages of a participant's experience, which allows Safer a degree of coordination when one of their Sheridan clients or a client from the ATCs leaves the system and goes down to a Safer regional office. The Safer regional offices act as a matching station for people leaving prison; direct service case managers network with different organizations to match people leaving prison with the services they need. While the regional offices offer employment training and mentoring, one of the major functions of the regional offices is to act as a coordinator between agencies, many of which have long-standing relationships with Safer clients.

ComALERT's Partnership with The Doe Fund

Like CEO, ComALERT, through a partnership with The Doe Fund, uses transitional employment to teach basic work skills that lead to full-time jobs. Program participants in Doe's Ready, Willing & Able program provide street cleaning and maintenance services that contribute to communities throughout New York City while learning the basic work skills and attitudes that are highly valued by employers.

Matching Job Seekers With the Right Job: What Are Those Jobs, and How Do We Find Them?

The previous section points out that many low- to medium-skilled jobs place a premium on customer-oriented skills. Fortunately, service industries are deemed to be in demand by the Department of Labor and are generally open to hiring people with criminal convictions (New York State Department of Labor, 2008). In fact, in the case of the Center for Employment Opportunities, service industry jobs account for more than half of total job placements each year. These industries are more open to people with criminal records than some other growing fields, such as some segments of health care or financial services, where there are outright employment bans of people with felony convictions (Independent Committee on Reentry and Employment, 2006). Although these exclusionary policies are the subject of policy debate and advocacy, for job seekers with convictions looking for work right now, they are real. Direct service organizations with responsibilities to place people in jobs today would be best off focusing on industries where someone with a criminal conviction can experience the rewards of work and advancement without experiencing the frustration of running into currently problematic barriers.

Employment intermediaries such as those highlighted in this chapter cultivate these industries and carefully match their job seekers with job openings in businesses that are open to hiring people with convictions. By offering free human resources, ongoing support, and financial incentives including tax credits for hiring disadvantaged people, these organizations provide a valuable service to both job seekers and employers.

Best Practice: Building Relationships With Employers Who Hire People With Criminal Convictions

Project RIO

Project RIO is a collaborative program between the Texas Department of Criminal Justice and the Texas Workforce Commission. Because RIO operates in part as an extension of the Texas Workforce Commission, RIO placement offices have access to the entirety of the Texas Workforce Commission's employment databases, and as such are able to provide their clients with specific, up-to-date information on job openings throughout the state. Additionally, Employment Specialists have access to lists of the 12,000 employers who have employed RIO graduates in the

(Continued)

(Continued)

past. Between 1985 and 1998, Project RIO placed 69% of its 100,000+ participants through its partnership with the Workforce Commission.

Center for Employment Opportunities (CEO)

CEO serves as a free employment and human resource provider, supplying qualified entry-level employees from CEO's pool of clients who have been vetted by their transitional work experience. In the last year, CEO has worked with 500 local employers, placing clients in industries as diverse as food services, retail/wholesale, manufacturing, human services, construction, maintenance, and warehouse. CEO's award-winning customized use of the Web-based Customer Relationship Management system Salesforce.com helps job developers carefully match their clients with viable, full-time jobs that use their skills and meet the needs of employers. In 2008, CEO made 1,220 full-time placements of people with a variety of convictions–all of them felonies.

In the past decade, CEO has made 10,000 full-time job placements.

Providing Ancillary Services That Affect Employment Rates

Organizations that meet the employment needs of people with criminal convictions also address ancillary issues that can decrease employment rates. In particular, it is considered best practice to help clients manage drug and alcohol use (either directly or in partnership with another service provider), build skills in basic education, and resolve problems involving the child support system.

Best Practice: Addressing Ancillary Needs

Drug Treatment: ComALERT and CEO both have partnerships with treatment providers that address substance abuse problems on an outpatient basis.

Child Support: CEO has a Responsible Fatherhood Program that assists clients with child support issues and provides workshops that help dads become better parents.

Education: The Safer Foundation offers a range of educational programs tailored to the needs of people with criminal histories inside correctional facilities and postrelease in communities.

Helping People Keep and Advance From the Jobs They Get

The post-placement stage of employment reentry can be understood as the final stage for securing the successful community reintegration of formerly incarcerated people. The outcomes of the previous sections manifest themselves here, and if everything has been carried out effectively, the result can be long lasting. The more people accustom themselves to the habits and the schedule of the work world, the more likely they are to make a meaningful, long-term transition to community life. Although this stage comes late in the reentry process, the needs of this period do not differ significantly from the needs of previous stages, and the same services are likely to be needed in a successful reentry program: coaching, skill training, and ancillary services such as substance abuse treatment and child support counseling as necessary. However, on the employment side, programs must focus not just on securing entry-level jobs but on helping people advance from those jobs into higher-wage sustainable employment. Compared with the literature and documented knowledge on initial job placement strategies, little quantitative information has been published about the long-term employment retention of people with criminal convictions. Retention is the newest employment focus of the reentry field, and so we can only discuss promising practices in this area.

Emerging Practices
in Job Retention and Advancement

... At ComALERT
The Doe Fund provides a $200 per-month stipend to participants who successfully find outside employment for the first five months of their employment.

... At CEO
CEO's incentive-based job retention program, Rapid Rewards, provides monthly payments to all participants who sign up for the program, up to a total of $600 in one year.

Participants get workplace counseling, crisis management, and long-term career planning from a team of CEO retention specialists; employers get tax credits and other incentives.

(Continued)

> (Continued)
>
> ### ... At the Safer Foundation
> Case managers maintain contact with placed participants (as well as those individuals and businesses that employ Safer graduates) for one year, and act as a mediator to resolve any difficulties a placed participant may be having on the job.
>
> Like CEO, Safer works to get employers tax credits that provide a positive incentive for employers to hire and to continually employ Safer graduates.

POLICY IMPLICATIONS

Using an experience of more than 15 years, in a nonprofit organization devoted to employment reentry at New York's Center for Employment Opportunities, Mindy Tarlow, Director of CEO, suggests what must be done to improve employment reentry and reduce the current barriers to employment for people with criminal convictions.

First, organizations that act as intermediaries between job seekers with criminal convictions and employers with appropriate job openings reduce barriers to employment for people with criminal convictions. Public and private funders must provide these organizations with adequate resources to serve the increasing number of people coming home from jail and prison to neighborhoods and communities. But the nonprofit community cannot do this on its own. Employment reentry needs champions at all levels of government. Former president Clinton championed hiring welfare recipients in the private sector; someone needs to do the same for formerly incarcerated people.

The government must create more job opportunities for people with criminal convictions and other hard-to-employ populations through public works programs and other legislative actions that increase the number of jobs available for people who need to gain a foothold in the labor market. There is a compelling social and economic argument for this: Employment reentry is cheaper than prison and gets results. More must be done to quantify and promote the social return on investment in employment. If the use of expensive prison beds is reduced and even a fraction of the savings is invested in employment reentry, we will have a healthier economy and safer streets.

Legislative action must be taken to reduce occupational and licensure bans to employment that don't make sense. Employers open to hiring formerly incarcerated people should be able to choose whom they hire. Employers wary of hiring people with criminal convictions need to be better educated about laws surrounding negligent hiring and employment discrimination and the services offered by employment intermediaries.

More must be done to bridge the gap between theory and practice. This can be accomplished by stronger partnerships between academics and practitioners, which will better document the importance of employment reentry. Academics need to spend more time in the field, and practitioners need to spend more time getting independent proof of their results.

Employment reentry is not just a public safety issue; it can reduce joblessness and poverty, improve the well-being of children and families, and build the economic prosperity of communities. Policymakers must address employment reentry as they consider all these areas of public concern.

DISCUSSION QUESTIONS

1. Imagine you work for an organization that gets jobs for people coming home from prison. You have a conversation with your neighbor, and she tells you that her son, who has a clean record, can't find a job. She knows what you do and says she doesn't understand why her tax dollars should support programs that help people who committed crimes get jobs when there's no program to help her son. What do you think is the most persuasive argument in support of employment reentry? Why do you think so?

2. Which government system is better positioned to support employment reentry: the criminal justice system or the workforce development system? Why?

3. Many prisons are located in communities that rely on them to employ local residents. How would you make the argument to these residents that closing prisons is better for the economy?

4. Which factor do you think is the biggest barrier to employment: race, education, age, or criminal conviction? Why do you think so?

REFERENCES

Bloom, D. (2007). *MRDC*. PowerPoint presentation to the U.S. Department of Health and Human Services, Administration for Children and Families Conference, June 4, Washington, DC.

Bloom, D. (2008). *Transitional jobs for ex-prisoners: Two-year results from a random assignment evaluation of the Center for Employment Opportunities (CEO)*. Presentation at the APPAM Annual Research Conference, Los Angeles, November 7, 2008.

Bryan, J. L. (2006). *Job losses with a rising GDP: An unsustainable mix for the US economy*. Internal document, available from the author upon request.

Bryan, J. L., Haldipur, J. N., & Williams, N. (2008). *"I'm worth more than that!": Race and ethnic conflict among low-wage workers after incarceration.* Paper presented at the annual meeting of the American Sociological Association, Boston. Retrieved January 29, 2009, from http://www.allacademic.com/meta/p241854_index.html

Buck, M. (2000). *Getting back to work: Employment programs for ex-offenders.* Field Report Series. Public/Private Ventures. Retrieved September 14, 2009, from http://eric.ed.gov/ERIC Docs/data/ericdocs2sql/content_storage_01/0000019b/80/16/cf/54.pdf

Campbell, R. (2003). *Dollars & sentences.* New York: Vera Institute of Justice.

Clear, T., Rose, D., & Ryder, J. (2001). Incarceration and the community: The problem of removing and returning offenders. *Crime & Delinquency, 47*(3), 331–335.

Conrad, C. (1999). *Soft skills and the minority work force: A guide for informed discussion.* Washington, DC: Joint Center for Political and Economic Studies.

Freeman, R. (1992). Crime and the employment of disadvantaged youth. In G. Peterson & W. Vorman (Eds.), *Urban labor markets and job opportunity* (pp. 201–237). Washington, DC: Urban Institute.

Freeman, R. (2003). *Can we close the revolving door?: Recidivism vs. employment of ex-offenders in the U.S.* Washington, DC: Urban Institute.

Freeman, R. (2008). Incarceration, criminal background checks, and employment in a low(er) crime society. *Criminology & Public Policy, 7*(3), 405–412.

Haberkern, R. (2003). Helping parents with criminal records find employment and achieve self-sufficiency. *Welfare Information Network, 7*(4).

Holzer, H. (1996). *What employers want: Job prospects of less-educated workers.* New York: Russell Sage Foundation.

Holzer, H. (2007, November). *What might improve the employment and advancement prospects of the poor?* Paper prepared for the conference of Federal Reserve Bank, Chicago.

Holzer, H., & Offner, P. (2002, January 3). Welfare: What about the men? *Washington Post,* p. A17.

Holzer, H., Raphael, S., & Stoll, M. (2003, May). *Employment barriers facing ex-offenders.* Paper presented at the Urban Institute Reentry Roundtable, New York.

Husock, H. (2008, May 20). *New York Post.*

Independent Committee on Reentry and Employment. (2006). *Report and recommendations to New York State on enhancing employment opportunities for formerly incarcerated people.* New York: The Doe Fund.

Justice Policy Institute. (August 30, 2002). More Black men in prison than college, study finds. *Drug War Chronicle.* Retrieved August 19, 2009, from http://stopthedrugwar.org/chronicle-old/252/jpistudy.shtml

Krisberg, B., & Marchionna, S. (2006). *Attitudes of US voters toward prisoner rehabilitation and reentry policies. Views from the National Council on Crime and Delinquency.* Retrieved September 14, 2009, from http://www.nccd-crc.org/nccd/pubs/2006april_focus_zogby.pdf

Levitan, M. (2004a, February). *A crisis of Black male employment, unemployment and joblessness in New York City, 2003.* A CSS annual report. New York: Community Service Society.

Levitan, M. (2004b). *Unemployment and joblessness in New York City, 2006.* New York: Community Service Society.

Levitan, M. (2005). *Unemployment and joblessness in New York City, 2004, better, but still a long way to go.* A CSS annual report. New York: Community Service Society.

Levitan, M. (2007). *Unemployment and joblessness in New York City, 2006. Recovery bypasses youth*. A CSS annual report. New York: Community Service Society.

Mason, K., & Williams-Mbengue, N. (2008). A different kind of jail. *State Legislatures, 34*(10), 30–32.

Maxwell, N. (2006). *The working life: The labor market for workers in low-skilled jobs.* Kalamazoo, MI: W.E. Upjohn Institute for Employment Research.

Moss, P., & Tilly, C. (2003). *Stories employers tell: Race, skill, and hiring in America*. New York: Russell Sage.

Mukamal, D. (2000). Confronting the employment barriers of criminal records: Effective legal and practical strategies. *Journal of Poverty Law and Policy, 33*(9/10), 597–606.

Mumola, C. (2006). *Parents under correctional supervision: Past estimates, new measures*. NIDA research meeting, North Bethesda, MD, November 6, 2006.

Nelson, A., & Turetsky, V. (2008). Second Chance Act of 2007: Community safety through recidivism prevention. *Center for Law and Social Policy: Legislation in brief.* Pub. law no. 110-199. Retrieved September 15, 2009, from http://www.clasp.org/admin/site/publications/files/0413.pdf

New York City Commission for Economic Opportunity. (2006, September). *Increasing opportunity and reducing poverty in New York City.* Report to Mayor Michael R. Bloomberg.

New York State Department of Labor. (2008). *Employment prospects to 2014, New York City region.* Retrieved January 27, 2009, from http://www.labor.state.ny.us/workforceindustry-data/descriptor_print.asp?reg=nyc&sort=s.soctitlel

Nightingale, D., & Watts, H. (1996). *Adding it up: The economic impact of incarceration on individuals, families, and communities. The unintended consequences of incarceration.* New York: Vera Institute of Justice.

Pager, D. (2007). *Marked: Race, crime, and finding work in an era of mass incarceration.* Chicago: University of Chicago Press.

Pager, D., & Quillian, L. (2005). Walking the talk? What employers say versus what they do. *American Sociological Review, 70,* 355–380.

Pager, D., & Western, B. (2005). *The realities of race and criminal record in a New York City job market.* NYC Commission on Human Rights Commission Conference. JEHT Foundation. Retrieved September 15, 2009, from http://www.princeton.edu/pager/race at work.pdf

Pager, D., Western, B., & Bonikowski, B. (2006). *Discrimination in low-wage labor markets.* Princeton, NJ: Princeton University.

Petersilia, J. (2004). What works in prisoner reentry: Reviewing the evidence. *Federal Probation, 68*(2), 4–8.

Robert D. Hart Research Associates. (2002). *Changing public attitudes toward the criminal justice system.* Open Society Institute. Retrieved July 14, 2008, from http://www.soros.org/initiatives/usprograms/focus/justice/articles_publications/publications/hartpoll_20020201

Rogers, W. M., III. (2008). African American and White differences in the impacts of monetary policy on the duration of unemployment. *American Economic Review, 98*(2), 382–386.

Scott, J. (2004, February 28). Nearly half of Black men found jobless. *New York Times.*

Solomon, A., Johnson, D. K., Travis, J., & McBride, E. (2004). *From prison to work: The employment dimensions of prisoner reentry.* A report of the Reentry Roundtable. Washington, DC: Urban Institute Justice Policy Center.

Solomon, P. (2004). Peer support/peer provided services underlying processes, benefits, and critical ingredients. *Psychiatric Rehabilitation Journal, 27*(4), 392–401.

Sum, A., McLaughlin, J., Khatiwada, I., & Palma, S. (2008). *The collapse of the 2008 summer teen job market: A record 60 year employment low for the nation's teens.* Boston: Center for Labor Market Studies.

Travis, J. (2005). *But they all come back: Facing the challenges of prisoner reentry.* Washington, DC: Urban Institute Press.

Travis, J. (2007). Reflections on the reentry movement. *Federal Sentencing Reporter, 20*(2), 84–87.

Uggen, C. (2000). Work as turning point in the life course of criminals: A duration model of age, employment and recidivism. *American Sociological Review, 67,* 529–546.

Uggen, C., Manza, J., & Thompson, M. (2006). Citizenship, democracy, and civic reintegration of criminal offenders. *Annals of the American Academy of Political and Social Science, 605*(1), 281–310.

U.S. Congress. (2007). Second Chance Act of 2007. 110th Congress, 1st Session, March 20, 2007. Retrieved June 23, 2008, http://www.sentencingproject.org/search/search.cfm?search_string= second+chance+act

U.S. Department of Health and Human Services. (2009, April). Office of Family Assistance (OFA). Administration for Children and Families. Retrieved September 15, 2009, from http://www .acf.hhs.gov/opa/fact_sheets/tanf_factsheet.html

U.S. Department of Labor. (2009). Monthly labor review. *U.S. Bureau of Labor Statistics, 132*(6), 3–64.

Western, B. (2002). The impact of incarceration on wage mobility and inequality. *American Sociological Review, 67,* 526–546.

Western, B. (2008). Criminal background checks and employment among workers with criminal records. *Criminology & Public Policy, 7*(3), 413–417.

Western, B., & Jacobs, E. (2006). *Report on the evaluation of the ComALERT prisoner reentry program.*

Zuckerman, D. (2000). Welfare reform in America: A clash of politics and research. *Journal of Social Issues, 56*(4), 587–599.

CHAPTER 14

Barriers to Reintegration

Andrea Leverentz

This chapter addresses challenges ex-prisoners face as they attempt to reintegrate into the community. These challenges include personal, interpersonal, and structural barriers to successful reentry. The chapter begins with a brief discussion of individual and contextual characteristics that may shape prisoners' experiences and how others respond to them. The second section explores a few of the primary structural barriers, such as employment and housing restrictions. The next section addresses personal and interpersonal concerns that ex-prisoners often must face in addition to these structural constraints. In the final section, policy implications are discussed to help reduce these barriers.

INDIVIDUAL AND NEIGHBORHOOD CHARACTERISTICS

An initial barrier for all returning prisoners is the label "convicted felon." Those who were convicted of a felony in Florida were more likely to recidivate than those who were sentenced to probation with a "withholding adjudication" of guilt finding (Chiricos, Barrick, Bales, & Bontrager, 2007). The "convicted" label itself shapes recidivism, especially for those who are otherwise less likely to recidivate, and perhaps they have more to lose by the label. Those who are most likely to recidivate (men, racial and ethnic minorities, and those with a more extensive criminal record) are less influenced by conviction (Chiricos et al., 2007).

Beyond the label "ex-prisoner" or "ex-offender," individual characteristics can shape one's likelihood of incarceration and experience after incarceration.

Prisoners are disproportionately male, African American, and from disadvantaged backgrounds (Pettit & Western, 2004; Travis, 2005; Western, Pettit, & Guetzkow, 2002). Black men are the largest percentage (35.4%) of inmates, followed by White men (32.9%) and Latino men (17.9%) (Sabol & Couture, 2008). The rate of Black male incarceration in 2007 was six times that of White men, and Black men aged 30–34 have the highest incarceration rate of any race, age, or gender group (Sabol & Couture, 2008).

This disproportionality is most extreme among men with lower education levels. Just over 40% of young Black men, ages 22–30, with less than a high school diploma were incarcerated on an average day in 1999, and more than half of Black high school dropouts in their early 30s had been incarcerated at some point in their lives (Western et al., 2002). Although a majority of male prisoners are employed at the time of their incarceration, they experience higher than average unemployment before incarceration (Greenfield & Snell, 1999; Travis, 2005). In addition, prisoners have lower than average levels of income in the months before their incarceration and lower than average educational attainment (Harlow, 2003; Solomon, Johnson, Travis, & Mcbride, 2004). Female inmates have lower incomes and lower employment than men and higher rates of welfare assistance receipt before their incarceration (Greenfield & Snell, 1999).

Incarceration, particularly at a young age, can lead to an accumulation of disadvantages over the life course, with future opportunities severely restricted (Sampson & Laub, 1993; Western, Kling, & Weinman, 2001). Because incarceration is so prevalent among Black men with low education levels, the impact on their individual wages also increases wage inequality on an aggregate level (Western, 2002). In addition, differential incarceration rates contribute to a stereotype of a young, Black male offender; this stereotype has negative consequences not only for offenders and ex-offenders but also for others who fit part of that stereotype (Pager, 2007; Western et al., 2001).

Although women are much less likely to be incarcerated, rates of female incarceration have been increasing much faster than rates of male incarceration. Women are approximately 24% of those on probation, 12% of those on parole, and 7% of those in prison (Glaze & Bonczar, 2007; Sabol & Couture, 2008). Female inmates may be seen as "double deviants," who have violated both gender and legal norms (Heimer & De Coster, 1999). Women who have been incarcerated often are seen as less feminine precisely because they were incarcerated. This may be especially pronounced among women of color. For African American women, "the sense of being marginalized within the context of a disenfranchised community has a profound impact on the ability of women to successfully reintegrate into it" (Richie, 2001, p. 383).

Prison inmates are drawn from and return to a small number of neighborhoods (see Lynch & Sabol, 2001). This concentration has increased in recent years, particularly in core urban counties (i.e., those that contain the central city of a metropolitan area). In 1996, for example, more than two thirds of prison inmates nationwide were released to core counties; often they are further concentrated in a small number of neighborhoods (Lynch & Sabol, 2001). These neighborhoods typically are characterized by high rates of poverty and other social disadvantages and are predominantly African American (Brooks, Visher, & Naser, 2006; La Vigne & Mamalian, 2004; La Vigne, Mamalian, Travis, & Visher, 2003; Lynch & Sabol, 2001; Watson et al., 2004).

Former inmates returning to disadvantaged neighborhoods are more likely to recidivate, controlling for individual-level characteristics (Kubrin & Stewart, 2006; Mears, Wang, Hay, & Bales, 2008). The concentration of offenders and ex-offenders may make it more difficult for them to avoid criminogenic social networks (Caspi & Moffitt, 1995; Gendreau, Little, & Goggin, 1996; Laub & Sampson, 2003; Warr, 1998) and to access resources such as drug treatment, housing, and employment (Cadora, Schwartz, & Gordon, 2003; La Vigne, Visher, & Castro, 2004). Returning prisoners also create an additional demand on already scarce resources in disadvantaged neighborhoods (Brooks, Solomon, Keegan, Kohl, & Lahue, 2005; Cadora et al., 2003; La Vigne et al., 2004; Lynch & Sabol, 2001; Petersilia, 1999). For these reasons, neighborhood change is a common self-described turning point (Laub & Sampson, 2003; La Vigne et al., 2004). A change in neighborhood context offers an opportunity to redefine roles, lifestyle, and sense of self and a change in social networks (Laub & Sampson, 2003; Warr, 1998). There is some evidence that such a residential change can lead to a reduction in recidivism (Kirk, 2009, but see Maruna & Roy, 2007).

STRUCTURAL BARRIERS

In addition to individual and social contextual factors shaping the experience of reentry, criminal records and incarceration lead to certain formal restrictions that limit the options available to returning prisoners. Two of the most commonly mentioned barriers to successful reentry are securing employment and housing. In addition, some types of offenses, particularly drug offenses and sex offenses, lead to additional restrictions. In this section, some of these barriers are detailed.

Employment

One of the most frequently cited precursors to successful reentry and criminal desistance is employment (Uggen, 1999, 2000; Uggen & Thompson, 2003). Employment provides a stake in conformity, new routines, prosocial ties, and legal income. For these reasons, employment, particularly high-quality employment, is often cited as a primary cause of decreased recidivism (Sampson & Laub, 1993; Uggen, 1999, 2000; Uggen & Thompson, 2003). High-quality employment can be conceptualized both in terms of stability and economic compensation and in extra-economic terms of gaining a sense of meaning from one's work (Laub & Sampson, 2003; Maruna, 2001; Uggen, 1999). In one test of high-quality employment, Uggen (1999) found an overall negative relationship between job quality (estimated using mean overall job satisfaction scores) and recidivism, controlling for prior criminality, drug use, and economic indicators. Maruna (2001) expands this idea somewhat by including "a variety of productive pursuits" through which ex-offenders translate their criminal history into wisdom "as a drug counselor, youth worker, community volunteer, or mutual-help group participant" (p. 117). In the latter case, the emphasis is on the meaning that the ex-offenders gain from their work, whether it is paid employment or volunteer work.

Despite the value of employment for reducing recidivism, ex-offenders face several barriers to securing employment. Those with felony convictions are legally barred from some occupations. Occupations with state or regulatory restrictions include those that work with vulnerable populations, such as childcare, home health care, or nursing, and private sector jobs such as barber, beautician, pharmacist, embalmer, optometrist, plumber, and real estate professional (Lucken & Ponte, 2008; Petersilia, 2003). Some of these restricted occupations, such as barber, are the same jobs in which prisoners are trained while incarcerated (Petersilia, 2003).

A study of Los Angeles employers found that businesses that perform background checks are less likely to hire those with a criminal record. However, when firms are not statutorily required to do background checks but do them anyway, there is no difference in hiring from firms that do not perform background checks (Stoll & Bushway, 2008). Stoll and Bushway conclude that the effect of performing background checks on hiring is driven almost entirely by statutes requiring such checks and restricting employment. They suggest that those who perform unrequired background checks may be concerned with the possibility of negligent hiring lawsuits but may use the information to make "risk-assessed" hiring decisions (Stoll & Bushway, 2008). Lucken and Ponte

(2008) make a similar argument in suggesting a "bona fide occupational qualification" standard to employment restrictions, wherein licensing agencies may restrict employment but must justify such a restriction in terms of how a certain conviction may negatively affect job tasks or the nature of the business.

In many states, employers are allowed to deny jobs to those with a criminal record and sometimes merely an arrest record (Legal Action Center, 2004; Petersilia, 2003). Many employers are resistant to hiring ex-offenders because of perceptions of trustworthiness and dependability and concerns about legal liability if they reoffend at work (Holzer, Raphael, & Stoll, 2001; Lucken & Ponte, 2008; Petersilia, 2003). In one series of surveys, more than 60% of employers would probably not or definitely not hire those with a criminal record (Holzer et al., 2001). In contrast, most would consider hiring a former or current welfare recipient (92%), workers with a GED instead of a high school diploma (96%), or workers with a spotty employment history (59%) (Holzer et al., 2001). Pager (2005) found that a higher percentage (approximately 62%) said they were willing to hire those with a drug conviction, but a much smaller percentage actually invited those with a drug conviction to interview.

There is evidence that the stigma of a criminal record and stereotypes about who is likely to have a criminal record play an important role in hiring decisions. Pager (2003, 2007) conducted an experimental audit in which pairs of White and Black young men applied for entry-level jobs, with one in each pair claiming to have a felony drug conviction and time served in prison. Pager constructed similar résumés, carefully selected testers, and trained them how to interact with potential employers (Pager, 2007). In doing so, she controlled for other common explanations of the lack of employment success among ex-offenders, such as a lack of social capital, a lack of education and work experience, and poor self-presentation. She found that both race and criminal history played a role in employer responses, with Blacks with a criminal record the least likely (5%) to receive a callback, followed by Blacks without a criminal record (14%), Whites with a criminal record (17%), and Whites without a criminal record (34%) (Pager, 2003, 2007).

Former inmates who do find work after their release usually find it through friends or family (La Vigne et al., 2004; Travis, 2005). Although programs assisting ex-offenders with employment have demonstrated some success, these programs are limited in capacity and geographic reach (Solomon et al., 2004). Among those who find work, there also is an issue of retention. Among a three-state sample of former inmates, for example, 65% had been employed at some point 8 months after release, but only 45% were working at the end of that time period (Visher, Debus, & Yahner, 2008). In addition to the difficulty of finding and keeping a job, the kinds of jobs for which ex-prisoners are most likely to be hired (e.g., manufacturing) are decreasing in number, and many of the types of jobs available to ex-prisoners are unlikely to be stable, well-paid, meaningful jobs that contribute to desistance (Giordano, Cernkovich, & Rudolph, 2002; Lucken & Ponte, 2008; Travis, 2005; Uggen, 1999). Being incarcerated also has a depressive effect on future earnings and thus can reinforce existing structures of inequality (Western, 2002; Western et al., 2001).

Housing

Arguably even more important to former prisoners than stable employment is secure housing. Many newly released former prisoners live with family members. In one Urban Institute study, approximately three quarters of Chicago releasees planned to live with family, and an even higher percentage (88%) were living with family 4–8 months later (La Vigne et al., 2004). This is not always an easy or possible choice, as family members may have victimized or been victimized or otherwise hurt by the returning person previously. Female offenders experience high rates of abuse and victimization, often at the hands of family members, in both childhood and adulthood (Chesney-Lind, 2002; Harlow, 1999; Richie, 2001). One study of female releasees in Chicago found that 30% reported physical or sexual abuse by family members while growing up, and nearly half were first exposed to drug and alcohol use by family members (Leverentz, 2006a). Twelve percent of male Chicago releasees report being physically abused or threatened by a family or household member in the months before incarceration; more than half report drug or alcohol use by family members (La Vigne et al., 2004). In addition to fraught relationships, those who have relatives who are involved with criminal activity may be prohibited from living with them as conditions of their parole or supervised release (Petersilia, 2003).

Ex-prisoners face numerous barriers in locating housing: They may be denied tenancy on the basis of their criminal history, and they may be unable to afford market rent or provide references, a security deposit, or an employment history (Travis, 2005). Public housing authorities in most states make individualized determinations of eligibility; in many states, these determinations may be based on arrest records and conviction records (Legal Action Center, 2004). Housing authorities have the power to deny residency and to evict tenants on the basis of criminal or drug activity on the part of the tenant, a household member, or anyone "under the tenant's control" (U.S. Code 42, sec. 1437d (1) (6), cited in Travis, 2005, p. 231). Estimates of homelessness among parolees range from 10% to 50% (Petersilia, 2003; Travis, 2005). Although halfway houses provide one promising alternative, at least for transitional housing, they have limited capacity and often face community resistance (Sadovi, 2005; Travis, 2005).

Those convicted of sex offenses face additional restrictions in securing housing. Forty-seven states and the federal government have some type of "Megan's Law" requiring those convicted of sex offenses to register. This registration, among other restrictions, makes offenders ineligible for public housing (Travis, 2005). In addition, 31 states have some version of "Jessica's Law," which imposes further residency rules on convicted sex offenders (such as not living within a certain distance of a school or park). These laws have so severely limited housing options in some jurisdictions that there are almost no legal options, contributing to an increase in the number of homeless offenders (Vick, 2009).

Additional Barriers for Drug Offenders

Although employment and housing are the most frequently mentioned hurdles to successful reentry, those with felony drug convictions face additional legal restrictions. The Personal Responsibility and Work Opportunity and Reconciliation Act of 1996 imposes a lifetime ban for Temporary Assistance for Needy Families (TANF) and food stamps on those convicted of a felony drug charge (Rubinstein & Mukamal, 2002). This ban is implemented differently across states, with some states opting out altogether and others narrowing the scope. Although the ban applies to the offender only, not children or other family members, it reduces the overall household income (Rubinstein & Mukamal, 2002). Because female prisoners are more likely to be receiving public assistance before their incarceration and are more likely to be custodial parents at the time of their incarceration, the ban disproportionately affects women (Petersilia, 2003). Approximately a third of female inmates are serving drug sentences, and they are the fastest-growing segment of the prison population (Greenfield & Snell, 1999).

Drug-related restrictions also affect drug offenders' ability to improve their situations. In some states, TANF benefits are dependent on participation in drug treatment, although this requirement may conflict with the welfare-to-work requirements of working a certain number of hours per day. Welfare benefits and food stamps also help fund room and board in drug treatment facilities; restrictions on eligibility make it more difficult for people to pay for drug treatment (Petersilia, 2003). In addition to TANF restrictions, drug-related offenses also may affect student loan eligibility. Although most ex-offenders are eligible for student loans, those who are convicted of drug-related offenses while receiving federal financial aid may be ineligible for federal student loans (U.S. Department of Education, 2008).

Prison and Reentry Programming

Prison programming can improve outcomes and decrease recidivism among prisoners. Unfortunately, although the prison population has grown dramatically in recent years, funding for programming has not, meaning fewer inmates have access to these programs (Lawrence, Mears, Dubin, & Travis, 2002). In addition, prisoners are often given some prerelease guidance before they are released, but this programming often does not translate into receipt of community services. Although 87% of respondents in an Urban Institute study of Chicago prisoners participated in prerelease programming, only 22% of them contacted a community program or accessed services through a referral when they were released (La Vigne et al., 2004). Similarly, ex-prisoners complain of the lack of relevance of their formal prerelease programming and information. One former prisoner from Chicago said of his reentry programming experience, "It's usually a package of papers that say go to this place or that place for what you need. I went there thinking they could help me, but they weren't there. It's frustrating" (Scott, Dewey, & Leverentz, 2006, p. 14). In part, this may reflect the difficulty of keeping information up to date and useful. It also may reflect capacity limitations of programs serving this population (Solomon et al., 2004). Similar problems emerge in reentry guides, which are often written at a level far above the abilities of a majority of former prisoners and include outdated or limited information (Mellow & Christian, 2008).

PERSONAL AND INTERPERSONAL DYNAMICS

Although the emphasis is often on structural barriers to reentry and the logistical needs involved in exiting prison, ex-prisoners also face more informal barriers to successful reentry. When leaving prison, many people hope to transition into a law-abiding lifestyle and to avoid future incarceration. Even those who participated in treatment and programming while incarcerated realize that the demands placed on them outside are quite different from those they experience in prison, and they must learn to negotiate new demands and new relationships. This section addresses the individual and interpersonal transitions involved with reentry.

Life Course Transitions and Cognitive Transformations

Much of our thinking on the life course transitions of offenders has been influenced by the work of Robert Sampson and John Laub (Laub, Nagin, & Sampson, 1998; Laub & Sampson, 2003; Sampson & Laub, 1990, 1993). They analyzed extraordinarily rich data originally collected by Sheldon and Eleanor Glueck, beginning in 1939 and continuing into the 1960s (Sampson & Laub, 1993). Laub and Sampson then collected criminal history information on all the surviving men from the original sample and interviewed a subsample of 52 men (Laub & Sampson, 2003). Among these men, experiencing transitions such as marrying a prosocial spouse, gaining employment, and joining the military led to desistance from offending.

Findings based on more contemporary samples are mixed, however. For example, Giordano et al.'s (2002) follow-up of a group of adolescent offenders who came of age in the 1980s found very low rates of the "complete package" of marriage and employment. Although average or above-average happiness in marriage and an above-poverty wage job did reduce the likelihood of adult offending, it added only a small amount to the explained variance. In addition, only 8% of the sample fell into this group, ranging from no African American men to 12% of White men. Although these bonds did seem to play some role in desistance, there was much variability that was not explained. Similarly, employment was not a prominent theme in the respondents' narratives of change, although marital partners and children were commonly mentioned. One possible explanation is that rewarding employment was less likely to lead to change among Giordano's sample because unemployment and unstable employment are much more widespread now than in the post–World War II era of the Glueck men (Giordano et al., 2002; Laub & Sampson, 2003).

Researchers also are emphasizing the importance of how offenders view themselves and their life chances and how cognitive transformations of ex-prisoners may shape their desistance. In other words, ex-prisoners may reframe how they think about their offending and what they want for their future. Maruna (2001, p. 7) argues that "ex-offenders need to develop a coherent, prosocial identity for themselves" in which they make sense of their criminal pasts in a way that allows a "reformed" future. Those who adopt such a narrative are more likely to desist from offending, whereas those who adopt a "condemnation script" are much more likely to continue to offend. Those who continue to offend view their lives as unchangeable and themselves as lacking any personal efficacy to change (Maruna, 2001).

Similarly, Giordano et al. (2002) expand beyond "hooks for change," such as employment and marriage, and emphasize the need for openness to change, the ability to reflect and envision an appealing conventional self, and, finally, a change in the way the person views a deviant lifestyle. They argue that being open to change is insufficient, but it is a minimal starting point, and a "solid replacement self" may be the most important piece in long-term behavior change (Giordano et al., 2002, p. 1002; see also Maruna & Roy, 2007). Laub and Sampson (2003) also emphasize the role of human agency and routine activities and the importance of looking at both structure and choice in desistance or continued offending.

Romantic Relationships

In addition to self-conceptions, the relationships former prisoners have are central to their reentry experiences. One of the most commonly discussed types of relationships is that with romantic partners (Giordano et al., 2002; Horney, Osgood, & Marshall, 1995; Huebner, 2007; King, Massoglia, & Macmillan, 2007; Leverentz, 2006b; Sampson, Laub, & Wimer, 2006). Among male offenders, marriage has a positive effect of reducing offending by increasing social control, changing routine activities, and decreasing time spent with offending peers (Horney et al., 1995; Laub et al., 1998; Warr, 1998). The effect for women is less clear (Giordano et al., 2002; King et al., 2007; Leverentz, 2006b).

Evidence suggests that there is a "good marriage" effect for men in part because male offenders are more likely to "marry up" with women who are not involved in criminal activity (Laub et al., 1998; Laub & Sampson, 2003). The effect of marriage on offending is gradual and cumulative, reflecting the importance of a high-quality bond that develops over time (Horney et al., 1995; Laub et al., 1998). In addition, there seems to be a large selection effect; the effect of marriage on offending is reduced when the likelihood of selecting into good relationships is taken into account (King et al., 2007). Although there is a consistent positive effect of marriage for men, incarceration reduces the likelihood of marriage, particularly among White men (Huebner, 2007). For White men, incarceration reduces the likelihood of marriage by 58%, compared with 32% for Blacks and 34% for Latinos (Huebner, 2007).

The effect of marriage on female offenders is less well understood, although evidence suggests that the effect is smaller or nonexistent for many women (King et al., 2007). Giordano and colleagues (2002) found marriage to be relevant to both men and women, though in different and gendered ways. Given the proportion of male and female prisoners and offenders, it is much less likely that a female offender will enter into a relationship with a male partner with no history of offending or drug use. However, women can enter into or continue relationships with men who are also desisting from offending and drug use, and these relationships may support conventional behavior in similar ways to purely prosocial relationships (Leverentz, 2006b). In addition, relationships may be conventionalizing, even while low in attachment (Giordano et al., 2002). Same-sex relationships also may have similar dynamics between partners but may face additional social stigma (Giordano et al., 2002; Leverentz, 2006b).

The relationships prisoners have before and during periods of incarceration often continue and may influence future recidivism or desistance. Long-standing relationships, even when one or both partners have a history of offending, may evolve into mutually supportive and noncriminal relationships (Leverentz, 2006b). However, these relationships face many challenges. Just as rates of recidivism are high, the chances of rearrest and reincarceration are high. This potential may cause strain and distrust. Continuing relationship partners need to adjust to changing expectations, lifestyles, and power dynamics (Oliver & Hairston, 2008). Men returning from prison may resent a newfound independence and self-sufficiency in their partners. In combination with their own perception of a lack of efficacy and other stressors related to reentry, this may increase the likelihood of domestic violence (Oliver & Hairston, 2008). The strains involved in incarceration or the lifestyle changes (or lack thereof) after incarceration break up many marriages and romantic partnerships (Braman, 2004; Leverentz, 2006b; Oliver & Hairston, 2008).

The gender imbalance in some neighborhoods with high incarceration rates also shapes men's and women's approaches to romantic relationships. Women often feel the need to have low standards for behavior, and men feel they can take advantage of the dearth of men by dating multiple women or ending relationships (Braman, 2004). An additional path that is often important for female offenders is to avoid romantic relationships and to instead focus on their own independence and their own children's needs (Giordano et al., 2002; Leverentz, 2006b). For these women, the absence of this type of social tie contributes to their desistance. Because men are often implicated in female offending, some women feel the need to distance themselves from previous, or all, romantic partners as they adjust to life after prison (Leverentz, 2006b).

Children

Just over half of the prisoners in U.S. state and federal prisons have minor children; two thirds of women and half of men in prison are parents (Glaze & Maruschak, 2008). The current caregiver of the children of incarcerated fathers is usually the child's mother (88%). In contrast, only 37% of those with incarcerated mothers live with their fathers; these children are most likely to live with a grandparent (45%) or other relatives (23%) (Glaze & Maruschak, 2008). Both men and women often hope to reestablish relationships with their children once they are released from prison.

The relationships between incarcerated men, their children, and the mothers of their children are often strained, not only because of incarceration but also because of the criminal activity and drug use that preceded it. Some men, particularly older fathers, use the experience of incarceration to try to reestablish ties with their children (Edin, Nelson, & Paranal, 2001). Although many men work to retain or improve bonds with their children, children tend to be more key to women's self-conception, and their children are often a more central theme in their narratives of change (Giordano et al., 2002). Having children usually does not lead to desistance, but in many cases they play an important role in mothers' narratives of desistance (Giordano et al., 2002; Leverentz, 2006a; Richie, 2001).

Peer Relationships

Understanding peer networks and the likelihood of returning to criminogenic social networks, particularly among male offenders, is a focus of much desistance research (Scott, 2004; Warr, 1998). Those who resume pre-incarceration patterns of behavior, including spending time with old friends, looking for easy money, or engaging in side relationships or one-night stands, were more likely to be reincarcerated than those who socially isolated themselves or those who engaged in more prosocial behavior and relationship patterns (Seal, Eldrige, Kacanek, Binson, & Macgowan, 2007). Yet for some, rejoining criminal networks may seem like one of few options available to ex-prisoners, even when they know this may be self-defeating (Scott, 2004).

Many former prisoners lose or break ties with friends or acquaintances. Nearly half of the Chicago Urban Institute sample reports no close friends 8 months after release (La Vigne et al., 2004). Some may choose to distance themselves from co-offending peers, whereas others lose a sense of commonality if they are desisting from offending and drug use. Some may create new networks, and others socially isolate themselves. Both of these approaches may be an attempt to create a lifestyle that is more conducive to desistance (Laub & Sampson, 2003; Leverentz, 2006a; Sampson & Laub, 1993; Seal et al., 2007).

Family Dynamics

Desisting former prisoners often choose to distance themselves from still-offending acquaintances, but many are embedded in networks of offending family members, the bonds to which are much more difficult to break (Braman, 2004; Leverentz, 2006a). Although all ex-prisoners experience a "hangover identity" from their previous status as offender, this residual role may be especially pronounced in long-term relationships (Ebaugh, 1988; Goffman, 1963). As mentioned earlier, these relationships often are fraught with tension and history related to offending and drug use, yet they also may provide beneficial support and continuity. In one study of Florida inmates, prisoners were most likely to be visited, and visited more often, by parents (Bales & Mears, 2008). They also found that visits, and more frequent visits, were related to reduced recidivism. Male inmates reporting positive family relationships before their incarceration had lower recidivism rates than those reporting negative family relationships (La Vigne et al., 2004).

A majority of male prisoners in a Chicago study relied on female relatives (including mother, sisters, and wives or girlfriends) for financial and material support after their release (Scott et al., 2006). In contrast, a sample of women, also being released in Chicago, were much more likely to be financially independent or to rely on social service support (Leverentz, 2006a). Part of the difference between these two groups may reflect the recruitment strategies of the two studies: The men were randomly selected from among releasees, whereas the women were recruited through their participation in a halfway house program (both samples were largely African American). However, it also seems to reflect, at least in part, racial and gender differences in sources of support and expectations of support. Both the women's real and expected financial independence and the importance of family in their lives are consistent with research on African American women's roles and African American families (Collins, 2000; Davis, 1981; Huebner, 2007; Kane, 2000). In addition, although women continued to rely on their families for support, they also returned to previous roles as caregivers for children, parents, and occasionally siblings (Leverentz, 2006a).

Although strong familial bonds may encourage desistance, family ties also may serve as a barrier to successful reentry. The return of a prisoner creates tension in family life and often an added financial burden (Braman, 2004; Oliver & Hairston, 2008). For some former prisoners, returning to family means returning to victims or victimizers (Braman, 2004; Richie, 2001, 2002). Parents seeking to regain custody of their children also may create tension with caregivers or face an additional time demand as they balance many competing requirements and expectations. Women, in particular, may feel compelled to return to family caregiver roles (Leverentz, 2006a). For custodial parents, negotiating childcare needs while trying to secure employment, participate in drug treatment, meet the conditions of parole, and other reentry demands is an additional challenge (Richie, 2001).

Community Context

As stated earlier, prisoners are not evenly distributed across the population. This concentration of ex-prisoners suggests a need to look at the neighborhood context into which they are being released and how community members receive them. Although much of the research on public attitudes toward crime focuses on individual attitudes, there is emerging evidence that neighborhood characteristics and context may affect community members' response to returning ex-offenders (Bottoms & Wilson, 2004; Leverentz, 2008). Bottoms and Wilson tested the idea of neighborhood variation in attitudes toward crime in the United Kingdom. They found that punitiveness varied substantially, even in similarly high-crime areas. Punitiveness was positively correlated with negative attitudes toward multiculturalism, perceived threats to the social order, perceived social and physical disorder, and a lack of informal social control.

Thus, there was a neighborhood effect on attitudes, but not one that was shaped entirely by crime itself. This is consistent with other work that concludes that public attitudes about punishment may not reflect concerns about crime or risk of victimization but rather concerns over social conditions (Tyler & Boeckmann, 1997). In addition, there is emerging evidence that the local culture of how crime is framed may shape attitudes of punitiveness (Leverentz, 2008). Communities that frame the crime problem as a general and amorphous issue may be less tolerant of returning prisoners than those who have a more nuanced and individual-level understanding of offenders and former prisoners. For example, residents of and workers in one high-crime area made a distinction between "good kids," who nonetheless may have been involved in crime, and the small number of people who caused significant problems in the community. Overall, residents in this community were less punitive than those in another high-crime community that displayed a much more abstract and general understanding of the crime problem (Leverentz, 2008). Other studies similarly have found a level of acceptance of offenders in some neighborhoods, even as they condemned criminal activity (Pattillo-McCoy, 1999; Venkatesh, 2000, 2006; Warner & Rountree, 1997). This greater tolerance is likely to be extended to former offenders.

Residents in neighborhoods with high numbers of returning ex-prisoners may be more exposed to the situational explanations of crime, and they may be more likely to know people who have spent time in prison, which may lead to lower levels of punitiveness and greater levels of acceptance (Cullen, Clark, Cullen, & Mathers, 1985; Leverentz, 2008; Maruna & King, 2008). Thus, despite recidivism studies demonstrating that offenders in neighborhoods of higher inequality have a greater likelihood of reoffending (Kirk, 2009; Kubrin & Stewart, 2006; Mears et al., 2008), some evidence suggests that ex-prisoners may face less resistance reentering some high-crime communities. Returning to communities with a more nuanced understanding of incarceration and offenders might allow desisting ex-prisoners to redefine themselves as role models in the neighborhood (Giordano et al., 2002; Maruna, 2001; Sommers, Baskin, & Fagan, 1994). This ties back to ideas of cognitive transformations and the redemptive script that desisters adopt (Giordano et al., 2002; Maruna, 2001).

The reduced stigma of being a former prisoner in a high-crime neighborhood with a concentration of ex-prisoners may be limited to life in that neighborhood, however. This benefit is unlikely to carry outside the neighborhood, and indeed the stigma may be magnified outside the neighborhood (Travis, 2005). In other words, although aspects of daily life, and perhaps housing and other neighborhood-based needs, may be easier to access, the stigma of being an ex-prisoner (particularly an African American man) coming from a high-crime neighborhood is likely to be greater.

POLICY IMPLICATIONS

Ex-prisoners face many demands, the co-occurrence of which creates a "complex web of concerns and stressors that often compete with and exacerbate one another" (Richie, 2001, p. 380). Looking individually at each component of the demands and stressors that prisoners face deemphasizes how they interact with one another; it is important to consider the complexity of the issues.

Studies cited in this chapter illustrate that the barriers ex-prisoners face come from personal weaknesses and disadvantages, many of which can be addressed through programming in prison or after release. In addition, however, they face numerous barriers based on legal restrictions and informal stigma.

There are several ways in which policies may better meet the needs of returning ex-prisoners. First, although programs do exist that can help prisoners make the transition back to the community, aiding with employment, housing, and relational needs, they do not exist in the numbers necessary to respond to the high numbers of returning prisoners (Lawrence et al., 2002; Solomon et al., 2004). Expanding services, both in correctional facilities and in communities (particularly those facing a large number of returning prisoners), can help prisoners and their families adjust to the community and desist from offending. Although successful implementation of such programs is challenging, there is evidence that, if implemented well, these programs can reduce recidivism and improve reintegration efforts among participants (Lawrence et al., 2002).

Targeting interpersonal needs also has a strong positive association with reduced recidivism (Dowden & Andrews, 1999). One aspect of prison and reentry programming should be an acknowledgment and awareness of the complex networks in which many prisoners are embedded. Rather than encourage prisoners and former prisoners to avoid criminogenic social networks, as do many 12-step programs, service providers and programs should help prisoners build skills in negotiating relationships with those who may remain actively involved in criminal activity or drug use but who also may be the child, parent, or sibling of the prisoner. In addition, working with offenders and their family members may better prepare them to negotiate changing relationship dynamics that come with a return to their families and communities.

Programs and policies should encourage changing self-conceptions to help ex-prisoners believe in a "replacement self" (Giordano et al., 2002; Maruna, 2001). One way to encourage this transformation is through strength-based approaches such as reentry courts (Maruna & LeBel, 2003). Strength-based approaches seek to identify the assets that offenders have to offer rather than the deficits they have to correct. Using such an approach encourages hope, a future orientation, and a willingness to take responsibility (Maruna & LeBel, 2003; Richie, 2001). Ex-offenders may give back by working with others who are incarcerated or who suffer from drug addictions. These "professional exes" use their experience to help others. For those receiving such mentoring, it is often valuable to work with someone with first-hand experience of the same struggles (Brown, 1991; Maruna, 2001; Maruna & LeBel, 2003; Richie, 2001). For those providing the services, their offending past is reframed as meaningful to their present and future, helping foster the generative scripts that contribute to desistance (Maruna, 2001).

These efforts may be publicly recognized, as with certificates of rehabilitation, which can provide psychological and social benefits for the ex-offenders and serve as a signal to employers and others that the person is a worthy risk (Legal Action Center, 2004; Maruna, 2001; Maruna & LeBel, 2003). In addition to certificates of rehabilitation, third-party intermediaries and case management may increase the confidence employers have in hiring ex-prisoners (Solomon et al., 2004). A strength-based approach may help change community attitudes toward ex-offenders and encourage a more individualized and nuanced approach (Leverentz, 2008; Maruna & LeBel, 2003).

In addition to encouraging individual transformations and strengthening prosocial relationships, policies also may address formal restrictions such as required background checks and employment licensing restrictions. Stoll and Bushway (2008) conclude that the effect of reduced hiring of those with a criminal record is primarily a result of the formal requirement to perform background checks. Therefore, they suggest a reduction in legally required background checks. In contrast, Freeman (2008) suggests offering more information in background checks, not reducing their number or restricting the information released. More information, he suggests, would allow employers to make more informed decisions. Lucken and Ponte (2008) suggest a bona fide occupational qualification, which would remove some of the broad restrictions in occupational licensing while also providing some liability protection to employers in the case of reoffending.

In addition to reducing employment of ex-prisoners, requiring background checks and restrictions on occupational licensing also sends a symbolic message that one's criminal record is important, even when the importance to the particular job is not immediately clear. Thus, narrowing such requirements also limits the symbolic importance. In a similar vein, some U.S. cities, such as Boston and San Francisco, are removing questions about criminal histories from job applications for municipal jobs. They may still conduct background checks at a later stage, but they cannot use this information to screen initial applicants (Associated Press, 2009; Lucken & Ponte, 2008). This allows ex-offenders to get a foot in the door and requires employers to justify decisions to not hire those with a criminal record who otherwise have been deemed qualified. Again, this also sends a symbolic message to other employers about standards for evaluating criminal backgrounds. Restricting background checks, limiting licensing restrictions, and providing more information with background checks, including evidence of successful rehabilitation efforts, may encourage a reformed self to emerge and may reduce recidivism.

SUMMARY

Ex-prisoners face many challenges to successful community reintegration. Ex-offenders, especially those convicted of drug or sex offenses, face many formal barriers to meeting their needs. Two of the most pressing and immediate challenges are securing employment and housing. In addition to formal restrictions, they face additional stigma and discrimination, based on their ex-offender status and because of their race, sex, offense history, and neighborhood context.

Beyond social bonds such as employment, ex-offenders are strongly influenced by their own self-conceptions. Those who can envision a successful noncriminal lifestyle and believe in their own efficacy to achieve these goals are more likely to desist from offending. In addition, their relationships with romantic partners, children, other family members, and friends may ease or further challenge reentry efforts. Many ex-offenders are embedded in criminogenic social networks, of both friends and family. Learning to negotiate these relationships and to respond to changing dynamics as a result of incarceration is necessary for successful reentry.

Policy approaches to easing the barriers to reentry should include approaches that foster an alternative, redemptive self-conception. Such approaches may include volunteer or professional work with offenders or addicts, reentry courts, and certificates of rehabilitation. In addition, policies should encourage community and business support, to help ex-prisoners reintegrate back into their community and to meet their tangible and social needs. Possible policy approaches include revised use of criminal background checks and the adoption of strength-based approaches to reentry.

DISCUSSION QUESTIONS

1. What are the most important considerations in structural barriers to reentry? If you were in a position to hire or provide housing to an ex-offender, what would you want to know about him or her? What might influence your decision? How might your concerns be addressed?

2. What are the most important considerations in family reunification?

3. Design a program to aid prisoners in their reentry. What do you think the most important components are? How would you measure effectiveness?

4. How might you sell such a program to the public? What concerns do you anticipate? How would you address these concerns?

SUGGESTED READINGS

Braman, D. (2004). *Doing time on the outside: Incarceration and family life in urban America.* Ann Arbor: University of Michigan Press.

Hagan, J., & Coleman, J. P. (2001). Returning captives of the American war on drugs: Issues of community and family reentry. *Crime and Delinquency, 47*(3), 352–367.

Maruna, S. (2001). *Making good: How ex-convicts reform and rebuild their lives.* Washington, DC: American Psychological Association.

O'Brien, P. (2001). *Making it in the "free world": Women in transition from prison.* Albany: State University of New York Press.

Pager, D. (2007). *Marked: Race, crime, and finding work in an era of mass incarceration.* Chicago: University of Chicago Press.

Richie, B. (2001). Challenges incarcerated women face as they return to their communities: Findings from life history interviews. *Crime and Delinquency, 47*(3), 368–389.

Travis, J. (2005). *But they all come back: Facing the challenges of prisoner reentry.* Washington, DC: The Urban Institute Press.

REFERENCES

Associated Press. (2009). Cities ease crime history queries. *Boston Globe.* January 11, 2009, Retrieved September 16, 2009, from http://www.boston.com/jobs/news/articles/2009/01/11/cities_ease_crime_history_queries

Bales, W. D., & Mears, D. P. (2008). Inmate social ties and the transition to society: Does visitation reduce recidivism? *Journal of Research in Crime & Delinquency, 45*(3), 287–321.

Bottoms, A., & Wilson, A. (2004). Attitudes to punishment in two high-crime communities. In A. Bottoms, S. Rex, & G. Robinson (Eds.), *Alternatives to prison: Options for an insecure society* (pp. 366–405). Cullompton, UK: Willan.

Braman, D. (2004). *Doing time on the outside: Incarceration and family life in urban America.* Ann Arbor: University of Michigan Press.

Brooks, L. E., Solomon, A., Keegan, S., Kohl, R., & Lahue, L. (2005). *Prisoner reentry in Massachusetts.* Washington, DC: The Urban Institute.

Brooks, L. E., Visher, C. A., & Naser, R. L. (2006). *Community residents' experiences with reentry in selected Cleveland neighborhoods.* Washington, DC: The Urban Institute.

Brown, J. D. (1991). The professional ex-: An alternative for exiting the deviant career. *The Sociological Quarterly, 32*(2), 219–230.

Cadora, E., Schwartz, C., & Gordon, M. (2003). Criminal justice and Health and Human Services: An exploration of overlapping needs, resources, and interests in Brooklyn neighborhoods. In J. Travis & M. Waul (Eds.), *Prisoners once removed: The impact of incarceration and reentry on children, families, and communities* (pp. 285–312). Washington, DC: The Urban Institute Press.

Caspi, A., & Moffitt, T. E. (1995). The continuity of maladaptive behavior: From description to understanding in the study of antisocial behavior. In D. Cicchetti & D. J. Cohen (Eds.),

Developmental psychopathology. Vol. 2: *Risk, disorder, and adaptation* (pp. 472–511). New York: Wiley.

Chesney-Lind, M. (2002). Imprisoning women: The unintended victims of mass imprisonment. In M. Mauer & M. Chesney-Lind (Eds.), *Invisible punishment: The collateral consequences of mass imprisonment* (pp. 79–94). New York: The Free Press.

Chiricos, T., Barrick, K., Bales, W., & Bontrager, S. (2007). The labeling of convicted felons and its consequences for recidivism. *Criminology, 45*(3), 547–581.

Collins, P. H. (2000). *Black feminist thought: Knowledge, consciousness, and the politics of empowerment.* New York: Routledge.

Cullen, F. T., Clark, G. A., Cullen, J. B., & Mathers, R. A. (1985). Attribution, salience, and attitudes toward criminal sanctioning. *Criminal Justice and Behavior, 12*(3), 305–331.

Davis, A. Y. (1981). *Women, race, and class.* New York: Random House.

Dowden, C., & Andrews, D. A. (1999). What works for female offenders: A meta-analytic review. *Crime and Delinquency, 45*(4), 352–438.

Ebaugh, H. R. F. (1988). *Becoming an ex: The process of role exit.* Chicago: University of Chicago Press.

Edin, K., Nelson, T. J., & Paranal, R. (2001). *Fatherhood and incarceration as potential turning points in the criminal careers of unskilled men.* Working paper series, Institute for Policy Research. Evanston, IL: Northwestern University.

Freeman, R. (2008). Incarceration, criminal background checks, and employment in a low(er) crime society. *Criminology and Public Policy, 7*(3), 405–412.

Gendreau, P., Little, T., & Goggin, C. (1996). A meta-analysis of adult offender recidivism: What works? *Criminology, 34*(4), 575–607.

Giordano, P. C., Cernkovich, S. A., & Rudolph, J. L. (2002). Gender, crime, and desistance: Towards a theory of cognitive transformation. *American Journal of Sociology, 107*(4), 990–1064.

Glaze, L. E., & Bonczar, T. P. (2007). *Probation and parole in the United States, 2006.* Bureau of Justice Statistics Bulletin. Washington, DC: U.S. Department of Justice.

Glaze, L. E., & Maruschak, L. M. (2008). *Parents in prison and their minor children.* Special report. Washington, DC: Bureau of Justice Statistics.

Goffman, E. (1963). *Stigma: Notes on the management of spoiled identity.* New York: Simon & Schuster.

Greenfield, L. A., & Snell, T. L. (1999). *Women offenders.* Washington, DC: Bureau of Justice Statistics, U.S. Department of Justice.

Harlow, C. W. (1999). *Prior abuse reported by inmates and probationers.* Washington, DC: Bureau of Justice Statistics, U.S. Department of Justice.

Harlow, C. W. (2003). *Education and correctional populations.* Washington, DC: U.S. Department of Justice, Office of Justice Programs.

Heimer, K., & De Coster, S. (1999). The gendering of violent delinquency. *Criminology, 37*(2), 277–318.

Holzer, H., Raphael, S., & Stoll, M. (2001). *Will employers hire ex-offenders? Employer preferences, background checks, and their determinants.* Working paper series, Center for the Study of Urban Poverty. Los Angeles: University of California.

Horney, J., Osgood, D. W., & Marshall, I. H. (1995). Criminal careers in the short-term: Intra-individual variability in crime and its relation to local life circumstances. *American Sociological Review, 60*(5), 655–673.

Huebner, B. M. (2007). Racial and ethnic differences in the likelihood of marriage: The effect of incarceration. *Justice Quarterly, 24*(1), 156.

Kane, E. W. (2000). Racial and ethnic variations in gender-related attitudes. *Annual Review of Sociology, 26,* 419–439.

King, R. D., Massoglia, M., & Macmillan, R. (2007). The context of marriage and crime: Gender, the propensity to marry, and offending in early adulthood. *Criminology, 45*(1), 33–65.

Kirk, D. (2009). A natural experiment of the effect of residential change on recidivism: Lessons from Hurricane Katrina. *American Sociological Review, 74*(3), 484–505.

Kubrin, C. E., & Stewart, E. A. (2006). Predicting who reoffends: The neglected role of neighborhood context in recidivism studies. *Criminology, 44*(1), 165–195.

Laub, J. H., Nagin, D. S., & Sampson, R. J. (1998). Trajectories of change in criminal offending: Good marriages and the desistance process. *American Sociological Review, 63*(2), 225–238.

Laub, J. H., & Sampson, R. J. (2003). *Shared beginnings, divergent lives: Delinquent boys to age 70.* Cambridge, MA: Harvard University Press.

La Vigne, N. G., & Mamalian, C. A. (2004). *Prisoner reentry in Georgia.* Washington, DC: The Urban Institute.

La Vigne, N. G., Mamalian, C. A., Travis, J., & Visher, C. (2003). *A portrait of prisoner reentry in Illinois.* Washington, DC: The Urban Institute.

La Vigne, N. G., Visher, C., & Castro, J. (2004). *Chicago prisoners' experiences returning home.* Washington, DC: The Urban Institute.

Lawrence, S., Mears, D. P., Dubin, G., & Travis, J. (2002). *The practice and promise of prison programming.* Washington, DC: The Urban Institute.

Legal Action Center. (2004). *After prison: Roadblocks to reentry. A report on state legal barriers facing people with criminal records.* New York: Author.

Leverentz, A. (2006a). *"I put her through a particular hell": The role of family and friends in onset and desistance.* Los Angeles: American Society of Criminology.

Leverentz, A. (2006b). The love of a good man? Romantic relationships as a source of support or hindrance for female ex-offenders. *Journal of Research in Crime and Delinquency, 43*(4), 459–488.

Leverentz, A. (2008). *Neighborhood context of attitudes towards crime and reentry.* American Sociological Association annual meeting, Boston.

Lucken, K., & Ponte, L. M. (2008). A just measure of forgiveness: Reforming occupational licensing regulations for ex-offenders using BFOQ analysis. *Law & Policy, 30*(1), 46–72.

Lynch, J., & Sabol, W. (2001). *Prisoner reentry in perspective.* Crime policy report. Washington, DC: The Urban Institute.

Maruna, S. (2001). *Making good: How ex-convicts reform and rebuild their lives.* Washington, DC: American Psychological Association.

Maruna, S., & King, A. (2008). Giving up on the young. *Current Issues in Criminal Justice, 20*(1), 129–134.

Maruna, S., & LeBel, T. P. (2003). Welcome home? Examining the "reentry court" concept from a strengths-based perspective. *Western Criminology Review, 4*(2), 91–107.

Maruna, S., & Roy, K. (2007). Amputation or reconstruction? Notes on the concept of "knifing off" and desistance from crime. *Journal of Contemporary Criminal Justice, 23,* 104–124.

Mears, D. P., Wang, X. I. A., Hay, C., & Bales, W. D. (2008). Social ecology and recidivism: Implications for prisoner reentry. *Criminology, 46*(2), 301–340.

Mellow, J., & Christian, J. (2008). Transitioning offenders to the community: A content analysis of reentry guides. *Journal of Offender Rehabilitation, 47*(4), 339–355.

Oliver, W., & Hairston, C. F. (2008). Intimate partner violence during the transition from prison to the community: Perspectives of incarcerated African American men. *Journal of Aggression, Maltreatment & Trauma, 16*(3), 258–276.

Pager, D. (2003). The mark of a criminal record. *American Journal of Sociology, 108*(5), 937–975.

Pager, D. (2005). Walking the talk: What employers say versus what they do. *American Sociological Review, 70*(3), 355–380.

Pager, D. (2007). *Marked: Race, crime, and finding work in an era of mass incarceration.* Chicago: University of Chicago Press.

Pattillo-McCoy, M. (1999). *Black picket fences: Privilege and peril in the Black middle class.* Chicago: University of Chicago Press.

Petersilia, J. (1999). Parole and prisoner reentry in the United States. In M. Tonry & J. Petersilia (Eds.), *Prisons* (pp. 479–529). Chicago: University of Chicago Press.

Petersilia, J. (2003). *When prisoners come home: Parole and prisoner reentry.* Oxford: Oxford University Press.

Pettit, B., & Western, B. (2004). Mass imprisonment in the life course. *American Sociological Review, 69*(4), 151–169.

Richie, B. (2001). Challenges incarcerated women face as they return to their communities: Findings from life history interviews. *Crime and Delinquency, 47*(3), 368–389.

Richie, B. (2002). The social impact of mass incarceration on women. In M. Mauer & M. Chesney-Lind (Eds.), *Invisible punishment: The collateral consequences of mass imprisonment* (pp. 136–149). New York: The New Press.

Rubinstein, G., & Mukamal, D. (2002). Welfare and housing: Denial of benefits to drug offenders. In M. Mauer & M. Chesney-Lind (Eds.), *Invisible punishment: The collateral consequences of mass imprisonment* (pp. 37–49). New York: The Free Press.

Sabol, W. J., & Couture, H. (2008). Prison inmates at midyear 2007. *Bureau of Justice Statistics Bulletin.* Washington, DC: U.S. Department of Justice.

Sadovi, C. (2005, January 31). 10.5% of sex offenders put in single city zip code: Sending parolees to South Side group homes angers neighbors. *Chicago Tribune,* p. 1.

Sampson, R. J., & Laub, J. H. (1990). Crime and deviance over the life course: The salience of adult social bonds. *American Sociological Review, 55*(5), 609–627.

Sampson, R. J., & Laub, J. H. (1993). *Crime in the making: Pathways and turning points through life.* Cambridge, MA: Harvard University Press.

Sampson, R. J., Laub, J. H., & Wimer, C. (2006). Does marriage reduce crime? A counterfactual approach to within-individual causal effects. *Criminology, 44,* 465–508.

Scott, G. (2004). "It's a sucker's outfit": How urban gangs enable and impede the reintegration of ex-convicts. *Ethnography, 5*(1), 107–140.

Scott, G., Dewey, J., & Leverentz, A. (2006). *Community reintegration trajectories: A qualitative comparative study of gang-affiliated and non–gang-affiliated ex-offenders.* Chicago: Illinois Criminal Justice Information Authority.

Seal, D. W., Eldrige, G. D., Kacanek, D., Binson, D., & Macgowan, R. J. (2007). A longitudinal, qualitative analysis of the context of substance use and sexual behavior among 18- to 29-year-old men after their release from prison. *Social Science & Medicine, 65*(11), 2394–2406.

Solomon, A. L., Johnson, K. D., Travis, J., & Mcbride, E. C. (2004). *From prison to work: The employment dimensions of prisoner reentry. A report of the Reentry Roundtable.* Washington, DC: The Urban Institute.

Sommers, I., Baskin, D., & Fagan, J. (1994). Getting out of the life: Crime desistance by female street offenders. *Deviant Behavior, 15,* 125–149.

Stoll, M. A., & Bushway, S. D. (2008). The effect of criminal background checks on hiring ex-offenders. *Criminology & Public Policy, 7*(3), 371–404.

Travis, J. (2005). *But they all come back: Facing the challenges of prisoner reentry.* Washington, DC: The Urban Institute Press.

Tyler, T. R., & Boeckmann, R. J. (1997). Three strikes and you are out, but why? The psychology of public support for punishing rule breakers. *Law & Society Review, 31*(2), 237.

Uggen, C. (1999). Ex-offenders and the conformist alternative: A job quality model of work and crime. *Social Problems, 46*(1), 127–151.

Uggen, C. (2000). Work as a turning point in the life course of criminals: A duration model of age, employment, and recidivism. *American Sociological Review, 65*(4), 529–546.

Uggen, C., & Thompson, M. (2003). The socioeconomic determinants of ill-gotten gains: Within-person changes in drug use and illegal earnings. *American Journal of Sociology, 109*(1), 146.

U.S. Department of Education. (2008). *Funding education beyond high school: The guide to federal student aid 2009–2010.* Washington, DC: U.S. Department of Education.

Venkatesh, S. A. (2000). *American project: The rise and fall of a modern ghetto.* Cambridge, MA: Harvard University Press.

Venkatesh, S. A. (2006). *Off the books: The underground economy of the urban poor.* Cambridge, MA: Harvard University Press.

Vick, K. (2009, January 2). Sex offender laws are leading to homelessness. *Boston Globe.* Retrieved February 1, 2009, from http://www.boston.com/news/nation/articles/2009/01/02/sex_offender_laws_are_leading_to_homelessness

Visher, C., Debus, S., & Yahner, J. (2008). *Employment after prison: A longitudinal study of releasees in three states.* Washington, DC: The Urban Institute.

Warner, B. D., & Rountree, P. W. (1997). Local social ties in a community and crime model: Questioning the systemic nature of informal social control. *Social Problems, 44*(4), 520–536.

Warr, M. (1998). Life-course transitions and desistance from crime. *Criminology, 36*(2), 183–216.

Watson, J., Solomon, A. L., La Vigne, N. G., Travis, J., Funches, M., & Parthasarathy, B. (2004). *A portrait of prisoner reentry in Texas.* Washington, DC: The Urban Institute.

Western, B. (2002). The impact of incarceration on wage mobility and inequality. *American Sociological Review, 67*(4), 526–546.

Western, B., Kling, J. R., & Weinman, D. F. (2001). The labor market consequences of incarceration. *Crime and Delinquency, 47*(3), 410–427.

Western, B., Pettit, B., & Guetzkow, J. (2002). Black economic progress in the era of mass imprisonment. In M. Mauer & M. Chesney-Lind (Eds.), *Invisible punishment: The collateral consequences of mass imprisonment* (pp. 165–180). New York: The Free Press.

CHAPTER 15

Rehabilitation, Reentry, and Reintegration in Criminal Justice Education

Lior Gideon

Some of the first images that come to mind when we think about corrections are prison walls, armed guards, and hardened criminals. Often, it seems as though *correction* has lost its meaning and that the exclusive focus of incarceration is incapacitation and punishment. Indeed, to a large extent students seeking education in the field of corrections are introduced to philosophies of punishment, causes of crime, alternatives to incarceration (e.g., community forms of supervision), and ideas on how correction systems can function better by reducing recidivism rates, improving public safety, and becoming more cost effective. These foci come as no surprise given the huge number of people currently under criminal justice supervision in the United States; 2.1 million people are incarcerated in federal or state prisons or local jails (Harrison & Beck, 2005), and an additional 4.8 million people are serving some kind of community supervision such as probation or parole (Glaze & Palla, 2005). In fact, the incarceration rate in the United States has quadrupled in the last 30 years, leaving

Author's note: The author would like to thank Debbie Mukamal, from the Reentry Institute at John Jay College, for her advice and comments on earlier drafts of this manuscript. The author would also like to thank Gail Yuhsu Hsiao for her assistance in completing the database and preparing it for analysis.

us with the highest rate of incarceration in the industrialized world. In fact, the Bureau of Justice Statistics (2008) indicates that on June 30, 2007, there were 2,299,116 prisoners in federal, state, and local jails, an increase of 1.8% from year-end 2006.

One result of the explosion in our criminal justice system has been a corresponding increase in the number of students seeking a criminal justice education. In particular, students are interested in pursuing careers in law enforcement and legal studies, and to a lesser degree in corrections, the starting point of this work.

Despite the increased interest among students, only a handful of those studying criminal justice end up specializing in corrections and, in particular, in prisoner reentry. This trend is linked to the common understanding of what corrections entails. When students and others are asked to explain what the field of corrections means to them, the most common response is, "Corrections deals with prisons, and studying corrections teaches you how to be a correction officer or guard in jail or prison." Such views are shared by many who teach corrections and also by those who advise criminal justice students. This is particularly true of first-year students. Such limited understanding of the field and its potential may also explain policy and program trends in the criminal justice system over the last 30 years, which focus more on crime control and punishment and less on offender rehabilitation and reintegration.

It is perhaps not surprising that students have a limited view of criminal justice. One of the major problems of the American criminal justice system is an approach of locking up offenders rather than effectively addressing the problems fueling their criminal behavior. According to Mauer (1999), this is a direct result of the "get tough" movement that gained political momentum in the late 1970s and throughout the 1980s and 1990s. Consider the enormous number of people cycling through the criminal justice system. Approximately 700,000 people will leave state and federal prisons this year. Another 8 to 10 million people will cycle in and out of local jails each year, serving a life sentence in installments. In fact, nationally about 66% of prisoners will be rearrested within 3 years, and about 47% will be convicted for a new crime (Langan & Levin, 2002). Travis and Petersilia (2001) attribute this failure rate primarily to the fact that "prisoners are less prepared for reintegration and less connected to community-based social structures" (p. 291). Most released prisoners are released to parole supervision, despite the fact that parole supervision has not been proven effective at reducing recidivism rates (Petersilia & Turner, 1993). In fact, about 60% of all returns to prison stem from technical violations and minor crimes during the period of supervision, when offenders are subject to closer surveillance and monitoring (Beck, 2000; MacKenzie & De Li, 2002).

Therefore, it is important to reconsider reintegration as an essential topic to be covered independently in any criminal justice curriculum.

Given the fourfold increase in people going to and leaving prison over the last three decades and students' growing interest in the field of criminal justice, it is critical to develop courses that focus on the pressing topic of prisoner rehabilitation, reintegration, and reentry. Thus, the goal of this chapter is to stimulate interest and discussion about how to introduce such an important topic to college students in criminal justice and liberal arts programs. It is argued that although the rhetoric of many scholars in the field focuses on a paradigm of rehabilitation and reintegration, the practice of educating future practitioners and policymakers remains conservative and geared toward punishment.

CRIMINAL JUSTICE INTEREST IN REENTRY

The phenomenon of people leaving prison was called prisoner reentry at the end of the 1990s, when the director of the National Institute of Justice, Jeremy Travis, wrote, "But they all come back," reminding the criminal justice policymaking and practitioner communities that approximately a half million people return home from prison each year and directing attention to the need to address those people's transitions back to the community. Since that time, much attention has been appropriately paid by federal, state, and local governments, private foundations, the community, and faith-based providers to address this phenomenon (Austin, 2001; Jacobson, 2005). For instance, the Second Chance Act was initially introduced in the House of Representatives and Senate in 2004, and after long debates and revisions it was signed by President George W. Bush in April 2008. The act comprehensively addresses prisoner reentry issues by giving grants to states and localities, addressing legal barriers to reentry, authorizing research by the National Institute of Justice, awarding mentoring grants, and developing best practices in a number of arenas, including family issues, housing, and employment. However, the academic community has not kept pace with this flurry of interest and activity.

Reentry is the process of leaving prison and returning to society. Reentry is not a form of supervision, like parole. Reentry is not a goal, like rehabilitation or reintegration. Reentry is not an option. Reentry reflects the iron law of imprisonment: They all come back (Travis, 2005). Reentry is an issue affecting huge numbers of people and a range of systems, including corrections, health, workforce development, housing, drug treatment, welfare, law enforcement, families of released inmates, and communities in general (Clear, 2007). Many criminal justice practitioners—inside and outside correctional facilities—struggle with reentry, but there is insufficient research indicating what works.

METHOD

To achieve the goals of this study, we surveyed the course offerings of 80 universities and colleges across the United States.[1] We focused on universities that offer courses in criminology, criminal justice, and corrections. Using *U.S. News Report* for colleges and universities of 2008 as our sampling frame, we used a random sampling procedure to achieve a representative sample of schools from all over the United States. Specifically, we surveyed universities from the East Coast, the West Coast, the Midwest, the South, and the North. The majority of departments surveyed (about 64%) were criminal justice or criminology exclusively, whereas the remaining 36% combine criminal justice and criminology with another discipline such as sociology, political science, or law. We surveyed the programs using two phases. The first phase, in the fall of 2005, only 36 schools were selected. In the summer of 2008, we examined an additional 44 schools. The two sampling phases enabled us to examine developments in course offerings over a 3-year period. We examined each school's official Web site and their undergraduate and graduate course listings.

While surveying the Web sites, we identified 477 courses with some connection to the corrections discipline or to prisoners' experiences. Of those, about 28% were graduate-level courses, and another 28% were 400-level undergraduate courses. The remaining 44% were 100-, 200-, and 300-level courses, with 100-level courses being the least represented (less than 4%).

Some cautionary notes: Because we captured the data by reading course abstracts on the Web sites, we may have missed courses that are being taught but whose syllabi do not appear on the official Web sites of these departments. Moreover, because we relied on course abstracts, we may have overlooked courses whose abstracts do not describe prisoner or prisoner reentry issues but whose course contents may include such subjects. We relied exclusively on the descriptions provided by the departments as they appeared on their official Web sites; we did not make follow-up inquiries to the departments to determine whether additional courses were currently taught or what the actual course content included. Although this limited our insight on the number and scope of courses being offered, it enabled us to appreciate and identify the rhetoric of course offerings, using prisms similar to those of potential students. In this preliminary examination of the topic, we acknowledge the need to further review additional universities' and colleges' Web sites and course offerings. However, we ask the reader to consider this work as an exploratory examination.

We would also like the reader to consider the goal of this study: to capture the visibility of the topic as it appears to interested potential students who search course offerings using these Web sites before enrolling.

FINDINGS

Despite the rapid increase in the number of students seeking formal education in the field of criminal justice, we were surprised to learn that only 477 courses were offered in the field of corrections. Keep in mind that this number is to be divided by the 80 schools we examined. Most of the schools we examined offered three to five courses on various levels (i.e., 100, 200, 300, and 400 levels), with only a few schools offering large numbers of correction-related courses. As listed in Table 15.1, a handful of schools are responsible for slightly more than 40% of courses. Despite the limitations of this exploratory study, this low number makes a point one cannot ignore: There is a famine in correctional course offerings. We return to this point after elaborating on the type of classes being offered to students interested in studying corrections and the ways in which the subject is covered.

Table 15.1 Universities and Colleges With More Than Nine Correction-Related Courses	
Institution	Number of Correction-Related Courses
John Jay College, City University of New York	22
University of Cincinnati	19
Rutgers State University	17
State University of New York, Albany; University of Nebraska, Omaha	16
Sam Houston State University	15
University of South Florida	13
Michigan State University; Minnesota State University, Mankato; Northeastern University	12
Florida State University; Metropolitan State College of Denver; University of Maryland, College Park; Pennsylvania State University	9–11

An examination of the course offerings revealed that there were no pure reentry courses, meaning that there were no courses with *reentry* or *reintegration* in their titles. In addition, we sought to identify how many courses include such issues in their course synopses. We also examined how many courses dealt with rehabilitation and treatment of offenders. Table 15.2 presents the distribution of course topics. Notice that none of the departments surveyed offered courses with *reentry* or *reintegration* in their titles. In addition, only about 9% of the course titles suggest that the course deals with treatment or rehabilitation.

On the other hand, about 18% of the course titles appearing on the official Web sites declared that the course deals with community supervision, probation, or parole. Also, about one fifth of the courses were geared toward correctional administration.

Table 15.2   Topics of Courses as They Appear on the Official Web Sites of the Departments Surveyed

Course Topic	Number of Courses	Percentage of Courses
Reentry and reintegration	0	0
Treatment and rehabilitation	42	8.8
Probation, parole, and community-based supervision	88	18.4
Introduction to corrections	58	12.2
Administration in corrections	90	18.9
Legal issues in corrections	43	9.0
Penology and sociology of punishment	32	6.7
Advanced seminars in corrections	49	10.3
Other various courses*	75	15.7
Total	477	100

*Courses in this category include "Understanding Sex Offenders," "Prison Environment," "Historical Development of Corrections," and the like.

However, as can be seen in Table 15.3, only about 8.4% of the course descriptions had some reference to reentry or reintegration, none of which were introductory courses. A better coverage was present for rehabilitation, with 19.5% of the course description mentioning that topic as a topic to be covered by the course. The same presentation was found in regard to treatment, where we found 19.5% of the course descriptions to deal with this issue. In regard to community supervision and community corrections (i.e., probation and parole), about 19% of the course descriptions address these topics. Additionally, according to Petersilia (2003) although parole was originally designed to ease the transition from prison back to the community, and thus serving the goal of reintegration among others, de facto "parole supervision has shifted away from providing services to parolees and more toward providing surveillance activities" (Petersilia, 2003, p. 88). This has to do a lot with newly hired parole officers who differ from their predecessors, who were mostly trained as social workers. Today's parole officers are now trained in criminal justice with a policing orientation:

> Newly hired parole officers often embrace the surveillance versus the rehabilitation model of parole, along with the quasi-policing role that parole has taken on in some locals. . . . At the end of 2002, the most common educational field, was criminal justice, an academic field spawned in the 1960s to professionalize law enforcement. (Petersilia, 2003, p. 90)

When we compared university course offerings in the first phase with course offerings in the second phase, a surprisingly dismal reality revealed itself:

Table 15.3 Numbers and Percentages of Course Descriptions With a Focus on Reentry, Rehabilitation, Treatment, or Community Supervision		
Course Topic	**Number of Courses**	**Percentage of Courses**
Reentry or reintegration	40	8.4
Rehabilitation	93	19.5
Treatment	93	19.5
Community supervision	90	18.9
None of the above	161	33.8
Total	477	100.1

Universities that offered courses on rehabilitation and reintegration in the first phase have reduced their course offerings in these fields. As can be seen in Table 15.4, rehabilitation course offerings dropped by half, from 32.1% to 16.6%, and courses on treatment dropped from 25% to about 14%, whereas no meaningful decline in course offerings was observed for community supervision (i.e., parole and probation) or reentry and reintegration.

Most criminal justice programs at the universities and colleges we surveyed offer courses on corrections, alternatives to incarceration, parole and probation, and community-based corrections, with only a handful offering any coursework on the topic of prisoner treatment and rehabilitation and no courses on reintegration and reentry, at least as evidenced by these institutions' official Web sites. Consequently, in the following pages we present a discussion of how reentry and reintegration courses can be incorporated into college corrections curricula.

Table 15.4 Numbers and Percentages of Course Descriptions With a Focus on Reentry, Rehabilitation, Treatment, or Community Supervision

Course Topic	2005 Percentage of Courses	2008 Percentage of Courses	Percentage Point Change
Reentry and reintegration	6.9	6.4	−0.5
Rehabilitation	32.1	16.6	−15.5**
Treatment	25.2	13.9	−11.3*
Community supervision	20.6	20.3	−0.3
Total	131	187	

$*p \leq .05.$ $**p \leq .001.$

COURSE LEVELS AND DESIGN

Given the inevitable fact that nearly all prisoners will return home, all criminal justice students should be exposed to issues related to prisoner reentry during their first year. Thus, more emphasis should be placed on reentry and reinte-gration issues in introductory-level courses (i.e., 100-level courses). Furthermore, such important issues should be addressed at the beginning of the course and not left to the end of the semester. Exposing students to the burn-ing issues of reentry and reintegration in their first year of academic studies will lay the foundation for future courses that will emerge from the reentry and reintegration framework. Subsequent 200-, 300-, and 400-level courses should focus additional attention on the various practices that directly relate to reen-try and reintegration, pinpointing the critical issues faced by administrators and criminal justice practitioners. More advance courses should encourage stu-dents to survey the existing literature for new developments in reentry and rein-tegration while offering new directions of study. This should be the focus of all graduate courses in the field.

WHAT MIGHT A CORRECTIONS COURSE ON REENTRY COVER?

- Issues inside and outside prison, including what has fueled the incarcera-tion rate in the United States over the last three decades, what knowledge and tools are available for inmates upon incarceration and immediately before and after their release, and what social support networks are avail-able to released inmates.
- Program issues, including the components of a successful reentry model, with lessons learned from national demonstration initiatives such as the Serious and Violent Offender Initiative, Ready4Work Initiative, Mentoring Children of Prisoners Program, Council of State Governments' Reentry Policy Council, National Governors Association's Reentry Policy Academy, and Urban Institute Reentry Roundtable.
- Legislative and policy issues, including the evolution and extent of state and federal legal barriers and efforts to minimize them; efforts at the local, state, and federal levels to pass legislation to promote reentry, including the Second Chance Act; tax credits available to employers who hire people with criminal records (Pager, Western, & Bonikowski, 2006); sealing or expungement of criminal records for nonviolent low-risk offenders; and discrimination in employment, child support modifications, issuance of state-issued identification before release, certificates of rehabilitation, and access to criminal records. Additionally, a discussion of cross-agency, interdisciplinary collaboration is much needed.

- The impact of incarceration on families. In 1999, a majority of state (55%) and federal (63%) prisoners reported having a child under the age of 18 (Mumola, 2000).
- Costs of crime, for both individuals and communities. For individuals, a criminal record is associated with a 50% reduction in employment opportunities for Whites and 64% for African Americans (Pager, 2003). Also, between 1977 and 1999 state and local expenditures for corrections rose by 946%; in 2000 state budgets included $74 billion for corrections (Travis, 2005). Moreover, a book chapter written by Clear, Waring, and Scully (2005) demonstrates the devastating impact incarceration has on communities.

CONCLUSIONS AND POLICY IMPLICATIONS

"Reentry has become the new buzzword in correctional reform. . . . The concept means many things to many people and has varying levels of importance to various agencies" (Austin, 2001, p. 314). However, our study reveals a very different scenario: a lack of courses covering the subject of prisoner reentry. According to Braithwaite and Mugford (1994, p. 141), "the specter of failure hunts modern criminology and penology. Deep down many feel what some say openly: 'nothing works.'" Martinson's (1974) negative conclusion remains a leading assumption in correctional practice. This claim is supported by Cullen and Gendreau (2001, p. 314), who argue that scholars have been trained to show what does not work, as opposed to showing what does work. Such ideology blocks the development of studies in corrections and, in turn, the development of much-needed courses to expose students to new and emerging topics affecting people who are trying to reenter society after release from jail and prison. In the words of Cullen and Gendreau (2001, p. 314), such ideology "has been dysfunctional to the extent that it has inhibited academic criminology's ability to create an evidence-based agenda for how best to correct offenders." Furthermore, it is argued that such inhibition is the core reason for the scarcity of courses focused on rehabilitation and reintegration, a scarcity that may also affect future practitioners' ability to rehabilitate and reintegrate offenders.

These observations lead us to a wider concern about the way in which we socialize future practitioners and policymakers to deal with the growing problems of people under criminal justice supervision. In Weisburd's words (2000, p. 185), "the political climate is less sympathetic . . . because in good part, public policy in the USA has taken a much more punitive turn in the past decade."

For this reason, we might better understand the paradox presented at the beginning of this chapter, according to which more and more students are enrolling in criminal justice programs to gain education in this field, but few courses are offered in corrections. Even fewer students are majoring in this field, which might explain the decrease in the percentages of courses offered in the field, and the majority of criminal justice students are majoring in law enforcement and legal studies. At least this is how it appears from the official Web sites of the departments we examined.

We believe that our sample adequately reflects the course offerings available to students in criminal justice programs offered by American universities. The reader must keep in mind that although there are tens of thousands of courses in criminology, penology, criminal justice, and legal studies, this chapter's focus is limited to corrections-related courses. However, this preliminary review makes the crucial point that substantial college curriculum development is needed to educate the next generation of criminal justice thinkers about prisoner reentry. Mauer (1999) concludes his book by citing leaders in policing who suggest that "we can't arrest our way out of the problem" (p. 192). However, the philosophies of incarceration and rehabilitation and reintegration are not incompatible, as can be seen in Scandinavian countries such as Sweden and Denmark (Finn, 1988) and in states such as Minnesota where much effort is directed at rehabilitation, reintegration, and community safety (Harris, 1996). We must find and develop new ways to educate society's future generation in rehabilitation, reintegration, and reentry to better conceptualize the problems of mass incarceration, reentry, and recidivism. This important topic is not covered adequately by most corrections or criminal justice textbooks; at best, these subjects are covered in rudimentary chapters that call for additional discussion, a discussion that often is missing.

Because Web sites serve as the face of academic departments to the outside world and, in particular, to students, they must provide information about course availability and new courses under development. Departments should keep their Web sites current to reflect all course offerings on offender rehabilitation and prisoner reentry issues. These sites should enable potential students to learn more about the various practices in corrections.

Finally, we hope that the ideas conveyed in this chapter, in conjunction with the resources made available by the Second Chance Act of 2008, will generate a much wider, fertile discussion that will lead to the development of effective college curricula on the important topics of rehabilitation, reentry, and reintegration. The chapter concludes with a suggested set of resources.

AVAILABLE RESOURCES

The following list of resources on prisoner reentry is not intended to be comprehensive. For additional materials, readers should conduct literature reviews on the various topics related to prisoner reentry.

- *After Prison: Roadblocks to Reentry* is a state-by-state compendium of legal barriers in the areas of employment, housing, welfare, driver's license privileges, parental rights, voting rights, and access to records (http://www.lac.org/lac/index.php/roadblocks.html).
- *Every Door Closed: Barriers Facing Parents With Criminal Records,* by the Center for Law and Social Policy and Community Legal Services, documents the legal challenges parents with criminal justice involvement face in their attempts to rebuild their lives and families (http://www.clasp.org/publications/every_door_closed.pdf).
- *Reentry Policy Council Report* offers consensus-based, bipartisan recommendations for reducing public spending and increasing public safety by promoting the safe and successful return of offenders to the community. The report is organized by topic area and covers issues from admission into correctional facilities to return to the community (http://www.reentrypolicy.org).
- *Second Chance Act of 2007* is federal legislation designed to ensure the safe and successful return of prisoners to the community. The act was signed by President George W. Bush in March 9, 2008 (http://reentry policy.org/government_affairs/second_chance_act).
- *Invisible Punishment: The Collateral Consequences of Imprisonment,* edited by Marc Mauer and Meda Chesney-Lind (The New Press, 2002). Leading scholars and advocates in criminal justice explore the far-reaching consequences of 30 years of "get tough" policies on prisoners, on ex-felons, and on families and communities who have committed no crimes (http://www.sentencingproject.org/doc/publications/cc_mauer-focus.pdf).
- *Civil Penalties, Social Consequences,* edited by Christopher Mele and Teresa A. Miller (Routledge Taylor and Francis Group, 2005), offers an analysis of the challenges faced by people with criminal records upon reentry into society. Such penalties include a lifetime ban on receiving welfare and food stamps for people convicted of drug felonies and barriers to employment, child rearing, and housing opportunities. The book contains pieces by scholars in law, criminology, and sociology (http://www.brennancenter.org/programs/downloads/cj_book_civilpenalties.pdf).

- *National Governors Association Center for Best Practices, "Improving Prisoner Re-Entry Through Strategic Policy Innovations,"* outlines prisoner reentry issues and challenges facing the states and suggests strategies that governors and other policymakers can use to initiate long-term improvements (http://www.nga.org/portal/site/nga/menuitem.9123e83a1f 6786440ddcbeeb501010a0/?vgnextoid=205eea48adc26010VgnVCM 1000001a01010aRCRD&vgnextchannel=4b18f074f0d9ff00VgnVCM 1000001a01010aRCRD).

- *When Prisoners Come Home: Parole and Prisoner Reentry,* by Joan Petersilia (Oxford University Press, 2003), describes how the current parole system is failing, explores the harsh realities of prisoner reentry, and offers specific solutions to prepare inmates for release, reduce recidivism, and restore them to full citizenship while balancing the demands of public safety (http://www.oup.com/us/catalog/general/subject/Sociology/ CriminalJustice/Criminology/?view=usa&ci=019516086X).

- *But They All Come Back: Facing the Challenges of Prisoner Reentry,* by Jeremy Travis (The Urban Institute Press, 2005), describes the new realities of punishment in America and explores the nexus of returning prisoners with seven policy domains: public safety, families and children, work, housing, public health, civic identity, and community capacity. Travis proposes a new architecture for our criminal justice system, organized around five principles of reentry, that will encourage change and spur innovation.

- *From Prison to Home: The Dimensions and Consequences of Prisoner Reentry,* by Jeremy Travis, Amy Solomon, and Michelle Waul (The Urban Institute, 2001), is a monograph that describes the reentry process, the challenges for reentry, and the consequences of prisoner reentry along several key dimensions (http://www.urban.org/UploadedPDF/from_ prison_to_home.pdf).

- *Life on the Outside: The Prison Odyssey of Elaine Bartlett,* by Jennifer Gonnerman (Farrar, Straus and Giroux, 2004), is the first major work of journalism on the subject of reentry. It documents the story of Elaine Bartlett, who spent 16 years behind bars for selling cocaine—a first offense—under New York's controversial Rockefeller drug laws. The book opens on the morning of January 26, 2000, when she walks out of Bedford Hills prison. The book was selected as a finalist for the 2004 National Book Award (http://www.lifeontheoutside.com).

- *Doing Time on the Outside: Incarceration and Family Life in Urban America,* by Donald Braman (University of Michigan Press, 2004), is a compelling account of the unintended social, financial, and personal consequences of incarceration for the families of prisoners. Braman delivers a number of genuinely new arguments. Among these is the compelling assertion that incarceration is not holding offenders accountable to their communities, their victims, and their families and that the stigma of incarceration divides members of impoverished neighborhoods against one another (http://www.press.umich.edu/titleDetailDesc.do?id=17629).

- *Making Good: How Ex-Convicts Reform and Rebuild Their Lives,* by Shadd Maruna (American Psychological Association Books, 2001), is a narrative analysis of the lives of repeat offenders who, by all statistical measures, should have continued on the criminal path but instead have created lives of productivity and purpose. This examination of the phenomenology of "making good" includes an encyclopedic review of the literature on personal reform and a practical guide to the use of narratives in offender counseling and rehabilitation (http://www.apa.org/books/431645A.html).
- *Reentry Today: Programs, Problems, and Solutions,* by the American Correctional Association, contains short research reports and studies by leading scholars on the challenges faced by convicted offenders, society, and policymakers. The manuscript also brings together data from national surveys on the availability of reintegration programs and other related reentry programs. The manuscript can be obtained from the American Correctional Association (http://www.aca.org/store/bookstore/view.asp?product_id=1039&origin=results&QS='&YMGHFREproduct_name=Reentry+Today&pagesize=10&top_parent=188).
- *The Prisoner Reentry Institute at John Jay College of Criminal Justice in New York.* A committee of academics from the fields of criminal justice, criminology, and sociology developed a model reentry curriculum in the spring and fall of 2006. The materials developed by the committee are available through the Prisoner Reentry Institute for use by academic departments (http://www.jjay.cuny.edu/centersinstitutes/pri/x.asp).

NOTE

1. A sample of 80 schools is also sufficient enough to adhere to a statistical power of .80, as suggested by Cohen (1988), to allow enough sensitivity to examine our assumption in regard to the rhetoric of many scholars in the field to focus on punishment rather than rehabilitation. Consequently, we assumed a large effect size with binomial statistical tests.

REFERENCES

Austin, J. (2001). Prisoner reentry: Current trends, practices, and issues. *Crime and Delinquency, 47*(3), 314–334.

Beck, A. (2000). *Prisoners in 1999.* NCJ 183476. Washington, DC: U.S. Department of Justice, Bureau of Justice Statistics.

Braithwaite, J., & Mugford, S. (1994). Conditions of successful reintegration ceremonies: Dealing with juvenile offenders. *British Journal of Criminology, 34*(2), 139–171.

Bureau of Justice Statistics. (2008). *Prison statistics.* Retrieved September 18, 2008, from http://www.ojp.usdoj.gov/bjs/prisons.htm

Clear, R. T. (2007). *Imprisoning communities: How mass incarceration makes disadvantaged neighborhoods worse.* Oxford: Oxford University Press.

Clear, R. T., Waring, E., & Scully, K. (2005). Communities and reentry: Concentrated reentry cycling. In J. Travis & C. Visher (Eds.), *Prisoner reentry and crime in America* (pp. 179–208). New York: Cambridge University Press.

Cohen, J. (1988). *Statistical power analysis for behavioral sciences.* Hillsdale, NJ: Erlbaum.

Cullen, F. T., & Gendreau, P. (2001). From nothing works to what works: Changing professional ideology in the 21st century. *The Prison Journal, 81*(3), 313–338.

Finn, H. (1988). Corrections in two social welfare democracies: Denmark and Sweden. *The Prison Journal, 68*(1), 63–82.

Glaze, L. E., & Palla, S. (2005). *Probation and parole in the United States, 2004.* NCJ 210676. Washington, DC: U.S. Department of Justice, Bureau of Justice Statistics.

Harris, K. M. (1996). Key differences among community corrections acts in the United States: An overview. *The Prison Journal, 76*(2), 192–238.

Harrison, P. M., & Beck, A. J. (2005). *Prison and jail inmates at midyear 2004.* NCJ 208801. Washington, DC: U.S. Department of Justice, Bureau of Justice Statistics.

Jacobson, M. (2005). *Downsizing prisons: How to reduce crime and end mass incarceration.* New York: New York University Press.

Langan, P., & Levin, D. (2002). *Recidivism of prisoners released in 1994.* Bureau of Justice Statistics special report. NCJ 193427. Washington, DC: U.S. Department of Justice, Office of Justice Programs.

MacKenzie, D. L., & De Li, S. (2002). The impact of formal and informal social controls on the criminal activities of probationers. *Journal of Research in Crime and Delinquency, 39*(3), 243–276.

Martinson, R. (1974). What works? Questions and answers about prison reform. *The Public Interest, 35,* 22–54.

Mauer, M. (1999). *Race to incarcerate: The sentencing project.* New York: The New Press.

Mumola, C. (2000). *Incarcerated parents and their children.* NCJ 182335. Washington, DC: U.S. Department of Justice, Bureau of Justice Statistics.

Pager, D. (2003). Mark of a criminal record. *American Journal of Sociology, 108,* 937–975.

Pager, D., Western, B., & Bonikowski, B. (2006). *Discrimination in low-wage labor markets.* Princeton, NJ: Princeton University Press.

Petersilia, J. (2003). *When prisoners come home: Parole and prisoner reentry.* Oxford: Oxford University Press.

Petersilia, J., & Turner, S. (1993). Intensive probation and parole. In M. Tonry & N. Morris (Eds.), *Crime and justice: A review of research* (Vol. 17, pp. 281–335). Chicago: University of Chicago Press.

Second Chance Act of 2005 (H.R. 1593/S. 1060). Retrieved September 18, 2008, from http://reentrypolicy.org/government_affairs/second_chance_act

Travis, J. (2005). *But they all come back: Facing the challenges of prisoner reentry.* Washington, DC: The Urban Institute Press.

Travis, J., & Petersilia, J. (2001). Reentry reconsidered: A new look at an old question. *Crime and Delinquency, 47*(3), 291–313.

Weisburd, D. (2000). Randomized experiments in criminal justice policy: Prospects and problems. *Crime and Delinquency, 46*(2), 181–193.

CHAPTER 16

Conclusion

Integrative Triple R Theory: Rehabilitation, Reentry, and Reintegration

Lior Gideon and Hung-En Sung

The grim statistics presented in this book demonstrate a consensus according to which American incarceration rates are unjustifiably high, thus placing the United States at the top of a very dubious list of countries that compete over the highest incarceration rates in the world. Such an achievement is not something America should be proud of as a leading democracy. It is in this context that we hope to teach the reader, our students, and policymakers that there are better alternatives to incarceration and, when incarceration is warranted, that there are ways to ensure that offenders' needs will be addressed to minimize their chances of recidivating while promoting public safety and improving our communities.

We began by examining public attitudes toward rehabilitation and punitiveness, as the first step toward understanding of society's reaction to the crime problem. Examining public attitudes is also the same token that politicians and policymakers use to pass new legislation and to tally electoral votes. Gideon and Loveland (chapter 2) affirm that such attitudes are essential to correctional practice and policy. Moreover, they show that the majority of the surveyed public support rehabilitation and reintegration initiatives, and so it is no wonder that on April 9, 2008, President George W. Bush signed the Second

Chance Act, giving federal support to initiatives that aim to ease the transition of inmates from incarceration to the community. The Second Chance Act also promotes research initiatives to examine what practices are effective in rehabilitating and reintegrating convicted offenders. Therefore, chapter 3, by Jeglic, Maile, and Calkins-Mercado, focuses on assessing the risk and needs of different groups of offenders.

Through the chapters in this book, the reader comes to understand that such an assessment is crucial for rehabilitation and its consequence, successful reintegration. As mentioned by Sung and Gideon (chapter 4), the words of Sutherland (1939) become clear, that in order to treat and rehabilitate offenders we need to know who these offenders are, and the treatment must be individualized. This important insight draws its roots from the medical model, which acknowledges that not all people are alike. Indeed, different offenders have different needs, and they are also characterized by different risk levels. Such distinctions are crucially important when aiming at successful rehabilitation and reintegration. Jeglic and her colleagues (chapter 3) discuss the importance of risk and needs assessment for different offenders and describe the risk–need–responsivity model. Porter's chapter on diversion programs and specialized courts (chapter 6) also addresses the needs of offenders and alternatives to incarceration that address such needs. Welsh's chapter (chapter 7) on substance-abusing offenders adds another layer to this discussion. Using a thorough review of evidence-based research, Welsh systematically demonstrates how substance abuse programs can reduce future substance abuse and recidivism. Guerrero's (chapter 8) discussion on educational and vocational programs addresses another dismal fact: Most offenders are uneducated and lack basic vocational skills. In this chapter, Guerrero demonstrates how prison-based vocational and educational programs addressing such dire need can achieve promising results. These arguments are supported by Tarlow (chapter 13). Tarlow argues that employment barriers are a chief reason for relapse and reoffending, and this argument is supported by Leverentz (chapter 14). Lussier, Dahabieh, Deslauriers-Varin, and Thomson's chapter on violent and sexual offenders (chapter 9) presents another angle to the discussion focusing on high-risk offenders, making the argument that such offenders are the ones who need the full attention of the system and also benefit the most from such attention in terms of lower recidivism rates. Lussier and his colleagues present a Canadian approach to dealing with such offenders. Corzine McMullan's discussion on medical and psychiatric attention (chapter 10) adds another dimension to the discussion of these offenders' needs and the potential risks to the community from overlooking such needs. Shifting the discussion from hard-core needs, Frazier (chapter 11) discusses a different yet equally important dimension: spiritual needs. Using symbolic interaction theory with an emphasis on the pivotal role of social capital, she discusses the importance of spiritual capital, enabling the reader to grasp the importance of faith in the rehabilitation process and in our communities. Taxman's chapter on parole supervision (chapter 12) focuses on what is probably the most important stage of reintegration: the reentry point. Taxman argues that certain actions by supervision agents can increase offenders' access to and retention in treatment programs and advocates a seamless system of care that brings public health and criminal justice agencies together in the pursuit of crime and recidivism reduction.

Leverentz (chapter 14) presents a thorough discussion of the barriers to reintegration, describing the multiple needs and impediments faced by released offenders as they seek housing, employment, and new personal relationships. Leverentz argues that service providers should help prisoners build the social skills they need to navigate difficult situations that often constitute the first impediment to successful reintegration: dealing with old friends and family members who are engaged in criminal and other unlawful behavior. Leverentz's chapter strengthens the argument that we need to rethink our correctional practices to focus on rehabilitation and reintegration of offenders into the normative society. Finally, Gideon's chapter on college curricula (chapter 15) argues that we must also rethink ways in which we educate the practitioners of the future. This chapter makes the argument that academic programs must be more open to the field of corrections, particularly rehabilitation, while developing course offerings and curricula in the specific niche of offender treatment, rehabilitation, and reintegration. Such consciousness is an essential stage in how we think about corrections and how we educate the next generation of thinkers.

RETHINKING CORRECTIONS: THE TRIPLE R THEORETICAL MODEL

The emergence of the reentry movement in the early 1990s was followed by a flurry of definitions and explanations of what reentry is and what it means. How different are rehabilitation and reintegration? And in particular, how different is reentry from reintegration and rehabilitation? Are they the same? Reading previously published work and the chapters submitted for this book, we came to realize that such definitions are murky. Therefore, we will try to clear some of the mist that surrounds these definitions by presenting a theoretical model that brings the three concepts—rehabilitation, reentry, and reintegration—together as different components of a lengthy correctional process (Figure 16.1).

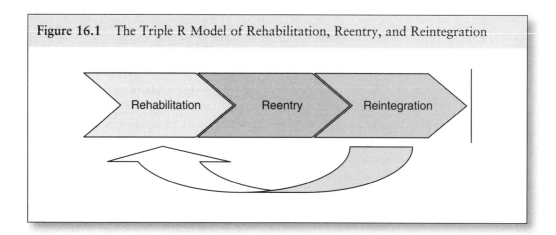

Figure 16.1   The Triple R Model of Rehabilitation, Reentry, and Reintegration

Assessment and Rehabilitation

The Triple Rs are integral parts of an ongoing process. The process begins with the initial rehabilitation of the offender as a result of the deliberate effort of criminal justice authorities and self-motivated participation of or passive compliance from the offender. We believe that the lack of systematic implementation of evidence-based rehabilitation interventions in our prisons is responsible for the unacceptable fact that 67.5% of state prison inmates were rearrested within 3 years of their release (Langan & Levin, 2002). Too many offenders have gone through their correctional experiences without meaningful exposure to research-informed rehabilitative interventions, which are always guided by careful need assessment, risk evaluation, and service matching such as the screening suggested by the risk–need–and responsivity (RNR) model. Once the risks and needs of the offender are assessed, a corresponding intervention should be planned and administered. An initial risk and need assessment should be done at an earlier stage, preferably before sentencing, as is usually done in the presentence investigation report and initial intake screening in jails. This is important to identify the actual risks and needs that may have initially contributed to the present offense and for potential diversion purposes. A similar conceptual framework was illustrated by Taxman (chapter 12) in regard to a seamless system of care for substance-abusing offenders in the community. A second, more systematic screening and assessment should be conducted during the initial stages of processing in the correctional system. That does not mean that an assessment should not be conducted before sentencing decisions. After the assessment, treatment that is aimed at addressing the specific needs of the offender (e.g., substance abuse, lack of formal education, medical, mental, spiritual) and even the addressing of some of the needs of his or her family is desirable, although we acknowledge the difficulty in implementing such family intervention. It is in this rehabilitative stage that we must plant the seeds for successful reintegration, hence the arrow from rehabilitation to reintegration in Figure 16.1.

Once intervention is completed, another assessment should follow. This assessment should reexamine the progress made during treatment while addressing the risks and needs of the offender before his or her discharge to the community. Rehabilitation should be examined in the exact same way we examine medical rehabilitation. In that regard we recommend that offenders be treated while incarcerated.

Reentry

Despite the common misconception, *reentry* refers not to intervention strategies or programs but to the natural transition from an institutionalized existence to a law-abiding and productive lifestyle in the community. It refers to the physical relocation (a physical dimension), with all its social and psychological demands, that every released inmate has to confront and manage. For this reason it is called reentry—the offender reenters and rejoins society. Despite the universality of this physical transition, individual ex-offenders display behavioral outcomes co-determined by their prior rehabilitation experiences and ongoing progress in reintegration. The shock of reentry can be overwhelming to newly released inmates who served longer sentences. As optimistic as one may be, leaving prison or jail with nothing to look forward to and no one to catch you can undermine successful reintegration. Differently put, the experiences of the first seconds, minutes, and hours after one returns to the community are extremely important to the smooth and lasting adjustment to the demands of reentry and will determine the direction and length of the reintegration process. It is helpful to use an analogy from the medical practice. People who are discharged from long hospitalization periods are usually escorted by a family member or a caregiver, with a detailed discharge plan and recommendations for continuing treatment and checkups. Without a deliberate effort to sustain the therapeutic gains beyond release, the benefits of treatment may be quickly lost. Consequently, as suggested by Gideon (2009), release from prison or jail should not be done without proper supervision in the community. Such supervision should be for at least a year after release. During this year, the reintegration process begins.

Reintegration

Reintegration is the functional aspect, as opposed to the physical dimension, of the transition from incarceration to community. As such, it can be understood as an outcome evaluation stage in that it allows us to examine how the seeds of rehabilitation developed to guide and support the offender in meeting the mundane and yet daunting challenges of normative life. For this reason, an arrow is drawn back from reintegration to rehabilitation in Figure 16.1. Reintegration comprises the availability and use of transitional services and the psychosocial adaptation of the ex-offender. It can progress or stall, succeed or fail. Thus, reintegration is somewhat similar to rehabilitation: Both processes depend on the planned interventions by correctional authorities and the individual contributions made by the ex-offender. In this context it becomes appropriate to discuss evidence-based practices and their effect on recidivism reduction. We now have sufficient evidence to show that treatment is effective for many substance abusers and that vocational and educational programs— and particularly college-level education—are effective in promoting successful reintegration for many offenders. We also know that helping released offenders gain a legitimate source of employment is associated with reduced recidivism. But more than anything else, we know that properly developed rehabilitation interventions that address the needs of individual offenders can later be evaluated in the reintegration stage. Once we identify individual needs and sources and level of risk, we can address these factors throughout the process. In evaluating the success of reintegration, we can look at the baseline needs and risks identified to confidently say whether and how they were addressed.

Discharge Plan

This discussion will not be complete without another dimension: the discharge plan. Discharge plans provide the critical link between the prison-based rehabilitation process and the transition from incarceration to community. According to Mellow et al. (2008, p. 5), a "primary goal of discharge plan is to link inmates with appropriate health and human service providers in the community to address their problems early on, before they violate their conditions of community supervision, or be arrested for a new offense." Discharge planning is an essential effort that directs the to-be-released inmate in the right direction or to the right stepping stone that will enable the offender to reach his or her goal. In fact, the entire rehabilitation, reentry, and reintegration process should be coordinated with the community to promote collaborative efforts that will ensure a continuum of care during the reentry process for the purpose of successful reintegration. Indeed, community supervision agencies and public health agencies often work together to achieve the best outcomes. This was also suggested by many released offenders, who reported that supervision in the community was one of the major driving forces of their success (see Gideon, 2009). It is also interesting to note that many of the offenders interviewed by Gideon perceived supervision not as a punitive measure but as a guiding hand for the first few months after release.

To summarize, *rehabilitation* is the actual intervention and treatment, guided by a thorough assessment of risks and needs, administered during incarceration. The intervention or treatment must correspond with the results of the assessment. *Reentry* is the physical resettlement and participation in the community of a former inmate. Consequently, reentry is a crucial part of a lengthy natural process that the ex-offender has to adjust to and manage. *Reintegration* is the continuation of the rehabilitation process and underpins the reentry process. It is a continuous struggle to "make good" (Maruna, 2001), maintained by the interaction between correctional authorities and the returning ex-offender and supported by the individual's family and community. The ex-offender plays new prosocial roles, experiments with new patterns of thinking and conduct, learns to satisfy his or her psychosocial needs through legitimate means, and tries to foster a new public image and self-perception. Depending on the needs of the individual offender, eligibility for services varies. At the end of this process, we can evaluate the outcomes of rehabilitation to derive evidence-based conclusions that will direct future policy. Therefore, the entire process of rehabilitation, reentry, and reintegration is characterized by a feedback loop that can benefit policymakers by providing tangible evidence. Although measuring successful rehabilitation and reentry is difficult, we can easily point at measurable outcomes that contribute to successful reintegration. A feedback loop also becomes apparent when the process fails to break the cycle of crime and recidivism and the released offender is returned to further incarceration, where the assessment and corresponding intervention are resumed. For example, we can talk about gaining legitimate employment, enrolling in college, avoiding alcohol and other drugs, and supporting oneself and other family members as clear, measurable outcomes that indicate successful reintegration. Correspondingly, these will also be outcomes of the rehabilitation process. However, rehabilitation can be deemed successful if it puts offenders in a better position to deal with the challenge of post-incarceration communal living. Reentry by itself, as a natural and universal experience, cannot have any measurable outcomes as it relates to the reintegration process. Its effectiveness can be measured only at the end of the process, as a measure of successful reintegration.

In chapter 12 Taxman describes the seamless system using an organizational approach to explain the need for coordinated service delivery between criminal justice agencies and care providers in the community. The discussion revolves around how the boundaries of these organizations should be expanded to provide a better delivery system that will be based on a continuum of care. In our Triple R model we seek to supplement this approach. The chapters of this book systematically argue that careful assessment of risks and needs is desired to tailor an appropriate intervention. Such an intervention should address the needs of the client while preparing him or her to reenter the civil society and begin his or her integration process. Therefore, we suggest that the seamless approach can be expanded to include a systematic approach of coordinated service delivery and to include the ways in which we view our correctional practices in regard to rehabilitation, reentry, and reintegration of offenders, an interlocking process.

SUMMARY

Rehabilitation as a correctional practice can be characterized as a swinging pendulum. However, the need to rehabilitate offenders is constant, and the idea of successful rehabilitative and reintegration practices has become a focal point of today's correctional practice and policy. Although the reentry movement is fairly new, its ideas are well established, and their roots can be traced to previous centuries. No matter how brutal corporal punishments were, they were built on shame and reintegration (when they did not result in death), or what we call "restorative justice" today, meeting society's need to avenge while restoring the peace and reintegrating the wrongdoer back into the community.

Again the pendulum has swung, and we now understand that punitive attitudes promote only the illusion of safety. When more than 700,000 inmates are returning from prison to the community and millions are being released from jails every year, without properly addressing their needs we do not promote public safety. The burden of high rates of imprisonment and reentry over the past two decades has strained the capacity of many communities, particularly some of the most vulnerable, to maintain successful civic life. The key tasks that communities are known for—raising children, providing a sense of security and pride, providing a healthy environment for families, providing jobs, and sustaining open exchanges and support—are jeopardized when large portions of the population, including young people, are going in and out of correctional facilities without ever being treated. More than half of our prison and jail inmates are diagnosed with some mental health problem. This is a direct result of the drastic reduction in the number of beds available to treat such people in a nonpunitive environment, which has shifted the responsibility for treating them to those who are less qualified to do so: correctional personnel. This has yielded a nasty backlash in specific communities and in society at large.

It is clear that education is essential practice for most incarcerated offenders, as it improves their self-esteem and gives them a new chance at social mobility by enabling them to obtain legitimate employment. We now know that educating offenders and providing substance abusers with adequate treatment is cost effective, particularly for drug offenders. From the chapters of this book and the many evidence-based studies they cite, we learn that intervention in the rehabilitation and reintegration stages is highly effective for those considered to be high-risk offenders. Consequently, the public, politicians, and policymakers acknowledge that something must be done. After decades of blindly following the Rockefeller drug laws, New Yorkers have initiated a heated and healthy debate on the rationality, effectiveness, and morality of existing penal philosophies and practices. We are certain that policymakers and the public in the rest of the country will also engage in similar dialogues, if they have not already done so. If we want to "correct" offenders we must think of better ways to do so, including labeling less, treating more, and saving incarceration for offenders who really deserve to be isolated from society. Although this book includes much discussion about prison-based interventions, we do not accept unconditionally America's current reliance on imprisonment for making communities safer and more just. On the contrary, we recognize the urgent need for a profound reexamination and overhaul of our penal options and believe that no society can expect its correctional system to fix all the mammoth social problems resulting from the failure of its educational, economic, familial, and communitarian institutions. Evidence-based rehabilitation can be effective in changing many criminal offenders and should be embraced because of its efficacy, but it does not address the root causes of crime, including many forms of inequality and injustice. It's time to rethink corrections in the broader context of social justice and the ways in which we rehabilitate and reintegrate those who have caused us harm.

REFERENCES

Gideon, L. (2009). "What shall I do now?" Released offenders' expectations to be supervised upon release. *International Journal of Offender Therapy and Comparative Criminology, 53*(1), 43–56.

Langan, P. A., & Levin, D. J. (2002, June). *Recidivism of prisoners released in 1994.* NCJ 193427. Washington, DC: Bureau of Justice Statistics.

Maruna, S. (2001). *Making good: How ex-convicts reform and rebuild their lives.* Washington, DC: American Psychological Association.

Mellow, J., Hoge, S. K., Lee, D. J., Natarajan, M., Yu, S. S. V., Greifinger, R. B., et al. (2008, Spring). *Mapping the innovation in correctional health care service delivery in New York City.* Retrieved September 16, 2009, from http://www.jjay.cuny.edu/centersinstitutes/pri/publications/asp

Sutherland, E. H. (1939). *Principles of criminology* (3rd ed.). Chicago: J.B. Lippincott.

Index

About the Editors

Lior Gideon, Ph.D., is an associate professor at John Jay College of Criminal Justice in New York. He specializes in corrections-based program evaluation and focuses his research on rehabilitation, reentry, and reintegration, particularly by examining offenders' perceptions of their needs. His research interests also involve international and comparative corrections-related public opinion surveys and their effect on policy. Dr. Gideon has published several manuscripts on these topics and is completing his third book on offenders' needs during reintegration, to be published by Springer. Dr. Gideon earned his Ph.D. from the Institute of Criminology at the Hebrew University in Jerusalem and completed a postdoctoral fellowship at the University of Maryland's Bureau of Governmental Research.

Hung-En Sung, Ph.D., is an associate professor at John Jay College of Criminal Justice. He specializes in substance abuse and comparative analysis of crime and justice and has published extensively on these issues. In the area of substance abuse policy and practice, his current work focuses on the diversion and treatment of chronic offenders with co-occurring disorders and the practice and impact of faith-based substance abuse treatment. His comparative research has revolved around the impact of democratization on political corruption and the administration of criminal justice.

About the Contributors

Cynthia Calkins-Mercado, Ph.D., is an assistant professor of psychology at John Jay College of Criminal Justice in New York. Her research examines empirical evidence underlying legislation and policy on sex offenders. Dr. Mercado is also involved in a major study of the causes and context of sexual abuse of minors by Catholic clergy.

Melissa Dahabieh has an M.A. in criminology from Simon Fraser University. Her research interests include risk management and community reintegration for high-risk sexual offenders. She works as a researcher for the government of Canada.

Nadine Deslauriers-Varin is a Ph.D. student at the School of Criminology, Simon Fraser University, British Columbia, Canada. Her Ph.D. thesis aims to investigate innovations in modus operandi and offending patterns of high-risk sex offenders. She holds the prestigious Vanier Canada Graduate Scholarship. Her research focuses on police investigation and police interrogation.

Beverly D. Frazier is an assistant professor at John Jay College of Criminal Justice. She earned her Ph.D. in social welfare from the University of Pennsylvania, where she completed a cross-sectional prisoner reentry study in Philadelphia. Dr. Frazier is also a nonresident fellow at the Center for African Studies and Program for Research on Religion and Urban Civil Society, both at the University of Pennsylvania, and has researched and written extensively on various aspects of prisoner reentry.

Georgen Guerrero is a faculty member at Texas State University and earned his Ph.D. in criminal justice with a specialization in criminology from Sam Houston State University. His areas of expertise include criminology, juvenile delinquency, penology, and ethics. Dr. Guerrero's research focuses primarily on incarcerated populations and unethical practices by criminal justice practitioners.

His research has led to several refereed publications in the areas of criminology, penology, and juvenile justice. In 2008 he was awarded the William L. Simon/Anderson Publishing Outstanding Student Paper Award and the Academy of Criminal Justice Affirmative Action Mini-Grant Award for his research in corrections. He is a member of the Academy of Criminal Justice Sciences, American Society of Criminology, Southwestern Association of Criminal Justice, and Texas Association of Criminal Justice Educators. Dr. Guerrero has more than 10 years of field experience in several criminal justice agencies working in many supervisory and nonsupervisory positions, such as adult probation officer, juvenile probation officer, detention shift supervisor, and detention intake supervisor.

Gail Y. Hsiao is a doctoral student at American University. She has a law degree from the National Cheng-Chi University and a master's degree in criminal justice from John Jay College of Criminal Justice in New York. Ms. Hsiao is involved in several funded research projects on the treatment of substance abusers, the performance of victim service agencies, and the comparative analysis of public attitudes toward correctional policies.

Elizabeth L. Jeglic, Ph.D., is an associate professor of psychology at John Jay College of Criminal Justice in New York. Her research interests include the treatment and assessment of sex offenders and sex offender legislation. Along with her colleague, Dr. Cynthia Calkins-Mercado, she recently received a National Institute of Justice Grant to study sex offender placement decisions in New Jersey.

Andrea Leverentz is an assistant professor of sociology and the director of the graduate certificate program in forensic services at the University of Massachusetts, Boston. She earned her Ph.D. from the Department of Sociology at the University of Chicago. She previously worked in the office of the Illinois attorney general, where she conducted research on community development, delinquency prevention programs, and law enforcement responses to street gangs. Her primary research interests are ex-prisoner reentry, public attitudes toward crime and reentry, and communities and crime. Her current research addresses the reentry experiences of women and how communities construct the "crime problem." Her work has appeared in the *Journal of Research in Crime and Delinquency;* in addition, she is completing a book manuscript on the social context of women's reentry from prison.

Natalie Loveland earned her M.A. in criminal justice, with a specialization in criminology and deviance, from John Jay College of Criminal Justice. Her thesis, "Public's Perception on Prisoner Reentry, Reintegration, and Rehabilitation," has been incorporated into this book. She trained as a police officer at the St. Johns River Community College, where she graduated as a squad leader and second academically in her graduating class. Currently she is a law enforcement officer with the Gainesville Police Department in Florida.

Patrick Lussier, Ph.D., is an assistant professor in the School of Criminology at Simon Fraser University. He is the co-director of the Centre for Research on Sexual Violence and a member of the Centre for Social Responsibility at Simon Fraser University. Lussier is the co–principal investigator of the Vancouver Longitudinal Study, which examines the psychosocial development of a cohort of at-risk children. His major research interest is the origins of aggression and violence. His research focuses on the risk factors and developmental pathways of sexual aggressors of women and children. His work has appeared in *Criminology, Criminal Justice and Behavior, Journal of Interpersonal Violence, Justice Quarterly,* and *Journal of Criminal Justice.*

Doris Layton MacKenzie is a professor in the Department of Criminology and Criminal Justice at the University of Maryland and director of the Evaluation Research Group. She earned her Ph.D. from Pennsylvania State University; was on the faculty of the Louisiana State University, where she was honored as a Researcher of Distinction; and was awarded a visiting scientist position at the National Institute of Justice. As visiting scientist, she provided expertise to federal, state, and local jurisdictions on correctional boot camps, correctional policy, intermediate sanctions, research methodology, experimental design, statistical analyses, and evaluation techniques. As an expert in criminal justice, Dr. MacKenzie has consulted with state and local jurisdictions and has testified before U.S. Senate and House committees. She has an extensive publication record on such topics as examining what works to reduce crime in the community, inmate adjustment to prison, the impact of intermediate sanctions on recidivism, long-term offenders, methods of predicting prison populations, self-report criminal activities of probationers, and boot camp prisons. She has directed several funded research projects and has served as chair of the American Society of Criminology's Division on Corrections and Sentencing, vice president of the American Society of Criminology (ASC), and president of the Academy of Experimental Criminology (AEC). She has been elected fellow in the ASC and AEC. In 2007, she was awarded a Fulbright Research Scholar grant to study the new community corrections programs in China.

Christian Maile is a doctoral student in the clinical forensic psychology program at John Jay College of Criminal Justice, City University of New York. His research interests include the assessment and etiology of sex-offending behavior and the development and application of psychological techniques to enhance self-disclosure of sensitive information.

Elizabeth Corzine McMullan is an assistant professor at Troy University. She has served as the key academic advisor to the Jacksonville Re-entry Center and Jacksonville Mental Health Court. She earned her Ph.D. in administration of justice with a graduate minor in educational research from the University of Southern Mississippi. Her work has been published in *Women & Criminal Justice,* the *Journal of Interpersonal Violence,* and the *Journal of Criminal Justice and Popular Culture.*

Rachel Porter, M.A., is a senior researcher at the Center for Court Innovation and teaches in the Department of Sociology at John Jay College as an adjunct professor. She is working toward her Ph.D. at the City University of New York graduate center in sociology.

Mindy S. Tarlow is chief executive officer and executive director of the Center for Employment Opportunities (CEO). She began her association with CEO as a program director at the Vera Institute of Justice in 1994, where she managed the successful spin-off of CEO from Vera. Before joining CEO, Ms. Tarlow spent almost 10 years at the New York City Office of Management and Budget. Ms. Tarlow co-authored the mayor's Safe Streets, Safe City Omnibus Criminal Justice Program. She is a member of the National Advisory Board of the Vera Institute of Justice National Associates Program and the Prisoner Reentry Institute Advisory Board at John Jay College of Criminal Justice; a founding board member of the Workforce Professionals Training Institute; and vice president of the New York City Employment & Training Coalition. Most recently, Ms. Tarlow served on the Mayor's Commission for Economic Opportunity and the Governor's Transition Team on Criminal Justice. She is also an adjunct professor at New York University's Robert F. Wagner Graduate School of Public Service.

Faye S. Taxman is a professor in the Administration of Justice Department, co-director of the Network for Justice Health, and director of the research program in evidence-based corrections and treatment at George Mason University. Dr. Taxman is recognized for her work in the development of seamless systems of care models that link criminal justice with other service delivery systems and in reengineering probation and parole supervision services and organizational change models. She is the senior author of *Tools of the Trade: A Guide to Incorporating Science Into Practice,* a publication of the National Institute on Corrections that provides a guidebook to implementation of science-based concepts. She is on the editorial boards of the *Journal of Experimental Criminology* and *Journal of Offender Rehabilitation.* She has published articles in the *Journal of Quantitative Criminology, Journal of Research in Crime and*

Delinquency, Journal of Substance Abuse Treatment, Journal of Drug Issues, Alcohol and Drug Dependence, and *Evaluation and Program Planning.* She received the University of Cincinnati award from the American Probation and Parole Association in 2002 for her contributions to the field. She is a fellow of the Academy of Experimental Criminology and a member of the Correctional Services Accreditation Panel of England. In 2008, the American Society of Criminology's Division of Sentencing and Corrections recognized her as a distinguished scholar. She has a Ph.D. from Rutgers University's School of Criminal Justice and a B.A. from the University of Tulsa.

Chris Thomson has worked in the field of corrections for 30 years and has specialized in training staff to assess and supervise high-risk offenders in the community. He has been the coordinator for the Sex Offender Awareness Program at the Justice Institute of British Columbia, developing and implementing training programs for staff and nongovernment agencies dealing with sexual abusers. He taught as an adjunct professor at John Jay College of Criminal Justice in the Law and Police Sciences Department. He also served as a high-risk offender analyst for the British Columbia Corrections Branch and is currently an instructor in the Corrections and Community Justice Division at the Justice Institute of British Columbia.

Wayne N. Welsh, Ph.D., is an expert in substance abuse treatment in criminal justice settings, corrections, violence, and organizational theory. Dr. Welsh has collaborated with state correctional agencies on several large, multisite studies of prison-based drug treatment. His projects include a National Institute of Justice–funded project to develop a model academic and justice research partnership with a state correctional agency. He subsequently led a quasiexperimental, multisite study that examined individual and programmatic factors associated with drug treatment outcomes. Dr. Welsh also conducted a randomized experiment examining drug treatment programs at the State Correctional Institution in Chester, Pennsylvania, a facility specializing in substance abuse treatment. His books include *Criminal Violence: Patterns, Causes and Prevention,* co-authored with Marc Riedel (Oxford University Press, 2008), and *Criminal Justice Policy and Planning* (LexisNexis/Anderson, 2008).

Supporting researchers
for more than 40 years

Research methods have always been at the core of SAGE's publishing program. Founder Sara Miller McCune published SAGE's first methods book, *Public Policy Evaluation*, in 1970. Soon after, she launched the *Quantitative Applications in the Social Sciences* series—affectionately known as the "little green books."

Always at the forefront of developing and supporting new approaches in methods, SAGE published early groundbreaking texts and journals in the fields of qualitative methods and evaluation.

Today, more than 40 years and two million little green books later, SAGE continues to push the boundaries with a growing list of more than 1,200 research methods books, journals, and reference works across the social, behavioral, and health sciences. Its imprints—Pine Forge Press, home of innovative textbooks in sociology, and Corwin, publisher of PreK–12 resources for teachers and administrators—broaden SAGE's range of offerings in methods. SAGE further extended its impact in 2008 when it acquired CQ Press and its best-selling and highly respected political science research methods list.

From qualitative, quantitative, and mixed methods to evaluation, SAGE is the essential resource for academics and practitioners looking for the latest methods by leading scholars.

For more information, visit **www.sagepub.com**.